J. Worth Carnahan

Manual of the Civil War and key to the Grand Army of the Republic

and kindred societies

J. Worth Carnahan

Manual of the Civil War and key to the Grand Army of the Republic
and kindred societies

ISBN/EAN: 9783337010812

Printed in Europe, USA, Canada, Australia, Japan

Cover: Foto ©ninafisch / pixelio.de

More available books at **www.hansebooks.com**

MANUAL OF THE CIVIL WAR

AND

KEY

TO THE

GRAND ARMY OF THE REPUBLIC

AND

KINDRED SOCIETIES

BY

J. WORTH CARNAHAN

REVISED EDITION—ILLUSTRATED

Published by the
U S. ARMY AND NAVY HISTORICAL ASSOCIATION
WASHINGTON, D. C.
— 1899 —

Copyrighted 1897,
By J. WORTH CARNAHAN

ALL RIGHTS RESERVED.

TABLE OF CONTENTS.

	PAGE.
INTRODUCTION	11
DEDICATION	12

PART I.

CHAPTER I.—Causes which led to the Organization of the G. A. R. and its Co-Workers.. 13

CHAPTER II.—History of the G. A. R.—Its Origin—Objects—Eligibility—Political Tendencies—Grade System of Membership—Its Growth—Numerical Strength of Each Department—National Encampments—Past Commanders-in-Chief—National Officers—Department Officers—Post Officers—Description of the G. A. R. Badge.. 18

CHAPTER III.—History of the "Woman's Relief Corps" and the "Ladies of the G. A. R.".. 41

CHAPTER IV.—History of the "Sons of Veterans, U. S. A."—"Ladies' Aid Society, Auxiliary to the 'Sons of Veterans, U. S. A.'"—and "Daughters of Veterans"..................................... 47

CHAPTER V.—History of the "National Association of Naval Veterans of the United States"—The "Loyal Legion"—The "Union Veteran Legion"—The "Union Veterans' Union"—The "Veterans' Rights Union," and the "Union Ex-Prisoners of War Association".. 55

CHAPTER VI.—Veteran Societies—"Third Army Corps"—"Society of the Army of Tennessee"—"Society of the Army of the Ohio"—"Society of the Army of the Cumberland"—"The Signal Corps"—"Society of the Army of the James"—"Society of the Army of the Potomac"—"Society of the Burnside Expedition and Ninth Corps"—"Society of the Army and Navy of the Gulf"—"Society of the Army of West Virginia"—"Cincinnati Society of Ex-Army and Navy Officers"—"Pennsylvania Reserve Association"—Society of the Army of Arkansas......... 67

PART II.

SUB-DIVISIONS of the Union Army—How Designated—Officers in the Order of their Rank, including Navy.......................... 75
ENLISTMENTS from the Different States, with Particulars as to Loss by Death.. 82
CORPS ENGAGEMENTS and Corps Commanders........................ 88

PART III.

ALPHABETICAL LIST of Battles and Engagements of the Late Civil War, with Casualties.. 111
ALPHABETICAL LIST of Naval Engagements of the Civil War, with Casualties... 205

PART IV.

AN OUTLINE intended for preserving a copy of the soldier's or sailor's *Honorable Discharge*, followed by his Personal RECORD of SERVICE inserted in *certificate* form. Also memoirs of the Civil War, newspaper clippings relative to his regiment, reunions, camp-fires, and other reminiscences which the soldier or any member of his family desires to hand down to posterity............ 224

PART V.

PENSIONS and *Pension Statistics*............................... 250

ILLUSTRATIONS.

BADGES.
PAGE.

Army of Arkansas.. 66
" " The Cumberland, ⎫
" " The James,
" " The Potomac,   ⎬ 68
" " Tennessee,
" " West Virginia,   ⎭
Corps Badges... 74
G. A. R. Membership Badge......................... 18, 38, 68
" Officer's " (acting and past).................... 39
" Recognition Lapel Button........................18, 66
Ladies' Aid Society.. 51
Ladies of the G. A. R.................................... 44
" " " Button 66
Loyal Legion 60
Medal of Honor... 66
Sons of Veterans.......................................47, 68
Union Soldiers' Alliance................................ 68
Union Veteran Legion................................... 61
" " " Button 61
Union Veterans' Union.................................. 63
United States Navy (new style)........................ 55
" " " (old ").................................. 68
Woman's Relief Corps...............................41–68

MISCELLANEOUS.

Artillery (Emblem)....................................... 66
Cavalry (Emblem).. 66
Coat of Arms (S. of V.).................................. 50
Columbia (Emblem)...................................... 68
Defense of the Flag...................................... 67

ILLUSTRATIONS.

	PAGE.
Discharges (Infantry and Naval)	225, 227
Comrade Rankin's little son Paul	229
Faces of Generals	79
Good-Bye	13
History (Emblem)	68
Hospital	40
Infantry (Emblem)	66
Keyboard to Colors used in Badges	68
Lessons in Patriotism	16
Navy (Emblem)	66
On the Field	14
Picking Lint	17
Sailor and Soldier	21
Woman's Work	15

Introduction.

To my Comrades of the Army and Navy:

As a *convenient reference* to all matters pertaining to the Civil War, the G. A. R. and Kindred Societies, I consider Carnahan's *"Manual"* a most valuable work.

It has never before been my pleasure to find so much *valuable information* couched in such *concise* and *agreeable* form.

The *record of service* feature in connection therewith is *especially* commendable; affording as it does an opportunity for preserving to our children and our children's children a history of our *personal* services during those four bleeding years of civil strife, in connection with a history of the *War* itself and a history of our *Grandest* of *Organizations*,— the *proper place for it.*

In F. C. & L.,

[signature]

DEDICATION.

To the brave "boys in blue," who, on land or sea participated in that memorable struggle for the preservation of our Union, and to the mothers, wives, daughters, and friends, who, at home and in the hospital, so nobly did their part, this little volume is respectfully dedicated by the author.

GRAND ARMY OF THE REPUBLIC

AND

KINDRED SOCIETIES.

CHAPTER I.

CAUSES WHICH LED TO THE ORGANIZATION OF THE G. A. R. AND ITS CO-WORKERS.

OVER a quarter of a century ago the people of the North were startled as never before by the report that Fort Sumter had been fired upon, and that the war between the North and the South had indeed commenced in earnest. A call for volunteers to defend the "Stars and Stripes" was made. That call was answered. Brave men left the farm, the workshop, the office, the store, home, and loved ones—everything, and rushed forward to protect the nation's honor. Battles were lost— battles were won. Long and weary were the marches, and fierce and bloody were the battles that marked the years from 1861 to 1865. The comrade who, at morning, answered "here," at eventide could nevermore respond. Never before in the annals of history was any similar struggle waged on so grand a scale or  with so great a destruction of men and material as in this "the great American conflict."

At last the final day came. The South, no longer able to withstand the prowess and overwhelming forces of the North, was compelled to surrender, and then "The Brave Boys in Blue" marched home again; but not until nearly half a million of their number were killed outright on the field, died of disease and wounds, or were crippled or maimed for life.

Many returned home to find themselves penniless and helpless, but strong in their determination to grapple with the world. The promises made to the men who left their families to go forth to fight for the integrity of the nation were but poorly kept, and though some were provided with employment by the Government, and many patriotic citizens, who remembered and appreciated their services, came nobly forward and gave them the preference in their enterprises, still a great number remained unemployed and unprovided for. This state of affairs caused deep anxiety in the hearts of their more fortunate comrades, who had stood shoulder to shoulder with these men during the death storm of battle, but who had come out of the war with happier fortune, and who were now better able to cope with the world.

It was this condition of affairs that caused the pioneers in the Grand Army of the Republic to conceive the idea of forming an organization that would, to a certain extent, look after the disabled and unemployed veterans, and to the welfare of the widows and orphans of those who had fallen in the conflict. Such were the circumstances which led to the organization of the G. A. R., made brothers under the cloud of war, brothers in a thousand common dangers, brothers in a thousand common sufferings, brothers they must remain in the sunshine of peace.

The history of "The Great American Conflict" would be incomplete without a record of the heroism and self-denying deeds of the mothers, wives, and daughters of those who sprang to arms to support the integrity of the Republic and the honor of the "Stars and Stripes."

Thousands of Northern women of all classes and every rank of society, willingly sacrificing much of what is dear to woman, urged their friends and loved ones to rally around the flag; and they eagerly sought the privilege, as they deemed it, of doing what they could for the cause. At home they managed the business, the factory, or the farm, at the same time caring for the little ones; and when tidings of defeat or disaster reached them, their hearts trembled with anxiety for the welfare of their loved ones and the success of the cause.

Every moment of the day and night of that trying time, hearts were lifted up in silent prayer to the "God of Battles" that the right might prevail and the absent ones be returned safe in peace and honor. In the stillness of the night, as the little ones were put to rest, their young voices were taught to lisp a prayer, that "God might spare papa and preserve the Union." Nor was this all. What a woman does, she does with her whole heart. Almost every home in the North was turned into a manufactory of lint; the closets and chests were ransacked and valued articles of linen were cheerfully brought forth and sacrificed to be shredded into lint for "the poor wounded soldiers."

Societies were organized throughout the country, and the women vied with each other in offering delicacies and dainties, to be sent to the hospitals for the weak and suffering who had been wounded on Southern battlefields. How devotedly they worked in the interest of the "Christian Commission" and the "Sanitary Commission." Their busy fingers even found time, in numerous cases, to pen words of cheer and encouragement to the brave men, strangers to them, except that they were bound together by the strong bonds of loyalty and patriotism.

Nor can we forget those dauntless ones, who, not tied by the cares of a family, so gladly volunteered for active service as nurses on the battlefield and in the hospital; who left the ease and refinement of home to suffer toil and privations to administer to the wants of the wounded. As ministering angels, they passed from cot to cot, stopping here to breathe a word of encouragement to a young sufferer racked with pain and far away from friends and home, and pausing there to raise the pillow of another that he might rest a little more comfortably. At times she was to be found writing a last message to loved ones from one about passing away, and whispering words of hope and consolation—in short, in a thousand different ways doing what only a woman, with her tact, gentleness, and sympathy, can do.

After the struggle was over and the sword was turned into the pruning-hook—when the gallant defenders returned to the vocations of peace; alas, many of them, incapacitated by wounds or disease, were unable to resume their former calling, and helplessly saw their families without proper provision for their maintenance, the women, faithful to their interests and true in their devotion, sprang to the rescue and organized the various auxiliaries known as the "Woman's Relief Corps," "Loyal Ladies' League," or the "Ladies of the G. A. R.," etc., etc.

The lessons of patriotism learned at the knee of their mothers were not lost on the children of the soldiers. On the return of their fathers and brothers from the conflict, the stories of battles and victory were told and retold by the fireside, and such was their charm that they were ever new. Their words burned into the hearts of the young listeners, and they made such an impression that with advancing years the children came to feel that they, too, could claim a common interest and heritage in the deeds of their fathers. This feeling seemed to unite them and form a common tie, leading eventually to the organization of the "Sons of Veterans," "Ladies' Aid Societies," and the "Daughters of Veterans," respectively.

"PICKING LINT"

CHAPTER II.

"THE GRAND ARMY OF THE REPUBLIC."

BADGE.

THE cradle of the "Grand Army of the Republic" was a soldier's tent. On the march to Meridian was born the idea that was to crystallize and develop, and finally produce that brotherhood of soldiers known as the G. A. R.

During Sherman's expedition to Meridian, in February, 1864, Maj. B. F. Stephenson and Chaplain W. J. Rutledge became tentmates and close friends. As they spoke in glad anticipation of the time when they might exchange the hardships and trials of the field for the shelter and comfort of their homes, Chaplain Rutledge suggested that when the troops were finally mustered out of the service, it would be but natural to suppose that men who had shared so much suffering, privation, and danger would wish to form some sort of association, that they might meet again to preserve the friendships and memories of the past. This topic became the subject of frequent conversation

G. A. R. BUTTON.

and they agreed to assist one another in the development of such a project, if they were spared.

This mutual agreement was not forgotten, especially by Dr. Stephenson, when he returned home after the close of his army service. The more he thought of an organization of perpetual comradeship, the more he was enthused with the idea. He could not forget the many deeds of valor daily performed by his comrades, or the many bloody battlefields won by their prowess. When his thoughts returned to the scenes of that trying time, he could again hear the roar of his comrades' deadly artillery, the terrible crash and racket of their muskets, and the ringing and clanging of their sabres, when they crossed with those of the enemy. He could again see the many battle-fields covered with the dead and wounded, and the ground made red with their hearts' blood. He could again hear the vain cry for "water" to sustain the fast ebbing life stream, and the sacred messages whispered in his ear by sufferers racked with pain and far away from home and loved ones, as he bent over them in performance of the duties required by his profession. His duty, as a physician, often called him to the bedside of comrades, who had returned home from the service crippled and maimed for life, and these interviews constantly reminded him of "the groan of the gray-haired sire on learning the sad news; the indescribable look of despair of the widow, on learning that her last prop was taken from her; the shriek of the newly-made bride; the suppressed anguish of the betrothed maiden; and the piteous wail of the bereaved mother, as, with quivering lips, she imparted the sad news to the little ones, who henceforth would be fatherless, and, perhaps, homeless."

Considerable correspondence on the subject of the organization of the Order, which is now known as the "Grand Army of the Republic," passed between Dr. Stephenson and Mr. Rutledge, until they met, by appointment, in Springfield, Ill., in March, 1866, to arrange for the compilation of a ritual for the proposed Order. The first

Post was organized at Decatur, Ill., April 6, 1866, by Maj. B. F. Stephenson, and a ritual was printed under his supervision. The first State Convention was held in Springfield, Ill., July 12, 1866.

As Commander-in-Chief, Dr. Stephenson issued a general order, dated October 31, 1866, calling the first National Convention of the "Grand Army of the Republic." The convention met in Indianapolis, Ind., November 20, 1866, and representatives were present from Illinois, Missouri, Kansas, Wisconsin, New York, Pennsylvania, Ohio, Iowa, Kentucky, Indiana, and the District of Columbia.

OBJECTS OF THE ORDER.

The objects of the G. A. R., as originally set forth in their Constitution, are: *First*, the preservation of those kind and fraternal feelings, which have bound together, with the strong cords of love and affection, the comrades in arms of many battles, sieges, and marches; *second*, to make these ties available in works and results of kindness, of favor and material aid to those in need of assistance; *third*, to make provision, where it is not already done, for the support, care, and education of soldiers' orphans, and for the maintenance of the widows of deceased soldiers; *fourth*, for the protection and assistance of disabled soldiers, whether disabled by wounds, sickness, old age, or misfortune; *fifth*, for the establishment and defense of the late soldiery of the United States, morally, socially, and politically, with a view to inculcate a proper appreciation of their services to the country, and to a recognition of such services and claims by the American people."

The Indianapolis Convention, held November 20, 1866, added the word "sailors" to the Springfield Constitution, and also a new section, taken from the Constitution of the "Loyal Legion," which reads as follows: "The maintenance of true allegiance to the United States of America, based upon paramount respect for and fidelity to the National Constitution and Laws, manifested by the discountenancing of whatever may tend to weaken loyalty, incite to insurrection, treason, or rebellion, or in any manner impairs the efficiency and permanency of our free institutions, together with a defense of universal liberty, equal rights, and justice to all men."

ELIGIBILITY TO MEMBERSHIP.

According to the Rules and Regulations of the Grand Army of the Republic, A. D. 1893, all "Soldiers and Sailors of the United States Army, Navy, or Marine Corps, who served between April 12, 1861, and April 9, 1865, in the war for the suppression of the Rebellion, and those having been honorably discharged therefrom after such service, and of such State regiments as were called into active service and subject to the orders of the U. S. General officers, between the dates mentioned, shall be eligible to membership in the Grand Army of the Republic. No person shall be eligible to membership who has at any time borne arms against the United States."

POLITICAL TENDENCIES.

Many prominent citizens, not bound by kindred ties to the Grand Army of the Republic, are of the opinion that it is little more than a political organization, and, therefore, take no interest in it. There are, also, a great many soldiers throughout the country who would be enrolled as members were it not that they, too, are of the same opinion. This is a great injustice to the Order, as the following bit of history will show that the Post-room is a place "where the partisan and sectarian are not heard."

During the political campaign of 1866, the disputes between President Johnson and the majority in Congress were the means of greatly hindering the growth of the G. A. R.; for, notwithstanding the fact that a great many soldiers who entered the war as Democrats returned with different political opinions, and that the great mass of the soldier vote in 1866 was Republican, it was by no means a unit, for many thousands of gallant soldiers, who were Democrats when they enlisted in the service, returned as such; and during this political campaign hundreds of political clubs were organized among the Veterans, some advocating the principles of the Republican, and others, the Democratic party. Naturally, when a question of a political nature found its way into a Post-room, any argument in its favor was sure to be hotly rebutted by some representative of the opposite party.

This condition of affairs soon caused a discord in the Post-room, and comrades by the hundred withdrew from the Order, especially those with Democratic views; as a result, the public soon began to look upon the G. A. R. as a political organization, and the tendency of the whole Democratic party was to work against any move that would tend to strengthen the ranks of the Order.

The leaders of the G. A. R. soon saw that even the discussion of political questions in the Order was greatly detrimental to its best interests. They realized that as the Rebellion was put down by "individual efforts united," on this principle alone could they secure legislation in behalf of the soldiers' orphans, widows, and dependent parents; or, for the maintenance of homes for disabled Veterans, and for the more successful carrying out of the principles and objects for which they were organized. They were not long, therefore, in taking steps to repair the breach which the political tendencies of the Order had made in its ranks, and in January, 1868, at the National Encampment, held in Philadelphia, Pa., while declaring that it was the purpose of the Grand Army "to secure the rights of the defenders of their country by all moral, social, and political means in their control," the following clause was added to the fifth section of their Declaration of Principles, "yet this Association does not design to make nominations for office, or to use its influence as a secret organization for partisan purposes."

In the next year, 1869, the following article was added to the

Rules and Regulations of the Order: "No officer or comrade of the 'Grand Army of the Republic' shall, in any manner, use this organization for partisan purposes, and no discussion of partisan questions shall be permitted at any of its meetings; nor shall any nominations for political office be made." Under this law, which has never been changed, the "Grand Army of the Republic" grew very rapidly.

THE GRADE SYSTEM OF MEMBERSHIP.

Another great drawback to its growth was the adoption of "The Grade System," which, according to Past Commander Robert B. Beath's "History of the Grand Army of the Republic," provided for three distinct grades of membership: 1. The grade of "Recruit;" 2. The grade of "Soldier;" 3. The grade of "Veteran." The "Recruits" could only be advanced to the grade of "Soldier" after two months' service, and were not eligible to office, or privileged to act, speak, or vote. All business was transacted by the second grade, or "Soldiers," except that pertaining to advancement to the third grade. The "Soldier" could not be advanced to the third grade until he had been a member of the second grade at least six months. "The third grade, or 'Veterans,' only were eligible to National or Department offices, or to membership in National or Department Encampments, or to offices filled by appointment of Commander-in-Chief or Department Commanders; and to the offices of Post-Commander, Vice-Commanders, Adjutant, Quartermaster, Surgeon, Chaplain, Officer of the Day, or Officer of the Guard."

Many members strongly objected to such complicated manœuvres as was required in passing from one grade to another in the "Grand Army," and "Recruits," full of enthusiasm when they joined, were disgusted at having to wait two months before having a vote. "After a two years' trial, this 'Grade System' of membership was entirely abolished." Since that time the Order has flourished and grown until, to-day, it is a powerful influence for good, and no one can deny that it has done much to remove from the nation "the shame of permitting men, who saved its life, to live, die, and be buried as paupers in the land they helped to save."

I cannot better express my opinion of the G. A. R. than to quote the words of Past Commander-in-Chief William Warner, in his report of the administration of his office, to the twenty-third annual session of the National Encampment of the G. A. R., held in Milwaukee, Wis., August 28, 1889:

"The Grand Army of the Republic is the grandest civic organization the world has ever seen—its list of membership is the Nation's roll of honor, containing the most illustrious names in history, the names of the brave men who, in the darkest days of the rebellion, followed the Stars and Stripes as the emblem, not of a confederacy of States bound together by ropes of sand, but as the emblem of an indissoluble Union of indestructible States.

"They followed that flag, whether in sunshine or in storm, victory or defeat, with more confidence and greater reverence than did the children of Israel the pillar of cloud by day and of fire by night. The men who compose this organization are they who, when others faltered, laid 'their lives, their fortunes, and their sacred honors' upon the altar of liberty and Union, that 'a government of the people, by the people and for the people' should not perish from the earth.

"As the war recedes the men who shared together the privations of the frozen camp, the hardships of the forced march, the dangers of the battlefield, the sufferings of the field hospital and the untold agonies of the prison pen, long for the touch of a comrade's elbow as of old, and seek the Post-room, where the partisan and sectarian are not heard. The teachings of the Grand Army of the Republic are so conservative, its practices so patriotic, its comradeship so universal, that all honorably discharged Union soldiers and sailors of '61 and '65, who have done nothing in civil life to cast a stain upon their honorable record in liberty's cause, feel that they are at home when in the Post-room, in the house of their friends.

" It is there that the general and the private, the merchant prince and the clerk, the millionaire and the laborer, sit side by side as comrades, bound each to the other by ties the tenderest yet the most enduring of any in this world, outside of the family circle.

> "' There are bonds of all sorts in this world of ours,
> Fetters of friendship and ties of flowers,
> And true lovers' knots, I ween;
> The boy and the girl are bound by a kiss,
> But there is never a bond, old friend, like this—
> We have drank from the same canteen.'

" The membership of the Grand Army of the Republic constitutes the great conservative element of the Nation, the champion of civil and religious liberty, recognizing the dignity of labor, but having no sympathy with anarchy or communism, recognizing no flag but the Stars and Stripes, believing that loyalty is a virtue and that treason is a crime."

When we come to consider the true American principles which form the foundation of the Order, is it any wonder that its membership, in about twenty-seven years, has reached the gigantic proportions of 7,626 Posts, and a membership, in good standing, of more than 400,000 men? What true American citizen can consider for a moment the vast amount of labor, time, and money expended yearly by the Grand Army of the Republic, in order that the soldier's widow might be comforted and supported; that his orphans might be fed, clothed, and educated, and that society might be compelled to give them a home, alike comfortable and respectable, without acknowledging what a blessing to the welfare of our country this Grand Soldier Organization has been, and how faithfully they have adhered to their motto of " Friendship, Charity and Loyalty "?

GROWTH OF THE ORDER.

A recapitulation of the Adjutant-General's report, at the National Encampment held in Indianapolis, Ind., Sept., A. D. 1893, shows the following figures:

In 1873 the number of comrades in the Grand Army of the Republic, in good standing, was 27,100; in 1878 it was 31,016; in 1883, 215,446; in 1888, the number was 372,960; in 1889, the number was 397,974; in 1890, 409,484; this appears to have been the high-water mark in its history. In 1891 it was 407,781. The total membership, in good standing, June 30, 1892, was 399,880; gained by muster, 24,954; gained by transfer, 7,034; gained by reinstatement, 10,283; total gains, 56,368; aggregate, 456,248. The losses were as follows: By death, 7,002; by honorable discharge, 1,707; by transfer, 8,168; by suspension, 35,298; by dishonorable discharge, 233; delinquent reports, 6,617; total losses, 59,025; net loss, during the year, 2,657. Total membership, in good standing, June 30, 1893, 397,223.

Adjt.-Gen. E. B. Gray states that 4,070 of those reported June 30, 1893, as delinquent are really in good standing, but were not so reported by inefficient Post officers. Therefore, the total membership of the G. A. R., in good standing, Sept. 10, 1893, was 401,293. This number added to the 35,298 suspended members makes a total membership for the Grand Army of the Republic of 436,591.

NUMERICAL STRENGTH OF EACH DEPARTMENT.

The following is a list of the forty-five State Departments of the Grand Army of the Republic, with date and place of organization; also, the number of active Posts, with total membership in good standing of each State or Department, A. D. 1893. Compiled from official sources.

Where two dates of organization are mentioned, the last is always that of permanent organization and national recognition.

ALABAMA.—Department organized March 12, 1889. Number of Posts, 13; total membership, 263.

ARIZONA.—Department organized at Phœnix, January 17, 1888. Number of Posts, 9; total membership, 288.

ARKANSAS.—Department permanently organized at Hot Springs, April 18, 1884. Number of Posts, 89; total membership, 2,872.

CALIFORNIA AND NEVADA.—Department organized at San Francisco, February 21, 1868. Number of Posts, 116; total membership, 6,678.

COLORADO AND WYOMING.—Formerly "The Mountain Department," was first organized at Laramie, Wyoming Territory, December 11, 1879; reorganized at Denver, Col., July 31, 1882. Number of Posts, 82; total membership, 3,394.

CONNECTICUT.—Department organized at Hartford, April 11, 1867. Number of Posts, 67; total membership, 7,852.

DELAWARE.—Department organized at Wilmington, January 14, 1881. Number of Posts, 22; total membership, 1,138.

FLORIDA.—Department permanently organized July 9, 1884. Number of Posts, 18; total membership, 565.

GEORGIA.—Department organized at Atlanta, January 25, 1889. Number of Posts, 10; total membership, 560.

IDAHO.—Department organized at Boise City, January 11, 1888. Number of Posts, 20; total membership, 738.

ILLINOIS.—Department organized at Springfield, July 12, 1866. Number of Posts, 582; total membership, 30,211.

INDIANA.—Department organized at Indianapolis, August 20, 1866; reorganized at Terre Haute, October 3, 1879. Number of Posts, 530; total membership, 24,078.

INDIAN TERRITORY —Department was organized 1889. Number of Posts, 14; total membership, 318.

IOWA.—Department first organized at Davenport, September 26, 1866; re-organized at Des Moines, January 23, 1879. Number of Posts, 449; total membership, 18,870.

KANSAS.—Department organized at Topeka, January 9, 1868;

recognized as a permanent Department March 16, 1880. Number of Posts, 468; total membership, 17,562.

KENTUCKY.—Department organized at Covington, January 16, 1883. Number of Posts, 172; total membership, 6,721.

LOUISIANA AND MISSISSIPPI.—Department permanently organized at New Orleans, May 15, 1884. Number of Posts, 17; total membership, 1,312.

MAINE.—Department organized at Portland, January 10, 1868. Number of Posts, 165; total membership, 10,564.

MARYLAND.—Department organized January 8, 1868; reorganized June 9, 1876. Number of Posts, 52; total membership, 2,825.

MASSACHUSETTS.—Department organized at New Bedford, May 7, 1867. Number of Posts, 210; total membership, 24,105.

MICHIGAN.—Department organized at Detroit, October 1, 1867; reorganized at Grand Rapids, January 22, 1879. Number of Posts, 397; total membership, 19,617.

MINNESOTA.—Department first organized at St. Paul, October 16, 1866; reorganized at Stillwater, August 17, 1881. Number of Posts, 185; total membership, 9,432.

MISSOURI.—Department first organized May 7, 1867; reorganized at Kansas City, April 22, 1882. Number of Posts, 436; total membership, 19,391.

MONTANA.—Department organized at Helena, March 10, 1885. Number of Posts, 16; total membership, 975.

NEBRASKA.—Department organized at Omaha, June 11, 1877. Number of Posts, 276; total membership, 8,324.

NEW HAMPSHIRE.—Department organized at Portsmouth, April 30, 1868. Number of Posts, 94; total membership, 5,837.

NEW JERSEY.—Department organized at Newark, December 10, 1867. Number of Posts, 115; total membership, 7,757.

NEW MEXICO.—Department organized at Santa Fé, July 14, 1883. Number of Posts, 11; total membership, 253.

NEW YORK.—Department organized at Albany, April 3, 1867. Number of Posts, 661; total membership, 40,306.

NORTH DAKOTA.—Department organized at Yankton, February 27, 1883. Number of Posts, 32; total membership, 928.

OHIO.—Department organized at Columbus, January 30, 1867. Number of Posts, 697; total membership, 42,680.

OKLAHOMA.—Department organized June 23, 1890. Number of Posts, 27; total membership, 464.

OREGON.—Department organized at Portland, September 28, 1882. Number of Posts, 50; total membership, 2,665.

PENNSYLVANIA.—Department organized at Philadelphia, January 16, 1867. Number of Posts, 619; total membership, 43,181.

POTOMAC.—Department organized at Washington, D. C., February 13, 1869. Number of Posts, 16; total membership, 3,936.

RHODE ISLAND.—Department organized at Providence, March 24, 1868. Number of Posts, 26; total membership, 3,522.

SOUTH DAKOTA.—Department organized February 27, 1883. Number of Posts, 94; total membership, 3,927.

TENNESSEE.—Department first organized August 18, 1868; reorganized at Nashville, February 26, 1884. Number of Posts, 88; total membership, 4,975.

TEXAS.—Department first organized at Austin, February 12, 1872; reorganized March 25, 1885. Number of Posts, 55; total membership, 1,637.

UTAH.—Department organized at Salt Lake City, October 8, 1883. Number of Posts, 3; total membership, 191.

VERMONT.—Department organized at Montpelier, October 23, 1868. Number of Posts, 110; total membership, 5,863.

VIRGINIA.—Department organized at Richmond, July 27, 1871. Number of Posts, 45; total membership, 1,592.

WASHINGTON AND ALASKA.—Department organized at Olympia, June 20, 1883. Number of Posts, 71; total membership, 3,782.

WEST VIRGINIA.—Department first organized at Wheeling, April 9, 1868; reorganized at Clarksburg, February 20, 1883. Number of Posts, 108; total membership, 3,267.

WISCONSIN.—Department organized at Madison, June 7, 1866. Number of Posts, 272; total membership, 15,871.

NATIONAL OFFICERS.

The supreme power of the Grand Army of the Republic is lodged in the *National Encampment*, which is "held annually between April and November, as may be fixed by the Commander-in-Chief, by consent of the Council of Administration, and at such place as shall have been determined at the previous stated meeting."

"Special meetings may be convened by order of the Commander-in-Chief, by and with the advice and consent of the National Council of Administration."

The National officers of the Grand Army of the Republic are as follows: Commander-in-Chief, Senior Vice-Commander-in-Chief, Junior Vice-Commander-in-Chief, Adjutant-General, Quartermaster-General, Inspector-General, Judge Advocate-General, Surgeon-General, Chaplain-in-Chief, and a Council of Administration, consisting of the above-named officers, and one comrade from each Department.

These officers, with the exception of the Adjutant-General, Quartermaster-General, Inspector-General, and Judge Advocate-General, who are appointed by the Commander-in-Chief as his staff, are elected by ballot at each National Encampment, and enter upon the duties of their respective offices immediately after the adjournment of the meeting at which they were elected.

Vacancies occurring during the year are filled by the Council of Administration.

DUTIES OF NATIONAL OFFICERS.

Article VI, of Chapter IV, of the Rules and Regulations of the Grand Army of the Republic, for 1893, reads as follows:

"SECTION 1. The Commander-in-Chief shall enforce the Rules and Regulations of the Grand Army of the Republic, and the orders of the National Encampment and Council of Administration, and for this purpose he may issue such orders as may be necessary."

"He shall preside in the National Encampment and Council of Administration, decide all questions of law or usage, subject to an appeal to the National Encampment; approve all requisitions properly drawn on the Quartermaster General, and shall hold all securities given by National officers, as trustee for the Grand Army of the Republic. He shall appoint immediately after entering his office, the Adjutant-General, the Quartermaster-General, the Inspector-General, the Judge Advocate-General, an Assistant Adjutant-General, as many Assistant Inspectors-General on the nomination of the Inspector-General and as many Aides-de-Camp as he may deem necessary. He shall appoint all other national officers and committees not otherwise provided for, and may remove these officers at his pleasure. He shall promulgate through the proper officers the national countersign, and may change the same at his discretion, and shall issue to all Departments, regularly organized, suitable charters, and appoint Provisional Commanders in States and Territories where there is no Department organization.

"SEC. 2. The Vice Commanders-in-Chief shall assist the Commander-in-Chief by counsel and otherwise, and in his absence or disability they shall fill his office according to seniority.

"SEC. 3. The Adjutant-General shall keep correct records of the proceedings of the National Encampment and Council of Administration; he shall conduct its correspondence and issue the necessary orders, under the direction of the Commander-in-Chief. All returns received by him from Departments shall be turned over to the proper officers.

"He shall prepare all books and blanks required for use of the Grand Army of the Republic, under the direction of the Commander-in-Chief. He shall draw requisitions on the Quartermaster-General, to be approved by the Commander-in-Chief, and shall perform such other duties and keep such other books and records as the Commander-in-Chief or the National Encampment may require him. He shall give security for the faithful discharge of his duties, to be approved by the Commander-in-Chief, and shall receive as compensation for his services such sum as the National Encampment may from time to time determine.

"SEC. 4. The Quartermaster-General shall hold the funds, securities, and vouchers of the National Encampment, and fill all requisitions drawn upon him by the Adjutant-General and approved by the Commander-in-Chief. He shall distribute all books and blanks required for the use of the Grand Army of the Republic, and, under the direction of the Commander-in-Chief, charge a reasonable and uniform price for the same. He shall give good and sufficient security, in a sum to be approved by the Council of Administration, for the faithful discharge of his duties, and shall receive such compensation for his services as the National Encampment may from time to time determine.

"SEC. 5. The Inspector-General shall perform such duties as are required of him by Chap. V, Art. V, and shall receive such compensation for his services as the National Encampment may from time to time determine.

"SEC. 6. The Surgeon-General shall perform the duties properly appertaining to that office.

"SEC. 7. The Chaplain-in-Chief shall perform such duties in connection with his office as the Commander-in-chief or the National Encampment may require.

"SEC. 8. The Judge Advocate-General shall perform the duties belonging to that office.

"SEC. 9. The National Council of Administration shall meet at such place as may be determined by the National Encampment at their stated meeting, and at such other times and places as the Commander-in-Chief may order; and ten members shall constitute a quorum. It shall audit the accounts of the various National officers, may propose plans of action, and shall represent in all matters the National Encampment in the interval between its sessions. It shall keep full and detailed records of its proceedings, and present the same as its report at the stated meeting of the National Encampment, for the consideration of that body.

"SEC. 10. The several staff officers shall present to the National Encampment, at each annual session, full and detailed reports, in print, of the operations of their respective departments; and when retiring from their office shall deliver to their successors all moneys, books, and other property of the Grand Army of the Republic in their possession or under their control."

NATIONAL ENCAMPMENTS.

The National Encampments of the Grand Army of the Republic were held as follows:

1st Session, Indianapolis, Ind., November 20, 1866.
No Session was held in the year 1867.
2d Session, Philadelphia, Pa., January 15, 1868.
3d " Cincinnati, O., May 12, 1869.
4th " Washington, D. C., May 11, 1870.
5th " Boston, Mass., May 10, 1871.
6th " Cleveland, O., May 8, 1872.
7th " New Haven, Conn., May 14, 1873.
8th " Harrisburg, Pa., May 13, 1874.
9th " Chicago, Ill., May 12, 1875.
10th " Philadelphia, Pa., June 30, 1876.
11th " Providence, R. I., June 26, 1877.
12th " Springfield, Mass., June 4, 1878.
13th " Albany, N. Y., June 17, 1879.
14th " Dayton, O., June 8, 1880.
15th " Indianapolis, Ind., June 15, 1881.
16th " Baltimore, Md., June 21, 1882.
17th " Denver, Col., July 25, 1883.
18th " Minneapolis, Minn., July 23, 1884.
19th " Portland, Me., June 24, 1885.
20th " San Francisco, Cal., August 4, 1886.
21st " St. Louis, Mo., September 28, 1887.
22d " Columbus, O, September 12, 1888.

23d Session, Milwaukee, Wis., August 28, 1889.
24th   "   Boston, Mass., August 8, 1890.
25th   "   Detroit, Mich., August 5, 1891.
26th   "   Washington, D. C., September 21, 1892.
27th   "   Indianapolis, Ind., September 7, 1893.
28th   "   Pittsburg, Pa., September 10, 1894.
29th   "   Louisville, Ky., September 11, 1895.
30th   "   St. Paul, Minn.. September 3, 1896.
31st   "   Buffalo, N. Y., August 26, 1897.
32d   "   Cincinnati, O., September 5, 1898.

PAST COMMANDERS-IN-CHIEF OF THE G. A. R.

B. F. STEPHENSON, of Illinois, the founder of the Order, served as Commander-in-Chief of the G. A. R. from 1866 to 1867.
STEPHEN A. HURLBUT, of Illinois, from 1867 to 1868.
JOHN A. LOGAN, of Illinois, from 1868 to 1871.
AMBROSE E. BURNSIDE, of Rhode Island, from 1871 to 1873.
CHARLES DEVENS, JR., of Massachusetts, from 1873 to 1875.
JOHN F. HARTRANFT, of Pennsylvania, from 1875 to 1877.
JOHN C. ROBINSON, of New York, from 1877 to 1879.
WILLIAM EARNSHAW, of Ohio, from 1879 to 1880.
LOUIS WAGNER, of Pennsylvania, from 1880 to 1881.
GEORGE S. MERRILL, of Massachusetts, from 1881 to 1882.
PAUL VAN DER VOORT, of Nebraska, from 1882 to 1883.
ROBERT B. BEATH, of Pennsylvania, from 1883 to 1884.
JOHN S. KOUNTZ, of Ohio, from 1884 to 1885.
S. S. BURDETT, of Washington, D. C., from 1885 to 1886.
LUCIUS FAIRCHILD, of Wisconsin, from 1886 to 1887.
JOHN P. REA, of Minnesota, from 1887 to 1888.
WILLIAM WARNER, of Missouri, from 1888 to 1889.
RUSSELL A. ALGER, of Michigan, from 1889 to 1890.
W. G. VEASEY, of Vermont, from 1890 to 1891.
JOHN PALMER, of New York, from 1891 to 1892.
A. G. WEISSERT, of Wisconsin, from 1892 to 1893.
JOHN G. B. ADAMS, of Lynn, Mass., from 1893 to 1894.
THOMAS G. LAWLER, Rockford, Ill., from 1894 to 1895.
I. N. WALKER, Indianapolis, Ind., from 1895 to 1896.
T. S. CLARKSON, Omaha, Neb., from 1896 to 1897.
J. P. S. GOBIN, Lebanon, Pa., from 1897 to 1898.
JAMES A. SEXTON, Chicago, Ill., from 1898 to 1899.

DEPARTMENT OFFICERS.

The Department Officers are: *First,* Department Commander; *second,* Senior Vice Department Commander; *third,* Junior Vice Department Commander; *fourth,* Assistant Adjutant-General; *fifth,* Assistant Quartermaster-General; *sixth,* Department Inspector; *seventh,* Judge Advocate; *eighth,* Chief Mustering Officer; *ninth,* Medical Director; *tenth,* Department Chaplain, and the Council of Administration, consisting of the above-named officers and five members by election.

These officers, except the Assistant Adjutant-General, the Assistant Quartermaster-General, the Inspector, the Judge-Advocate, and the Chief Mustering Officer, who are appointed by the Department Commander immediately after entering upon his office, are elected by ballot at the Annual Encampment of the Department, which is held between January 1 and July 1 of each year.

The officers thus elected enter upon their respective duties immediately after the adjournment of the meeting at which they were chosen, and hold office until their successors are duly installed.

The Council of Administration fills all vacancies in elective offices.

DUTIES OF DEPARTMENT OFFICERS.

According to Article VI of Chapter III of the Rules and Regulations of the Grand Army of the Republic for 1893, the duties of the Department Officers are as follows:

"SECTION 1. The Department Commander shall, immediately after entering upon his office, appoint an Assistant Adjutant-General, an Assistant Quartermaster-General, an Inspector, a Judge Advocate, and a Chief Mustering Officer, and may remove these officers at his pleasure. He may appoint as many Assistant Inspectors, on the nomination of the Inspector of the Department, and as many Aides-de-Camp as he may deem necessary. He shall preside at all meetings of the Department Encampment and Council of Administration, shall forward the reports and dues to National Headquarters, and see that all orders received from thence are properly published and obeyed, shall issue suitable charters to all Posts organized in his Department, and perform such other duties as are incumbent on officers of like position.

"SEC. 2. The Vice Commanders shall assist the Commander by counsel or otherwise, and in his absence or disability they shall fill his office according to seniority.

"Sec. 3. The Assistant Adjutant-General shall keep correct records of the proceedings of the Department Encampment and of the Council of Administration; he shall conduct the correspondence and issue all orders under direction of the Commander, draw all requisitions upon the Assistant Quartermaster-General, make out all returns to the National Headquarters, and transmit the same, through the Department Commander, to the Adjutant-General, countersign all charters issued by the Commander, keep an Order Book, a Letter Book, an Indorsement and Memorandum Book, and files of all orders, reports, and correspondence received and remaining in his office, and perform such other duties and keep such other records in connection with his office as may be required of him by the Commander or the Department Encampment. He shall receive, as compensation for his services, such sum as the Department Encampment may from time to time determine.

"Sec. 4. The Assistant Quartermaster-General, shall hold the funds, securities, vouchers, and property of the Department, and fill all requisitions drawn by the Assistant Adjutant-General and approved by the Commander and shall give good and sufficient security, to be approved by the Council of Administration, for the faithful discharge of his duties.

"Sec. 5. The Inspector shall perform such duties as are prescribed in Chap. V, Art. V, and shall receive such compensation for his services as the Department Encampment shall from time to time determine.

"Sec. 6. The Judge Advocate and the Chief Mustering Officer shall perform the duties properly belonging to their offices.

"Sec. 7. The Medical Director shall require such returns from Post Surgeons as may be needed and called for by the Surgeon-General, and shall make returns to that officer.

"Sec 8. The Chaplain shall perform such duties in connection with his office as the Commander of the Department may require of him.

"Sec. 9. The Council of Administration shall have charge of the working interests of the Department, shall audit the accounts of the various officers, shall keep a full and detailed record of its proceedings, and shall present the same for the consideration of the Department Encampment at each stated meeting thereof.

"Sec. 10. The various staff officers shall make to the Department Encampment, at each stated meeting, full and complete reports, in writing, of the operations of their Departments, and when retiring from office shall deliver to their successors all moneys, books, and other property of the Department in their possession or under their control."

POST OFFICERS.

The officers of each Post of the Grand Army of the Republic are as follows: Post-Commander, Senior Vice-Post-Commander, Junior Vice-Post-Commander, Adjutant, Quartermaster, Surgeon, Chaplain, Officer of the Day, Officer of the Guard, Sergeant-Major, and Quartermaster-Sergeant. In addition to the above, the Commander details an Inside Sentinel, Outside Sentinel, and Color Sergeant.

ELECTION OF OFFICERS.

These officers (the Adjutant, Sergeant-Major, and Quartermaster Sergeant excepted) are elected at the first stated meeting in December, by ballot, unless a ballot be dispensed with by unanimous consent, and are installed into their respective offices at the first stated meeting in January following.

INSTALLATION OF OFFICERS.

At the installation of officers, which is generally held publicly at a special meeting called for that purpose, the Commander appoints the Adjutant, Sergeant-Major, and Quartermaster-Sergeant. These officers the Commander can remove, if he so desires. All officers, whether elected or appointed, hold office until their successors are duly installed.

No part of the opening or closing services, or signs of recognition, of the Grand Army of the Republic, are made use of at a public installation of officers, but an evening spent in witnessing an occasion of this kind, especially by one who never attended an installation of Grand Army officers, will certainly never be regretted, as it is a very entertaining ceremony.

DUTIES OF POST OFFICERS.

Article VIII, of Chapter II, of the Grand Army of the Republic Rules and Regulations for 1893, give the duties of the Post officers as follows:

"SECTION 1. It shall be the duty of the Post Commander to preside at all meetings of the Post, to enforce a strict observance of the Rules and Regulations and By-Laws, and all orders from proper authority, to detail all officers and committeees not otherwise provided for, to approve all orders drawn upon the Quartermaster for appropriations of money made and passed at a stated meeting of the Post, to forward the returns required by Chap. V, Art. II, and to perform such other duties as his charge may require of him.

"SEC. 2. The Vice-Post Commanders shall perform such duties as are required of them by the Ritual, and, in the absence of the Commander, shall take his place in the order of their rank. If neither of them are present the Post shall elect a Commander *pro tempore*.

"SEC. 3. The Adjutant shall keep in books properly prepared:—
"1. The Rules and Regulations of the Grand Army of the Republic and the By-Laws of the Post, to be signed by every comrade on his becoming a member.

"THE GRAND ARMY OF THE REPUBLIC."

"2. A Descriptive Book, ruled to embrace every fact contained in the application as well as the date of acceptance and muster, and a column for general remarks.

"3. A Journal of the Proceedings of the Post, after the same shall have been corrected and approved.

"4. An Order Book, in which shall be recorded all orders and circulars issued by the Post Commander.

"5. A Letter Book.

"6. An Indorsement and Memorandum Book.

"7. A Black Book, in which shall be recorded the names of all rejected candidates, also of all members of the Grand Army who have been dishonorably discharged.

"He shall attest by his signature all actions of the Post, and draw all orders on the Quartermaster, to be approved by the Post Commander; shall notify in writing newly-elected members, and shall, under the direction of the Post Commander, prepare all reports and returns required of him. He shall perform such other duties as appertain to his office, and shall transfer to his successor, without delay, all books, papers, and other property.

"SEC. 4. The Quartermaster shall hold the funds, securities, vouchers, and other property of the Post, and fill all requisitions drawn by the Adjutant and approved by the Post Commander; he shall collect all moneys due the Post, giving his receipt therefor; he shall keep an account with each member, and notify all comrades in arrears; he shall render a monthly account in writing to the Post of its finances, which shall be referred to an auditing committee appointed by the Post. He shall make and deliver to the Post Commander all reports and returns required of Post Quartermasters by Chap. V, Art. II, and shall deliver to his successor in office, or to any one designated by the Post, all moneys, books, and other property of the Post in his possession or under his control. He shall give security for the faithful discharge of his duties as provided in Chap. V, Art. VII.

"SEC. 5. The Surgeon shall discharge such duties in connection with his office as may be required of him.

"SEC. 6. The Chaplain shall officiate at the opening of the Post and at the funeral of the comrades when attended by the Post, and perform such other duties in connection with his office as the Post may require.

"SEC. 7. The Officer of the Day and the Officer of the Guard shall perform such duties as may be required by the Ritual or by the Post Commander.

"SEC. 8. The Sergeant-Major and Quartermaster-Sergeant shall assist the Adjutant and Quartermaster respectively in their duties.

"SEC. 9. The Trustees of the Post shall have the care, custody, and management of such property of the Post as the Post by vote shall place in their possession, or under their control, subject to the direction of the Post as to its management and investment; and all leases or conveyances of lands or buildings, by or to the Posts, shall be in the names of such Trustees and their successors in office.

"SEC. 10. Trustees of the Relief Fund shall have the care, custody, and management of the Relief Fund of the Post, subject to the direction of the Post, and all investments of the Relief Fund shall be in the names of such Trustees and their successors in office.

"SEC. 11. Posts may make By-Laws regulating the manner in which Trustees of the Post or Relief Fund shall perform their duties, and respecting the reports of such Trustees.

"SEC. 12. No change shall be made by the Trustees in any investment of Post or Relief Funds, or in the title to Post or Relief Fund Property, or any money paid therefrom, without the concurrence in writing of all the Trustees.

"SEC. 13. The Quartermaster of the Post shall turn over to the Trustees such property and funds of the Post as the Post by vote may direct."

DESCRIPTION OF THE G. A. R. BADGE.

MEMBERSHIP BADGE.

The membership badge of the Grand Army of the Republic consists of the figure of an Eagle, with Cross-Cannon and Ammunition, representing Defense; the Eagle hovering over with a sword, and always ready to protect from insult or dishonor the National Flag, which is also the emblem and ribbon of the Order.

One end of this flag-ribbon is attached to the figure of the above-described eagle, cross-cannon, etc., and the other end is fastened to a five-pointed star, in the centre of which is "the figure of the Goddess of Liberty, representing Loyalty; on either side a soldier and a sailor clasping hands, representing Fraternity, and two children receiving benediction and assurance of protection from the comrades, representing Charity. On each side of the group is the National Flag and the Eagle, representing Freedom; and the Axe, or Bundle of Rods, or Fasces, representing Union.

"In each point of the star is the insignia of the various arms of the service, viz.: the Bugle for Infantry, Cross-cannon for Artillery, Cross-muskets for the Marine, Cross-swords for Cavalry, and the Anchor for Sailors.

"Over the Central Group are the words, 'Grand Army of the Republic,' and under the word and figures, '1861—Veteran—1866,' commemorating the commencement and close of the Rebellion, and also the date of organization of the Order."

OFFICIAL BADGES OF THE G. A. R.

ACTING OFFICER'S BADGE.   PAST OFFICER'S BADGE.

As the above cuts will show, the difference between the membership and the official badge of the G. A. R. is that the ribbon of the latter is wider and ornamented by a buff, cherry red, or a lighter blue border—(Buff for National officers, Red for Department officers, and Blue for Post officers)—and that on the active officer's badge the eagle is supplanted by a miniature strap one and one-half inches long and one-half inch wide, enameled with a gold or gilt border one-sixteenth of an inch in width. The color of this strap for National or Department officers is black, for Post officers dark blue.

On the badge worn by Past officers this strap is clasped upon their proper ribbon, between the star and the eagle of the membership badge.

A miniature shield in gold or gilt, with the coat of arms of the State, may be worn pendant to the official strap, to distinguish the different State Departments.

The bronze used in the manufacture of the Grand Army badge and button is that of cannon captured in different decisive battles of the late Civil War.

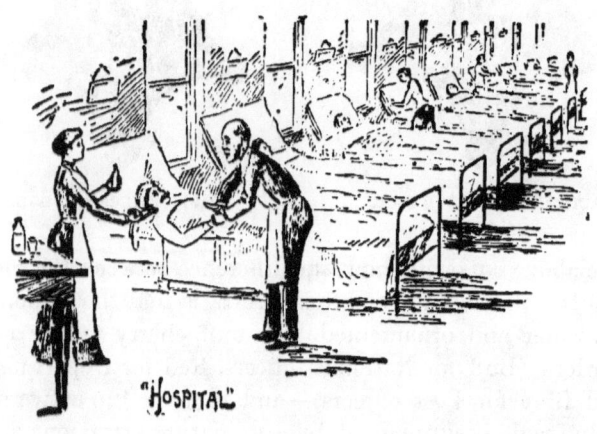

CHAPTER III.

"WOMAN'S RELIEF CORPS."

TO the State of Maine belongs the honor of having within its boundaries the first organization of ladies who have always so nobly seconded the efforts of the G. A. R. in the discharge of the principles and duties of that body, to co-operate with them as a G. A. R. Post.

As early as 1869, the "Bosworth Relief Corps" was formed in Portland, Maine, for the purpose of aiding the "Bosworth Post," of that city, to relieve the unfortunate and needy comrades and their families. So well did they acquit themselves in their destined work, and so successfully did they administer to the wants of the needy and suffering that in a short time it became evident that their co-operation was a necessity, and corps after corps was organized in every direction; but it was not until ten years later that a State organization was formed. In April, 1879, the first State organization was perfected at Fitchburg, Mass., under the title of "Woman's Relief Corps," as advocated by the ladies of Massachusetts.

ELIGIBILITY TO MEMBERSHIP.

The membership did not rest upon kinship to Veterans, but the assistance and sympathy of all loyal women were asked, and the only requirements for admission as a member were loyalty and the observance of the principles of the Order.

OBJECTS OF THE ORDER.

The objects of the "Woman's Relief Corps are: "*First*, to especially aid and assist the Grand Army of the Republic and to perpetuate the memory of their heroic dead; *second*, to assist such Union Veterans as need our help and protection, and to extend needful aid to their widows and orphans, to find them homes and employment, and assure them of sympathy and friends; *third*, to cherish and emulate the deeds of our army nurses, and of all loyal women who rendered loving service to their country in her hour of peril; *fourth*, to inculcate lessons of patriotism and love of country among our children and in the communities in which we live; *fifth*, to maintain true allegiance to the United States of America; *sixth*, to discountenance whatever tends to weaken loyalty, and to encourage the spread of universal liberty and equal rights to all men."

Notwithstanding their valuable services, nothing substantial was done by the G. A. R. to encourage the growth of these Societies, nor were they accorded the official recognition they merited until 1881, when Chaplain-in-Chief Rev. Joseph F. Lovering urged upon the National Encampment the necessity of their being given their due recognition and support. A resolution was then adopted approving the work of the "Woman's Relief Corps," and they were also authorized to add to their title "Auxiliary to the G. A. R."

It soon became evident that a National organization and the uniformity of rules governing them would strengthen the "Woman's Relief Corps" and increase their usefulness. Accordingly, in 1883, Commander-in-Chief Paul Van Der Voort invited representatives from all existing Ladies' Auxiliaries to meet at Denver, Colorado, at the time the National Encampment of the G. A. R. met there, to arrange for a union of all the Societies. This invitation was accepted, and a large delegation met at Denver, July 25, 1883, and Mrs. E. F. Barker, President of the "Woman's Relief Corps" of

Massachusetts, was appointed President, and Mrs. Kate B. Sherwood, of "Forsyth Post Relief Corps" of Toledo, Ohio, was appointed Secretary. Owing to some difference of opinion regarding eligibility to membership, the delegation from New Jersey declined to unite with the "Woman's Relief Corps," and maintained their organization under the title " Loyal Ladies' League," later known as " Ladies of the G. A. R."

The plan of organization of the "Woman's Relief Corps" was very similar to that of the G. A. R. The National organization was called the "National Convention, Woman's Relief Corps, Auxiliary to the Grand Army of the Republic;" the State organizations were called departments, and the local associations were termed corps.

The record of the successful organization of the "Woman's Relief Corps" was received with great satisfaction by the National Encampment of the G. A. R., and the following resolution was adopted in order to be transmitted: "*Resolved*, That we cordially hail the organization of the ' Woman's Relief Corps,' and extend our greeting to them. We return our warmest thanks to the loyal women of the land for their earnest work, support, and encouragement, and bid them Godspeed in their patriotic work."

How rapidly this organization has spread may be judged from the fact that, at the present time, there are upward of two thousand Posts in the United States, with a membership of about one hundred thousand, who contribute annually more than one hundred thousand dollars ($100,000). This is a representation of their strength in figures, but who can measure the value of their kindly sympathy, their visits at the bedsides of suffering Veterans, their tender care for the widows and orphans, their loving work in the many channels of usefulness which their tact has found them. It is, indeed, as priceless as the patriotic devotion which actuated them to devote their time and money to the cause they love so well, and the " Woman's Relief Corps " will ever stand as a living monument of the love of American women for the cause of truth and justice: American women, true daughters of their brave ancestors, who fought and suffered for liberty in the days of " '76."

" LADIES OF THE G. A. R."

(Formerly Known as " Loyal Ladies' League.")

The movement of patriotic women, "Auxiliary to the Grand Army of the Republic," which was first inaugurated at Portland, Me., in 1869, spread rapidly throughout the country. The ladies of New Jersey were second to none in their enthusiastic support of it. A number of societies or leagues were soon formed throughout the State, which were, however, not perfectly uniform in their rules and management. To secure a more thorough co-operation in the work for which they were destined, a request was issued in general orders by Commander Charles Houten, Department of New Jersey, asking all the ladies to send representatives to Trenton, with a view of forming a State organization. The delegates met at Trenton, N. J., December 15, 1881, and after some debate an organization was perfected under the title, " Loyal Ladies' League, Auxiliary to the Grand Army of the Republic, Department of New Jersey." The new Order adopted a charter, badge, and rules, and began its work with eight subordinate leagues, Mrs. Carrie N. Burgee, of **Vineland**, N. J., being elected its president.

ELIGIBILITY TO MEMBERSHIP.

Only such were admitted to membership as were of good moral character, and who were related as mother, wife, sister, or daughter to an honorably discharged soldier, sailor, or marine, who served in the late Rebellion.

OBJECTS OF THE ORDER.

The objects of the "Loyal Ladies' League," as set forth in these rules, were as follows: " To unite with loyalty—love for each other; to practice the precepts of true fraternity of feeling toward all sisters of our Order, thus emulating the spirit which unites our fathers, husbands, and brothers; to honor the memory of those fallen; to perpetuate and keep forever sacred 'Memorial Day'; to assist the 'Grand Army of the Republic' in its high and holy mission; aid, encourage, and sympathize with them in their noble work of charity; to extend needful aid to members in sickness and distress; to aid sick soldiers, sailors, and marines; to do all in our power to alleviate suffering."

In July, 1883, Mrs. S. D. Hugg and Mrs. Laura McNeir were sent as delegates from New Jersey to Denver, Colorado, to meet with the delegates from the Ladies' Auxiliary Societies in the different States, who were called together by a request issued by Paul Van Der Voort, Commander-in-Chief of the National Encampment of the G. A. R., with a view of forming a National organization to better carry out the objects for which they were organized. At this convention the delegates from New Jersey were opposed to making all loyal women eligible to membership, and on the adoption of that rule by a majority of the delegates present, they declined to become a part of the "Woman's Relief Corps," as they thought that the membership should be restricted to the immediate relatives of Veterans. In this view they were supported by their State Convention, and New Jersey remained an independent department.

On November 18, 1886, delegates from the various Leagues in New Jersey, Pennsylvania, Kansas, California, Ohio, Delaware, and West Virginia met in convention at Chicago, Ill., for the purpose of effecting a National organization. After some discussion and a few slight changes in the rules, a union was effected with an organization in Illinois, known as "Ladies of the G. A. R." This name was adopted by the Convention for the National Order, and Mrs. Laura McNeir, of Camden, N. J., was elected as its National President. The membership at the present time is about thirty-five thousand, who have, by their activity and fidelity to the purpose of their Order, done much to aid and support the Grand Army of the Republic.

The organization formed, as it is, by the immediate relatives of the Veterans, is united by the strongest kind of bonds. Those ties of comradeship which were formed and strengthened by mutual privation and suffering on the field and in the camp, amidst hunger, thirst, and disease in Southern swamps, Confederate prisons, and which are such a marked feature, many of the comrades of the G. A. R. bore to be communicated to their mothers, wives, sisters, and daughters, who, by the fireside, and in the hospital, did their part so bravely in the great struggle, sharing their mutual joys and woe: these ties binding them together have made them, as it were, one great family having a common cause and a common interest.

CHAPTER IV.

"SONS OF VETERANS OF THE UNITED STATES OF AMERICA."

BADGE.

SHORTLY after the organization of the G. A. R., the plan of forming a Cadet Corps of the Sons of the Veterans was discussed from time to time, but it was not until 1878 that any decisive action was taken in the matter. At a meeting of the "Anna M. Ross Post, No. 94," of Philadelphia, Pa., August 27, 1878, the subject was taken up, and, on motion of Comrade James P. Holt, a committee of five was appointed to devise means of forming a G. A. R. Cadet Corps, to be attached to that Post. On the 17th of September following, the committee reported and submitted a plan of organization, which was at once adopted by the Post, and on the 29th of September, 1878, the first Camp of the "Sons of Veterans" was formally organized, under the title, "Anna M. Ross Camp No. 1, of Philadelphia, Order of Sons of Veterans." Other Camps were soon organized in Philadelphia and throughout the State, and in July, A. D. 1880, a division organization was completed, with Comrade Linder as Colonel.

The Order spread rapidly in the States of New York, New Jersey, Pennsylvania, and Delaware, in 1881, and during the same year a National organization was formed, and Alfred Cope was elected Commander.

About the same time Maj. A. P. Davis, of Pittsburgh, Pa., was organizing the "Sons of the Veterans," of that city, and on the 12th of November, 1881, he instituted an organization under the title, "Sons of Veterans of the United States of America," and prepared for it a Constitution, rules and regulations, and ritual, which provided for a National organization and State and Local associations.

In 1883, owing to misunderstanding and dissensions in the Order first above mentioned, thirty-three of its Camps withdrew and united with the Order founded by Maj. Davis, leaving but three Camps of the original Order, but the National division remained intact, and Commander Cope created a provisional division in Pennsylvania, appointing L. M. Wagner as Provisional Colonel. A permanent organization, however, was formed for Pennsylvania, February 22, 1882, and the original Order continued to exist until August, 1886, when it was consolidated with the "Sons of Veterans, U. S. A."

In his address at the National Encampment of the G. A. R., held at Columbus, Ohio, in 1888, Commander-in-Chief John P. Rea alluded to the order of "Sons of Veterans" as follows: "It will be but a short period until our ranks are so meagre and the surviving comrades so weighed down with the burden of years that our organization will have ceased to be an active force in the works of loyal love and charity which it has ordained. The tender ceremonies of 'Memorial Day' will then be performed by others, or not at all. It seems to me that it would be the part of wisdom for us, while yet in our vigor, to establish such relationship between our Order and the 'Sons of Veterans' as to properly recognize that organization."

Afterward, at the same Encampment, the following resolution was passed: "*Resolved*, That this Encampment indorse the objects and purposes of the Order of 'Sons of Veterans, U. S. A.,' and hereby gives to the Order the official recognition of the Grand Army of the Republic, and recommend that comrades aid and encourage the institution of Camps of the 'Sons of Veterans, U. S. A.'"

ELIGIBILITY TO MEMBERSHIP

The requirements for admission to membership are that the applicant must not be less than eighteen years of age, and that he must be the son of a deceased or honorably discharged Union soldier or sailor, or a son of a member of the Order of "Sons of Veterans."

PRINCIPLES.

The principles of the "Sons of Veterans, U. S. A.," are " a firm belief and trust in Almighty God, and a realization that under His beneficent guidance the free institutions of our land, consecrated by the services and blood of our fathers, have been preserved, and the integrity and life of the nation maintained. True allegiance to the Government of the United States of America, based upon a respect for and devotion and fidelity to its Constitution and laws, manifested by the discountenancing of anything that may tend to weaken loyalty, incite to insurrection, treason, or rebellion, or in any manner impair the efficiency and permanency of our National Union."

OBJECTS.

The objects of the Order are: "*First*, To keep green the memory of our fathers and their sacrifices for the maintenance of the Union; *second*, To aid the members of the Grand Army of the Republic in caring for their helpless and disabled veterans; to extend aid and protection to the widows and orphans; to perpetuate the memory and history of their heroic dead; and the proper observance of Memorial Day; *third*, To aid and assist worthy and needy members of the Order; *fourth*, To inculcate patriotism and love of country, not alone among our membership, but among all the people of our land, and to spread and sustain the doctrine of equal rights, universal liberty, and justice to all."

The Order is organized on strictly military principles, and is officered and governed according to army regulations. The National organization, which has its one Commandery-in-Chief, corresponds to an army; the State organizations, or Divisions, are officered and governed as regiments, while the local organizations, or Camps, correspond to companies, and are regulated as such. The officers of the Camp are Captain, First Lieutenant, and Second Lieutenant, who are elected by ballot. In addition to these, the Captain appoints a staff, consisting of the following officers: First Sergeant, Quartermaster Sergeant, Chaplain, Color Sergeant, Sergeant of the Guard, Corporal of the Guard, Musician, Camp Guard, and Picket Guard. Each Camp is organized as a company, and every officer is required to discharge his duties in precisely the same manner as though he were regularly enlisted. The Captain presides at the meetings of the Camp, and in his absence his place is filled by the First or Second Lieutenant, in the order of his rank. The Chaplain's duties are indicated by his title. The First Sergeant keeps the records of the Camp, and makes a quarterly report to Division Headquarters through the Captain. The Quartermaster Sergeant has charge of the funds of the Camp, and likewise, through the Captain, makes a quarterly report to Division Headquarters.

COAT OF ARMS OF THE SONS OF VETERANS.

The Order has spread rapidly throughout the entire Union, from the Atlantic to the Pacific. It has now on its roll more than ninety thousand active members. As Commander-in-Chief Rea intimated in his address, that time will gradually decimate the ranks of the G. A. R., and old age will enfeeble the survivors, there should be a union of younger men upon whom they could lean for support, who would be worthy of their charge and who would foster and perpetuate the purpose for which they suffered and bled. When the necessity for such an organization became apparent, the Order of the "Sons of Veterans, U. S. A.," sprang into existence to meet that necessity; and well have they met it, its membership being made up of the best blood of the land, young men well drilled in military tactics, who are devoted to their country, and who cherish the memory of the brave deeds of their fathers. At a call of their country they would be among the first to spring to arms, and, incited by the deeds of their fathers, they would soon rival them in their devotion to preserve the honor and integrity of the "Stars and Stripes."

"LADIES' AID SOCIETY."

AUXILIARY TO THE "SONS OF VETERANS, U. S. A."

BADGE.

The "Ladies' Aid Society" was organized in Philadelphia, Pa., A. D. 1883, but it was not until the 29th day of August, 1884, at a meeting of the "Sons of Veterans" held in Philadelphia that it was duly recognized and practically acknowledged as an "Auxiliary to the Sons of Veterans, U. S. A."

Prior to June 13, 1885, this Order consisted of but seven Societies, and was not known outside of Eastern Pennsylvania. In September, 1885, at an annual meeting held at Grand Rapids, Mich., the "Sons of Veterans" passed the following resolution:

"*Resolved*, That all brothers of our Order be requested to encourage the movement to extend the Association of 'Ladies' Aid Societies,' in order that they might become a National body, and to give the movement such support as their situation and circumstances will admit of, and that the Commander-in-Chief, Grand Division, Division, and Camp Commanders, and all others interested aid in the establishment of Societies, and that in accordance with the request of the President, Miss Laura F. Martin, of Lancaster, Pa., they advance to her Order in the shape of a temporary loan such moderate amounts as her appeal indicates will be sufficient to meet the requirements of the case."

The passing of this resolution is credited to Maj. A. P. Davis, of Pittsburgh, Pa., the founder of the "Sons of Veterans, U. S. A.," and to him the more perfect and thorough organization of the Order as it now stands is largely due.

The rapid growth of the Order is clearly demonstrated by the fact that its first National Encampment was held at Akron, Ohio, September 7 to 9, 1887, just two years after the passing of the above resolution, and since that time the Order has been repeatedly indorsed by the National Encampments of the "Sons of Veterans" as their only authorized auxiliary. It now embraces about three hundred and fifty Societies, with thirteen States organized into permanent Divisions, and has a total membership of over eight thousand.

ELIGIBILITY TO MEMBERSHIP.

This Order admits to membership: *First*, "mothers, wives, and sisters of deceased or honorably discharged soldiers, sailors, or marines who served in the Union Army or Navy during the Civil War of 1861–1865; *second*, female lineal descendants not less than sixteen years of age of soldiers, sailors, or marines; *third*, wives of Sons of Veterans."

PRINCIPLES OF THE ORDER.

Its principles are: *First*, "a firm belief and trust in Almighty God, and a realization that under His beneficent care and guidance the free institutions of our land—by the assistance and sacrifices of our soldiers—have been preserved, and the integrity and life of the nation maintained; *second,* true allegiance to the Government of the United States of America, and a respect for and a devotion and fidelity to its Constitution and laws, with a firm opposition to anything that may tend to weaken loyalty or in any manner impair the efficiency and permanency of our National Union."

OBJECTS.

The objects of the Order are: *First,* "to assist the 'Sons of Veterans' in keeping green the memories of our soldiers, and their sacrifices for the maintenance of the Union; *second,* to aid the members of the 'Grand Army of the Republic' in caring for their helpless and disabled veterans, to extend aid and protection to their widows and orphans, to perpetuate the memory and history of their heroic dead, and the proper observance of Memorial Day; *third,* to aid and assist the 'Sons of Veterans' in all their objects, both financially and otherwise; *fourth,* to aid and assist worthy and needy members of our Society; *fifth,* to inculcate true patriotism and love of country, not only among our membership, but all the people of our land, and to spread and sustain the doctrine of equal rights, universal liberty, and justice to all."

The Order takes its name from a society organized in Philadelphia, Pa., the week following the fall of Fort Sumter in 1861, under the title of "Ladies' Aid Society." This Society was composed of about two hundred loyal ladies of that city, and was organized for the purpose of providing nurses for the sick and wounded soldiers, and to care for suffering and bereaved soldiers' families. In short, as an organization to aid and encourage the Union soldiers in their struggle for the maintenance of the Union.

As the Order of the "Sons of Veterans, U. S. A.," will likely continue as an organization for many years to come, owing to the fact that it was organized for the purpose of aiding and continuing the work begun, and thus far so faithfully carried out by the "Grand Army of the Republic," and, inasmuch as it has been demonstrated in the past that the "Woman's Relief Corps" and the "Ladies of the G. A. R.," both auxiliaries to the G. A. R., have been a source of great aid to that organization, it is reasonable to suppose that the "Ladies' Aid Society, Auxiliary to the Sons of Veterans," will continue to grow in favor until it becomes a mighty factor in carrying out the principles and objects of the "Sons of Veterans," upon which its structure is based and reared.

"DAUGHTERS OF VETERANS."

This Society is located principally in the West, but is rapidly spreading in all directions. It is, in many respects, similar to the "Sons of Veterans," and is entirely independent and auxiliary to no other organization.

It was organized at Massilon, Ohio, May 30, 1885, and has a National organization and local Societies, known as "Tents."

The Order admits to membership "all daughters and granddaughters of honorably discharged soldiers, sailors, and marines who served in the Union army or navy during the Rebellion of 1861–65, who have attained the age of fifteen years," and has for its objects, as follows: "To perpetuate the memories of our fathers, grandfathers, and brothers, their loyalty to the Union, and their unselfish sacrifices for the perpetuity of the same; to keep green the memory and history of those who participated in that heroic struggle for the maintenance of our free government; to aid them and their widows and orphans when helpless and in distress; to assist the Grand Army to commemorate the deeds of their fallen comrades on the 30th of May, until such time as it shall devolve upon their descendants."

There is a Floral Committee attached to each Tent, whose duty it is to provide floral offerings for the funeral of any deceased soldier or sailor in the vicinity.

CHAPTER V.

"THE NATIONAL ASSOCIATION OF NAVAL VETERANS OF THE UNITED STATES."

BADGE.

THE objects for which the Grand Army of the Republic was organized appeal as strongly to the loyal sailor as to his soldier brother. Naturally, therefore, the G. A. R. early absorbed into its ranks large numbers of Naval Veterans, and it was not because of any change in principles that many old sailors in the course of time decided to withdraw from the G. A. R., and form Naval Associations, but rather that the Naval Veterans might be united in closer bonds of fraternity.

Prior to the year 1887 a number of Independent Societies, composed exclusively of Naval Veterans, had been formed at various times in different sections throughout the country, and on the 13th day of January, 1887, eight of these Veteran societies met in convention at New York city, where the "National Association of Naval Veterans of the United States" was formed, with Charles W. Adams, of Illinois, as first Commodore. At this convention, a constitution, together with a uniform, national badge, and a recognition lapel button, was adopted and other important matters for the welfare of the local associations decided upon.

OBJECTS OF THE ORDER.

The objects of this National Organization are "to cherish the memory and association of the War of the Rebellion; to perpetuate the glorious name and deeds of our Navy; to strengthen the ties of fraternal fellowship and sympathy; to extend relief to worthy members; to bury their dead; and to maintain the honor of the American flag;" in short, "mutual benefit, better recognition by Federal, State, and municipal authorities, a higher elevation of our old messmates, and a cementing of the bonds of friendship, which were begun more than a quarter of a century ago, and an independent, but concerted, action of Naval Veterans throughout the country."

ELIGIBILITY TO MEMBERSHIP.

" To become a member of this Order, the applicant must have been an officer, seaman, landsman, fireman, or marine; or one who served in the United States Navy from 1861 to 1865, or who was in the revenue cutter service during that period, and who resigned or was honorably discharged from the service." "Shipmates" who are isolated and not within easy reach of a local association may become " Associate Members " by the payment of a small fee, and thus become entitled to wear the uniform, badge, and button, and parade with the Order annually.

Ten "Shipmates" can form an association, and upon the payment of five dollars ($5) receive from the Rear Admiral commanding a charter, set of rituals, and service books.

The association has a uniform and rank insignia, not unlike that worn by the officers of the " Old Navy," in which they served, and flies the " Union Jack " as its service colors.

The work of this organization is carried on much after the manner of the Grand Army of the Republic, yet purely distinctive of naval routine and customs. A National Convention is held yearly in connection with the G. A. R. encampments, and the national officers for the following year are then elected. At the Twenty-sixth Annual Encampment of the G. A. R., held at Washington, September 20, 1892, over one thousand "Shipmates" were added to the National Roster of the Order, which now contains the names and addresses of about nine thousand living Naval Veterans.

The Association is noted for the interest and enthusiasm of its members and the strong ties of friendship and comradeship existing among the "Shipmates." There are a large number of Naval Veterans in the G. A. R. Posts of all State Departments: in fact, most of the members of this Association have also a membership in the G. A. R.

Most of the Naval Veteran Associations meet regularly once or twice a month, and all of them hold yearly reunions, where the old "Blue-jackets" spin over their yarns, fight over their battles, and, perhaps, "splice the main brace."

The old Veterans are rapidly "losing the number of their mess," and, in a few short years, there will be left but a "quarter watch" of useless human hulks. "May they find happiness and contentment as they lie moored in the still waters of the stream of life, calmly awaiting the inevitable hour when the frail cable shall part and they drift away into the great ocean of eternity."

The following is a list of the active Naval Veteran Societies of the United States:

Farragut Association Naval Veterans, Philadelphia, Pa.
Farragut Association Naval Veterans, New York.
Naval Veterans' Association of Connecticut, Hartford, Conn.
Farragut Association, Chicago, Ill.
Essex Naval Veterans' Association, Salem, Mass.
Cushing Naval Veterans' Association, Milwaukee, Wis.
Naval Veterans' Association of the Gulf, New Orleans, La.
D. D. Porter Naval Veterans' Association, Columbus, Ohio.
Admiral Dahlgren Naval Veterans' Association, Dayton, Ohio.
Farragut Naval Veterans' Association, Providence, R. I.

D. D. Porter Naval Veterans' Association, Louisville, Ky.
Maryland Naval Veterans' Association, Baltimore, Md.
Illinois Naval Veterans' Association, Chicago, Ill.
Thos. A. Budd Naval Veterans' Association, Buffalo, N. Y.
Naval Veterans' Legion, Philadelphia, Pa.
Potomac Naval Veterans' Association, Washington, D. C.
Cumberland Naval Veterans' Association, New Bedford, Mass.
Central New York Naval Veterans' Association, Amsterdam, N. Y.
Michigan Naval Veterans' Association, Detroit, Mich.
Herrick Blue Naval Veterans' Association, Zanesville, Ohio.
Monitor Naval Veterans' Association, Brooklyn, N. Y.
Cincinnati Naval Veterans' Association, Cincinnati, Ohio.
Minnesota Naval Veterans' Association, St. Paul, Minn.
Admiral Du Pont Naval Veterans' Association, Fort Worth, Tex.
Commodore Perry Naval Veterans' Association, Cleveland, Ohio.
Shirk Naval Veterans' Association, Erie, Pa.
Kearsarge Naval Veterans' Association, Portsmouth, N. H.
Black Hawk Naval Veterans' Association, Indianapolis, Ind.
Dahlgren Naval Veterans' Association, Lowell, Mass.
Kennebec Naval Veterans' Association, Bath, Me.

At this writing, October 20, 1893, there are Associations almost ready for charter in Boston, Philadelphia, Pittsburgh, and Annapolis.

At the last National Convention, held in Indianapolis, Ind., September 7, 1893, the "Union Jack" was substituted for the red, white, and blue ribbon formerly attached to the badge of the Association, and the following officers were elected:

Rear Admiral Commanding—B. S. Osbon, 429 Broadway, New York.
Commodore—Cyrus Sears, 423 Lafayette Avenue, Baltimore, Md.
Captain—R. N. Hopkins, 128 South Clark Street, Chicago, Ill.
Commander—C. H. Leaman, Market and Jefferson Streets, Dayton, Ohio

Lieutenant Commander—Samuel B. Dixon, 63 Brady, corner John R. Street, Detroit, Mich.
Senior Lieutenant—Benj. D. Blanchard, 372 West Forty-sixth Street, New York.
Lieutenant—Joseph Chace, Jr., 33 Belmont Avenue, Providence, R. I.
Surgeon—C. Marion Dodson, 1408 Madison Avenue, Baltimore, Md.
Paymaster—Erdix F. Dustin, 90 Friendship Street, Providence, R. I.
Engineer—John B. Wirt, 8 Indiana Avenue, Indianapolis, Ind.
Chaplain—Rev. Samuel Alman, 227 Division Avenue, Brooklyn, N. Y.
National Secretary—George W. Bostwick, 52 Atlantic Street, Brooklyn, N. Y.
National Boatswain—W. E. Goodnough, 503 East Street, New Haven Conn.
Senior Aide, Chief of Staff—Commander Will E. Atkins, Cherry Street, North Chase Avenue (Cumminsville) Cincinnati, Ohio.
National Historian—Past Commander Wm. Simmons, 1432 Wharton Street, Philadelphia, Pa.

"THE MILITARY ORDER OF THE LOYAL LEGION OF THE UNITED STATES."

The "Loyal Legion" owes its origin to a meeting of Col. S. B Wylie Mitchell, Lt.-Col. T. Ellwood Zell, and Capt. Peter D. Keyser, M. D., which was held on the day following the assassination of President Lincoln, when they met in Lt.-Col. Zell's office in Philadelphia to arrange for a meeting of the ex-officers of the Army and Navy to adopt a set of resolutions relative to the death of the President.

The advisability of forming a permanent organization was discussed, and they agreed to consider the matter, and take more definite action at a future meeting.

On the 20th of April, 1865, another meeting was held, at which it was decided to form a permanent organization, and they adjourned to meet in the hall of the Hibernia Fire Company, of Philadelphia, May 3, 1865.

BADGE.

During the month of May a Constitution and By-Laws were adopted, which provided for the following officers: Commander, Senior and Junior Vice-Commanders, Recorder, Correspondent, Treasurer, Chancellor, Chaplain, and Council. The plan of organization provides for a National organization or Commandery-in-Chief, State Organizations or Grand Commanderies, Local or District Commanderies.

The first Commander-in-Chief was Lt.-Col. T. Ellwood Zell, who was succeeded by Maj.-Gen. George Cadwalader, Maj.-Gen. Winfield S. Hancock, Maj.-Gen. Rutherford B. Hayes, Gen. Philip H. Sheridan, and Rear-Admiral John J. Almy respectively.

The memberships are divided into three classes: *First*, Commissioned Officers of the Army or Navy who were actively engaged in suppressing the Rebellion, or, the eldest male lineal descendants of such deceased officers, provided such descendants be twenty-one years of age or over; *second*, the eldest sons of living companions or members of the first class, provided they be twenty-one years of age or over; *third*, gentlemen in civil life, who were conspicuous for loyalty to the National Government during the Rebellion.

The objects of the Association are: "To cherish the memories and associations of the war waged in defense of the unity and indivisibility of the Republic; to strengthen the ties of fraternal fellowship and sympathy, formed from the companionship in arms; to advance the best interests of the soldiers and sailors of the United States; to extend all possible relief to their widows and children; to foster the cultivation of military and naval science, and, in general, to maintain national honor, unity, and independence."

The "Loyal Legion" has grown and prospered, and has now more than eleven thousand members on its rolls, with active Commanderies in nineteen States and the District of Columbia.

The interests of the "Loyal Legion" and the Grand Army are nearly identical, and many Veterans have a membership in both organizations.

"UNION VETERAN LEGION."

BADGE.

As originally organized in Pittsburgh, Pa., in March, 1884, membership in the "Union Veteran Legion" was restricted to "officers, soldiers, and marines of the Union Army, Navy, or Marine Corps during the War of the Rebellion, who volunteered, prior to July 1, 1863, for a term of three years, and were honorably discharged for any cause, after a continuous service of two years, or were at any time discharged by reason of wounds received in the line of duty; but no drafted person, nor substitute, nor any one who has at any time borne arms against the United States is eligible."

The clause relative to eligibility to membership was changed at the annual meeting held at Youngstown, Ohio, February 22, 1888, and those, also, were made eligible to membership who volunteered for a term of two years; prior to July 22, 1861, and served their full term of enrollment, unless discharged for wounds received in the line of duty.

The Order has a National Encampment, also Local Organizations, or Encampments, with the following officers: Colonel-Commander, Lieutenant-Colonel, Major, Officer of the Day, Adjutant, Quartermaster, Chaplain, Officer of the

U. V. L. BUTTON.

Guard, Surgeon, Sergeant-Major, Quartermaster-Sergeant, Color-Bearer, Sentinel, and Drummer, or Bugler.

The executive authority is conferred upon the National officers, there being no Department organizations, as in the Grand Army.

The first National Encampment was held at Pittsburgh, Pa., February 18, 1887, when George B. Chalmers, of Pittsburgh, was chosen its first National Commander.

The objects of the "Union Veteran Legion" are: "*First*, the cultivation of true devotion to the American Government and institutions; *second*, the moral, social, and intellectual improvement of its members and their relief, and the relief of their widows and orphans, in sickness and distress; *third*, the preservation of friendly relations among those who fought for the safety of the American Union; *fourth*, by the personal example and influence of its members to perpetuate the three great principles of 'Fraternity, Charity, and Patriotism,' and to promote the interests of humanity; *fifth*, all things being equal, to give preference to its members in all business relations, and to assist them, as far as possible, in all honorable ways."

"UNION VETERANS' UNION."

This organization was formed at Washington, D. C., June 18, 1886, through the efforts of M. A. Dillon, who was also elected its first Commander-in-Chief.

It has a National organization and subordinate commands, with the following officers: Colonel, Lieutenant-Colonel, Major, Surgeon, Chaplain, Officer of the Day, Officer of the Guard, Adjutant, Quartermaster, Sergeant-Major, Quartermaster-Sergeant, Drum-Major, Color-Bearer, and Sentinel.

Eligibility to membership consists in having had at least six months' continuous service, unless discharged on account of wounds (part of which must have been at the front), in the Army, Navy, or Marine Corps of the United States, between April 12, 1861, and April 30, 1865, and an honorable discharge from the same.

The society also admits to honorary membership gentlemen of good moral character, not entitled to join as comrades, who are willing to co-operate with the Command in promoting the objects of the " Union Veterans' Union."

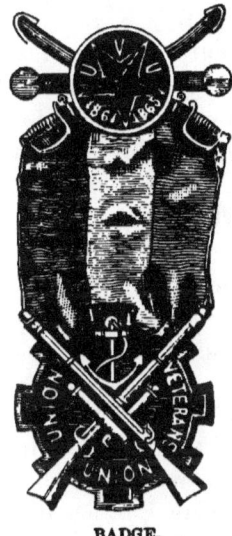
BADGE.

The objects of the "Union Veterans' Union" are: "*First*, to preserve and perpetuate the principles for which we contended on many battle-fields; *second*, to recognize the rights of the soldier to positions of public trust, and the preferment of our members over others for employment by the Government, or by individuals, other things being equal; *third*, to demand of this Government a proper appreciation of their services and a just recognition of their claims; *fourth*, to support, aid, and assist in the election to positions of public trust any and all true friends of the Union Soldier, irrespective of politics, creed, or party; *fifth*, to extend to our comrades, their widows and orphans, in time of need, that charity that knows no end."

"THE VETERANS' RIGHTS UNION."

The tendency of heads of departments and government officials to discriminate against the old soldier in filling positions of trust and profit in their respective departments, and to ignore the rights of Veterans of the late War, who, in every respect, were worthy and competent to fill such positions, aroused the righteous indignation of all their old comrades in arms. To remedy this and secure for them, at least, an equal chance to fill positions in the Civil Government, when there were vacancies which they were competent to fill, a convention was called, at the solicitation of

Post No. 135, Department of New York, to meet in New York city, October 13, 1882, " to consider the best means of advancing the interests of Veterans employed, or seeking to be employed, in the Local, State, and National Governments."

In response to this call, about one hundred and fifty Posts of the G. A. R. sent representatives, and the " Veterans' Rights Union " was formed, the members pledging themselves, in the resolutions adopted, " by all legitimate methods, to maintain the rights and assert the privileges of the Veteran Soldiers and Sailors of this land, whenever, wherever, and by whomsoever those rights and privileges shall be menaced."

An Executive Committee of five was chosen, with full power to act for the Society, and they pledged themselves not to accept any position of trust or profit under the Government, during the time for which they were chosen.

The object, as explained in their communications, was to secure to those who served under the Government of the United States, during the late War, the privileges and rights guaranteed to them by the statutes of the United States, or any State law that has been or may be enacted for their benefit.

After much perseverance and hard work, the Committee succeeded in securing, directly and indirectly, the passage of a number of laws in the interest of their cause, and, also, the ruling of the Civil Service Commission of the United States, as follows: " Any applicant honorably discharged for such cause (by reason of disability, resulting from such wounds and sickness incurred in the line of duty), who, as the result of an examination, had been placed upon a register as eligible for an appointment, should be certified in preference to any other person thereon, not entitled to such preference, examined for the same part of the service, even though such persons are graded higher."

The Association, through its various committees, has done a great deal for the best intersts of the Veterans, and deserves much credit for the tireless energy of its members in their behalf.

"UNION EX-PRISONERS OF WAR ASSOCIATION."

Soon after the close of the war a number of attempts were made to form societies, composed exclusively of soldiers who had been confined in Confederate prisons, but these attempts were not successful until April 9, 1874, when the "National Union of Andersonville Survivors" was organized at Worcester, Massachusetts; Warren Lee Goss, of Norwich, Connecticut, being chosen President.

At the end of the meeting held at Hartford, Connecticut, April 19, 1877, the title was changed to "National Union of Survivors of Andersonville, and other Southern Military Prisons." This title was again changed to "National Association of Ex-Union Prisoners of War" at a meeting held in Cleveland, Ohio, September 19, 1883.

The meeting for 1887 was held in Chicago, Illinois, September 22 and 23, when the title was finally changed to "Union Ex-Prisoners of War Association," by which title it is known now, and all State Associations were abolished.

The membership of the Order is over two thousand, and its objects are "to strengthen the ties of fraternal fellowship and sympathy, formed by companionship in arms during the Civil War among the survivors of Rebel military prisons; to perpetuate the name and fame of those who have fallen in the prison pens of the South, and in the line of duty; to bind together in the most friendly ties the survivors of the above prisons by joint action of its members in any direction which will secure justice to the living and honor to the dead, and to assist such of our fellow-prisoners as need help and protection, and to extend needful aid to the widows and orphans of those who have fallen."

66 MISCELLANEOUS EMBLEMS, ETC.

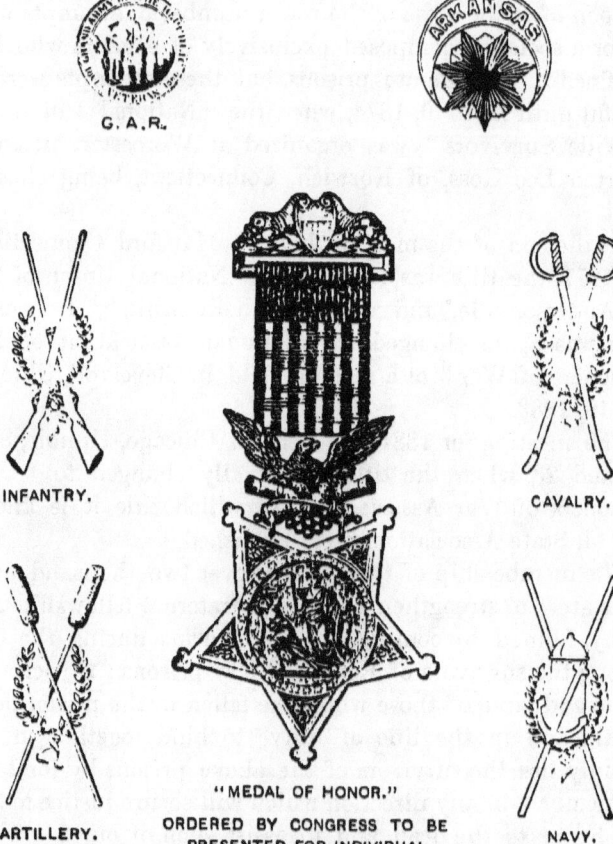

G.A.R.

INFANTRY.

CAVALRY.

ARTILLERY.

NAVY.

"MEDAL OF HONOR."
ORDERED BY CONGRESS TO BE
PRESENTED FOR INDIVIDUAL
ACTS OF BRAVERY.

CHAPTER VI.

VETERAN SOCIETIES.

We recognize no flag but the Stars and Stripes.

WHEN peace again prevailed throughout our land, and the brave boys in blue gladly laid aside the grim implements of war to return to their firesides, a tinge of sadness marred the change, welcome as it was; the ties between congenial spirits that were formed amidst the dangers and privations of a great campaign were not easily broken. Strong men, who were never known to quail in the face of danger, wept like children when the day of parting finally came.

The memories of the camp and battle-field were not easily to be forgotten, and but few regiments disbanded that did not provide for future reunions, when they could meet again under more peaceful auspices, and recall what was pleasant of their former associations. This same spirit led to the organization of that greatest brotherhood of men, known in modern times, "The Grand Army of the Republic," as well as the other organizations of those engaged in special arms of the service.

The first of these Societies was the

THIRD ARMY CORPS UNION

which was formed March 16, 1862, and at first had for its object the raising of funds for embalming and sending home for burial

68   MISCELLANEOUS BADGES, ETC.

Key-Board to the Colors used in the following badges:

the bodies of officers killed in battle or dying in hospitals at the front.

Gen. Sickles was elected its first President, and held that position until prevented from acting by disability.

The Society developed into a permanent institution to which all officers or enlisted men who enlisted in the 3d Corps or participated in the battles of the 3d Corps are eligible.

Meetings are held annually on May 5, the anniversary of the battle of Williamsburg.

SOCIETY OF THE ARMY OF THE TENNESSEE.

This Society owes its origin to a meeting held in the Senate Chamber of the State Capitol at Raleigh, N. C., April 14, 1865. Brig.-Gen. W. B. Woods presided, and a committee of five was appointed to prepare a plan of organization.

At an adjourned meeting held in the same place on the 25th of April a plan of organization was reported, in which the membership was restricted to officers who had served in the "Old Army of the Tennessee." This was afterward amended to admit into membership the relative of any deceased member to whom such membership should descend by bequest, and in default of such declaration the eldest son should inherit his father's title to enrollment in the Society. Maj.-Gen. John A. Rawlins was elected its first President.

The objects, as set forth in the Constitution, are: "To keep alive and preserve that kindly and cordial feeling, which has been one of the characteristics of this Army during its career in the service, and which has given it such harmony of action, and contributed, in no small degree, to its glorious achievements in our country's cause; the fame and glory of all officers belonging to this army who have fallen, either on the field of battle or in the line of their daily duty, shall be a sacred trust to this Society, which shall cause proper memorials of their services to be collected and preserved, and thus to transmit their names with honor to posterity; the families of all such officers who shall be in indigent circumstances will have a claim upon the generosity of the Society, and will be relieved by the voluntary contributions of its members whenever brought to their attention; in like manner, the suffering families of those officers who may hereafter be stricken by death in the hands of the survivors."

THE SOCIETY OF THE ARMY OF THE OHIO.

This Society was organized at a reunion of the Western Societies held in Chicago, Illinois, December 15, 1868, and Maj.-Gen. John M. Schofield was elected its first President.

On the same occasion the "Society of the Army of Georgia" was formed, of which Maj.-Gen. Henry W. Slocum was chosen President.

THE SOCIETY OF THE ARMY OF THE CUMBERLAND.

On the 16th of February, 1868, the organization of this Society was completed at Cincinnati, Ohio, Maj.-Gen. George H. Thomas being elected President.

The Society admits to membership all officers and enlisted men who served in the Army of the Cumberland; its badge, as formally adopted, is very unique, being in part made up of a combination of the corps badges of the 4th, 14th, and 20th Army Corps.

SIGNAL CORPS.

There being no separate and distinct organization of the "Signal Corps," a meeting was called for that purpose in Boston, Mass., in 1867, and on the 14th of November of that year an organization was perfected, with Lieut. J. W. Willard Brown as President. Since 1879 meetings of the Society have been held annually.

SOCIETY OF THE ARMY OF THE JAMES.

This Society was organized in Boston, Mass., September 2, 1865, and Gen. Charles E. Devens was elected its first President. Meetings were held in 1871, 1874, and 1876, when the Society was incorporated with the Army of the Potomac.

SOCIETY OF THE ARMY OF THE POTOMAC.

All who served in the Army of the Potomac, or in the 10th and 18th Corps, Army of the James, are eligible to membership in this Society. It was first organized in New York city on the 5th of July, 1869, with Lieut. Philip H. Sheridan as its first President. Meetings have been held each year since that time, with the exception of 1875. The officers are elected annually, and consist of the following: President; one Vice-President from each of the Army Corps belonging to it, including the 10th and 18th Corps, Army of the James, and one each from the Artillery Corps, Cavalry Corps, Signal Corps, and General Staff, respectively; Treasurer; Recording Secretary, and Corresponding Secretary.

SOCIETY OF THE BURNSIDE EXPEDITION AND THE 9TH CORPS.

This Society was organized in New York city February 8, 1869, and Gen. A. E. Burnside was elected as its first President, which office he filled until his death in 1871, when Vice-President Gen. A. B. R. Sprague filled his position until the next re-union, at which Gen. John F. Parke was made President.

THE SOCIETY OF THE ARMY AND NAVY OF THE GULF.

This Society was made up of officers who had served in the Department of the Gulf, and was instituted at Long Branch, N. J., July 8, 1869. Admiral G. D. Farragut was its first President, holding that position until his death, when Gen. P. H. Sheridan succeeded him.

SOCIETY OF THE ARMY OF WEST VIRGINIA.

The survivors of the Army of West Virginia, organized at Moundsville, W. Va., September 22, 1870, with Gen. R. B. Hayes as President, and have held large and interesting re-unions annually since then.

"THE CINCINNATI SOCIETY OF EX-ARMY AND NAVY OFFICERS."

This Society was organized in Cincinnati, O., October 2, 1874, and Col. Stanley Matthews was elected its first President.

The object of the Society is: "To preserve the feeling of friendship and cordiality among those who served in our National forces during the struggle for the preservation of the Republic, and also to keep a record of its members."

Meetings are held quarterly, also annually on the third Thursday in January.

"PENNSYLVANIA RESERVE ASSOCIATION."

In 1861 Governor Curtin, of Pennsylvania, organized 15 Regiments which were known as "The Pennsylvania Reserve Corps," anticipating a call for troops to serve three years. These Regiments were engaged in active service from the time of their muster-in until the close of the war. A number of the surviving members met in Philadelphia July 3, 1866, and resolved to form a permanent organization, calling a meeting for that purpose at Lancaster, Pa., September 14, 1866, when they formally organized and elected Gov. A. G. Curtin President.

The object of the Society is: "To cherish the memories, perpetuate the friendships, and continue the associations formed in the field."

SOCIETY OF THE ARMY OF ARKANSAS.

This Society was organized in the United States Senate Chamber, Washington, D. C., in February, 1888. It has a total membership of about one thousand, derived from service with the troops constituting the Seventh Army Corps, west of the Mississippi, and the Army of the Frontier. Its object is much the same as Army Societies generally.

PART II.

CORPS BADGES.

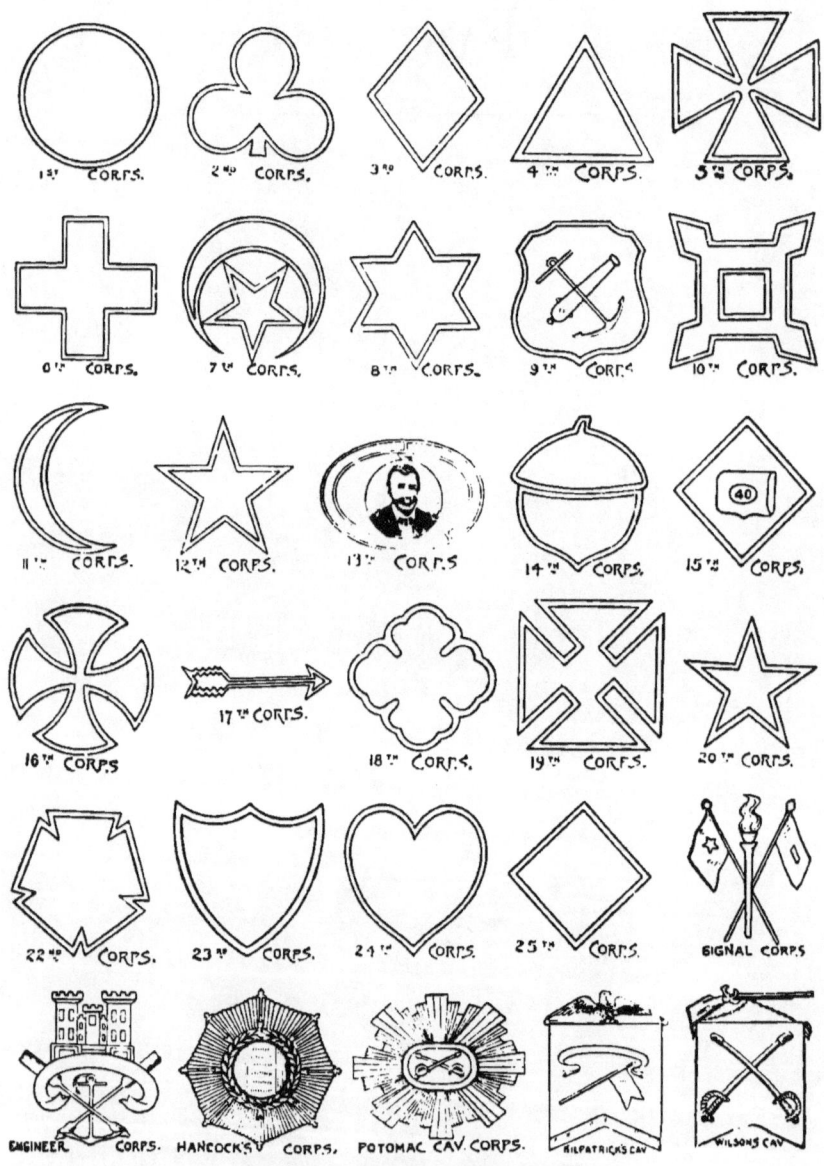

The 21st Corps never adopted a Badge.

THE UNION ARMY.
(SUBDIVIDED.)

IN addition to the Signal and Engineer Corps, which were distinct branches of the service, Hancock's Corps, composed of volunteer veterans, Sheridan's Cavalry Corps, Kilpatrick's Division of Cavalry, and Wilson's Cavalry, the Union Army during the war was subdivided into twenty-five Army Corps. These Corps were designated by the badges represented on the opposite page with the exception of the 21st Corps, which never adopted a badge, and the badge of the 13th Corps, which was adopted after the close of the war. These badges were originally stamped out of flannel cloth, and were worn conspicuously on the front of the soldiers' caps. The color of the badge indicated the Corps Division, namely, Red, the 1st Division; White, the 2d Division; Blue, the 3d Division; Orange, the 4th Division; and Green, the 5th Division. The idea of the Corps Badge appears to have originated in Philip Kearny's Division. In 1862, Kearny ordered his officers and men to wear a red patch on their caps, so that he might distinguish them from those of other commands. The Corps Badges were first officially ordered in the spring of 1863, and were immediately adopted by the Army of the Potomac, but in the Western armies they did not appear on the men's caps until 1864. These badges were also painted on the wagons of the Corps, and stenciled on all its articles of public property.

CORPS SUBDIVISIONS.

The various Army Corps were organized, for the most part, with three Divisions, each Division containing three Brigades, and each Brigade consisting of five Regiments, making forty-five Regiments of Infantry in a Corps, to which were added about nine Batteries of Light Artillery. The Infantry Regiments consisted of ten Companies, of one hundred and one men each; the Artillery and Cavalry Regiments consisted of twelve companies, of one hundred and three and one hundred and five men each.

This form of division was adhered to only as a general rule, and was varied at times to meet temporary exigencies. The greatest variation occurred in the Brigades, the depletion, at times, of some Regiments making additional ones necessary to keep up a proper effective strength. Occasionally a Corps would consist of from four to five Divisions, and during the Atlanta Campaign some Brigades of the Fourth and Fourteenth Corps contained as high as nine Regiments. Fifteen hundred men to a regiment was not an uncommon occurrence, but such irregularities were exceptional, and generally proved to be but temporary arrangements.

HOW DESIGNATED.

The Regiments enlisting from each State were numbered from one upward. The Companies of the Infantry Regiments were designated by the letters of the alphabet from A to K; the Companies or Troops of the Cavalry Regiments and the Companies or Batteries of the Artillery Regiments from A to M, the J being omitted in all cases.

OFFICIAL RANK.

The members of an Infantry Company, in the order of their rank, were as follows: Captain, First Lieutenant, Second Lieutenant, Sergeant, Corporal, Musician, Wagoner, and Private. The members of an Artillery Company, in the order of their rank, were the same as the Infantry, with the exception of the Bugler and Artificer. The members of a Cavalry Company were the same as the Infantry, with the exception of the Bugler, Blacksmith, Farrier, and Saddler.

The officers were either commissioned or non-commissioned. The commissioned officers of a Company were Captain, First Lieutenant, and Second Lieutenant.

The officers of an Infantry and Artillery Regiment, in the order of their rank, were Colonel, Lieutenant-Colonel, Major, Adjutant, Quartermaster, Surgeon, Assistant Surgeon, Chaplain, Sergeant-Major, Quartermaster-Sergeant, Commissary Sergeant, Hospital Steward, and Principal Musician. In addition to the above the Cavalry Regiments had a Chief Bugler or Trumpeter, Saddler-Sergeant, and Veterinary Surgeon.

The commissioned Field and Staff Officers of a Regiment were Colonel, Lieutenant-Colonel, Major, Surgeon, Assistant Surgeon, Adjutant, Quartermaster, and Chaplain.

The Corps, Divisions, Brigades, and different armies were commanded by Brigadier and Major-Generals, in the order of their rank and line of promotion.

The entire Union forces were subject to the orders of a Commander-in-Chief, who, in turn, was subservient to the orders of the War Department. Winfield S. Scott was Commander-in-Chief at the time the war broke out. He was succeeded by Gen. Geo. B. McClellan, November 1, 1861; McClellan was succeeded by Gen. H. W. Halleck, July 11, 1862, and Halleck was succeeded by Gen. U. S. Grant, March 9, 1864.

Prior to the restoration of the rank of Lieutenant-General, which was restored on the 26th day of February, 1864, by an act of Congress, Secretary of War Edwin M. Stanton persisted in exercising the power of the War Department to dictate to the Commander-in-Chief the movements of the Union forces. General Grant, when offered the Lieutenant-Generalship, said that he would accept it only on the condition that he should have "absolute control." Mr. Stanton was opposed to giving Grant so much power, but President Lincoln declared that Grant's request should be complied with, thus exercising the President's constitutional power of command over the entire army and navy. General Grant received his commission as Lieutenant-General on the 9th day of March, 1864, and three days later assumed command, relieving Major-General H. W. Halleck.

NAVAL OFFICERS.

The Naval officers, in the order of their rank, were as follows:

Rear-Admiral,	with the rank of	Major-General.
Commodore,	" " "	Brigadier-General.
Captain,	" " "	Colonel.
Commander,	" " "	Lieutenant-Colonel.
Lieutenant-Commander,	" " "	Major.
Lieutenant,	" " "	Captain.
Master,	" " "	First Lieutenant.
Ensign,	" " "	Second Lieutenant.

EXPLANATION OF OPPOSITE PAGE.

George Washington, the " Father of our Country."

Abraham Lincoln, President of the United States during the Civil War.

Lieutenant-General U. S. Grant, afterward commissioned "*General*" by an act of Congress, which rank extended to Sherman and Sheridan.

Major-General Wm. T. Sherman, Commander of the Western Army, and hero of the Atlanta Campaign and " Sherman's March to the Sea."

Major-General Phil. H. Sheridan, Cavalry Commander and hero of Cedar Creek.

Major-General George G. Meade, Commander of the Army of the Potomac and hero of Gettysburg.

Major-General W. S. Hancock, the "Superb" (and of Wilderness fame).

Major-General George H. Thomas, Commander of the Army of the Cumberland.

Rear-Admiral Farragut, Commander of the Naval Forces.

CORPS COMMANDERS.

First Corps.—Irwin McDowell, Jos. Hooker, J. F. Reynolds, John Newton.
Second Corps.—E. V. Sumner, D. N. Couch, W. S. Hancock, Wm. Hays, G. K. Warren, A. A. Humphreys.
Third Corps.—S. P. Heintzelman, Geo. Stoneman, D. E. Sickles, W. H. French.
Fourth Corps.—E. D. Keyes, Gordon Granger, O. O. Howard, D. S. Stanley, T. J. Wood.
Fifth Corps.—N. P. Banks, F. J. Porter, Daniel Butterfield, Geo. G. Meade, George Sykes, G. K. Warren.
Sixth Corps.—W. B. Franklin, W. F. Smith, J. Sedgwick, H. G. Wright.
Seventh Corps.—John A. Dix, Frederick Steele.
Eighth Corps.—J. E. Wood, Geo. Crook, Lew Wallace, E. O. Ord.
Ninth Corps.—A. E. Burnside, J. L. Reno, J. D. Cox, O. B. Wilcox, J. Sedgwick, W. F. Smith, J. G. Parke, R. B. Potter.
Tenth Corps.—O. M. Mitchell, J. M. Brannan, David Hunter, Q. A. Gilmore, D. B. Birney, A. H. Terry.
Eleventh Corps.—Frantz Siegel, O. O. Howard.
Twelfth Corps.—J. K. Mansfield, A. S. Williams, H. W. Slocum.
Thirteenth Corps.—U. S. Grant, J. A. McClernand, E. O. Ord, Gordon Granger.
Fourteenth Corps.—W. S. Rosecrans, Geo. H. Thomas, J. M. Palmer, J. C. Davis.
Fifteenth Corps.—W. T. Sherman, F. P. Blair, John A. Logan, P. J. Osterhaus.
Sixteenth Corps.—S. A. Hurlbut, G. M. Dodge, A. J. Smith.
Seventeenth Corps.—J. B. McPherson, F. P. Blair.
Eighteenth Corps.—J. G. Foster, J. M. Palmer, B. F. Butler, W. F. Smith, E. O. Ord, Godfrey Weitzel.
Nineteenth Corps.—N. P. Banks, Wm. B. Franklin, W. H. Emory, G. C. Grover.

Twentieth Corps.—A. McD. McCook, Jos. Hooker, H. W. Slocum, A. S. Williams, J. A. Mower.
Twenty-first Corps.—T. L. Crittenden.
Twenty-second Corps.—S. P. Heintzelman, J. G. Parke, C. C. Augur.
Twenty-third Corps.—G. L. Hartsuff, M. D. Manson, J. D. Cox, Geo. Stoneman, J. M. Schofield.
Twenty-fourth Corps.—E. O. Ord, A. H. Terry, Chas. Devens, J. Gibbon, J. W. Turner.
Twenty-fifth Corps.—Godfrey Weitzel.

LIST OF UNION ARMY REGIMENTS.

The following is a list of the regiments, etc. which served in the Union armies, with total loss, or number of officers and men who were killed, or who died of wounds, disease, accidents, in prisons, etc., according to the States from which they enlisted:

Connecticut Enlistments.

Connecticut had in the service twenty-nine Infantry Regiments, one Cavalry Regiment, two Heavy Artillery Regiments, and three Light Batteries.

Total loss of officers and men by death, 5,354.

Delaware Enlistments.

Delaware had in the service nine Infantry Regiments, one Cavalry Regiment, one Heavy Artillery Regiment, and one Light Battery.

Total loss of officers and men by death, **882**.

Illinois Enlistments.

Illinois had in the service one hundred and fifty-eight Infantry Regiments, including Sturgis Rifles, the Marine Brigade, and the Alton Battalion, seventeen Cavalry Regiments, two Light Artillery Regiments, and eight Independent Batteries.

Total loss of officers and men by death, 34,834.

Indiana Enlistments.

Indiana had in the service one hundred and fifty-six Infantry Regiments, thirteen Cavalry Regiments, one Heavy Artillery Regiment, and twenty-six Light Batteries.

Total loss of officers and men by death, 26,672.

Iowa Enlistments.

Iowa had in the service forty-eight Infantry Regiments, nine Cavalry Regiments, and four Light Batteries.

Total loss of officers and men by death, 13,001.

Kansas Enlistments.

Kansas had in the service seven Infantry Regiments, nine Cavalry Regiments and three Light Batteries.

Total loss of officers and men by death, 2,630.

Kentucky Enlistments.

Kentucky had in the service fifty-five Infantry Regiments, including "Patterson's Ky. Company" and the "State Defense Regiments," seventeen Cavalry Regiments, and five Light Batteries.

Total loss of officers and men by death, 10,744.

Maine Enlistments.

Maine had in the service thirty-two Infantry Regiments, also the 1st Maine Battalion and the "Maine Coast Guard," two Cavalry Regiments, one Heavy Artillery Regiment, and seven Light Batteries.

Total loss of officers and men by death, 9,398.

Maryland Enlistments.

Maryland had in the service nineteen Infantry Regiments, including the "Purnell Legion" and "Patapsco Guards," four Cavalry Regiments, and two Light Batteries.

Total loss of officers and men by death, 2,982.

Massachusetts Enlistments.

Massachusetts had in the service sixty-two Infantry Regiments, five Cavalry Regiments, four Heavy Artillery Regiments, the 1st Massachusetts Battalion, seventeen Light Batteries, and 1st and 2d Companies of Massachusetts Sharpshooters, also the 4th, 5th, and 6th Massachusetts "Three Months' Men," and the 5th, 6th, 8th, and 42d "Hundred Days' Men."

Total loss of officers and men by death, 13,942.

Michigan Enlistments.

Michigan had in the service thirty Infantry Regiments, eleven Cavalry Regiments, one Light Artillery Regiment, two Light Batteries, 1st Michigan Engineers, and two Companies of Sharpshooters.

Total loss of officers and men by death, 14,753.

Minnesota Enlistments.

Minnesota had in the service eleven Infantry Regiments, two Cavalry Regiments, one Heavy Artillery Regiment, three Light Batteries, and two Battalions.

Total loss of officers and men by death, 2,584.

Missouri Enlistments.

Missouri had in the service sixty-one Infantry Regiments, including Missouri Home Guards, thirty-four Cavalry Regiments, three Light Artillery Regiments, three Light Batteries, and "Bissell's" 1st Missouri Engineers.

Total loss of officers and men by death, 13,885.

New Hampshire Enlistments.

New Hampshire had in the service eighteen Infantry Regiments, one Cavalry Regiment, one Heavy Artillery Regiment, and one Light Battery.

Total loss of officers and men by death, 4,882.

New Jersey Enlistments.

New Jersey had in the service forty Infantry Regiments, three Cavalry Regiments, and five Light Batteries.
Total loss of officers and men by death, 5,754.

New York Enlistments.

New York had in the service one hundred and ninety-four Infantry Regiments, including "*Les Enfans Perdus;*" twenty-seven Cavalry Regiments, the 1st and 2d New York Mounted Rifles, thirteen Heavy Artillery Regiments, 1st New York Marine Artillery, 1st New York Light Artillery, thirty-three Independent Batteries, 1st, 15th, and 50th New York Engineers, 1st New York Sharpshooters, consisting of six Companies; one Independent Company, and the 8th, 69th, 71st, and 84th New York National Guards.
Total loss of officers and men by death, 46,534.

Ohio Enlistments.

Ohio had in the service one hundred and ninety-eight Infantry Regiments, including the Dennison and Trumbull Guards; thirteen Cavalry Regiments, two Heavy Artillery Regiments, one Light Artillery Regiment, twenty-four Light Batteries, 3d and 4th Ohio Independent Companies, three Battalions, McLaughlin's Squadron, and the 1st Ohio Battalion of Sharpshooters.
Total loss of officers and men by death, 35,475.

Pennsylvania Enlistments.

Pennsylvania had in the service two hundred and fifteen Infantry Regiments, twenty-three Cavalry Regiments, four Heavy Artillery Regiments, one Light Artillery Regiment, and one Independent Battery.
Total loss of officers and men by death, 33,183.

Rhode Island Enlistments.

Rhode Island had in the service twelve Infantry Regiments, three Cavalry Regiments, two Heavy Artillery Regiments, and one Light Artillery Regiment.
Total loss of officers and men by death, 1,321.

Tennessee Enlistments.

Tennessee had in the service six Infantry Regiments, one Mounted Infantry Regiment, and ten Cavalry Regiments.
Total loss of officers and men by death, 6,777.

Vermont Enlistments.

Vermont had in the service seventeen Infantry Regiments, one Cavalry Regiment, one Heavy Artillery Regiment, and three Light Batteries.
Total loss of officers and men by death, 5,224.

West Virginia Enlistments.

West Virginia had in the service sixteen Infantry Regiments, eight Cavalry Regiments, and one Light Artillery Regiment, consisting of eight Companies.
Total loss of officers and men by death, 4,017.

Wisconsin Enlistments.

Wisconsin had in the service fifty-three Infantry Regiments, three Cavalry Regiments, one Heavy Artillery Regiment, and thirteen Light Batteries.
Total loss of officers and men by death, 12,301.

Miscellaneous Enlistments.

In addition to the foregoing statistics, there were a number of

LIST OF UNION ARMY REGIMENTS.

Regiments enlisted from the Territories, Southern States, etc., with loss by death, as follows:

Alabama,	Total loss,	345.
Arkansas,	"	"	1,713.
California,	"	"	573.
Colorado,	"	"	325.
Dakota,	"	"	6.
District of Columbia,	"	"	290.
Florida,	"	"	215.
Georgia,	"	"	15.
Louisiana,	"	"	945.
Mississippi,	"	"	78.
Nebraska,	"	"	239.
New Mexico,	"	"	204.
Nevada,	"	"	33.
North Carolina,	"	"	360.
Oregon,	"	"	45.
Texas,	"	"	141.
Virginia,	"	"	42.
Washington Territory,	"	"	22.

United States Enlistments.

The United States had in the service nineteen Infantry Regiments, thirty-two Colored Infantry Regiments, six Cavalry Regiments, three Colored Cavalry Regiments, five Artillery Regiments, one Colored Heavy Artillery Regiment, and the 1st and 2d U. S. Sharpshooters.

Nineteen of the United States Regiments, namely, ten Infantry, four Artillery, and five Cavalry, constituted the regular Army prior to the Civil War.

Total loss of officers and men by death, 5,798.

Colored Troops.

There were, in all, one hundred and sixty-six Regiments of Colored Troops engaged in the Civil War, commanded by white officers.

The total loss by death of these Regiments, including officers, was 36,847, of which over 25,000 died of disease, wounds, and in Confederate prisons.

TOTAL LOSS AND COST.

The total loss of the Union Armies by death on the field, in hospitals, and prisons, by disease, accidents, etc., was 359,528 officers and men.

Total loss of life, including Union and Confederate Armies, nearly 800,000 officers and men.

Total cost of the War to the United States, over $4,000,000,000.

CORPS ENGAGEMENTS

OF THE

CIVIL WAR.

The engagements and skirmishes which occurred before the reorganization of the Union army by corps, also in which only detachments of corps participated, cannot properly be classed as corps engagements, and have therefore been omitted from the following list. For particulars as to all such engagements, also casualties of all important engagements, see *alphabetical list* beginning on page 111.

FIRST CORPS.
(Army of the Potomac.)

Commanders: Irwin McDowell, Joseph Hooker, J. F. Reynolds, John Newton.

ENGAGEMENTS:

Cedar Mountain or Slaughter Mountain, Va., Aug. 9, 1862.
Rappahannock or Kelly's Ford, Va., Aug. 21, 1862.
Gainesville, Va., Aug. 28, 1862.
Groveton, Va., Aug. 29, 1862.
2d Bull Run or Manassas, Va., Aug. 30, 1862.
South Mountain, Turner or Crampton's Gap, Md., Sept. 14, 1862.
Antietam or Sharpsburg, Md., Sept. 17. 1862.
Fitzhugh Crossing, Va., April 29, 30, 1863.
Chancellorsville, Va., May 1-4, 1863.
Gettysburg, Pa., July 1-3, 1863.
Mine Run or Locust Grove, Va., Nov. 26-28, 1863.

The 1st Corps as an organization discontinued in March, 1864, and the regiments were transferred to the 5th Corps, Robinson's Div. becoming the 2d Div. of the 5th Corps and Wadsworth's Div. the 4th Div. of the 5th Corps.

SECOND CORPS.
(Army of the Potomac.)

Commanders: E. V. Sumner, D. N. Couch, W. S. Hancock, Wm. Hays, G. K. Warren, A. A. Humphreys.

ENGAGEMENTS:

Yorktown, Va., April 5 to May 3, 1862.
Fair Oaks or Seven Pines, Va., May 31, and June 1, 1862.
Oak Grove, Va., June 25, 1862.
Gaines' Mills, Va., June 27, 1862.
Savage Station, Va., June 29, 1862.
Peach Orchard or Allen's Farm, Va., June 29, 1862.
White Oak Swamp or Glendale, Va., June 30, 1862.
Malvern Hill, Va., July 1, 1862.
Antietam or Sharpsburg, Md., Sept. 17, 1862.
Fredericksburg, Va., Dec. 13, 1862.
Chancellorsville, Va., May 1-4, 1863.
Gettysburg, Pa., July 1-3, 1863.
Auburn or Bristoe Station, Va., Oct. 14, 1863.
Mine Run or Locust Grove, Va., Nov. 26-28, 1863.
Morton's Ford, Va., Feb. 6, 1864.

Wilderness, Va., May 5-7, 1864.
Corbin's Bridge, Va., May 8, 1864.
Po River, Va., May 10, 1864.
Spottsylvania, Va., May 8-18, 1864.
North Anna, Va., May 23-27, 1864.
Totopotomoy, Va., May 29-31, 1864.
Cold Harbor, Va., June 1-12, 1864.
Petersburg, Va., June 15, 19, 20-30, 1864; April 2, 1865.
Weldon R.R., William's Farm, Davis Farm, or Jerusalem Plank Road, Va., June 22, 23, 1864.
Deep Bottom, New Market and Malvern Hill, Va., July 27, 28, 1864.
Mine Explosion, Petersburg, Va., July 30, 1864.
Strawberry Plains or Deep Bottom Run, Va., Aug. 14-18, 1864.
Ream's Station, Va., Aug. 25, 1864.
Preble Farm or Poplar Spring Church, Va., Sept. 30, 1864.
Hatcher's Run or Boydton Road, Oct. 27, 1864.
Boydton and White Oak Road, Va., March 31, 1865.
Sutherland Station, Va., April 2, 1865.
Sailor's Creek or Harper's Farm and Deatonsville, Va., April 6, 1865.
Farmville, Va., April 7, 1865.
Appomattox or Lee's Surrender, Va., April 9, 1865.

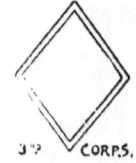

THIRD CORPS.

(Army of the Potomac.)

Commanders: S. P. Heintzelman, George Stoneman, D. E. Sickles, W. H. French.

ENGAGEMENTS:

Yorktown, Va., April 5 to May 3, 1862.
Williamsburg, Va., May 5, 1862.
Fair Oaks or Seven Pines, Va., May 31, and June 1, 1862.
Oak Grove, Va., June 25, 1862.
White Oak Swamp or Glendale, Va., June 30, 1862.
Malvern Hill, Va., July 1, 1862.
Bristoe Station or Kettle Run, Va., Aug. 27, 1862.
Groveton and Gainesville, Va., Aug. 28, 29, 1862.
2d. Bull Run or Manassas, Va., Aug. 30, 1862.
Chantilly or Ox Hill, Va., Sept. 1, 1862.
Fredericksburg, Va., Dec. 13, 1862.
Chancellorsville, Va., May 1-4, 1863.
Gettysburg, Pa., July 1-3, 1863.
Wapping Heights or Manassas Gap, Va., July 23, 1863.
Kelley's Ford, Va., Nov. 7, 1863.
Mine Run or Locust Grove, Va., Nov. 26-28, 1863.
The 3d Corps was discontinued March 23, 1864. The 1st

and 2d Divisions were transferred to the 2d Corps. The 3d Division to the 6th Corps.

1st Division under Gen. Birney; 2d Division, Gen. Mott; 3d Division, Gen. Ricketts.

FOURTH CORPS.

(Army of the Potomac and Cumberland.)

Commanders: E. D. Keyes, Gordon Granger, O. O. Howard, D. S. Stanley, T. J. Wood.

ENGAGEMENTS.

Army of the Potomac.
Yorktown, Va., April 5 to May 3, 1862.
Lee's Mills, Va., April 16, 1862.
Williamsburg, Va., May 5, 1862.
Fair Oaks or Seven Pines, Va., May 31, and June 1, 1862.
Oak Grove, Va., June 25, 1862.
Seven days' battle, Va., June 26 to July 1, 1862.
Antietam or Sharpsburg, Md., Sept. 17, 1862.

Army of the Cumberland.
Orchard Knob or Chattanooga, Tenn., Nov. 23, 1863.
Lookout Mountain, Tenn., Nov. 24, 1863.
Mission Ridge, Tenn., Nov. 25, 1863.
Dandridge, Tenn., Jan. 16, 17, 1864.
Buzzard's Roost, Tunnel Hill, Rocky Face Ridge, Ga., Feb. 25-27, 1864.
Rocky Face Ridge, Ga., May 5-9, 1864.
Resaca or Sugar Valley or Oostenaula, Ga., May 13-16, 1864.
Adairsville, Ga., May 17, 18, 1864.

Cassville, Ga., May 19-22, 1864.
Dallas or New Hope Church, Ga., May 25 to June 4, 1864.
Pickett's Mills, Ga., May 27, 1864.
Kenesaw Mountain, including Pine Mountain, Pine Knob, Golgotha, Culp House, McAfee's Cross Roads, Latimer's Mills, Noon-Day Creek, Powder Springs, Ga., June 9-30, 1864.
Nickajack Creek, Smyrna Camp Ground, Vining Station, Ga., July 2-5, 1864.
Peach Tree, Ga., July 20, 1864.
Siege of Atlanta, Ga., July 22-28 to Sept. 2, 1864.
Jonesboro, Ga., Aug. 31 to Sept. 1, 1864.
Lovejoy Station, Ga., Sept. 2-6, 1864.
Spring Hill or Mt. Carmel, Ga., Nov. 20, 1864.
Franklin, Tenn., Nov. 30, 1864.
Nashville, Tenn., Dec. 15, 16, 1864.
Occupation of Texas, June to December, 1865.

After the battle of Antietam Couch's Division became the 3d Division of the 6th Corps.

FIFTH CORPS.

(Army of the Potomac.)

Commanders: N. P. Banks, F. J. Porter, Daniel Butterfield, George G. Meade, George Sykes, G. K. Warren.

ENGAGEMENTS:

Hanover, C. H., Va., May 27, 1862.
Mechanicsville, Va., June 26, 1862.
Gaines' Mills, Va., June 27, 1862.
White Oak Swamp, or Glendale, Va., June 30, 1862.
Malvern Hill, Va., July 1, 1862.
2d Bull Run or Manassas, Va., Aug. 30, 1862.
Antietam or Sharpsburg, Md., Sept. 17, 1862.
Shepardstown or Blackfords Ford, Va., Sept. 20, 1862.
Fredericksburg, Va., Dec. 13, 1862.
Chancellorsville, Va., May 1-4, 1863.
Gettysburg, Pa., July 1-3, 1863.
Bristoe Station, Va., Oct. 14, 1863.
Rappahannock Station, Va., Nov. 7, 1863.
Mine Run or Locust Grove, Va., Nov. 26-28, 1863.
Wilderness, Va., May 5-7, 1864.
Alsop Farm, Va., May 10, 1864.
Laurel Hill, Va., May 18, 1864.
Spottsylvania, C. H., Va., May 8-18, 1864.
North Anna, Va., May 23-27, 1864.
Totopotomoy, Va., May 30, 31, 1864.
Bethesda Church, Va., May 30 to June 6, 1864.
Cold Harbor, Va., June 1-12, 1864.
Petersburg, Va., June 15-30 to Aug. 1-31, 1864, April 2, 1865.
Weldon R. R., Va., June 22, 23, 1864.
Mine Explosion, Va., July 30, 1864.
Six Mile House, Weldon R. R., Va., Aug. 18-21, 1864.
Preble's Farm and Poplar Spring Church, Va., Sept. 30 to Oct. 1, 1864.
Hatcher's Run or Boydton Road, Va., Oct. 27, 1864.
Dabney's Mills or Rowanty Creek, Vaughn Road, Hatcher's Run, Va., Feb. 5-7, 1865.
Quaker Road or Gravelly Run, Va., March 29, 1865.
Boydton and White Oak Road, Va., March 31, 1865.
Five Forks, Va., April 1, 1865.
Appomattox and Lee's Surrender, Va., April 9, 1865.

SIXTH CORPS.

(Army of the Potomac.)

Commanders: W. B. Franklin, W. F. Smith, J. Sedgwick, H. G. Wright.

ENGAGEMENTS.

West Point, Va., May 7, 8, 1862.
Gaines Mills, Va., June 27, 28, 1862.
Golding Farm, Va., June 28, 1862.
Savage Station, Va., June 29, 1862.
White Oak Swamp or Glendale, Va., June 30, 1862.
Malvern Hill, Va., July 1, 1862.
Bull Run Bridge, Va., Aug. 27, 1862.
South Mountain, Turner or Crampton's Gap, Md., Sept. 14, 1862.
Antietam or Sharpsburg, Md., Sept. 17, 1862.
Fredericksburg, Va., Dec. 13, 1862.
Marye's Heights and Salem Church, Va., May 3, 1863.
Bank's Ford, Va., May 4, 1863.
Gettysburg, Pa., July 1-3, 1863.
Funkstown, Md., July 12, 13, 1863.
Rappahannock, Va., Nov. 7, 1863.
Mine Run or Locust Grove, Va., Nov. 26-28, 1863.
Wilderness, Va., May 5-7, 1864.
Spottsylvania, Va., May 8-18, 1864.
Cold Harbor, Va., June 1-12, 1864.
Petersburg, Va., June 15-19, 1864.
Weldon R. R. or Jerusalem Road, Va., June 22, 23, 1864.
Monocacy, Md., July 9, 1864.
Fort Stevens (Washington), D.C., July 11, 12, 1864.
Snicker's Ferry or Island Ford, Va., July 18, 1864.
Winchester, Va., Aug. 17, 1864.
Summit Point, Va., Aug. 21, 1864.
Smithfield, Va., Aug. 29, 1864.
Opequon, Winchester or Belle Grove, Va., Sept. 19, 1864.
Fisher's Hill or Woodstock, Va., Sept. 22, 1864.
Cedar Creek or Middletown, Va., Oct. 19, 1864.
Fall of Petersburg, Va., April 2, 1865.
Sailor's Creek, Harper's Farm or Deatonville, Va., April 6, 1865.
Appomattox or Lee's Surrender, Va., April 9, 1865.*

SEVENTH CORPS.

Commanders: John A. Dix, Frederick Steele.

(Department of Virginia.)

Commander: John A. Dix.

ENGAGEMENTS:

Deserted House, Cassville or Kelly's Store, Va., Jan. 30, 1863.
Siege of Suffolk, Va., April 12 to May 4, 1863.

(Department of Arkansas.)

Commander: Frederick Steele.

ENGAGEMENTS:

Arkadelphia, Ark., March 28, 1864.
Okalona, Ark., April 3, 1864.
Elkin's Ford, Ark., April 4-6, 1864.
Prairie De' Ann, Ark., April 10-13, 1864.
Moscow, Ark., April 13, 1864.
Camden, Ark., April 2-24, 1864.
Mark's Mills, Ark., April 5-25, 1864.
Jenkins' Ferry, Ark., April 30, 1864.

EIGHTH CORPS.

(Army of West Virginia.)

Commanders: J. E. Wood, George Crook, Lew Wallace, E. O. Ord.

ENGAGEMENTS:

Cloyd's Mountain and New River Bridge, Va., May 9, 10, 1864.
Newmarket, Va., May 15, 1864.
Piedmont or Mount Crawford, Va., June 5, 1864.
Lynchburg, Va., June 17, 18, 1864.
Monocacy, Md., July 9, 1864.
Snicker's Ferry, or Island Ford, Va., July 18, 1864.
Winchester, Stevenson Depot, Carter Farm, Va., July 20-24, 1864.
Martinsburg, Va., July 25, 1864.
Halltown, Va., Aug. 24, 1864.
Berryville, Va., Sept. 3, 4, 1864.
Opequon, Winchester or Belle Grove, Va., Sept. 19, 1864.
Fisher's Hill or Woodstock, Va., Sept. 22, 1864.
Cedar Creek, Va., Oct. 19, 1864.
December 18, 1864, Thoburn's Brigades were transferred to 24th Corps.

NINTH CORPS.

(The Wandering Corps.)

Commanders: A. E. Burnside, J. L. Reno, J. D. Cox, O. B. Willcox, J. Sedgwick, W. F. Smith, J. G. Parke, R. B. Potter.

ENGAGEMENTS:

Roanoke Island, N. C., Feb. 7, 8, 1862.
Newbern, N. C., March 14, 1862.

Wilmington Island, Ga., April 16, 1862.
Camden, N. C., April 19, 1862.
James Island, S. C., June 10-13, 1862.
Groveton and Gainesville, Va., Aug. 28, 29, 1862.
2d Bull Run or Manassas, Va., Aug. 30, 1862.
Chantilly or Ox Hill, Va., Sept. 1, 1862.
South Mountain, Turner or Crampton's Gap, Md., Sept. 14, 1862.
Antietam or Sharpsburg, Md., Sept. 17, 1862.
Fredericksburg, Va., Dec. 13, 1862.
Siege of Vicksburg, Miss., May 18 to July 4, 1863.
Jackson, Miss., July 11-16, 1863.
Blue Springs, Tenn., Oct. 10, 1863.
Loudon, Tenn., Nov. 15, 1863.
Lenoir, Tenn., Nov. 15, 1863.
Campbell Station, Tenn., Nov. 16, 1863.
Fort Sanders, Tenn., Nov. 29, 1863.
Siege of Knoxville, Tenn., Nov. 17 to Dec. 4, 1863.
Strawberry Plains, Tenn., Jan. 10, 1864.
Wilderness, Va., May 5-7, 1864.
Ny River, Va., May 12, 1864.
Spottsylvania, Va., May 8-18, 1864.
North Anna, Va., May 23-27, 1864.
Bethesda Church, Va., May 30 to June 6, 1864.
Cold Harbor, Va., June 1-12, 1864.
Petersburg, Va., June 15 to Aug. 1-31, 1864; April 2, 1865.
Mine Explosion, Va., July 30, 1864.
Six Mile House, Weldon R. R., Va., Aug. 18-21, 1864.
Preble Farm, Poplar Spring Ch'ch, Va., Sept. 30, and Oct. 1, 1864.
Hatcher's Run or Boydton Road, Va., Oct. 27, 1864.
Fort Stedman, Va., March 25, 1865.
Fall of Petersburg, Va., April 2, 1865.
In December, 1864, Ferrero's Division, colored troops, was transferred to the 25th Corps.

TENTH CORPS.

(Army of the James.)

Commanders: O. M. Mitchell, J. M. Brannan, David Hunter, Q. A. Gilmore, D. B. Birney, A. H. Terry.

ENGAGEMENTS:

James Island, S. C., June 10-13, 1862.
Pocotaligo or Yemassee, S. C., Oct. 22, 1862.
Morris Island, S. C., July 10, 1863.
Fort Wagner, S. C., July 10 to Sept. 6, 1863.
Olustee, Ocean Pond, or Silver Lake, Fla., February 20, 1864.

CORPS ENGAGEMENTS.

Walthall Junc. or Chester, Va., June 16, 1864.
Swift Creek, or Arrowfield Church, Va., May 9, 10, 1864.
Drewry's Bluff or Fort **Darling**, Va., May 12-16, 1864.
Bermuda Hundred, Va., May 16-30, June 2, Aug. 24-25, 1864.
Cold Harbor, Va., June 1-12, 1864.
Petersburg, Va., June 15-30, 1864.
Strawberry Plains or Deep Bottom, Va., Aug. 14-18, 1864.
Newmarket or Chapin Farm, Va., Sept. 28-30, 1864.
Charles City Road, Va., Oct. 1, 1864.

Darbytown Road, Va., Oct. 7, 1864.
Fair Oaks, Va., Oct. 27, 28, 1864.
Fort Fisher, N. C., Jan. 13-15, 1865.
Sugar Loaf, N. C., Feb. 11, 1865.
Fort Anderson, N. C., Feb. 18, 1865.
Wilmington, N. C., Feb. 23, 1865.
On Dec. 30, 1864, the white regiments were transferred to the 24th Corps, and the colored regiment to the 25th Corps.
Ames' Division and Abbott's Brigade ordered to Ft. Fisher, and with Burger's Division of the 19th Corps reorganized the 10th Corps.

ELEVENTH CORPS.

(Army of the Potomac.)

Commanders: Franz Sigel, O. O. Howard.

ENGAGEMENTS:

McDowell, Va., May 8, 1862.
Cross Keys, Va., June 8, 1862.
Cedar (or Slaughter) Mountain, Va., Aug. 9, 1862.
Freeman's Ford, Va., Aug. 24, 1862.
Sulphur Springs, Va., Aug. 25, 1862.
2d Bull Run or Manassas, Va,. Aug. 30, 1862.
Chancellorsville, Va., May 1-4, 1863.

Gettysburg, Pa., July 1-3, 1863.
Wauhatchie, Tenn., Oct. 27, 1863.
Orchard Knob. Tenn., Nov. 23, 1863.
Lookout Mountain, Tenn., Nov. 24, 1863.
Mission Ridge, Tenn., Nov. 25, 1863.
In April, 1864, the two divisions of the 11th Corps were transferred to the 20th Corps.

TWELFTH CORPS.

(Army of the Potomac.)

Commanders: J. K. Mansfield, A. S. Williams, H. W. Slocum.

ENGAGEMENTS:

Winchester, Va., March 23, 1862.
Port Republic, Va., June 9, 1862.
Cedar (or Slaughter) Mountain, Va., August 9, 1862.
2d Bull Run or Manassas, Va., August 30, 1862.
Antietam, or Sharpsburg, Md., Sept. 17, 1862.
Chancellorsville, Va., May 1-4, 1863.
Gettysburg, Pa., July 1-3, 1863.
Wauhatchie, Tenn., Oct. 27, 1863.
Orchard Knob, Tenn., Nov. 23, 1863.
Lookout Mountain, Tenn., Nov. 24, 1863.
Mission Ridge, Tenn., Nov. 25, 1863.
Ringgold, Ga., Nov. 27, 1863.
In April, 1864, the corps was changed to the 20th.

THIRTEENTH CORPS.

Commanders: U. S. Grant, J. A. McClernand, E. O. Ord, Gordon Granger.

ENGAGEMENTS:

Chickasaw Bayou, Miss., Dec. 28, 29, 1862.
Fort Hinman or Arkansas Post, Ark., Jan. 10, 11, 1863.
Port Gibson, Miss., May 1, 1863.
Champion Hills, Miss., May 16, 1863.
Big Black River, Miss., May 17, 1863.
Siege of Vicksburg, Miss., May 18 to July 4, 1863.
Jackson, Miss., July 9-16, 1863.
Helena, Ark., July 4, 1863.
Grand Coteau or Carrion Crow Bayou, La., Nov. 3, 1863.
Sabine Cross Roads or Mansfield, La., April 8, 1864.
Cane River or Monetis Bluff, La., April 24, 1864.
Cloutierville, La., April 23, 24, 1864.
Spanish Fort, Ala., April 8, 1865.
Fort Blakeley, Ala., March 31 to April 9, 1865.

FOURTEENTH CORPS.
(Army of the Cumberland.)

Commanders: W. S. Rosecrans, Geo. H. Thomas, J. M. Palmer, Jeff. C. Davis.

ENGAGEMENTS:

Perryville or Chapin Hill, Ky., Oct. 8, 1862.
Nolensville or Knob Gap, Tenn., Dec. 26, 1862.
Stone River or Murfreesboro, Tenn., Dec. 31, 1862, to Jan. 2, 1863.
Hoover's Gap, Tenn., June 24, 1863.
Chickamauga, Ga., Sept. 19, 20, 1863.
Orchard Knob, Tenn., Nov. 23, 1863.
Lookout Mountain, Tenn., Nov. 24, 1863.
Mission Ridge, Tenn., Nov. 25, 1863.
Buzzard's Roost or Tunnel Hill, Ga., Feb. 25-27, 1864.

Resaca or Sugar Valley, Ga., May 13-16, 1864.
Rome, Ga., May 17, 18, 1864.
Dallas or New Hope Church, Ga., May 25 to June 4, 1864.
Kenesaw Mountain, Ga., June 9-30, 1864.
Peach Tree Creek, Ga., July 20, 1864.
Utoy Creek, Ga., Aug. 5, 6, 1864.
Siege of Atlanta, Ga., July 22 to Sept. 2, 1864.
Jonesboro, Ga., Aug. 31, 1864.
Lovejoy Station, Ga., Sept. 2-6, 1864.
Savannah, Ga., Dec. 10-21, 1864.
Averasboro, N. C., March 16, 1865.
Bentonville, N. C., March 19-21, 1865.

FIFTEENTH CORPS.
(Army of Tennessee.)

Commanders: W. T. Sherman, F. P. Blair, John A. Logan, P. J. Osterhaus.

ENGAGEMENTS:

Chickasaw Bayou, Miss., Dec. 28, 29, 1862.
Fort Hinman or Arkansas Post, Ark., Jan. 11, 1863.
Deer Creek, Miss., March 21, 1863.

Black Bayou Expedition, Miss., April 5-10, 1863.
Snyder's Bluff, Miss., April 30, '63.
Jackson, Miss., May 14, 1863.
Siege of Vicksburg, Miss., May 18 to July 4, 1863.

Jackson, Clinton, Rienzi or Canton, Miss., July 9-16, 1863.
Brandon, Miss., July 18-20, 1863.
Cane (or Bear) Creek or Tuscumbia, Ala., Oct 24-27, 1863.
Cherokee, Ala., Oct. 29, 1863.
Orchard Knob or Chattanooga, Tenn., Nov. 23, 1863.
Lookout Mountain, Tenn, Nov. 24, 1863.
Mission Ridge, Tenn., Nov. 25, 1863.
Ringgold or Pea Vine Creek, Ga., Nov. 27, 1863.
Resaca, Ga., May 13-16, 1864.
Dallas or New Hope Church, Ga., May 25 to June 4, 1864.
Big Shanty, Ga., June 6, 1864.
Kenesaw, Ga., June 9-30, 1864.
Nickajack Creek, Smyrna or Vining Station, July 2-5, 1864.
Siege of Atlanta, Ga., July 22 to Sept. 2, 1864.
Ezra Church, Ga., July 28, 1864.
Jonesboro, Ga., Aug. 31, 1864.
Lovejoy, Ga., Sept. 2-6, 1864.
Allatoona, Ga., Oct. 5, 1864.
Ship Gap or Taylor's Bridge, Ga., Oct. 16, 1864.
Griswoldville, Ga., Nov. 22, 1864.
Fort McAllister, Ga., Dec. 13, 1864.
River Bridge, Salkahatchie, S. C., Feb. 3-9, 1865.
Congaree Creek, S. C., Feb. 15, 1865.
Columbia, S. C., Feb. 15-17, 1865.
Lynch Creek, S. C., Feb. 26, 1865.
Bentonville, N. C., March 19-21, 1865.

SIXTEENTH CORPS.
(Army of Tennessee)

Commanders: S. A. Hurlbut, G. M. Dodge, A. J. Smith.

ENGAGEMENTS:

Hernando, Miss., April 18, 1863.
Coldwater, Miss., April 19, 1863.
Town Creek, Ala., April 28, 1863.
Siege of Vicksburg, Miss., May 18 to July 4, 1863.
Jackson, Clinton, Rienzi or Canton, Miss., July 9-16, 1863.
Collierville, Tenn., Nov. 3, 1863.
Pleasant Hill, La., April 9, 1864.
Snake Creek Gap, Ga., May 8, 1864.
Resaca or Sugar Valley, Ga., May 13-16, 1864.
Lay's Ferry, Ga., May 15, 1864.
Rome, Ga., May 16, 1864.
Bayou de Glaize or Old Oaks, La., May 18, 1864.
Dallas or New Hope Church, Ga., May 25 to June 4, 1864.
Big Shanty, Ga., June 6, 1864.
Lake Chicot or Old River Lake, Ark., June 6, 1864.

Kenesaw, Ga., June 9-30, 1864.
Brice's Cross Roads, near Guntown, Miss., June 10, 1864.
Ruff's Mills, Miss., July 4, 1864.
Tupelo, Miss., July 13-15, 1864.
Siege of Atlanta, Ga., July 22 to Sept. 2, 1864.
Ezra Church, Ga., July 28, 1864.
Tallahatchie River, Miss., Aug. 7-9, 1864.
College Hill, Oxford or Hurricane Creek, Miss., Aug. 21-2, 1864.
Jonesboro, Ga., Aug. 31, 1864.
Nashville, Tenn., Dec. 15, 16, 1864.
Spanish Fort, Ala., April 8, 1865.
Fort Blakely, Ala., March 31 to April 9, 1865.

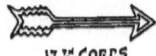

SEVENTEENTH CORPS.

(Army of Tennessee.)

Commanders: J. B. McPherson, F. P. Blair.

ENGAGEMENTS:

Port Gibson or Magnolia Hills, Miss., May 1, 1863.
Forty Hill or Hankinson's Ferry, Miss., May 3, 1863.
Raymond, Miss., May 12, 1863.
Jackson, Miss., May 14, 1863.
Champion Hill or Baker Creek, Miss., May 16, 1863.
Siege of Vicksburg, Miss., May 18 to July 4, 1863.
Jackson, Clinton, Rienzi or Canton, Miss., July 9-16, 1863.
Chattanooga or Orchard Knob, Tenn., Nov. 23, 1863.
Lookout Mountain, Tenn., Nov. 24, 1863.
Mission Ridge, Tenn., Nov. 25, 1863.
Ft. De Russy, Red River, La., March 14, 1864.
Monetis Bluff, La., April 23, 1864.
Cloutierville, La., April 23, 24, 1864.
Vaughn, Miss., May 12, 1864.
Marksville, La., May 14-16, 1864.
Bayou De Glaize, La., May 18, 1864.
Big Shanty, Ga., June 6, 1864.
Kenesaw, Ga., June 9-30, 1864.
Jackson, Miss., July 5, 6, 1864.
Nickajack Creek, Smyrna or Vining Sta., Ga., July 2-5, 1864.
Chattahoochie River, Ga., July 6-10, 1864.
Siege of Atlanta, Ga., July 22 to Sept. 2, 1864.
Ezra Church, Ga., July 28, 1864.
Jonesboro, Ga., Aug. 31, 1864.
Lovejoy, Ga., Sept. 2-6, 1864.
Ogeechee River or Jenk's Bridge, Ga., Dec. 7-9, 1864.
Nashville, Tenn., Dec. 15, 16, 1864.
Savannah, Ga., Dec. 10-21, 1864.
Pocataligo, S. C., Jan. 14-16, 1865.

Combahee River, S. C., Jan. 25, to Feb. 9, 1865.
Orangeburg, North Edisto River, S. C., Feb. 12, 1865.
Cheraw, S. C., March 2, 3, 1865.
Fayetteville, N. C., March 13, 1865.
Bentonville, N. C., March 19-21, 1865.

EIGHTEENTH CORPS.

(Army of the James.)

Commanders: J. G. Foster, J. M. Palmer, B. F. Butler, W. F. Smith, E. O. Ord, Godfrey Weitzel.

ENGAGEMENTS:

Kinston, N. C., Dec. 14, 1862.
Whitehall, N. C., Dec. 16, 1862.
Goldsboro, N. C., Dec. 17, 1862.
Washington, N. C., March 30 to April 4, 1863.
Suffolk, Va., April 12 to May 4, 1863.
Gum Swamp, N. C., May 22, 1863.
Bachelor's Creek, N. C., May 23, 1863.
Quaker Bridge or Comfort, N. C., July 6, 1863.
Port Walthall or Chester, Va., May 6, 7, 1864.
Arrowfield Church or Swift Creek, Va., May 9, 10, 1864.
Drewry's Bluff, Fort Darling, Va., May 12-16, 1864.
Bermuda Hundred, Va., May 16-30, 1864.
Cold Harbor, Va., June 1-12, 1864.
Petersburg, Va., June 15 to Aug. 31, 1864.
Mine Explosion, Va., July 30, 1864.
New Market, Chapin Farm or Ft. Harrison, Va., Sept. 28-30, 1864.
Fair Oaks, Va., Oct. 27, 28, 1864.
Fall of Richmond, Va., April 3, 1865.
Dec. 3, 1864. The White Regiments were transferred to the 24th Corps, and the colored regiments to the 25th Corps.

NINETEENTH CORPS.

(Middle Military Division.)

Commanders: N. P. Banks, W. B. Franklin, W. H. Emory, G. C. Grover.

ENGAGEMENTS:

Baton Rouge, La., Aug. 5, 1862.
Georgia Landing or Labadiesville, La., Oct. 27, 1862.
Bayou Teche, La., Jan. 14, 1863.
Fort Bisland, La., April 12, 1863.
Irish Bend, La., April 12-14, 1863.

CORPS ENGAGEMENTS.

Plains' Store, La., May 21, 1863.
Port Hudson, La., May 27 to July 9, 1863.
Thibodeaux or Hernando, La., June 20, 21, 1863.
Brashear City, La., June 23, 1863.
Donaldsonville or Kock's Plantation, La., July 13, 1863.
Sabine, Mansfield and Pleasant Grove, La., April 8, 1864.
Pleasant Hill, La., April 9, 1864.
Cloutierville, La., April 23, 24, 1864.
Monetis Bluff, Cane River, La., April 23, 1864.
Alexandria, La., May 1-8, 1864.
Mansura, La., May 14-17, 1864.
Bayou DeGlaize, La., May 18, 1864.
Atchafalaya, La., July 28, 1864.
Berryville, Va., Sept. 3, 4, 1864.
Opequon, Winchester or Belle Grove, Va., Sept. 19, 1864.
Fisher's Hill or Woodstock, Va., Sept. 22, 1864.
Cedar Creek or Middletown, Va., Oct. 19, 1864.

TWENTIETH CORPS.

(Army of the Cumberland.)

Commanders: A. McD. McCook, Joseph Hooker, H. W. Slocum, A. S. Williams, J. A. Mower.

ENGAGEMENTS:

Stone River or Murfreesboro, Tenn., Dec. 31, 1862, to Jan. 2, 1863.
Liberty Gap or Beach Grove, Tenn., June 25, 1863.
Chickamauga, Ga., Sept. 19, 20, '63.
Rocky Face Ridge, Ga., May 5-9, 1864.
Resaca or Sugar Valley, Ga., May 13-16, 1864.
Cassville, Ga., May 19-22, 1864.
Dallas or New Hope Church, Ga., May 25 to June 4, 1864.
Kenesaw, Pine Knob, Golgotha and Culp Farm, Ga., June 9-30, 1864.
Peach Tree, Ga., July 20, 1864.
Atlanta, Ga., July 22-28 to Sept. 2, 1864.
Monteith Swamp, Ga., Dec. 9, 1864.
Nashville, Tenn., Dec. 15, 16, 1864.
Savannah, Ga., Dec. 10-21, 1864.
Averasboro, N. C., March 16, 1865.
Bentonville, N. C., March 19-21, 1865.
April 4, 1864. The 11th and 12th Corps were consolidated, forming the 20th Corps.

TWENTY-FIRST CORPS.
(Army of the Cumberland.)

Commander: T. L. Crittenden.

ENGAGEMENTS:

Stone River or Murfreesboro, Tenn., Dec. 31, 1862, to Jan. 2, 1863.
Chickamauga, Ga., Sept. 19, 20, 1863.

After the battle of Chickamauga this corps was transferred to the 4th Corps, army of the Cumberland.

TWENTY-SECOND CORPS.
(Defences of Washington, D. C.)

Commanders: S. P. Heintzelman, J. G. Parke, C. C. Augur.

ENGAGEMENT:

Fort Stevens, Washington, D. C., July 11, 12, 1864.

TWENTY-THIRD CORPS.
(Department of the Ohio.)

Commanders: G. L. Hartsuff, M. D. Manson, J. D. Cox, George Stoneman, J. M. Schofield.

ENGAGEMENTS:

Blue Springs, Tenn., Oct. 10, 1863.
Campbell Station, Tenn., Nov. 16, 1863.
Siege of Knoxville, Tenn., Nov. 17 to Dec. 4, 1863.
Fort Sanders, Tenn., Nov. 29, 1863.
Talbot Station or Mossy Creek, Tenn., Dec. 29, 1863.
Strawberry Plains, Tenn., Jan. 10, 1864.

Dandridge, Tenn., Jan. 16, 17, 1864.
Rocky Face Ridge, Ga., May 5-9, 1864.
Resaca or Sugar Valley, Ga., May 13-16, 1864.
Cassville, Ga., May 19-22, 1864.
Dallas or New Hope Church, Ga., May 25 to June 4, 1864.
Kenesaw, Pine Mountain, Lost

Mountain and Culp Farm, Ga., June 9-30, 1864.
Chattahoochie River, Ga., July 6-10, 1864.
Siege of Atlanta, Ga., July 22, 28 to Sept. 2, 1864.
Decatur, Ga., Aug. 5, 1864.
Utoy Creek, Ga., Aug. 5, 6, 1864.
Lovejoy, Ga., Sept. 2-6, 1864.
Columbia, Duck River, Tenn., Nov. 24-28, 1864.
Spring Hill or Mount Carmel, Tenn., Nov. 29, 1864.
Franklin, Tenn., Nov. 30, 1864.
Nashville, Tenn., Dec. 15, 16, 1864.
Ft. Anderson, N. C., Feb. 18, 1865.
Town Creek, N. C., Feb. 20, 1865.
Wilmington, N. C., Feb. 23, 1865.
Kinston, N. C., March 14, 1865.
Goldsboro, N. C., March 21-24, 1865.

TWENTY-FOURTH CORPS.

(Army of the James.)

Commanders: E. O. Ord, A. H. Terry, Charles Devens, J. Gibbon, J. W. Turner.

ENGAGEMENTS:

Bermuda Hundred, Va., Dec. 3, 1864.
Fort Fisher, N. C., Dec. 24, 1864, to Jan. 15, 1865.
Fort Anderson, Va., Feb. 18, 1865.
Fort Gregg, Petersburg and
Rice's Station, Va., April 2, 1865.
Fall of Richmond, Va., April 3, 1865.
High Bridge, Va., April 6, 1865.
Appomattox or Lee's Surrender, Va., April 9, 1865.

TWENTY-FIFTH CORPS.

(COLORED.)

Commander: Godfrey Weitzel.

ENGAGEMENTS:

Bermuda Hundred, Va., Dec. 3, 1864.
Fort Fisher, N. C., Jan. 15, 1865.
Fort Gregg, Petersburg and Rice's Station, Va., April 2, 1865.
Fall of Richmond, Va., April 3, 1865.
Appomattox, Va., April 9, 1865.

CAVALRY CORPS.

(Army of the Potomac.)

Corps Commanders: George Stoneman, Alfred Pleasanton, Philip H. Sheridan.

POTOMAC CAV.CORPS. Division Commanders: Abram Buford, J. H. Wilson, Geo. A. Custer, A. T. A. Torbert, A. N. Duffie, Judson Kilpatrick, Wm. W. Averell, D. M. Gregg, Charles Devens, Wesley Merritt.

ENGAGEMENTS:

Stoneman's Raid, Va., April 27 to May 8, 1863.
Chancellorsville, Va., May 1-4, 1863.
Greenwich, Va , May 30, 1863.
Beverly Ford, Va., June 9, 1863.
Aldie, Va., June 17, 1863.
Middleburg, Va., June 19, 1863.
Upperville, Va., June 21, 1863.
Hanover, Pa., June 30, 1863.
Gettysburg, Pa., July 1-3, 1863.
Monterey, Md., July 4, 1863.
Fairfield, Pa., July 3-5, 1863.
Boonsboro, Md., July 7-9, 1863.
Hagerstown, Md., July 6-10, 1863.
Williamsport, Md., July 6-10, 1863.
Falling Waters, Md., July 14, 1863.
Shepardstown, Va., July 16, 1863.
Manassas Gap, Va., July 21, 1863.
Brandy Station or Rappahannock, Va., Aug. 1-3, 1863.
Averell's Raid, Va., Aug. 25-30, 1863.
Culpeper, Va., Sept. 13, 1863.
Raccoon Ford or Rapidan, Va., Sept. 14-19, 1863.
White's Ford, Va., Sept. 21, 1863.
Rapidan, Va., Oct. 10, 1863.
James City or Robertson's Run, Va., Oct. 10, 1863.
Culpeper or White Sulphur Springs, Va., Oct. 12, 13, 1863.
Buckland Mills, Va., Oct. 19, 1863.
Stevensburg, Va., Nov. 7, 1863.
Mine Run or Locust Grove, Va., Nov. 26, 1863.
Averell's Raid, Va., Dec. 8-21, 1863.
Barnett's Ford, Va., Feb. 7, 1864.
Kilpatrick's Raid, Va., Feb. 28 to March 4, 1864.
Kautz's Raid, Va., May 4-12, 1864.
Kautz's Raid on R. R., Va., May 12-17, 1864.
Todd's Tavern, Va., May 8, 1864.
Yellow Tavern, Va., May 11, 1864.
Meadow Bridge, Va., May 12, 1864.
Milford, Va., May 20, 1864.
Ashland, Va., May 11, 30, 1864.
Hanover C. H., Va., May 27-30, 1864.
Old Church, Va., May 30 and June 10, 11, 1864.
St. Mary's Church, Va., June 7, 1864.
Cold Harbor, Va., June 1-12, 1864.
Trevillian Station, Va., June 11, 12, 1864.
White House Landing, Va., June 21, 1864.

CORPS ENGAGEMENTS.

Wilson's Raid, Va., June 22-30, 1864.
Nottoway C. H., Va., June 23, 1864.
Staunton Bridge, Va., June 24, 1864.
Stony Creek, Va., June 28, 1864.
Ream's Station, Va., June 22-29, 1864.
Moorefield, W. Va., Aug. 7, 1864.
White Post or Sulphur Springs Bridge, Va., Aug. 11, 1864.
Smithfield, Shepherdstown or Kearneysville, Va., Aug. 25, 1864.
Ream's Station, Va., Aug. 25, 1864.
Berryville, Va., Sept. 3, 4, 1864.
Opequon, Winchester or Belle Grove, Va., Sept. 19, 1864.
Luray, Va., Sept. 24, 1864.
Waynesboro, Va., Oct. 2, 1864.
Newmarket and Darbytown Road, Va., Oct. 7-13, 1864.
Woodstock, Fisher's Hill or Strasburg, Va., Oct. 9, 1864.
Cedar Creek or Middletown, Va., Oct. 19, 1864.
Hatcher's Run or Boydton Road, Va., Oct. 27, 1864.
Newtown, Nineveh and Cedar Springs, Va., Nov. 12, 1864.
Rood's Hill, Va., Nov. 22, 1864.
Bellefield and Hicksford, Va., Dec. 9, 1864.
Sheridan's Raid, Va., Feb. 27, to Mch. 25, 1865.
Mount Crawford, Va., Feb. 28, 1865.
Waynesboro, Va., March 2, 1865.
Dinwiddie C. H., Va., March 31, 1865.
Five Forks, Va., April 1. 1865.
Amelia Springs or Jettersville, Va., April 5, 1865.
Sailor's Creek, Harper's Farm or Deatonsville, Va., April 6, 1865.
Appomattox or Lee's Surrender, Va., April 9, 1865.

CAVALRY CORPS.
(Armies of the West.)
Commander: J. H. Wilson.

DIVISION COMMANDERS:

E. M. McCook,
J. F. Knipe,
Geo. Stoneman,
Geo. Crook,
A. L. Lee,

Edw. Hatch,
Eli Long,
A. C. Gillem,
R. B. Mitchell,
Richard Arnold,

R. W. Johnson,
Emory Upton,
S. G. Burbridge,
D. S. Stanley.

ENGAGEMENTS:

Pea Ridge, Ark., March 6-8, 1862.
Lone Jack, Mo., Aug. 11-16, 1862.
Prairie Grove or Fayetteville, Ark., Dec. 7, 1862.

CORPS ENGAGEMENTS.

Stone River, Tenn., Dec. 31, 1862, to Jan. 2, 1863.
McMinnville, Tenn., April 20, 1863.
Streight's Raid, Ala. and Ga., April 27 to May 3, 1863.
Grierson's Raid, La. and Tenn., April 17 to May 2, 1863.
Middleton, Tenn., May 21 and June 24, 1863.
Franklin, Tenn., June 4, 1863.
Triune, Tenn., June 9, 1863.
Shelbyville and Guy's Gap, Tenn., June 27, 1863.
Jackson, Miss., July 13, 1863.
Canton, Miss., July 18, 1863.
Sparta, Tenn., Aug. 9, 1863.
Grenada, Miss., Aug. 13, 1863.
Graysville, Ga., Sept. 10, 1863.
Chickamauga, Ga., Sept. 19, 20, 1863.
Carter's Station, Tenn., Sept. 22, 1863.
Murfreesboro Road, Tenn., Oct. 4. 1863.
Farmington, Tenn., Oct. 7, 1863.
Blue Springs, Tenn., Oct. 10, 1863.
Byhalia or Ingham's Station, Miss., Oct. 12, 1863.
Wyatt's Ford or Tallahatchie, Miss., Oct. 13, 1863.
Maysville, Ala., Oct. 13, 1863.
Blountsville, Tenn., Oct. 13, 1863.
Sweetwater, Tenn., Oct. 24, 1863.
Moscow, Tenn., Nov. 4 and Dec. 4, 1863.
Ripley, Miss., Dec. 1, 1863.
Salisbury, Tenn., Dec. 3, 1863.
Morristown, Tenn., Dec. 10, 1863.
Bean Station, Tenn., Dec. 10-14, 1863
Mossy Creek or Talbot, Tenn, Dec. 29, 1863.
Dandridge, Tenn., Jan. 16, 17, 1864.
Fair Gardens or Kelly's Ford, Tenn., Jan. 27, 28, 1864.
Arkadelphia, Ark., March 28, 1864.
Camden, Ark., April 2-24, 1864.
Wilson Farm, La., April 7, 1864.
Sabine Cross Roads or Pleasant Grove, La., April 8, 1864.
Prairie De'Ann, Ark., April 10-13, 1864.
Natchitoches, La., March 31 and April 19, 1864.
Cane River or Monotis Bluff, La., April 23, 1864.
Jenkins' Ferry, Saline River, La., April 30, 1864.
Red Clay, Ga., May 3. 1864.
Varnell, Ga., May 9, 1864.
Tilton, Tenn., May 13, 1864.
Resaca, Ga., May 13-16, 1864.
Rome, Ga., May 16-18, 1864.
Kingston, Ga., May 18-24, 1864.
Dallas or New Hope Church, Ga., May 25 to June 4, 1864.
Ackworth, Ga., June 3, 4, 1864.
Kenesaw, Ga., June 9-30, 1864.
Brice's Cross Roads or Guntown, Miss., June 10, 1864.
McAfee's Cross Roads, Ga., June 12, 1864.
Powder Springs, Ga., June 20, 1864.
Noonday Creek, Ga., June 20, 1864.
Tupelo, Miss., July 13-25, 1864.
Decatur, Ga., July 22 and Aug. 5, 1864.

Lovejoy Station, Ga., July 29, 30, 1864.
Newman, Ga., July 30, 1864.
Hillsboro or Sunshine Church, Ga., July 31, 1864.
Fairburn, Ga., Aug. 18, 1864.
Red Oak, Ga., Aug. 19, 1864.
Jonesboro, Ga., Aug. 19, 20-31, 1864.
Pulaski, Tenn., Sept. 26, 27, 1864.
Osage River or Prince's Place, Mo., Oct. 6, 1864.
Boonville, Mo., Oct. 9-11, 1864.
Little Blue, Mo., Oct. 21, 1864.
Hurricane Creek, Miss., Oct. 23, 1864.
Big Blue, Mo., Oct. 23, 31, 1864.
Griswoldville, Ga., Nov. 22, 1864.
Waynesboro or Thomas Station, Ga., Nov. 27-29, 1864.
Franklin, Tenn., Nov. 29, 30, 1864.
Nashville, Tenn., Dec. 15, 16, 1864.
Ogeechee River, Ga., Dec. 7-9, 1864.
Cypress River, Ga., Dec. 7, 1864.
Rutherford, Tenn., Dec. 19, 1864.
Saltville, Va., Dec. 20, 1864.
Pulaski, Anthony's Hill or Sugar Creek, Tenn., Dec. 25, 1864.
Egypt Station, Miss., Dec. 28, 1864.
Salkahatchie, S. C., Feb. 6, 1865.
Rockingham, N. C., March 7, 1865.
Averasboro, N. C., March 16, 1865.
Bentonville, N. C., March 19-21, 1865.
Stoneman's Raid, Va. and N. C., March 20 to April 6, 1865.
Plantersville, Ala., April 1, 1865.
Selma, Ala., April 2, 1865.
Tuscaloosa, Ala., April 4, 1865.
Montgomery, Ala., April 12, 13, 1865.
Columbus, Ga., April 16, 1865.
Macon, Ga., April 20, 1865.
Wilson's Raid, Ala. and Ga., March 22 to April 20, 1865.
Talladega, Ala., April 22, 1865.
Capture of Jeff Davis, Irwinsville, Ga., May 10, 1865.

PART III.

ANNOUNCEMENT.

The alphabetical list of battles and engagements of the Civil War, beginning on the opposite page, followed by a similar list of naval engagements, pages 205-222 inclusive, *is the only compilation of the kind ever published.*

These lists contain the gist of ponderous volumes on file at Washington and in the archives of the different States, so far as they record the history of nearly five thousand sanguinary conflicts between the Blue and the Gray.

The absolute value of this *alphabetical* arrangement is apparent, as almost any soldier can remember the names of the battles in which he participated, but very few can remember the exact dates, without which knowledge it is extremely difficult to obtain information from any of the *chronological* lists heretofore published.

The following pages have, also, an *associated* value, in that they are necessary *supplements* to the soldier's or sailor's *individual Record of Service.* Not one of the *various styles* of *record of service picture* or "*escutcheon*" which have been sold by different firms throughout the country is *complete* without reference to an *alphabetical list* of engagements. *This Manual supplies that long-felt want.*

The *publishers* of this Manual are prepared to furnish in *certificate form*, over their corporate seal, the *Record of Service* of any *regiment*, or the *personal* Record of any soldier who served during the Civil War.

Address all inquiries to the

U.S. ARMY AND NAVY HISTORICAL ASS'N,

629 F Street, N.W.,

WASHINGTON, D.C.

List of Battles and Engagements.

ABBEVILLE and Oxford, Miss., Aug. 12, 1864. Cav. and Inf. of the 16th Corps.
Abbeville, Miss., Aug. 23, 1864. 10th Mo.; 14th Iowa; 5th and 7th Minn.; 8th Wis. Union, 20 wounded; Confed., 15 killed.
Abb's Valley, Va., May 8, 1864. (See Jeffersonville.)
Aberdeen, Ark., July 9, 1862. 24th, 34th, 43d, and 46th Ind. Casualties not reported.
Aberdeen and Butler Creek, Ala., Nov. 17, 1864. 2d Iowa Cav.
Abingdon, Va., Dec. 15, 1864. Cav. under Gen. Burbridge. (Stoneman's raid.)
Abo Pass, New Mexico, July 5, 1865.
Ackworth, Ga., June 3 and 4, 1864. Cav. of the 2d Div., Army of the Cumberland.
Acton, Minn., Sept. 2 and 3, 1862. (See Birch Coolie.) Indian fight.
Adairsville, Graves' House and Calhoun, May 17 and 18, 1864. 4th Corps, Army of the Cumberland.
Adamsville, Tenn., April 4, 1862. (See Crump's Landing.)
Ætna, Mo., July 22, 1861. 21st Mo.
Aiken, S. C., Feb. 11, 1865. Cav. Div. of Gen. Sherman's Army.
Albuquerque, New Mexico, April 9, 1862.
Aldie, Va., Oct. 9, 1862. Detachment of Cav. from Gen. Sigel's command.
Aldie, Va., Oct. 31, 1862. 1st N. J. and 2d N. Y. Cav.
Aldie, Va., June 17, 1863. 2d and 4th N. Y.; 6th Ohio; 1st Mass.; 1st Me. and 1st R. I. Cav. Union, 24 killed, 41 wounded, 89 missing; Confed., 100 wounded.
Alexandria, Va., May 24, 1861. Occupied by 1st N. Y. Zouaves.
Alexandria, La., April 26, 1864. 14th N. Y. and 16th Mo. Cav.
Alexandria, La., May 1 to 8, 1864. Portions of the Cav. of 13th and 19th Corps.
Alimosa, New Mexico (near Fort Craig), Oct. 4, 1861. Mink's Cav. and U. S. Regulars. Confed., 11 killed, 31 wounded.
Allatoona, Ga., Oct. 5, 1864. 7th, 12th, 50th, 57th, and 93d Ill.; 39th Iowa; 4th Minn.; 18th Wis.; 12th Wis. Battery. Union, 142 killed, 352 wounded, 212 missing; Confed., 231 killed, 500 wounded, 411 missing.
Allatoona Hills, Ga., May 25 to June 4, 1864. (See Dallas.)
Allen's Farm, Va., June 29, 1862. (See Peach Orchard.)
Alpine Gap, Ga., Sept. 11, 1863. (See Dug Gap.) [Bath.)
Alpine Sta., Va., Jan. 4, 1862. (See Alsop's Farm, Va., May 10, 1864.
Altoona Hills, Ga., May 25 to June 4, 1864. (See Dallas.)
Amelia Springs, or Jettersville, Va., April 5, 1865. Crook's Cav. Union, 20 killed, 96 wounded.
Amite River, La., June 27, 1862. (See Williams' Bridge.)
Amitie, La., March 28, 1863. 14th and 24th Me. Inf.
Amitie, La., March 18, 1865.
Anandale, Va., Dec. 4, 1861. Part of 3d N. J. Inf. Union, 1 killed; Confed., 7 killed.

Anderson's Cross Roads, Tenn., Oct. 2, 1863. McCook's Cav. Corps. Union, 70 killed and wounded; Confed., 200 killed and wounded.
Anderson's Gap, Tenn., Oct. 1, 1863. 21st Ky. Inf.
Anthony's Hill, Tenn., Dec. 25, 1864. (See Pulaski.)
Antietam, or Sharpsburg, Md., Sept. 17, 1862. 1st Corps, Maj.-Gen. Hooker; 2d Corps, Maj.-Gen. Sumner; 5th Corps, Maj.-Gen. Fitz-John Porter; 6th Corps, Maj.-Gen. Franklin; 9th Corps, Maj.-Gen. Burnside; 12th Corps, Maj.-Gen. Williams; Couch's Div., 4th Corps; Pleasonton's Div. of Cav. Union, 2,010 killed, 9,416 wounded, 1,043 missing; Confed., 3,500 killed, 16,400 wounded, 600 missing. Union, Brig.-Gen. Mansfield killed; Maj.-Gen's Hooker and Richardson and Brig.-Gen'ls Rodman, Weber, Sedgwick, Hartsuff, Dana, and Meagher wounded. Confed., Brig.-Gen'ls Branch, Anderson, Starke killed; Maj.-Gen. Anderson, and Brig.-Gen'ls Toombs, Lawton, Ripley, Rhodes, Gregg, Armstead, and Ransom wounded.
Antioch Sta., N. C., April 10, 1863. Detachment of 10th Mich. Union, 8 killed, 12 wounded.
Antoine, Ark., April 2, 1864. 13th Ill. and 1st Iowa Cav. (Steele's Expedition.)
Anxvois River, Tenn., Oct. 20, 1862, 10th Mo. Militia Cav.
Apache Cañon, or Glorietta, New Mexico, March 26 to 28, 1862. 1st and 2d Col. Cav. Union, 32 killed, 75 wounded, 35 missing; Confed., 36 killed, 60 wounded, 93 missing.
Apache Pass, Ariz. Ter., July 15, 1862. 2d Cal. Cav.
Appomattox, Va., April 9, 1865. (Lee's Surrender.) Armies of the Potomac and James. Confed., 26,000 prisoners.
Appomattox C. H., Va., April 8 and 9, 1865. 24th Corps; 1st Div., 25th Corps, and Sheridan's Cav. Union,

200 killed and wounded; Confed., 500 killed.
Arivapo Cañon, Ark., June 8, 1864.
Arkadelphia, Ark., Feb. 15, 1863. Troops under Capt. Brown.
Arkadelphia, Ark., March 28, 1864. Advance Cav. of 7th Corps.
Arkansas Post, Ark., Jan. 11, 1863. Captured by 13th Corps, Gen. McClernand; 15th Corps, Gen. Sherman; Army of the Mississippi, aided by Gunboats. Union, 129 killed, 831 wounded, 17 missing; Confed., 100 killed, 400 wounded, 5,000 prisoners.
Armstrong Ferry, Tenn., Jan. 22, 1864.
Arrowfield Church, Va., May 9 and 10, 1864. (See Swift Creek.)
Arrow Rock, Mo., July 29, 1862.
Arrow Rock, Mo., Oct. 12 and 13, 1863. (See Merrill's Crossing.)
Arthur's Swamp, Va., Aug. 29 and 30, 1864.
Arthur's Swamp, Va., Sept. 30 and Oct. 1, 1864. Gregg's Cav. Union, 60 wounded, 100 missing.
Ash Bayou, La., Nov. 19, 1864. (See Bayou La Fourché.)
Ashby's Gap, Va., Sept. 22, 1862. 2d Pa. and 1st W. Va. Cav.
Ashby's Gap, Va., July 12, 1863. 2d Mass. Cav. Union, 2 killed, 8 wounded.
Ashby's Gap, Va., July 18, 1864. Duffie's Cav. Union, 200 killed and wounded.
Ashby's Gap, Va., Feb. 18, 1865. Detachment of 14th Pa. Cav. Union, 6 killed, 19 wounded, 64 missing.
Ashepoo River, S. C., May 16, 1864. 34th U. S. Colored Troops.
Ashland, La., June 6 to 8, 1863. (See Milliken's Bend.)
Ashland, Va., May 11, 1864. 1st Mass. Cav.
Ashland, Va., May 30, 1864. 3C Div., Cav. Corps, Army of the Potomac.
Ashland, Va., March 15, 1865. 2d Brigade, 3d Div. Cav., Army of the Potomac.
Ashley's Mills, Ark., Sept. 7, 1863. Davidson's Cav. Div., Department of Missouri.

Ashley Sta., Ark., Aug. 24, 1864. (See Jones' Hay Station.)
Ashton, La., May 1, 1864.
Ashwood, Miss., June 25, 1864.
Ashwood Landing, La., May 1 to 4, 1864. 64th U. S. Colored Troops.
Atchafalaya, La., Sept. 9 and 10, 1863.
Atchafalaya River, La., Sept. 7, 1863. 2d Brigade, 2d Div., 13th Corps.
Atchafalaya River, La., July 28, 1864. Part of the 19th Corps.
Athens, Ala., Jan. 25, 1864.
Athens, Ala., Sept. 23, 1864. 106th, 110th, 114th U. S. Colored Troops; 3d Tenn. Cav.; 18th Mich. and 102d Ohio Inf. Union, 950 missing; Confed., 5 killed, 25 wounded.
Athens, Ala., Oct. 1 and 2, 1864. 73d Ind. Inf.
Athens, Ky., Feb. 23, 1863.
Athens, Mo., Aug. 5, 1861. Home Guards, 21st Mo. Union, 3 killed, 8 wounded; Confed., 14 killed, 14 wounded.
Athens Ranch, Col., Aug. 22, 1864.
Atlanta, Ga., July 22, 1864. (Hood's first sortie.) 15th, 16th, and 17th Corps, Maj.-Gen. McPherson. Union, 500 killed, 2,141 wounded, 1,000 missing; Confed., 2,482 killed, 4,000 wounded, 2,017 missing. Union, Maj.-Gen. McPherson and Brig.-Gen. Greathouse killed.
Atlanta, Ga., July 28, 1864. (Second sortie at Ezra Chapel.) 15th, 16th, and 17th Corps, Maj.-Gen. Howard. Union, 100 killed, 600 wounded; Confed., 642 killed, 3,000 wounded, 1,000 missing.
Atlanta, Ga., July 28 to Sept. 2, 1864. (See Siege of Atlanta.)
Atlanta, Ga., Sept. 2, 1864. Fall of Atlanta, and end of Campaign in Northern Georgia. Union loss, 37,200.
Atlanta, Ga., Nov. 9, 1864. 2d Div., 20th Corps. Union, 5 killed, 10 wounded; Confed. loss, 50.
Atlee, Va., March 1, 1864. Cav., Army of the Potomac.
Attack on Transport "Crescent City," Miss., May 18, 1863. 3d Iowa Inf.

Auburn, Ga., July 18, 1864. 9th Ohio and 4th Tenn. Cav. (Rousseau's Raid.)
Auburn, Va., Oct. 14, 1863. Part of 1st Div., 2d Corps, Army of the Potomac. Union, 11 killed, 42 wounded; Confed., 8 killed, 24 wounded.
Augusta, Ark., April 1, 1864. 3d Minn. and 8th Mo. Cav. Union, 8 killed, 16 wounded; Confed., 15 killed, 45 wounded.
Augusta, Ark., Sept. 2, 1864.
Austin, Ark., Aug. 31, 1863. Davidson's Cav. Div., Army of the Missouri.
Austin, Miss., Aug. 2, 1862. 8th Ind. Inf.
Averill's Raid, W. Va., Aug. 25 to 30, 1863. Union, 3 killed, 10 wounded, 60 missing.
Averill's Raid, S. W. Va., Dec. 8 to 21, 1863. Union, 6 killed, 5 wounded; Confed., 200 prisoners.
Averasboro', or Smith's Farm, N. C., March 16, 1865. 20th Corps and Kilpatrick's Cav. Div. of Gen. Sherman's Army. Union, 77 killed, 477 wounded; Confed., 108 killed, 540 wounded, 217 missing.
Avoyelle's Prairie, La., May 14 to 16, 1864. (See Mansura.)
Aylett's, Va., June 4 and 5, 1863.

BACHELOR'S Creek, N. C., Nov. 11, 1862. (See Newbern.)
Bachelor's Creek, N. C., May 23, 1863. 58th Pa. and 46th Mass. Inf.
Bachelor's Creek, Newport Barracks, and Newberne, N. C., Feb. 1 to 3, 1864. 132d N. Y.; 9th Ver.; 17th Mass.; 2d N. C.; 12th N. Y. Cav.; 3d N. Y. Artil. Union, 16 killed, 50 wounded, 280 missing; Confed., 5 killed, 30 wounded.
Bachelor's Creek, N. C., May 26, 1864. Torpedo Explosion. Present, 132d and 158th N. Y. and 58th Pa. Inf.
Bacon Creek, Ky., Dec. 26, 1862. Detachment of 2d Mich. Cav. Union, 23 wounded.

Bad Lands, Dak. Ter., Aug. 8, 1864. (See Two Hills.)
Bagdad, Ky., Dec. 12, 1861. 6th Ky. Inf.
Baker's Creek, Miss., May 16, 1863. (See Champion Hills.)
Baker's Creek, Miss., Feb. 4, 1864. (See Champion Hills.)
Baker's Springs, Ark., Jan. 24, 1864. 2d and 6th Kan. Cav. Union, 1 killed, 2 wounded; Confed., 6 killed, 3 wounded.
Baldwin, Miss., June 9, 1862. 2d Iowa and 2d Mich. Cav.
Baldwin, Miss., Oct. 2, 1862. Cav., Army of the Miss.
Baldwin's Ferry, Miss., May 13, 1863.
Ball's Bluff, also called Edward's Ferry, Harrison's Landing, Harrison's Island, and Leesburg, Va., Oct. 21, 1861. 15th and 20th Mass.; 40th N. Y.; 71st Pa.; Battery B, R. I. Artil. Union, 223 killed, 226 wounded; Confed., 36 killed, 264 wounded; Union, acting Brig.-Gen. E. D. Baker killed.
Ball's Cross Roads, Va., Aug. 27, 1861. Two companies, 23d N.Y. Union, 1 killed, 2 wounded.
Ball's Ferry, Ga., Nov. 24 and 25, 1864. 1st Ala. Cav.; Advance of the Army of the Tenn.
Ball's Mills, Mo., Aug. 28 and 29, 1861.
Baltimore, Md., April 19, 1861. Riots. 6th Mass.; 26th Pa. Union, 4 killed, 30 wounded; Confed., 9 killed.
Baltimore Cross Roads, Va., June 26, 1863. 4th Corps., Maj.-Gen. Keyes.
Baltimore Cross Roads, Va., July 2, 1863. Part of 4th Corps.
Barbee's Cross Roads and Chester Gap, Va. (also called Markham), Nov. 5, 1862. Gen. Pleasanton's Cav.
Barbee's Cross Roads, Va., Sept. 1, 1863. Detachment 6th Ohio Cav. Union, 2 killed, 4 wounded.
Barber's Place, St. Mary's River, Lake City, and Gainesville, Fla., Feb. 9 to 14, 1864. 40th Mass. Mounted Inf. and Independent Cav. Union, 4 killed, 16 wounded; Confed., 4 killed, 50 wounded.

Barboursville, or Red House, W. Va., July 12, 1861. 2d Ky. Union, 1 killed; Confed., 10 killed.
Barboursville, or Red House, W. Va., Sept. 18, 1861. Ky. Home Guards. Union, 1 killed, 1 wounded; Confed., 7 killed.
Bardstown, Ky., Oct. 4, 1862. Advance Troops of the Army of the Ohio.
Barnett's Ford, Va., Feb. 7, 1864. Brig.-Gen. Merritt's Cav. Union, 20 killed and wounded.
Barnwell's Island, S. C., Nov. 24, 1863. 33d U. S. Colored Troops.
Barrancas, Fla., July 22, 1864.
Barren Fork, Ind. Ter., Dec. 19, 1863. 1st and 3d Kan. Indian Home Guards. Confed., 50 killed.
Bartlett's Mills, Va., Nov. 26, 1863. (See Mine Run.)
Barton Sta., Miss., April 16, 1863.
Barton Sta., Miss., Oct. 20, 1863. Troops of Army of the Tenn.
Bastin Mountain, Mo., Nov. 9, 1862.
Batesville, Ark., July 14, 1862. 4th Iowa Cav. Union, 1 killed, 4 wounded.
Batesville, Ark., Feb. 4, 1863. Brigade of Cav. under Col. Geo. E. Waring.
Batesville, Ark., Feb. 19, 1864. 4th Ark.; 4th Mo. Cav. Union, 3 killed, 4 wounded; Confed., 6 killed, 10 wounded.
Bath, Va., Jan. 4, 1862. (Including skirmishes at Great Cacapon Bridge, Alpine Sta., and Hancock.) 39th Ill. Union, 2 killed, 2 wounded; Confed., 30 wounded.
Bath, Va., Sept. 8, 1863. 7th Pa. Cav.
Baton Rouge, La., Aug. 5, 1862. 14th Me.; 6th Mich.; 7th Ver.; 21st Ind.; 30th Mass.; 9th Conn.; 4th Wis.; 2d, 4th, and 6th Mass. Batteries, under Brig.-Gen. Thos. Williams. Union, 82 killed, 265 wounded, 34 missing; Confed., 84 killed, 316 wounded, 78 missing. Union, Brig.-Gen. Williams killed.
Baton Rouge, La., Sept. 8, 1863. 7th Pa. Cav.
Baton Rouge, La., March 8, May 3, and June 16, 1864.

Battery Huger, or Hill's Point, Va., April 18, 1863. Detachment of 89th N. Y. and 8th Conn.
Battle Creek, Tenn., June 21, 1862. 2d and 33d Ohio; 10th Wis.; 24th Ill.; 4th Ohio Cav.; 4th Ky. Cav., and Edgarton's Battery. Union, 4 killed, 3 wounded.
Baxter Springs, Ark., Oct. 6, 1863. Detachment of 3d Wis.; 14th Kan. Cav., and 83d U. S. Colored Troops. Union, 54 killed, 18 wounded, 5 missing. Prisoners robbed and murdered by Quantrell's forces.
Bayle's Cross Roads, La., Oct. 12, 1861. 79th N. Y. Union, 4 wounded.
Baylor's Farm, Va., June 15, 1864. 3d Div., 10th Corps.
Bayou Barnard, Ind. Ter., July 28, 1862. 1st, 2d, and 3d Kan. Indian Home Guards; 1st Kan. Battery.
Bayou Biddell, La., Oct. 15, 1864. 52d U. S. Colored Troops.
Bayou Boeuff, La., Dec. 13, 1863.
Bayou Boeuff, La., May 7, 1864. Portion of 16th Corps.
Bayou Bontecom, La., Nov. 21, 1862. 31st Mass. Inf.
Bayou Bourdeaux, La., Nov. 3, 1863. (See Grand Coteau.)
Bayou Cache, Ark., also called Cotton Plant, Round Hill, Hill's Plantation, and Bayou de View, July 7, 1862. 11th Wis.; 33d Ill.; 8th Ind.; 1st Mo. Light Artil.; 1st Ind. Cav.; 5th and 13th Ill. Cav. Union, 7 killed, 57 wounded; Confed., 110 killed, 200 wounded.
Bayou de Glaize, also known as Old Oaks, Simmsport, Yellow Bayou, and Calhoun Sta., La., May 18, 1864. 1st and 3d Divs., 16th Corps.; portion of 17th Corps and Cav., 19th Corps. Union, 60 killed, 300 wounded; Confed., 500 killed and wounded.
Bayou De Mora, La., May 12, 1864.
Bayou De View, Ark., July 7, 1862. (See Bayou Cache.)
Bayou La Fourché, or Ash Bayou, La., Nov. 19, 1864. 11th Wis. Inf.; 93d U. S. Colored Troops.
Bayou La Mourie, La., May 7, 1864.

Portion of 16th Corps. Union, 10 killed, 31 wounded.
Bayou Macon, La., May 10, 1863.
Bayou Mason, Miss., July —, 1864.
Bayou Metoe, Ark., Aug. 25, 1863. (See Brownsville.)
Bayou Metoe, Ark., Sept. 1, 1863. Rice's Div., Department of Arkansas.
Bayou Pierre, Miss., May 2, 1863.
Bayou Rapids, La., March 21, 1864. (See Henderson Hills.)
Bayou Roberts, La., May 8, 1864. Portion of 16th Corps.
Bayou Sara, Miss., Nov. 9, 1863.
Bayou St. Louis, Miss., Nov. 17, 1863.
Bayou Teche, La., Jan. 14, 1863. 8th Ver.; 16th and 75th N. Y.; 12th Conn.; 6th Mich.; 21st La.; 1st La. Cav.; 4th and 6th Mass. Battery; 1st Me. Battery, assisted by U. S. Gunboats "Calhoun," "Diana," "Kinsman," and "Estrella." Union, 10 killed, 27 wounded; Confed., 15 killed. Union, Commodore Buchanan killed; Confed., Gunboat "Cotton" destroyed.
Bayou Teché, La., April 12 and 14, 1863. (See Irish Bend.)
Bayou Tensas, La., June 30, 1863. Brigade of Inf. and Cav., under Col. Ellett.
Bayou Tensas, La., Aug. 10, 1863, July 30 and Aug. 26, 1864.
Bayou Tunica, La., Nov. 9, 1863.
Bayou Vermilion, La., April 17, 1863. Division of 19th Corps, under Brig.-Gen. Grover.
Bay Springs, Miss., Oct. 26, 1863. 1st Ala. Cav. Union, 14 killed, 25 wounded.
Beachtown, Ga., July 22, 1864.
Bealington, W. Va., July 8, 1861. (See Laurel Hill.)
Bealton and Rappahannock Bridge, Va., Oct. 24, 1863. 1st Div., Cav. Corps, Army of the Potomac.
Bealton, Va., Jan. 14, 1864. One company of 9th Mass. Union, 2 wounded; Confed., 3 killed, 12 wounded.
Bean's Sta., Tenn., Dec. 9, 1862.
Bean's Sta. and Morristown, Tenn., Dec. 10 to 14, 1863. Shackleford's Cav. Union, 700 killed and wound-

ed; Confed., 932 killed and wounded, 150 prisoners.
Bear Creek, Cherokee Sta., and Lundy's Lane, Ala. (or Hillsborough), April 17, 1863. 10th Mo. and 7th Kan. Cav.
Bear Creek, Ala., Oct. 26, 1863. (See Cane Creek.)
Bear Creek, Miss., Oct. 27, 1863.
Bear Creek, Mo., Feb. 5, 1863. 40th Mo. Militia.
Bear Creek Sta., Ga., Nov. 17, 1864. 2d Brigade, 3d Div., Cav., Army of the Cumberland.
Bear River, Wash. Ter., Jan. 26, 1863. Four Companies 2d Cal. Cav. and 1 Company, 3d Cal. Inf. (Indian fight.)
Bear-Skin Lake, Mo., Sept. 7, 1863. 2d Mo. Cav.
Bear Wallow, Ky., Dec. 25, 1862. Two Battalions, 12th Ky. Cav.
Beaver Creek, Ky., June 27, 1863. 39th Ky. Inf.
Beaver Creek, Mo., Nov. 24, 1862. 21st Iowa; 3d Mo. Cav.
Beaver Dam Lake, Miss., May 24, 1863. Marine Brigade of Cav. and Inf.
Beaver Dam Sta., Va., May 9, 1864. (See Sheridan's Cav. Raid.)
Beckwith Farm, Mo., Oct. 13, 1861. Tuft's Cav. Union, 2 killed, 5 wounded; Confed., 1 killed, 2 wounded.
Beech Creek, W. Va., Aug. 6, 1862. 4th W. Va. Inf. Union, 3 killed, 8 wounded; Confed., 1 killed, 11 wounded.
Beech Grove, Ky., Jan. 19 and 20, 1862. (See Mill Springs.)
Beech Grove, Tenn., June 25, 1863. (See Liberty Gap.)
Beersheba Springs, Tenn., Nov. 26, 1863. Detachments of Ala. and Tenn. Troops.
Beersheba Springs, Tenn., March 20, 1864. 5th Tenn. Cav.
Beher's Mills, Va., Sept. 2, 1861. 13th Mass. Inf. Confed., 3 killed, 5 wounded.
Belcher's Mills, Va., May 16, 1864. 3d N. Y.; 5th and 11th Pa.; 1st D. C. Cav. (Kautz's Raid.)

Belcher's Mills, Va., Sept. 17, 1864. Kautz's and Gregg's Cav. Union, 25 wounded.
Bellefield, Va., Dec. 9, 1864. 2d Div. Cav. Corps, Army of the Potomac. (Weldon R. R. Raid.)
Bellegrove, Va., Sept. 19, 1864. (See Opequan.)
Belmont, Mo., Nov. 7, 1861. 22d, 27th, 30th, and 31st Ill.; 7th Iowa; Battery B, 1st Ill. Art.; 2 Companies 15th Ill. Cav. Union, 90 killed, 173 wounded, 235 missing; Confed., 260 killed, 425 wounded, 278 missing.
Bennett's Mills, Mo., Sept. 1, 1861. Mo. Home Guards. Union, 1 killed, 8 wounded.
Benton, Miss., May 7, 1864. 11th, 72d, and 76th Ill. Inf., 7th Ohio Battery.
Bentonville, Ark., March 6, 1862. (See Pea Ridge.) [1863.
Bentonville, Ark., Feb. 20 and Aug. 15,
Bentonville, Mo., Feb. 19, 1862, and May 22, 1863.
Bentonville, N. C., March 19 to 21, 1865. 14th, 15th, 17th, and 20th Corps; Kilpatrick's Cav. Union, 91 killed, 1,168 wounded, 287 missing; Confed., 267 killed, 1,200 wounded, 1,625 missing.
Bent's Old Fort, Tex., Nov. 24, 1864. 1st Cal. Cav.
Bermuda Hundred, Va., May 4 and Dec. 13, 1864.
Bermuda Hundred, Va., May 16 to 30, 1864. 10th and 18th Corps, Army of the James. Union, 200 killed, 1,000 wounded; Confed., 3,000 killed, wounded, and missing.
Bermuda Hundred, Va., June 2, 1864. 10th Corps. Union, 25 killed, 100 wounded; Confed., 100 killed and wounded.
Bermuda Hundred, Va., Aug. 24 and 25, 1864. 10th Corps, Army of the James. Union, 31 wounded; Confed., 61 missing.
Bermuda Hundred, Va., Nov. 17, 1864. (See Chester Sta.)
Bermuda Hundred, Va., Nov. 30 to Dec. 4, 1864. Pickets of the 19th Colored Troops.

LIST OF BATTLES AND ENGAGEMENTS. 187

Berry's Ferry, Va., May 16, 1863. Detachment of 1st N. Y. Cav.
Berryville, Va., Nov. 30, 1862. (See Snicker's Ferry.)
Berryville, Va., Dec. 1, 1862. (See Charlestown.)
Berryville, Va., June 6, 1863. 67th Pa. Inf.
Berryville, Va., June 12, 1863. 1st Brigade, Milroy's Div.
Berryville, Va., Oct. 18, 1863. 34th Mass. and 17th Ind. Battery. Union, 2 killed, 4 wounded; Confed., 5 killed, 20 wounded.
Berryville, Va., Aug. 21, 1864. (See Summit Point.)
Berryville, Va., Sept. 3 and 4, 1864. 8th and 19th Corps; Torbett's Cav. Union, 30 killed, 182 wounded, 100 missing; Confed., 25 killed, 100 wounded, 70 missing.
Berryville, Va., April 17, 1865. (See Mosby's Surrender.)
Berryville Pike, Sulphur Springs Bridge, and White Post, Va., Aug. 10 and 11, 1864. Torbett's Cav. Union, 34 killed, 90 wounded, 200 missing.
Bertrand, Mo., Dec. 11, 1861. 2d Ill. Cav. Union, 1 wounded.
Berwick, La., April 26, 1864.
Berwick City, La., March 13, 1863. 160th N. Y. Inf.
Bethesda Church, Va., May 30 to June 6, 1864.
Beverly, W. Va., July 12, 1861. 4th and 9th Ohio. Confed., 600 prisoners.
Beverly, W. Va., April 24, 1863. 5th W. Va. Cav.
Beverly, W. Va., July 2, 1863. 10th W. Va. Inf. and Battery G, W. Va. Artil.
Beverly, W. Va., Oct. 29, 1864. 8th Ohio Cav. Union, 8 killed, 25 wounded, 13 missing; Confed., 17 killed, 27 wounded, 92 missing.
Beverly, W. Va., Jan. 11, 1865. 34th Ohio and 8th Ohio Cav. Union, 5 killed, 20 wounded, 583 missing.
Beverly Ford and Brandy Sta., Va., June 9, 1863. 2d, 3d, and 7th Wis.;
2d and 33d Mass.; 6th Me.; 86th and 104th N. Y.; 1st, 2d, 5th, and 6th U. S. Cav.; 2d, 6th, 8th, 9th, and 10th N. Y. Cav.; 1st, 6th, and 17th Pa. Cav.; 1st Md.; 8th Ill.; 3d Ind.; 1st N. J.; 1st Me. Cav. and 3d W. Va. Cav. Union, 500 killed, wounded, and missing; Confed., 700 killed, wounded, and missing.
Beverly Ford and Rappahannock Crossing, Va., Oct. 22, 1863. 2d Pa. and 1st Me. Cav. Union, 6 killed.
Bidnell Cross Roads, Va., March 1, 1864. (See Atlee.)
Big Beaver Creek, Mo., Nov. 7, 1862. 10th Ill.; 2 Com. Mo. Militia Cav. Union, 300 captured.
Big Bethel, Va., June 10, 1861, and April 4, 1862. (See Great Bethel.)
Big Black River, Miss., May 3, 1863.
Big Black River, Miss., May 17, 1863. Carr's and Osterhaus's Divs., 13th Corps, under Maj.-Gen. McClernand. Union, 29 killed, 242 wounded; Confed., 600 killed and wounded, 2,500 captured.
Big Black River, Miss., July 4 and 5, 1863. (See Bolton.)
Big Black River, Miss., Oct. 13, 1863. Cav. and Inf. under Gen. McPherson.
Big Black River, Miss., Feb. 4, 1864. (See Champion Hills.)
Big Black River Bridge, Miss., Aug. 12 and Sept. 11, 1863.
Big Black River Bridge, Miss., Nov. 27, 1864. 3d U. S. Colored Cav., and Artil. and Cav., under Col. Osband.
Big Blue, Mo., Oct. 23 and 31, 1864.
Big Creek, Ark., July 10, 1863.
Big Creek, Ark., July 26, 1864. (See Wallace's Ferry.)
Big Creek, Mo., Sept. 9, 1862.
Big Creek Gap, Tenn., March 10, 1862. (See Jacksboro'.)
Big Creek Gap, Tenn., Sept. 4, 1862. Detachment of 6th Tenn. Inf.
Big Hatchie River, Miss., Oct. 5, 1862. (See Metamora.)
Big Hill, Ky., Aug. 23, 1862. 3d Tenn.; 7th Ky. Cav. Union, 10 killed, 40 wounded and missing; Confed., 25 killed.

Big Hill Road, Ky., Oct. 23, 1862. (See Point Lick.)
Big Hurricane Creek, Mo., Oct. 19, 1861. 18th Mo. Union, 2 killed, 14 wounded; Confed., 14 killed.
Big Indian Creek, near Searcy Landing, Ark., May 27, 1862. 1st Mo. Cav. Union, 3 killed; Confed., 5 killed, 25 wounded.
Big Indian Creek, Mo., May 26, 1862.
Big Mound, Dak. Ter., July 24, 1863. 1st Minn. Cav.; 3d Minn. Battery; 6th, 7th, and 10th Minn. Inf. (Sioux Indian Fight.) [1864.
Big North Fork Creek, Mo., June 16,
Big Pigeon River, Tenn., Nov. 5 and 6, 1864. 2d N. C. Mounted Inf.
Big Pine Creek, Cal., April 10, 1863.
Big Piney, Mo., July 25 and 26, 1862. (See Mountain Store.)
Big River Bridge, Mo., Oct. 15, 1861. 40 men of 38th Ill. Union, 1 killed, 6 wounded, 33 captured; Confed., 5 killed, 4 wounded.
Big Sandy, Colo., Nov. 29, 1864. 1st and 3d Colo. Cav.
Big Sewell and Meadow Bluff, W. Va., Dec. 12, 1863. 12th Ohio Inf.
Big Shanty, Ga., June 6th and Oct. 3, 1864.
Big Shanty, Ga., June 9 to 30, 1864. (See Kenesaw Mountain.)
Big Shanty, Ga., Sept. 2, 1864. Detachment of Ohio Cav.
Big Springs, Ky., Jan. —, 1865.
Binniker's Bridge, S. C., Feb. 9, 1865. 17th Corps, Army of Tenn.
Birch Coolie, or Acton, Minn., Sept. 2 and 3, 1862. Indian Fight.
Bird Song Ferry, Miss., June 18, 1863.
Bird Song Ferry, Miss., July 4 and 5, 1863. (See Bolton.)
Bird's Point, Mo., Aug. 19, 1861. (See Charleston.)
Birmingham, Miss., April 24, 1863.
Bisland, La., April 12 and 14, 1863. (See Bayou Teche or Irish Bend.)
Black Bayou Expedition, Miss., April 5 to 10, 1863. Part of 15th Corps, under Maj.-Gen. Stelle.
Black Bayou, Miss., April 10, 1863, and March 19, 1864.

Blackburn's Ford, Va., July 18, 1861. 1st Mass.; 2d and 3d Mich.; 12th N. Y.; detachment of 2d U. S. Cav.; Battery E, 3d U. S. Art. Union, 19 killed, 38 wounded; Confed., 16 killed, 53 wounded.
Blackburn's Ford, Va., Sept. 19, 1862.
Blackburn's Ford, Va., Oct. 15, 1863. Part of 2d Corps, Army of the Potomac.
Black Cañon, Ariz. Ter., May 6, 1865.
Black Creek, Fla., July 27, 1864. (See Whiteside.)
Blackford's Ford and Shepherdstown, Va., Sept. 20, 1862. 5th Corps; Griffith's and Barne's Brigades. Union, 92 killed, 131 wounded, 103 missing; Confed., 33 killed, 235 wounded.
Black Jack Forest, Tenn., March 16, 1862. Detachments of 4th Ill. and 5th Ohio Cav. Union, 4 wounded.
Blackland, Miss., June 4, 1862. 2d Iowa Cav.; 2d Mich. Cav. Union, 5 killed, 14 wounded.
Black River, La., Nov. 1, 1864. 6th U. S. Colored Heavy Art.
Black River, Miss., July 1 and 2, 1863. Portion of 17th Corps.
Black River, Mo., Sept. 12, 1861. Three companies 1st Ind. Cav. Confed., 5 killed.
Black River, Mo., July 8, 1862. 5th Kan. Cav. Union, 1 killed, 3 wounded.
Black River, Mo., Sept. 17 to 20, 1864. (See Doniphan.)
Blackville, S. C., Feb. 11, 1865. 3d Cav. Div., Army of the Mississippi.
Black Walnut Creek, near Sedalia, Mo., Nov. 29, 1861. 1st Mo. Cav. Union, 15 wounded; Confed., 17 killed.
Black Warrior Creek, Ala., May 1, 1863. (See Sand Mountain.)
Black Water, Fla., Oct. 18, 1864. (See Pierce's Point.)
Black Water, or Black Water Mound, Mo., Dec. 18, 1861. (See Milford.)
Black Water, Mo., Oct. 12 and 13, 1863. (See Merrill's Crossing.)
Black Water, Mo., Sept. 23, 1864. One company 1st Mo. Militia Cav.
Black Water, Va., Sept. 28, 1862. 1st N. Y. Mounted Rifles.

LIST OF BATTLES AND ENGAGEMENTS. 119

Black Water, Va., Oct. 24, 1862. 39th Ill.; 62d Ohio; 1st N. Y. Mounted Rifles.
Black Water, Va., March 17, 1863. 11th Pa. Cav.
Blain's Cross Roads, Tenn., Dec. 16, 1863. Army of the Ohio.
Blair's Landing, La., April 12, 1864. (See Pleasant Hills.)
Block House No. 4, Tenn., Aug. 19, 1864. One company 115th Ohio Inf.
Block House No. 5, Tenn., Aug. 31, 1864. 115th Ohio. Union, 3 killed; Confed., 25 wounded.
Block House No. 2, Mill Creek, Chattanooga, Tenn., Dec. 2 and 3, 1864. Detachments of 115th Ohio Inf.; also 44th and two companies 14th U. S. Colored Troops.
Block House No. 7, Overall's Creek, Tenn., Dec. 4, 1864. Troops under Gen. Milroy. Union, 100 wounded; Confed., 100 killed and wounded.
Bloomfield, Mo., May 11, 1862. 1st Wis. Cav. Confed., 1 killed.
Bloomfield, Mo., July 29, 1862, March 1, and May 12, 1863.
Bloomfield, Mo., Aug. 25 and 29, 1862. 13th Ill. Cav. Confed., 20 killed and wounded.
Bloomfield, Mo., Sept. 11 to 13, 1862. 13th Ill.; 1st Wis. Cav.; Battery E, 2d Mo. Artil., assisted by Mo. Militia.
Bloomfield, Mo., April 29 and 30, 1863. (See Castor River.)
Bloomfield and Union, Va., Nov. 2 and 3, 1862. Pleasanton's Cav. Union, 2 killed, 10 wounded; Confed., 3 killed, 15 wounded.
Blooming Gap, Va., Feb. 13, 1862. 8th Ohio; 7th W. Va., and 1st W. Va. Cav. Union, 2 killed, 5 wounded; Confed., 13 killed.
Blount's Farm, Ala., May 2, 1863. 51st and 73d Ind.; 80th Ill.; 3d Ohio Mounted Inf.; 1st Ala. Cav. (Streight's Raid.)
Blount's Mills, N. C., April 9, 1863. 3d and 17th Mass.; 1st R. I. and 3d N. Y. Artil.
Blountsville, Tenn., Sept. 22, 1863. Foster's 2d Brig. of Cav. Union, 5 killed, 22 wounded; Confed., 15 killed, 50 wounded, 100 missing.
Blountsville, Tenn., Oct. 13, 1863. 3d Brig., Shackleford's Cav. Union, 6 wounded; Confed., 8 killed, 26 wounded.
Blue Gap, near Romney, Va., Jan. 7, 1862. 4th, 5th, 7th, and 8th Ohio; 14th Ind.; 1st W. Va. Cav. Confed., 15 killed.
Blue Island, Ind., June 19, 1863. Ind. Home Guards.
Blue Mills, Mo., July 24, 1861. 5th Mo. Reserves. Union, 1 killed, 12 wounded.
Blue Mills, or Blue Mills Landing, Mo., Sept. 17, 1861. 3d Iowa. Union, 11 killed, 39 wounded; Confed., 10 killed, 16 wounded.
Blue Mount, Ala., April 13, 1865. (See Mumford's Sta.)
Blue River, Mo., May 18, 1863.
Blue Spring, Mo., March 22, 1863. 1st and 5th Mo. Militia.
Blue Springs, Tenn., Oct. 5, 1863. Part of Gen. Burnside's Troops.
Blue Springs, Tenn., Oct. 10, 1863. 9th Corps, Army of the Ohio: Shackleford's Cav. Union, 100 killed, wounded, and missing; Confed., 66 killed and wounded, 150 missing.
Bluff Springs, Ala., March 25, 1865. (See Pine Barren Creek.)
Bluffton, S. C., June 4, 1863.
Bobb's Creek, Mo., March 7, 1862. (See Fox Creek.)
Bogg's Mills, Va., Jan. 24, 1865. (See Fort Brady.)
Bogler's Creek and Plantersville, or Ebenezer Church and Maplesville, Ala., April 1, 1865. 2d and 4th Div. Cav., and Military Div. of the Miss. (Wilson's Raid.)
Bole's Farm, Mo., July 23, 1862. (See Florida.)
Bollinger Co., Mo., Jan. 14, 1862.
Bollinger's Mills, Mo., July 29, 1862. Two Co's 13th Mo. Confed., 10 killed.
Bolivar, Miss., Aug. 25 and Sept. 20, 1862, and May 3, 1864.
Bolivar, Tenn., Aug. 30, 1862. 20th and 78th Ohio; 2d and 11th Ill.

Cav.; 9th Ind. Artil. Union, 5 killed, 18 wounded, 64 missing; Confed., 100 killed and wounded.
Bolivar, Tenn., Sept. 21, 1862; Feb. 13 and March 9, 1863.
Bolivar and Summerville, Tenn., Dec. 24, 1863. 7th Ill. Cav. Union, 3 killed, 8 wounded.
Bolivar, Tenn., Feb. 6, 1864. Detachment of 7th Ind. Cav. Union, 1 killed, 3 wounded; Confed., 30 wounded.
Bolivar, Tenn., March 29, 1864. 6th Tenn. Cav. Union, 8 killed, 35 wounded.
Bolivar, Tenn., May 3, 1864. Cav. under Gen. S. D. Sturgis.
Bolivar Heights, Va., July 14, 1863. 1st Conn. Cav.
Bolivar Heights and Md. Heights, Va., July 4 to 7, 1864. Maj.-Gen. Siegel's Reserve Div. Union, 20 killed, 80 wounded.
Bolivar Heights, Va., Oct. 16, 1861. Parts of 28th Pa.; 3d Wis., and 13th Mass. Union, 4 killed, 7 wounded.
Bolton and Bird Song Ferry, or Big Black River, Miss., July 4 and 5, 1863. Maj.-Gen. Sherman's Forces. Confed., 2,000 captured.
Bolton Depot, Miss., July 16, 1863. (See Jackson.)
Bolton Depot. Miss., Feb. 4, 1864.
Bone Yard, Tenn., Feb. 10, 1863. 18th Mo. Inf.
Bonfouca, La., Nov. 26, 1863. 31st Mass. Inf. and 4th Mass. Battery.
Boone, N. C., April 1, 1865. Stoneman's Raid.
Boone's C. H., W. Va., Sept. 1, 1861. 1st Ky. Inf. Union, 6 wounded; Confed., 30 killed.
Booneville, Mo., June 17, 1861. 2d Mo. Inf.; Batteries H and L, Mo. Light Artil. Union, 2 killed, 19 wounded; Confed., 15 killed, 20 wounded.
Booneville, Mo., Sept. 13, 1861. Mo. Home Guards. Union, 1 killed, 4 wounded; Confed., 12 killed, 30 wounded.
Booneville, Mo., Oct. 12 and 13, 1863.

Booneville, Mo., Oct. 9 to 11, 1864. 1st, 4th, 5th, 6th, and 7th Mo. Militia Cav.; 15th Mo. and 17th Ill. Cav.; Battery H, 2d Mo. Light Artil. (Price's Invasion.)
Booneville, Miss., May 30 and July 1, 1862. 2d Iowa Cav.; 2d Mich. Cav. Union, 45 killed and wounded; Confed., 17 killed, 65 wounded, 2,000 prisoners.
Boonsboro, Ark., Nov. 7, 1862.
Boonsboro, Ark., Nov. 28, 1862. (See Cane Hill.)
Boonsboro, Md., Sept. 15, 1862. Cav. Army of the Potomac.
Boonsboro, Md., July 7 to 9, 1863. Buford's and Kilpatrick's Cav. Union, 9 killed, 45 wounded.
Boston Mountain, Ark., Nov. 28, 1862. (See Cane Hill.)
Boston Mountain, Ark., Dec. 4 to 6, 1862.
Bottom's Bridge, Va., July 2, 1863. 5th Pa. Cav.
Bottom's Bridge, or Dry Creek, Va., Aug. 29, 1863. 1st N. Y. Mounted Rifles; 5th Pa. Cav.
Bowling Green, Ky., Feb. 1, 1862. One Company 2d Ind. Cav. Confed., 3 killed, 2 wounded.
Bowling Green, Ky., Feb. 15, 1862.
Boyd Troops, under Brig.-Gen. D. C. Buell.
Boyd's Sta., Ala., March 18, 1865. 101st U. S. Colored Troops.
Boyd's Sta., Nev., June 3, 1865.
Boydton Plank Road, Va., Oct. 8, 1864. Recon. by 5th and 9th Corps, Army of the Potomac.
Boydton Road, Va., Oct. 27, 1864. (See Hatcher's Run.)
Boydton and White Oak Roads, Va., March 31, 1865. 2d and 5th Corps. Union, 177 killed, 1,134 wounded, 556 missing; Confed., 1,000 wounded, 235 missing.
Boykan's Mills, S. C., April 18, 1864. 54th Mass.; U. S. Colored Troops. Union, 2 killed, 18 wounded.
Boykan's Mills, or Bradford's Springs, S. C., April 18, 1865. Troops of the Department of the South.

Bradford's Springs, S. C., April 18, 1865. (See Boykan's Mills.)
Bradyville, Tenn., March 1, 1863. 3d and 4th Ohio Cav.; 1st Tenn. Cav. Union, 1 killed, 6 wounded; Confed., 5 killed, 25 wounded, 100 captured.
Bradysville, Va., May 16, 1863. (See Cripple Creek.)
Branchville, Ivy Ford, or Joy Ford, Ark., Jan. 19, 1864. 5th Kan. Cav.
Brandenburg, Ky., July 8, 1863. Ind. Home Guards. (Morgan's Raid.)
Brandon, Miss., July 18 to 20, 1863. Part of Gen. Sherman's Troops.
Brandy Sta., Va., Aug. 20, 1862. Cav., Army of Va. Confed., 3 killed, 12 wounded.
Brandy Sta., Va., June 9, 1863. (See Beverly Ford.)
Brandy Sta., Va., Aug. 1 to 3, 1863. (See Rappahannock Sta.)
Brandy Sta., Va., Sept. 6, 1863. Cav., Army of Potomac.
Brandy Sta., Va., Nov. 8, 1863.
Brashear City, La., March 18, 1863. 1st La. Cav.
Brashear City, La., June 23, 1863. Detachments of 114th and 176th N. Y.; 23d Conn.; 42d Mass., and 21st Ind. Union, 46 killed, 40 wounded, 300 missing; Confed., 3 killed, 18 wounded.
Brawley Fork, Tenn., March 25, 1865.
Brazil Creek, Ind. Ter., Oct. 11, 1863.
Brazos de Santiago, Tex., Nov. 2, 1863. Portion of 13th Corps.
Brentsville, Va., Jan. 9, 1863.
Brentsville, Va., Feb. 14, 1863. 1st Mich. Cav. Union, 15 wounded.
Brentsville, Va., Feb. 14, 1864. 13th Pa. Cav. Union, 4 killed, 1 wounded.
Brentville, Tenn., Dec. 9, 1862. 25th Ill.; 8th Kan.; 81st Ind., and 8th Wis. Battery.
Brentwood, Tenn., Sept. 19, 1862.
Brentwood, Tenn., March 25, 1863. Detachment of 22d Wis. and 19th Mich. Union, 1 killed, 4 wounded, 300 prisoners; Confed., 1 killed, 5 wounded.

Brentwood, Tenn., Dec. 15 and 16, 1864. (See Nashville.)
Brewer's Lane, Ark., Sept. 11, 1864.
Briar, Mo., March 26, 1862. (See Warrensburg.)
Brice's Cross Roads, near Guntown, Miss., June 10, 1864. 81st, 95th, 108th, 113th, 114th, and 120th Ill.; 72d and 95th Ohio; 9th Minn.; 93d Ind.; 55th and 59th U. S. Colored Troops; Brig.-Gen. Grierson's Cav.; 4th Mo.; 2d N. J.; 19th Pa.; 7th and 9th Ill.; 7th Ind.; 3d and 4th Iowa, and 10th Kan. Cav.; 1st Ill. and 6th Ind. Batteries; Battery F, 2d U. S. Colored Art. Union, 223 killed, 394 wounded, 1,625 missing; Confed., 131 killed, 475 wounded.
Bridgeport, Ala., April 29, 1862. 3d Div., Army of the Ohio. Confed., 72 killed and wounded, 350 captured.
Bridgeport Ferry, Miss., July 1 and 2, 1863. (See Black River.)
Brier Creek, Ga., Dec. 4, 1864. (See Waynesboro.)
Briggen Creek, S. C., Feb. 25, 1865.
Brimstone Creek, Tenn., Sept. 10, 1863. 11th Ky. Mounted Inf.
Bristoe Sta., Va., Oct. 14, 1863. 2d Corps; portion of 5th Corps, and 2d Cav. Div., Army of Potomac. Union, 51 killed, 329 wounded; Confed., 750 killed and wounded, 450 missing; Union, Brig.-Gen. Malone killed; Confed., Brig.-Genls. Cooke, Posey, and Kirkland wounded.
Bristoe Sta., Va., April 15, 1864. 13th Pa. Cav. Union, 1 killed, 2 wounded.
Bristol, Tenn., Sept. 21, 1863. Shackleford's and Foster's Cav., Army of the Ohio.
Bristol, Tenn., Dec. 14, 1864. Gen. Burbridge's Cav. (Stoneman's Raid.)
Britton's Lane, Tenn., Sept. 1, 1862.
Broad River, S. C., April 8, 1863. Steamer "Geo. Washington" destroyed.
Broad River, S. C., Nov. 30, 1864. (See Honey Hill.)
Broad Run, Va., April 1, 1863. Detachment of 1st Ver. and 5th N. Y. Cav.

Brooklyn, Kan., Aug. 21, 1863. (See Lawrence.)
Brook's Plantation, Miss., March 31, 1864. (See Roach's Plantation.)
Brook's Turnpike, Fortifications of Richmond, Va., March 1, 1864. Cav., Army of the Potomac. (Kilpatrick's Raid.)
Brown's Cross-roads, Ga., Nov. 27 to 29, 1864. (See Waynesboro.)
Brown's Ferry, Tenn., Oct. 27, 1863. Detachments from 5th, 6th, and 23d Ky.; 1st, 6th, 41st, 93d, and 124th Ohio; 26th Ind. Inf. Union, 5 killed, 21 wounded.
Brown's Gap, Va., Sept. 26, 1864. 1st Cav. Div., Army of Potomac, and 2d Cav. Div., Army of W. Va.
Brown's Springs, Mo., July 27, 1862. 2d Iowa Cav.
Brownsville, Ark., July 25, 1863, and Aug. 25, 1864.
Brownsville, Ark., Aug. 25, 1863. Davidson's Cav. Div., Dept. of Mo.
Brownsville, Ark., Sept. 14 to 16, 1863. 5th Kan. Cav.
Brownsville, Ark., Oct. 30, 1864. 7th Iowa and 11th Mo. Cav. Union, 2 killed.
Brownsville, Miss., June 18, 1863, and Sept. 28, 1864.
Brownsville, Miss., Oct. 16 to 18, 1863. (See Canton.)
Brownsville, Hatchie River, Tenn. July 25, 1862. Cav., commanded by Maj. Wallace.
Brownsville, Tenn., July 29, 1862. One Company 15th Ill. Cav. Union, 4 killed, 6 wounded; Confed., 4 killed, 6 wounded.
Brunswick, Mo., Aug. 17, 1861. 5th Mo. Reserves. Union, 1 killed, 7 wounded.
Bryant's Plantation, Fla., Oct. 21, 1864.
Bubel's Bay, S. C., Feb. 11 to 19, 1865. Exp. under Gen. Potter, with Naval Force under Capt. Ridgely assisting.
Buchanan, Va., June 14, 1864.
Buckhannon, W. Va., July 6, 1861. (See Middle Creek Fork.)
Buckhannon, W. Va., July 26, 1862.
Buckhead Creek, Ga., Nov. 27 to 29, 1864. (See Waynesboro.)

Buckland Mills, Va., Oct. 19, 1863. 3d Div. of Kilpatrick's Cav. Union, 20 killed, 60 wounded, 100 missing; Confed., 10 killed, 40 wounded.
Buckstone Sta., Va., May 23, 1862. 3d Wis.; 27th Ind. Union, 2 killed, 6 wounded; Confed., 12 killed.
Buffalo, W. Va., Sept. 27, 1862. 34th Ohio Inf.
Buffalo Creek, Ga., Nov. 26, 1864. (See Sandersville.)
Buffalo Creek, Ind. Ter., Sept. 14, 1863. (See Seneca Sta.)
Buffalo Gap, W. Va., June 6, 1864. Gen. Hayes' Brigade, 2d Div., Army of W. Va.
Buffalo Hill, Ky., Oct. 4, 1861. Union, 20 killed; Confed., 50 killed.
Buffalo Mills, Mo., Oct. 22, 1861. Confed., 17 killed.
Buffalo Mountain, W. Va., Dec. 13, 1861. (See Camp Alleghany.)
Bullington Island, or St. George's Creek, O., July 19, 1863. 1st, 3d, 8th, 9th, 11th, and 12th Ky.; 8th, 9th, and 12th Mich.; 5th Ind. Cav.; 45th Ohio and 2d Tenn. Mounted Inf., assisted by Militia and U. S. Steamer "Moose." ((Capture of Morgan's Raiders.)
Buford's Gap, Va., June 21, 1864. 23d Ohio. Union, 15 killed.
Buford's Sta., Tenn., Dec. 23, 1864. Cav. under Gen. Thomas.
Bull Bayou, Ark., Aug. 26, 1864. 9th Kan. and 3d Wis. Cav.
Bull Creek, Ark., Aug. 6 and 27, 1864.
Bull Pasture Mountain, Va., May 8, 1862. (See McDowell.)
Bull Run (1st), or Manassas, Va., July 21, 1861. 2d Me.; 2d N. H.; 2d Vt.; 1st, 4th, and 5th Mass.; 1st and 2d R. I.; 1st, 2d, 3d Conn.; 8th, 11th, 12th, 13th, 16th, 18th, 27th, 29th, 31st, 32d, 35th, 38th, and 39th N. Y.; 2d, 8th, 14th, 69th, 71st, and 79th N. Y. Militia; 27th Pa.; 1st, 2d, and 3d Mich.; 1st and 2d Minn.; 1st and 2d Ohio: Detachments of 2d, 3d, and 8th U. S. Regulars; Battalion of Marines; Batteries D, E, G, and M, 2d U. S. Art.; Battery E, 3d U. S.

Art.; Battery D, 5th U. S. Art.; 2d R. I. Battery; Detachments of 1st and 2d Dragoons, and 2d Wis. Union, 481 killed, 1,011 wounded, 1,460 missing and captured; Confed., 269 killed, 1,483 wounded. Confed., Brig.-Gens. Bee and Barton killed.

Bull Run (2d), or Manassas, Va., Aug. 30, 1862. Same troops as engaged at Groveton and Gainesville, with the addition of Porter's 5th Corps. Union, 800 killed, 4,000 wounded, 3,000 missing; Confed., 700 killed, 3,000 wounded.

Bull Run Bridge, Va., Aug. 27, 1862. 11th and 12th Ohio; 1st, 2d, 3d, and 4th N. J. Union, Brig.-Gen. G. W. Taylor mortally wounded.

Bull's Gap, Tenn., Sept. 24, 1864. Cav. and Mounted Inf.

Bull's Gap, Tenn., Nov. 13, 1864. 8th, 9th, and 13th Tenn. Cav. Union, 5 killed, 36 wounded, 200 missing.

Bulltown, Va., Oct. 13, 1863. Detachments of 6th and 11th W. Va. Confed., 9 killed, 60 wounded.

Bunker Hill, Va., July 17, 1861. Portion of Gen. Patterson's command. Confed., 4 killed.

Burgess Farm, Va., Oct. 27, 1864. (See Hatcher's Run.)

Burkesville, Ky., July 2, 1863. (See Marrowbone.)

Burke's Sta., Va., March 10, 1862. One Company 1st N. Y. Cav. Union, 1 killed; Confed., 3 killed, 5 wounded.

Burke's Sta., W. Va., April 4, 1865.

Burned Church, Ga., May 26, 1864. Cav. of 1st Div., Army of the Cumberland.

Burned Hickory, Ga., May 25 to June 4, 1864. (See Dallas.)

Burned Hickory, Ga., July 4 and 5, 1864.

Burnt Ordinary, Va., Jan. 19, 1863. 5th Pa. Cav.

Burnt Ordinary, Va., April 16, 1864.

Burton's Ford, Va., March 1, 1864. (See Stanardsville.)

Bushy Creek, Ark., Dec. 9, 1861. Union Indians. [Ill. Cav.

Bushy Creek, Mo., May 28, 1863. 13th

Butler, Mo., Oct. — to Nov. 20, 1862.

Butler, Bates Co., Mo., May 15, 1862. 1st Iowa Cav. Union, 3 killed, 1 wounded.

Butler, Mo., May 26, 1862. 1st Iowa Cav.

Butler and Osage, or Island Mound, Mo., Oct. 29, 1862. 79th U. S. Colored Troops.

Butler Creek, Ala., Nov. 17, 1864. (See Aberdeen.)

Butler Creek, Tenn., Nov. 22, 1864. Part of 5th Cav. Div, Division of the Mississippi.

Butler's Bridge, N. C., Dec. 12, 1864.

Buzzard Roost, Tunnel Hill, and Rocky Face Ridge, Ga., Feb. 25 to 27, 1864. 4th and 14th Corps and Cav. Corps, Army of the Cumberland. Union, 17 killed, 272 wounded; Confed., 20 killed, 120 wounded.

Buzzard Roost Block House, Ga., Oct. 13, 1864. One company 115th Ill. Union, 5 killed, 36 wounded, 60 missing.

Buzzard Roost Gap, Ga., May 8, 1864. 4th Corps and Cav., Army of the Cumberland.

Byhalia, Miss., Oct. 12, 1863.

CABIN Creek, Ind. Ter., July 1 and 2, 1863. 3d Wis.; 6th and 8th Kan.; 2d Col. Cav.; 79th U. S. Colored Troops, and 3d Kan. Indian Home Guards.

Cabin Creek, Ind. Ter., July 5 and 20, 1863, and Nov. 4, 1864.

Cabin Creek, Ind. Ter., Sept. 19, 1864. 2d, 6th, and 14th Kan. Cav.; 1st and 2d Kan. Indian Home Guards.

Cabin Point, Va., Aug. 5, 1864. 1st U. S. Colored Cav.

Cabletown, Va., March 10, 1864. 1st N. Y. Veteran Cav.

Cabletown, Va., July 19 and Nov. 19, 1864.

Cacapon Bridge, Va., Sept. 6, 1862. 1st N. Y. Cav.

Cache River, Ark., April 22, 1864.

Cache River Bridge, Ark., May 28, 1862. 9th Ill. Cav.

8

Caddo Gap, Ark., Dec. 4, 1863.
Caddo Gap, Ark., Jan. 24, 1864. (See Baker Springs.)
Caddo Gap and Scott's Farm, Ark., Jan. 26, and Feb. 12 and 16, 1864. 2d Kan. Cav.
Caddo Mountains, Ark., Feb. 12, 1864. (See Caddo Gap.)
Cahawba River, Ga., April 8, 1865.
Cainsville, Tenn., Feb. 15, 1863. 123d Ill.; one company, 5th Tenn. Cav.
Cajou De Arivaypo, N. Mex., May 7, 1863.
Calf-Killer Creek, Tenn., Feb. 23, 1864. 5th Tenn. Cav.
Calf-Killer River, Tenn., March 18, 1864. 5th Tenn. Cav.
Calhoun, Ga., May 17 and 18, 1864. (See Adairsville.)
Calhoun, Mo., Jan. 4, 1862. Union, 10 wounded; Confed., 30 wounded.
Calhoun, or Hagnewood Prairie, Tenn., Sept. 26, 1863. Cav., Army of the Ohio. Union, 6 killed, 20 wounded, 40 missing.
Calhoun Sta., La., May 18, 1864. (See Bayou de Glaize.)
California, Mo., Oct. 9 to 11, 1864. 4th and 7th Mo. Militia Cav.; Batteries H and L, 2d Mo. Artil.
California House, Mo., Oct. 18, 1862.
Cambridge, Mo., Sept. 26, 1862. 9th Mo. Militia Cav.
Camden, Ark., April 2, 15, 16, 18, and 24, 1864. Advance troops of 7th Corps. (Steele's Campaign.)
Camden, or South Mills, N. C., April 19, 1862. 9th and 89th N. Y.; 21st Mass.; 51st Pa.; 6th N. H. Union, 12 killed, 98 wounded; Confed., 6 killed, 19 wounded.
Camden Point, Mo., July 13, 1864.
Cameron, Mo., Oct. 12, 1861. James' Cav. Union, 1 killed, 4 wounded; Confed., 8 killed.
Cameron, Va., Jan. 27, 1864.
Campaign in N. Ga., May 5 to Sept. 8, 1864.
Camp Advance, or Munson's Hill, Va., Sept. 29, 1861. 69th Pa. fired, by mistake, into 71st Pa., killing 9 and wounding 25.

Camp Alleghany, or Buffalo Mountain, W. Va., Dec. 13, 1861. 9th and 13th Ind.; 25th and 32d Ohio; 2d W. Va. Union, 20 killed, 107 wounded; Confed., 20 killed, 96 wounded.
Camp Babcock, Ark., Nov. 25, 1862. 3d Kan. Indian Home Guards.
Campbell Sta., Tenn., Nov. 16, 1863. 9th Corps; 2d Div., 23d Corps; Sander's Cav. Union, 60 killed, 340 wounded; Confed., 570 killed and wounded.
Campbellton, Ga., July 28, 1864. Portion of McCooke's Cav.
Campbellville, Tenn., Sept. 5, 1864. Rousseau's Cav.
Campbellville and Lynnville, Tenn., Nov. 24, 1864. 5th Cav. Div., Military Div. of Mo.
Campbellville, Tenn., Sept. 24, 1864.
Camp Cole, Mo., June 18, 1861. 800 Mo. Home Guards. Union, 70 killed and wounded; Confed., 4 killed, 20 wounded.
Camp Crittenden, Mo., Sept. 22, 1861. (See Elliott's Mills.)
Camp Jackson, Mo., May 10, 1861. 1st, 3d, and 4th Mo. Reserve Corps; 3d Mo. Inf. Confed., 639 prisoners.
Camp Meringo, La., Sept. 14, 1864.
Camp Moore, La., May 15, 1863. Troops under Col. Davis.
Campti, La., March 26 and April 4, 1864. 35th Iowa; 5th Minn.; 2d and 18th N. Y. Cav.; 3d R. I. Cav. Union, 10 killed, 18 wounded; Confed., 3 killed, 12 wounded.
Camp Verdigris, Ind. Ter., Sept. 2, 1864.
Canadian River, Ind.Ter.,Aug. 21, 1864.
Cane Creek, also Bear Creek, or Tuscumbia, Ala., Oct. 26, 1863. 1st Div., 15th Corps. Union, 2 killed, 6 wounded; Confed., 10 killed, 30 wounded.
Cane Creek, Ala., June 10, 1864. 106th Ohio Inf.
Cane Hill, Boston Mountain, and Boonsboro, Ark., Nov. 28, 1862. 1st Div., Army of the Frontier. Union, 4 killed, 36 wounded; Confed., 75 killed, 300 wounded.

Cane Hill, Ark., Dec. 20, 1862, and Jan. 2, 1863. Portion of the Army of the Frontier.
Cane River, La., April 24, 1864. (See Monetis Bluff.)
Cane River Crossing, La., April 23, 1864. (See Monetis Bluff.)
Cañon De Chelly, La., Jan. 10, 1864. Troops under Col. Kit Carson (Indian Fight).
Canton, Ky., Aug. 22, 1864.
Canton, Miss., July 17 and 18, 1863. 76th Ohio; 25th and 31st Iowa; 3d, 13th, and 17th Mo.; 2d Wis. Cav.; 5th Ill. Cav.; 3d and 4th Iowa Cav.; one Battery of Art.
Canton, Miss., Sept. 28th, 1863.
Canton, Brownsville, and Clinton, Miss., Oct. 15 to 18, 1863. Portion of 15th and 17th Corps. Confed., 200 killed and wounded.
Canton, Miss., Feb. 27 and 28, 1864. Foraging detachments of 3d and 32d Iowa. Union, 2 killed, 6 wounded; Confed., 3 killed, 15 wounded.
Cape Fear River, N. C., Jan. 16, 1865. Evacuation of Fort Caswell.
Cape Girardeau, Mo., April 26, 1863. 32d Iowa; 1st Wis. Cav.; 2d Mo. Cav.; Batteries D and L, 1st Mo. Light Art. Union, 6 killed, 6 wounded; Confed., 60 killed, 275 wounded and missing.
Cape Girardeau, Mo., Feb. 5, 1864. 2d Mo. Militia Cav. Confed., 7 killed.
Capture of Fort Hell, Jerusalem Plank Road, Va., Sept. 10, 1864. 99th Pa.; 20th Ind.; 2d U. S. Sharpshooters. Union, 20 wounded; Confed., 90 prisoners.
Capture of Jefferson Davis, at Irwinsville, Ga., May 10, 1865. 1st Wis. and 4th Mich Cav. Union, 2 killed, 4 wounded, owing to the pursuing firing into each other.
Capture of Rebel Ram "Fair Play," near Milliken Bend, La., Aug. 18, 1862. 58th and 76th Ohio. Confed., 40 prisoners.
Carlisle, Pa., July 1st, 1863. 12th Ill. Cav.
Carnifax Ferry, Va., Sept. 10, 1861.

9th, 10th, 12th, 13th, 28th, and 47th Ohio. Union, 16 killed, 102 wounded.
Carolina Bend, Miss., July 24, 1864. (See Steamer "Clara Bell.")
Carrick's Ford, W. Va., July 14, 1861. 14th Ohio; 7th and 9th Ind. Union, 13 killed, 40 wounded; Confed., 20 killed, 10 wounded, 50 prisoners.
Carrion Crow Bayou, La., Nov. 3, 1863. (See Grand Coteau.)
Carrion Crow Bayou, La., Nov. 18, 1863. 6th Mo. Cav.
Carroll Co., Ark., April 4, 1863. 1st Ark. Cav.
Carrollton, Ark., March 10, 1863.
Carrollton Landing, Miss., July 24, 1864. (See Steamer "Clara Bell.")
Carrollton Store, Va., March 13, 1864. 1st N. Y. Mounted Rifles; 11th Pa. Cav.
Carrsville, Va., Oct. 15, 1862. One company of 7th Pa. Cav.
Carrsville, or Cassville, Va., Jan. 30, 1863. (See Deserted House.)
Carrsville and Suffolk, or Holland House, Va., May 15 and 16, 1863. Exp. under Gen. Foster.
Carrsville, Va., May 18, 1863. 170th N. Y. Inf.
Carter's Creek, Tenn., April 27, 1863.
Carter's Farm, Va., July 20, 1864. (See Winchester.)
Carter's Sta., Ark., Sept. 27, 1864.
Carter's Sta., Tenn., Dec. 30, 1862. (See Wautauga Bridge.)
Carter's Sta., Tenn., Sept. 22, 1863. 3d Brigade, Cav. Div., Army of the Ohio.
Carter's Sta., Tenn., April 25 and 26, 1864. (See Wautauga Bridge.)
Carter's Sta., Wautauga River, Tenn., Sept. 27, 1864. Cav. and Mounted Inf., under Gen. Ammen.
Carthage, Ark., Nov. 27, 1862. 2d Kan. Cav.
Carthage, La., Jan. 23, 1863.
Carthage, or Dry Forks, Mo., July 5, 1861. 3d and 5th Mo.; 1 Battery of Mo. Artil. Union, 13 killed, 31 wounded; Confed., 30 killed, 125 wounded, 45 prisoners.
Carthage, Mo., March 23, 1862. 6th Kan. Cav. Union, 1 wounded.

Carthage, Mo., Jan. 13, June 27 and 28, and Oct. 2d, 1863, Sept. 22 and Oct. 26, 1864.

Carthage, Mo., May 16 and 24, 1863. 7th Mo. Militia Cav.

Cashtown, Md., July 5, 1863.

Cass Co., Mo., Nov. 3, 1862. (See Harrisonville.)

Cassville, Ga., May 19 to 22, 1864. 20th Corps, Maj.-Gen. Hooker commanding. Union, 10 killed, 46 wounded.

Cassville, Mo., Sept. 21, 1862. 1st Ark. Cav.

Cassville Sta., Ga., May 25, 1864. 1st and 11th Ky. Cav. Union, 8 killed, 16 wounded; Confed., 2 killed, 6 wounded.

Castor River and Bloomfield, Mo., April 29, 1863. 1st Wis. Cav.

Catawba River, N. C., April 19, 1865. Gen. Stoneman's Troops.

Catlett's Sta., Va., Aug. 21 to 23, 1862. Purnell's Legion and 1st Pa. Rifles.

Catlett's Sta., Va., Oct. 24, 1862. Detachment of 3d W. Va. Cav.

Catlett's Sta., Va., Jan 10, 1863.

Cedar Bluffs, Col., May 3, 1864. One company, 1st Col. Cav.

Cedar Creek or Middletown (Sheridan's Ride), Va., Oct. 19, 1864. 6th Corps; 8th Corps, and 1st and 2d Divs., 19th Corps; Merritt's, Custer's and Torbett's Cav. Union, 588 killed, 3,516 wounded, 1,891 missing; Confed., 3,000 killed and wounded, 1,200 missing. Union, Brig.-Gens. Bidwell and Thorburn killed, and Maj.-Gens. Wright, Ricketts, and Grover, and Brig.-Gens. Ketchem, McKenzie, Penrose, Hamlin, Devins, Duval, and Lowell wounded; Confed., Maj.-Gen. Ramseur, killed, and Maj.-Gens. Battle and Conner wounded.

Cedar Fork, Utah Ter., April 2, 1863.

Cedar Keys, Fla., Feb. 16, 1865. 2d U. S. Colored Troops.

Cedar Mountain, also known as Slaughter Mountain, Southwest Mountain, Cedar Run, and Mitchell's Sta., Va., Aug. 9, 1862. 2d Corps, Maj.-Gen. Banks; 3d Corps, Maj.-Gen. McDowell; Army of Va., under command of Maj.-Gen. Pope. Union, 450 killed, 660 wounded, 290 missing; Confed., 229 killed, 1,047 wounded, 31 missing. Union, Brig.-Gens. Augur, Carroll, and Geary wounded; Confed., Brig.-Gen. C. S. Winder killed.

Cedar Run and Mitchell's Sta., Va., Aug. 9, 1862. (See Cedar Mountain.)

Cedar Run Church, Va., Oct. 17, 1864. Detachment of 1st Ky. Cav.

Cedars, Tenn., Dec. 5 to 8, 1864. (See Murfreesboro.)

Cedar Springs, Va., Nov. 12, 1864. (See Newtown.)

Celina, Ky., April 20, 1863. 5th Ind. Cav.

Celina, Tenn., Dec. 7, 1863. 13th Ky. Cav.

Centralia, Mo., Sept. 27, 1864. Three companies, 39th Mo. Inf., massacred by Price. Union, 122 killed, 2 wounded.

Centre Creek, Mo., Feb. 20, 1865.

Centreville, Ala., April 1, 1865. 2d Brig., 1st Div., Cav. Corps, Military Div. of the Miss. (Wilson's Raid.)

Centreville, La., April 13, 1863. (See Irish Bend.)

Centreville and Pine Factory, Tenn., Nov. 3, 1863. Detachments from various regiments under Lieut.-Col. Scully. Confed., 15 killed.

Centreville, Tenn., Sept. 29, 1864. 2d Tenn. Mounted Inf. Union, 10 killed, 25 wounded.

Chackahoola Sta., La., June 24, 1863. Five companies, 9th Conn. Inf.

Chalk Bluffs, Mo., May 15, 1862. 1st Wis. Cav. Union, 1 killed, 3 wounded.

Chalk Bluffs, Ark., March 19 and 25, 1863.

Chalk Bluffs, Ark., April 1, 1863. One company, 2d Mo. Militia Cav.

Chalk Bluffs and St. Francis River, Ark., April 30 and May 1, 1863. 2d Mo. Militia; 3d Mo. Cav.; 1st Iowa Cav.; Battery E, 1st Mo. Light Artil. Union, 2 killed, 11 wounded.

Chalk Bluffs, Ark., May 11, 1865. Surrender of Jeff Thompson's command

LIST OF BATTLES AND ENGAGEMENTS. 127

to Gen. Dodge. Confed., 7,454 prisoners.
Chambersburg, Pa., July 30, 1864. Burned by Confederates.
Champion Hills, or Baker's Creek and Edward's Sta., Miss., May 16, 1863. Hovy's Div., 13th Corps and 17th Corps. Union, 426 killed, 1,842 wounded, 189 missing. Confed., 2,500 killed and wounded, 1,800 missing.
Champion Hills, Baker's Creek, Raymond and Bolton Depot, or Big Black River, Miss., Feb. 4, 1864. 10th Mo.; 4th Iowa; 5th and 11th Ill.; Foster's Battalion Ohio Cav. and a portion of 17th Corps.
Chancellorsville, Va., May 1 to 4, 1863. (Including battles of 6th Corps, at Fredericksburg and Salem Heights.) Army of Potomac, Maj.-Gen. Hooker; 1st Corps, Maj.-Gen. Reynolds; 2d Corps, Maj.-Gen. Couch; 3d Corps, Maj.-Gen. Sickle; 5th Corps, Maj.-Gen. Meade; 6th Corps, Maj.-Gen. Sedgwick; 11th Corps, Maj.-Gen. Howard; 12th Corps, Maj.-Gen. Slocum. Union, 1,512 killed, 9,518 wounded, 5,000 missing; Confed., 1,581 killed, 8,700 wounded, 2,000 missing. Union, Maj.-Gen. Berry and Brig.-Gen. Whipple killed. Brig.-Gens. Devan and Kirby wounded. Confed., Brig.-Gen. Paxton killed. Lieut.-Gen. J. S. Jackson, Maj.-Gen. A. P. Hill and Brig.-Gens. Hoke, Nichols, Ramseur, McGowan, Heth, and Pender wounded.
Chantilly, or Ox Hill, Va., Sept. 1, 1862. McDowell's Corps, Army of Va.; Hooker's and Kearney's Divs. of 3d Corps, Army of Potomac, and Reno's Corps. Union, 1,300 killed, wounded, and missing. Confed., 800 killed, wounded, and missing. Union, Maj.-Gen. Kearney and Brig.-Gen. Stevens killed.
Chapel Hill, Tenn., March 2 and 4, 1863. (See Petersburg.)
Chapin's Farm, Va., Sept. 28 to 30, 1864. (See New Market Heights.)
Chapin's Farm, Va., Nov. 4, 1864.

Chapin Hills, Ky., Oct. 8, 1862. (See Perryville.)
Chapmansville, W. Va., Sept. 25, 1861. 1st Ky. and 34th Ohio. Union, 4 killed, 9 wounded. Confed., 20 killed, 50 wounded.
Chariton Bridge, Mo., Aug. 3, 1862. 6th Mo. Cav. Union, 2 wounded; Confed., 11 killed, 14 wounded.
Chariton River, Mo., Aug. 9, 1862. Mo. Militia.
Chariton River, Mo., Aug. 10 to 13, 1862. (See Grand River.)
Charles City Cross Roads, Va., June 30, 1862. (See White Oak Swamp.)
Charles City Cross Roads, Va., Nov. 16, 1863. Cav. Exp. under Col. West.
Charles City Cross Roads, Va., June 13, 1864. (See White Oak Swamp Bridge.)
Charles City Cross Roads, Va., Oct. 1, 1864. Recon. by Spear's Cav. Brigade, and Terry's Brigade, 10th Corps, Army of Potomac.
Charles City Road, Va., Oct. 27, 1864.
Charleston, Ill., March 28, 1864. Attack on a portion of 54th Ill. while returning to the front from a veteran furlough, by a mob of Copperheads. Union, 2 killed, 8 wounded; Confed., 3 killed, 4 wounded, 12 prisoners.
Charleston, Mo., Jan. 8, 1862. 10th Iowa Inf.
Charleston, S. C., Feb. 18, 1865. Surrender of Ft. Sumter and evacuation of the city. Troops of the Dep't of the South, assisted by U. S. Naval Fleet.
Charleston, Tenn., Dec. 28, 1863. Detachments of 2d Mo. and 4th Ohio Cav. guarding wagon-train. Union, 2 killed, 15 wounded; Confed., 8 killed, 39 wounded, 121 captured.
Charlestown, Va., Oct. 6, 1862. 6th U. S. Cav.
Charlestown, Va., Oct. 16, 1862. Recon. by Army of Potomac.
Charlestown and Berryville, Va., Dec. 1, 1862. 2d Div., 12th Corps. Confed., 5 killed, 18 wounded.

LIST OF BATTLES AND ENGAGEMENTS.

Charleston, or Bird's Point, Mo., Aug. 19, 1861. 22d Ill. Union, 1 killed, 6 wounded; Confed., 40 killed.
Charlestown, Va., March 7, 1862.
Charlestown and Harper's Ferry, W. Va., May 28, 1862.
Charlestown, W. Va., Sept. 12, 1862. 4th W. Va.; 34th Ohio Inf.
Charlestown, W. Va., Oct. 8, 1863.
Charlestown, W. Va., Oct. 18, 1863. 9th Md. Inf. Union, 12 killed, 13 wounded, 379 missing.
Charlestown, W. Va., June 27, 1864. 1st Div. Army of W. Va.
Chattahoochee River, Ga., July 6 to 10, 1864. Army of the Ohio, Maj.-Gen. Schofield; Army of the Tenn., Maj.-Gen. McPherson; Army of the Cumberland, Maj.-Gen. Thomas; Army of the Miss., Maj.-Gen. W. T. Sherman. Union, 80 killed, 450 wounded, 200 missing.
Chattanooga, Tenn., Aug. 21, 1863. Artil. of Gen. Rosecran's Army.
Chattanooga, or Orchard Knob, Tenn., Nov. 23, 1863. 4th and 14th Corps, Army of the Cumberland, Maj.-Gen. Geo. H. Thomas; 11th, Geary's Div. of the 12th, and 15th Corps, Army of the Tenn., Maj.-Gen. W. T. Sherman. Union, 757 killed, 4,529 wounded, 330 missing; Confed., 361 killed, 2,181 wounded, 6,142 missing. (Losses include Lookout Mountain, on the 24th, and Missionary Ridge, on the 25th.
Chattanooga, Tenn., Dec. 2 and 3, 1864. (See Block House No. 2.)
Chattanooga, Tenn., Feb. 5, 1865.
Cheat Mountain, W. Va., Sept. 12 and 13, 1861. 13th, 14th, 15th, and 17th Ind.; 3d, 6th, 24th, and 25th Ohio; 2d W. Va. Inf. Union, 9 killed, 12 wounded; Confed., 80 wounded.
Cheek's Cross Roads, Tenn., March 14, 1864. Cav. under Col. Garrard and 7th Ohio Cav.
Cheese Cake Church, Va., May 4, 1862. 3d Pa.; 1st and 6th U. S. Cav.
Cheraw, S. C., March 2 and 3, 1865. Advance of 17th Corps.

Cherokee Nation, Ind. Ter., Jan. 18, 1863.
Cherokee Sta., Ala., April 17, 1863. (See Bear Creek.)
Cherokee Sta., Ala., Oct. 21, 1863. 1st Div., 15th Corps. Union, 17 killed, 37 wounded; Confed., 40 killed and wounded.
Cherokee Sta., Ala., Oct. 29, 1863. 1st Div., 15th Corps. Casualties not recorded.
Cherry Creek, Miss., July 10, 1864.
Cherry Grove, Mo., June 26, 1862.
Cherry Grove, Va., April 14, 1864. (See Smithfield.)
Chesterfield, S. C., March 2, 1865. Advance of the 20th Corps.
Chester Gap, Va., Nov. 5, 1862. (See Barbee's Cross Roads.)
Chester Gap, Va., July 21 and 22, 1863. 8th N. Y.; 3d Ind.; 12th Ill.; advance Cav., Army of Potomac. Union, 35 killed, 102 wounded; Confed., 300 killed and wounded. (Including loss at Manassas Gap, July 21.)
Chester Sta. (sometimes called Bermuda Hundred), Va., Nov. 17, 1864. (See Bermuda Hundred.)
Chewa Sta., Montgomery and West Point R. R., Ga., July 18, 1864. 8th Ind.; 5th Iowa and 4th Tenn. Cav.
Chickahominy, Va., May 24, 1862. Davidson's Brigade of 4th Corps. Union, 2 killed, 4 wounded.
Chickahominy, Va., June 27, 1862. (See Gaines' Mill, or Seven Days' Retreat.)
Chickahominy River, Va., May 12, 1864. (See Meadow Bridge.)
Chickamcomico, N. C., Oct. 5, 1861. 20th Ind., assisted by Navy.
Chickamauga, Ga., Sept. 19 and 20, 1863. Army of the Cumberland, Maj.-Gen. Rosecrans; 14th Corps, Maj.-Gen. Thomas; 20th Corps, Maj.-Gen. McCook; 21st Corps, Crittenden; Reserve Corps, Maj.-Gen. Granger. Union, 1,644 killed, 9,262 wounded, 4,945 missing; Confed., 2,389 killed, 13,412 wounded, 2,003 missing. Union,

Brig.-Gen. Lytle killed; and Brig.-Gens. Starkweather, Whittaker, and King wounded. Confed., Brig.-Gens. Preston, Smith, Deshler, and Helm killed; and Maj.-Gen. Hood, Brig.-Gens. Adams, Brown, Bunn, Gregg, McNair, Preston, Cleburne, Benning, and Clayton wounded.

Chickamauga Sta., Ga., Nov. 26, 1863.

Chickasaw Bayou and Chickasaw Bluffs, Miss., Dec. 28 and 29, 1862. Army of Tenn., Maj.-Gen. W. T. Sherman; Brig.-Gens. G. W. Morgan's, Steele's, N. L. Smith's, and A. J. Smith's Div. of the Right Wing. Union, 191 killed, 982 wounded, 756 missing; Confed., 207 wounded. Union, Maj.-Gen. N. L. Smith wounded.

Childsburg, Va., May 9, 1864. 6th Ohio and 1st N. J. (Sheridan's Raid.)

Chippewa Steamer, Ark., Feb. 17, 1865.

Choctaw Nation, Ind. Ter., Oct. 7 and Nov. 9, 1863.

Christmas Prairie, Cal., Dec. 26, 1863.

Chulahoma, Miss., Nov. 30, 1862. Advance Cav. of Gen. Grant's Army.

Chunky Sta., Miss., Feb. 12, 1864. 20th, 29th, 31st, 45th and 124th Ill. Inf.; 17th Corps. (Exp. to Meridian.)

Church-in-the-woods, Mo., Aug. 6, 1862. (See Montavallo.)

"City Belle" (Steamer), La., May 3, 1864. 120th Ohio Inf.; 72d U. S. Colored Troops.

City Point, Va., Aug. 9, 1864. Explosion of ammunition, 70 killed, 130 wounded.

Civiques Ferry, La., May 10, 1863. 14th and 24th Me.; 177th N. Y.; 21st N. Y. Battery.

Clarendon, Ark., Aug. 13, 1862. Brig.-Gen. Hovey's Div., 13th Corps. Confed., 700 captured.

Clarendon, Ark., March 15, 1864. 8th Mo. Cav. Union, 1 killed, 2 wounded.

Clarendon, or Pikesville, St. Charles River, Ark., June 25 to 29, 1864. 126th Ill. and 11th Mo.; 9th Iowa and 3d Mich. Cav.; Battery D, 2d

Mo. Art. Union, 200 wounded; Confed., 200 wounded, 200 missing.

Clarendon, Ark., July 14, 1864.

Clarendon Road, Ark., Jan. 15, 1863. (See Helena.)

Clarke's Hollow, W. Va., May 1, 1862. Company C, 23d Ohio Inf. Union, 1 killed, 21 wounded.

Clarke's Neck, Ky., Aug. 27, 1863. 39th Ky. Inf.

Clarkson, Mo., Oct. 28, 1862. Detachment of 2d Ill. Art. Confed., 10 killed, 2 wounded.

Clarksville, Ark., Oct. 28, 1863, May 18, and Sept. 28, 1864. 3d Wis. Cav.

Clarksville, Ark., Nov. 8 and 24, 1863. 3d Wis. Cav. Union, 2 killed.

Clarksville, Ark., Jan., 18, 1865.

Clarksville, Tenn., Aug. 19, 1862. 71st Ohio, under Col. Mason, who surrendered after having offered only slight resistance.

Clarksville, or Rickett's Hill, Tenn., Sept. 7, 1862. 11th Ill.; 13th Wis.; 71st Ohio; 5th Iowa Cav.; two Batteries.

Clay Co., Mo., July 4, 1864. 9th Mo. Militia Cav.

Claysville, Ala., March 14, 1864.

Clayton, Ala., March 14, 1864. (See Claysville.)

Clear Creek, Ark., Aug. 19, 1862, and Feb. 11, 1865.

Clear Creek, or Taberville, Mo., Aug. 2, 1862. Four companies, 1st Iowa Cav. Union, 5 killed, 14 wounded; Confed., 11 killed.

Clear Creek, Mo., May 16, 1864. Two companies, 15th Kan. Cav.

Clear Lake, Ark., March 11, 1865. 3d Wis. Cav.

Clear Springs, Md., July 29, 1864. 12th and 14th Pa. Cav. Confed., 17 killed and wounded.

Clendenin's Raid, Va., May 20 to 28, 1863. 8th Ill. Cav., under Lt.-Col. G. R. Clendenin (below Fredericksburg).

Cleveland, Tenn., Nov. 27, 1863. 2d Brigade, 2d Cav. Div. Confed., 200 captured.

Cleveland, Tenn., Dec. 22, 1863.
Cleveland, Tenn., April 2 and 13, 1864. 1st Wis. Cav.
Cleveland, Tenn., Aug. 17, 1864. 6th Ohio Heavy Art.
Clinch Mountain, Tenn., Dec. 6, 1863. Cav., Army of the Ohio.
Clinton, Ga., Nov. 22, 1864. Advance of 15th Corps.
Clinton, La., Dec. 28, 1862; May 1 and Aug. 25, 1864.
Clinton, La., June 4, 1863. 6th Ill. Cav.
Clinton and Liberty Creek, La., Nov. 15, 1864. Exp. under Gen. A. L. Lee.
Clinton, La., March 2, 1865. 4th Wis. Cav.
Clinton, Miss., July 8 and 16, 1863.
Clinton, Miss., Oct. 17, 1863. Detachment of Army of Tenn., under Gen. McPherson.
Clinton and Jackson, Miss., Feb. 5, 1864. Portion of the 17th Corps and Cav. (Exp. to Meridian.)
Clinton, Miss., July 4, 1864. 2d Wis. Cav.
Clinton, Miss., July 7, 1864. 11th Ill.; 2d Wis. Cav.; Battery of 2d Ill. Art.
Clinton, Mo., July 9, 1862.
Clinton, N. C., May 19, 1862.
Cloutierville, La., April 23 and 24, 1864. (See Monetts Bluff.)
Clover Hill, Va., April 8 and 9, 1865. (See Appomattox C. H.)
Cloyd's Mountain and New River Bridge, Va., May 9 and 10, 1864. 12th, 23d, 34th, and 36th Ohio; 9th, 11th, 14th, and 15th W. Va.; 3d and 4th Pa. Reserves. Union, 126 killed, 585 wounded; Confed., 600 killed and wounded, 300 missing.
Coahoma Co., Miss., Aug. 2, 1862. 11th Wis. Inf. Union, 5 wounded.
Cochran's Cross Roads, Miss., Sept. 10, 1862. (See Cold Water.)
Coffeeville, Miss., Dec. 5, 1862. 1st, 2d, and 3d Cav. Brigades, Army of the Tenn. Union, 10 killed, 54 wounded; Confed., 7 killed, 43 wounded.

Cold Harbor, Va., June 27, 1862. (See Gaines' Mill and Seven Days' Retreat.)
Cold Harbor, Va., June 1 to 12, 1864. (Including Gaines' Mills, Salem Church, and Hawes' Shop.) 2d, 5th, 6th, 9th, and 18th Corps, together with Sheridan's Cav. Union, 1,905 killed, 10,570 wounded, 2,456 missing; Confed., 1,200 killed and wounded, 500 missing. Union, Brig.-Gens. Brookes and Byrnes killed, and Tyler, Stannard, and Johnson wounded; Confed., Brig.-Gens. Doles and Keitt killed, and Brig.-Gens. Kirkland, Finnegan, Law, and Lane wounded.
Cold Knob Mountain, or Sinking Creek, or Frankfort, Va., Nov. 26, 1862. 2d W. Va. Cav.
Coldwater, Miss., May 11, July 24, Nov. 8 and 9, 1862; Feb. 19 and July 28, 1863.
Coldwater, Miss., Sept. 10, 1862. 6th Ill. Cav. Confed., 4 killed, 80 wounded.
Coldwater, Miss., April 19, 1863. (See Hernando.)
Coldwater, Miss., Aug. 21, 1863. 3d and 4th Iowa Cav.; 5th Ill. Cav. Union, 10 wounded.
Coldwater Creek, Miss., Sept. 8 and 11, 1862. Portion of 34th and 37th Ohio.
Coldwater Grove, Mo., Oct. 24, 1864. Kan. Cav., Army of the Frontier.
Coldwater Grove, Tenn., April 19, 1863.
Coldwater Sta., Miss., Nov. 29, 1862. 1st Ind. Cav.
Coldwater Sta., Tenn., March 17, 1863.
Cole Camp, Mo., Oct. 5, 1862, and June 8, 1863.
Cole Co., Mo., Oct. 6, 1864. (See Prince's Place.)
Cole Creek, Miss., Oct. 4, 1864.
Coleman's, Miss., March 5, 1864. Miss. Marine Brigade.
Coleman's Plantation, near Port Gibson, Miss., July 4 and 5, 1864. 52d U. S. Colored Troops; Miss. Marine Brigade. Union, 6 killed, 18 wounded.

College Hill, or Oxford Hill and Hurricane Creek, Miss., Aug. 21 and 22, 1864. 4th Iowa; 11th and 21st Mo. Inf.; 3d Iowa Cav.; 12th Mo. Cav. Confed., 15 killed.
Collinsville, Miss., June 23, 1864. Train attack on the Charleston & Miss. R. R.
Colliersville, Tenn., Oct. 11, 1863. 69th Ind. Inf; 13th U.S. Regulars. Union, 15 killed, 50 wounded.
Colliersville, Tenn., Oct. 25, 1863.
Colliersville, Tenn., Nov. 3, 1863. Cav. Brig., 16th Corps.
Colliersville, Tenn., Dec. 27 and 28, 1863. Cav., Army of the Tenn.
Columbia, Ky., July 3, 1863. 1st Ky.; 2d Ohio Cav.; 45th Ohio Mounted Inf. (Morgan's Raid.)
Columbia, La., Feb. 4, 1864.
Columbia, La., June 6, 1864. (See Lake Chicot.)
Columbia, S. C., Feb. 16 and 17, 1865. 15th Corps, Army of the Tenn.
Columbia, Tenn., Sept. 9, 1862. 42d Ill. Inf. Confed., 18 killed, 45 wounded.
Columbia, Duck River, Tenn., Nov. 24 to 28, 1864. Capron's Brigade, 1st Cav. Div.; 4th and 23d Corps.
Columbia, Tenn., Dec. 19, 1864.
Columbia, Va., Oct. 7 and 8, 1864.
Columbus, Ga., April 16, 1865. 4th Div. Cav., Military Div. of the Miss. (Wilson's Raid.)
Columbus, Ky., Jan. 18, 1865. Detachment of Tenn. Cav.
Columbus, Mo., Jan. 9, 1862. 7th Kan. Cav. Union, 5 killed.
Columbus, Mo., July 23, 1862. 7th Mo. Cav. Union, 2 wounded.
Combahee River and River's Bridge, Salkahatchie, S. C., Jan. 25 to Feb. 9, 1865. 15th and 17th Corps. Union, 138 killed and wounded.
Comfort, N. C., July 6, 1863. (See Quaker Bridge.)
Como, Miss., Oct. 7, 1863.
Como, Tenn., Sept. 19, 1863.
Compton Ferry, Mo., Aug. 10 to 13. 1862. (See Grand River.)
Concha's Springs, New Mexico, July 22, 1863. One company of New Mexico Cav.
Concordia Bayou, La., Aug. 5, 1864.
Conne Creek, Clinton, La., Aug. 25, 1864. Part of Cav., Dep't of the Gulf.
Congaree Creek, S. C., Feb. 15, 1865. 15th Corps, Army of the Tenn.
Construction Train, Tenn., Jan. 25, 1863.
Convalescent Corral, near Corinth, Miss., July 7, 1863. One company, 39th Iowa Inf.
Conyersville, Tenn., Sept. 5, 1863.
Cook's Cañon, Nev., July 24, 1863.
Coon Creek, or Lamar, Mo., Aug. 24, 1862. Union, 2 killed, 22 wounded.
Coosa Creek, Ala., April 1, 1865.
Coosa River, Ala., July 13, 1864.
Coosa River, Ga., Oct. 25, 1864.
Coosaw River, S. C., Dec. 4, 1864. 25th Ohio Inf.
Corinth Road, Miss., April 8, 1862. Recon. by 3d Brig., 5th Div., Army of Tenn.; 4th Ill. Cav.
Corinth, Miss., April 30 to May 30, 1862. (Siege of Corinth.) Evacuated May 30, when Gen. Halleck's Army took possession.
Corinth, Miss., May 17, 1862. Brig.-Gen. Smith's Brigade. Union, 10 killed, 31 wounded; Confed., 12 killed.
Corinth, Miss., Oct. 3 and 4, 1862. McKean's, Davies', Hamilton's, and Stanley's Divs., Army of the Miss. Union, 315 killed, 1,812 wounded, 232 missing; Confed., 1,423 killed, 5,692 wounded, 2,248 missing. Union, Brig.-Gens. Hackleman killed, and Oglesby wounded.
Corinth, Miss., Aug. 16, 1863.
Corinth, Miss., June 10, 1864. 2d N. J. Cav. (Guntown Exp.)
Corydon, Ind., July 9, 1863. Ind. Home Guards. (Morgan's Raid.)
Cosby Creek, Tenn., Jan. 14, 1864. (See Terrisville.)
Cottage Grove, Tenn., March 21, 1863.
Cotton Gap, Ark., Sept. 1, 1863. (See Devil's Back-bone.)
Cotton Hill, W. Va., Sept. 11, 1862. 34th and 37th Ohio; 4th W. Va. Inf.

Cotton Plant, Ark., July 7, 1862. (See Bayou Cache.)
Cotton Plant, Cache River, Ark., April 21, 1864. 8th Mo. Cav. Union, 2 killed, 3 wounded.
Courtland, Ala., July 25 and 27, 1864. 18th Mich.; 32d Wis. Inf.
Courtland, Tenn., Aug. 22, 1862. 42d Ill. Union, 2 wounded; Confed., 8 killed.
Courtland Bridge, Ala., July 25, 1862. Two companies, 10th Ky. Inf.; 2 companies, 1st Ohio Cav. Union, 100 captured.
Courtland Road, Ala., May 26 and 27, 1864. (See Decatur.)
Courtney's Plantation, Miss., April 11, 1863.
Cove Creek, N. C., Nov. 18, 1862. 3d N. Y. Cav.
Cove Mountain, or Grassy Lick, or Wytheville, Va., May 9 and 10, 1864, 14th Pa.; 1st, 2d, and 3d W. Va.; 34th Ohio Mounted Inf.
Covington, Tenn., March 10, 1863. 6th and 7th Ill. Cav. Confed., 25 killed.
Cow Creek, Kan., Nov. 14 to 28, 1864. 54th U. S. Colored Troops; 3d Kan. Indian Home Guards.
Cow Creek, Kan., June 12, 1865.
Cowskin Creek, Mo., Aug. 5 to 7, 1864. 8th Mo. Militia Cav.
Coxe's Bridge, N. C., March 24, 1865. Provisional Corps under Gen. Terry.
Coyle Tavern (near Fairfax, C. H.), Va., Aug. 24, 1863. 2d Mass. Cav. Union, 2 killed, 3 wounded; Confed., 3 killed, 4 wounded.
Crab Orchard, Ky., Aug. 22, 1862. 9th Pa. Cav.
Craig's Meeting House, Va., May 5, 1864. 3d Div. Cav., Army of Potomac.
Crampton's Ferry, Mo., Aug. 11, 1862. (See Grand River.)
Crampton's Gap, Md., Sept. 14, 1862. (See Turner's Gap.)
Crane Creek, Mo., Oct. 29 and 30, 1864. (See Newtonia.)
Crawford Co., Ark., Aug. 11, 1864. (See Van Buren.)

Crawford Co., Mo., Nov. 25, 1862. Mo. and enrolled Militia.
Creek Agency, Ind. Ter., Oct. 15 and 25, 1863. 1st Kan., Indian Home Guards; 2d Ind. Battery.
Creelsboro, Ky., and Celina, Tenn., Dec. 7, 1863. 13th Ky. Cav. Confed., 15 killed. [Malvern Hill.)
Crew's Farm, Va., July 1, 1862. (See Cripple Creek, or Bradyville, Va., May 16, 1863. Detachment of 5th Tenn. Cav.
Crooked Creek, Ala., May 1, 1863. (See Sand Mountain.)
Crooked Creek, Mo., Aug. 24, 1862.
Crooked River, Oregon, May 18, 1864. 1st Oregon Cav.
Crooked Run, Front Royal, Va., Aug. 15, 16, 1864. 1st and 2d Brigades, 1st Cav. Div., Army of Potomac. Union, 13 killed, 58 wounded; Confed., 30 killed, 150 wounded, 300 captured.
Cross Bayou, La., Sept. 14, 1863.
Cross Hollow and Fayetteville, or Oxford Bend, Ark., Oct. 18 and 28, 1862. One Div., Army of Frontier, under Brig.-Gen. Herron.
Cross Keys, or Union Church, Va., June 8, 1862. 8th, 39th, 41st, 45th, 54th, and 58th N. Y.; 2d, 3d, 5th, and 8th W. Va.; 25th, 32d, 55th, 60th, 73d, 75th, and 82d Ohio; 1st and 27th Pa.; 1st Ohio Battery. Union, 125 killed, 500 wounded; Confed., 42 killed, 230 wounded; Confed., Brig.-Gens. Stewart and Elzey wounded.
Cross Lanes, or Summerville, W. Va., Aug. 26, 1861. 7th Ohio Inf. Union, 5 killed, 40 wounded, 200 captured.
Cross Timbers, Mo., July 28, 1862.
Cross Timbers, Mo., Oct. 16, 1863. 18th Iowa Inf. Confed., 2 killed, 8 wounded.
Croton Springs, Ariz. Ter., July 14, 1865.
Crump's Hill, or Pine Woods, La., April 2, 1864. 14th N. Y. Cav.; 2d La.; 2d Ill. and 16th Mo. Cav.; 5th U. S. Colored Artil. Union, 20 wounded; Confed., 10 killed, 25 wounded.

Crump's Landing, or Adamsville, Tenn., April 4, 1862.

Culpeper (near Culpeper), Va., July 12, 1862. 1st Md.; 1st Vt.; 1st W. Va.; 5th N. Y. Cav. Confed., 1 killed, 5 wounded.

Culpeper, Va., Sept. 13, 1863. 1st, 2d, and 3d Divs., Cav. Corps, Army of Potomac. Union, 3 killed, 40 wounded; Confed., 10 killed, 40 wounded, 75 missing.

Culpeper, or White Sulphur Springs, or Warrenton Springs, Va., Oct. 12 and 13, 1863. Cav. Corps, Army of Potomac. Union, 8 killed, 46 wounded.

Culp's House, Ga., June 22, 1864. (See Kenesaw Mountain.)

Cumberland, or Flock's Mills, Md., Aug. 1, 1864. Troops under Gen. Kelley.

Cumberland Gap, Tenn., June 18, 1862. Troops under Gen. G. W. Morgan.

Cumberland Gap, Tenn., Sept. 9, 1863. Shackleford's Cav. Confed., 2,000 captured.

Cumberland Gap, Tenn., Jan. 29, 1864.

Cumberland Gap, Tenn., Feb. 22, 1864. One company 91st Ind.

Cumberland Iron Works, Tenn., Aug. 26, 1862. 71st Ohio Inf.; 5th Iowa Cav.

Cumberland Iron Works, Tenn., Feb. 3, 1863. (See Fort Donelson.)

Cumberland Mountain, Tenn., April 28, 1862. 16th and 42d Ohio; 22d Ky. Inf.

Cuyler's Plantation, Monteith Swamp, Ga., Dec. 9, 1864. 14th Corps, Military Division of the Mississippi.

Cynthiana, Ky., July 17, 1862. 18th Ky.; 7th Ky. Cav., and Home Guards. (Morgan's Raid.) Union, 17 killed, 34 wounded; Confed., 8 killed, 29 wounded.

Cynthiana and Kellar's Bridge, Ky., June 10, 1864. 168th and 171st Ohio. Union, 21 killed, 71 wounded, 980 captured. (Morgan's Raid.)

Cynthiana, Ky., June 11, 1864. Burbridge's attack on Morgan's Raiders.

Union, 150 killed and wounded; Confed., 300 killed and wounded, 400 captured.

Cypress Bridge, Ky., Nov. 17, 1861. Union, 10 killed, 15 wounded.

Cypress Swamp, Ga., Dec. 7, 1864. (See Ebenezer Creek.)

DABNEY'S Mills, or Rowanty Creek and Baughn Road, Hatcher's Run, Va., Feb. 5 to 7, 1865. 5th Corps and 1st Div. of the 6th Corps, together with Gregg's Cav. Union, 232 killed, 1,062 wounded, 186 missing; Confed., 1,200 killed and wounded. Union, Brig.-Gens. Morrow, Smythe, Davis, Gregg, Ayres, Sickel, and Gwyn wounded; Confed., Gen. Pegran killed, and Sorrell wounded.

Dallas, Ark., Jan. 28, 1864.

Dallas, also called New Hope Church, Burned Hickory, Pumpkinvine Creek, and Altoona Hills, Ga., May 25 to June 4, 1864. 4th, 14th, 20th, and Cav. Corps, Army of the Cumberland, Maj.-Gen. Thomas; 23d Corps, Maj.-Gen. Schofield; 15th, 16th, and 17th Corps, Army of the Tennessee, Maj.-Gen. McPherson; Army of the Mississippi, Maj.-Gen. Sherman. Union, 2,400 killed, wounded, and missing; Confed., 3,000 killed, wounded, and missing. Confed., Maj.-Gen. Walter killed.

Dallas, Mo., Sept. 2, 1861. 11th Mo. Inf. Union, 2 killed.

Dallas, Mo., Aug. 24, 1862. 12th Mo. Militia Cav. Union, 3 killed, 1 wounded.

Dallas, N. C., April 19, 1865. Stoneman's Raid.

Dallas Co., Mo., Sept. 19, 1864.

Dalton, Ga., Jan. 21, 1864. 28th Ky. Mounted Inf.; 4th Mich. Cav.

Dalton, Ga., May 9, 1864. 23d Corps, Army of the Ohio.

Dalton, Ga., Aug. 14 to 16, 1864. 2d Mo. Inf.; 14th U. S. Colored Troops.

Dalton, Ga., Oct. 13, 1864. 44th U. S. Colored Troops. Union, 400 missing.

Dam No. 4, Potomac, Va., Dec. 11, 1861.
  12th Ind. Inf.
Dandridge, Tenn., Jan. 16 and 17, 1864.
  4th Corps and Cav. Div., Army of
  the Ohio. Union, 150 wounded.
Danville, Ark., March 28, 1864. 2d
  Kan. Cav.   [Home Guards.
Danville, Ky., Aug. 26, 1862. Ky.
Danville, Ky., March 24, 1863. 18th
  and 22d Mich.; 1st Ky. Cav.; 2d
  Tenn. Cav.; 1st Ind. Battery.
Danville, Miss., June 6, 1864. (Exp. to
  Guntown.)
Darbytown Road, near New Market
  Heights, Va., Oct. 7, 1864. 10th Corps
  and Custer's Cav.
Darbytown Road, Va., Oct. 13, 1864.
  Recon. by 1st and 3d Divs., 10th
  Corps; Custer's Cav.
Dardanelle, Ark., Sept. 9 and 12, 1863.
  2d Kan. Cav.; 2d Ind. Battery.
Dardanelle, Ark., May 10, 1864. 6th
  Kan. Cav.
Dardanelle, Ark., Nov. 29, 1864.
Dardanelle, Ark., Jan. 14, 1865. 2d
  Kan. Cav.; Ohio Cav.
Darksville, Va., July 19, 1864. Averill's
  Cav. (Including Steven's Depot and
  Winchester, on the 20th.) Union, 37
  killed, 175 wounded; Confed., 300
  wounded, 200 captured.
Darksville, Va., Sept. 3, 1864. 3d Cav.
  Div., Army of Potomac.
Darnestown, Va., Sept. 15, 1861. (See
  Pritchard's Mills.)
Davis Bend, La., June 2 and 29, 1864.
Davis' Cross Roads, Ga., Sept. 11,
  1863. (See Dug Gap.)
Davis' Farm, Va., June 22 and 23,
  1864. (See Weldon R. R.)
Davis' Mills, Miss., Dec. 21, 1862. Six
  companies, 25th Ind.; 2 companies,
  5th Ohio Cav.
Davis' Mills, Miss., March 14, 1863.
Day's Gap, Ala., April 30, 1863. Forces
  on Streight's Raid.
Dayton, Ark., Dec. 23, 1861.
Dayton, Mo., April 27, 1864.
Dead Buffalo Lake, Dak. Ter., July 26,
  1863. 1st Minn. Cav.; 6th, 7th, and
  10th Minn. Inf.; 3d Minn. Battery.
  (Sioux Indian Fight.)

Deatonsville, Va., April 6, 1865. (See
  Sailor's Creek.)
Decatur, Ala., July 15, 1862. Detach-
  ment of 1st Ohio Cav.
Decatur, Ala., March 7, 1864. Army
  of the Tenn. under Gen. Dodge.
Decatur, Ala., April 17, 1864. 25th
  Wis. Inf. Union, 2 wounded.
Decatur, Courtland Road, Ala., May
  26 and 27, 1864. 1st, 3d, and 4th
  Ohio Cav.; Cav. Corps and 3d
  Brigade, 4th Div., 16th Corps.
Decatur, Ala., Aug. 18, 1864. 2d Cav.
  Div., Army of the Cumberland; 1st
  U. S. Colored Artil.
Decatur, Ala., Oct. 26 to 29, 1864. 18th
  Mich.; 102d Ohio; 68th Ind.; 14th
  U. S. Colored Troops. Union, 10
  killed, 45 wounded, 100 missing;
  Confed., 100 killed, 300 wounded.
Decatur, Ala., Dec. 27 and 28, 1864.
  Troops of Provisional Div. under
  Gen. Steadman.
Decatur, Ga., July 22, 1864. 2d Brigade,
  4th Div., 16th Corps. Confed., Maj.-
  Gen. Walker killed.
Decatur, Ga., Aug. 5, 1864. 2d Cav.
  Div., Army of the Cumberland.
Decatur, Miss., Feb. 12, 1864. Portion
  of 16th Corps. (Exp. to Meridian.)
Decatur, Tenn., July 15, 1862. De-
  tachment of 1st Ohio Cav. Union,
  4 wounded.
Decatur, Tenn., Aug. 18, 1864.
Deep Bottom, Va., July 21, 1864. 1st
  Div., 10th Corps, Army of the
  James.
Deep Bottom, New Market, and Mal-
  vern Hill, Va., July 27 and 28, 1864.
  1st Div., 10th Corps, Cav., Army of
  the James; 2d Corps and 1st and 2d
  Divs., Cav. Corps, Army of Potomac.
Deep Bottom, or Deep Bottom Run,
  Va., Aug. 14 to 18, 1864. (See Straw-
  berry Plains.)
Deep Bottom, Va., Sept. 2 and 6 and
  Oct. 1 and 31, 1864.
Deep Creek, N. C., Feb. 5, 1864. (See
  Quallatown.)
Deep Creek, Va., April 5, 1865.
Deep Gully, N. C., March 13 and 14,
  1863.

LIST OF BATTLES AND ENGAGEMENTS. 135

Deep River Bridge, N. C., April 4, 1865. (Stoneman's Raid.)
Deep Water Creek, Mo., Oct. 15, 1863.
Deer Creek, Dak. Ter., May 21, 1865.
Deer Creek, near Greenville, Miss., Feb. 23, 1863. Gen. Burbridge's Div., 13th Corps.
Deer Creek, Miss., March 21 and April 8 and 12, 1863.
Denver, Kan., Sept. 7, 1864.
Des Allemands, La., Sept. 9, 1862. 21st Ind. and 4th Wis. Inf. Confed., 12 killed.
Des Arcs, Ark., Jan. 16, 1863. (See Duvall's Bluff.)
Des Arcs, Ark., July 26, 1864. 11th Mo. Cav.
Des Arcs, Ark., Dec. 6, 1864.
Deserted House, or Carrsville and Kelly's Ford, near Suffolk, Va., Jan. 30, 1863. Portion of Maj.-Gen. Peck's Forces, under Gen. Corcoran and Col. Spear. Union, 24 killed, 8 wounded; Confed., 50 wounded.
Deveaux Neck, or Mason's Bridge and Gregory's Farm, also Tillafinny River, S. C., Dec. 6 to 9, 1864. 26th, 32d, 33d, 34th, and 102d U. S. Colored Troops; 54th and 55th Mass. Colored Troops; 56th, 127th, and 155th N. Y.; 25th and 107th Ohio; 3d R. I. Artil. and U. S. Gunboat. Union, 39 killed, 390 wounded, 200 missing; Confed., 400 killed and wounded.
Devil's Back-bone, or Ft. Smith and Cotton Gap, Ark., Sept. 1, 1863. 1st Ark.; 6th Mo. Militia; 2d Kan. Cav.; 2d Ind. Battery. Union, 4 killed, 12 wounded; Confed., 25 killed, 40 wounded.
Diamond Grove, Mo., April 14, 1862. 6th Kan. Cav. Union, 1 wounded.
Diamond Grove, Mo., June 3 and Aug. 21, 1864.
Dickson Sta., Ala., April 19 and 23 and Oct. 20, 1863.
Dinwiddie C. H., Va., March 31, 1865. 1st, 2d, and 3d Cav. Divs., Army of Potomac. Union, 67 killed, 354 wounded; Confed., 400 killed and wounded.

Disputant's Sta., Va., Nov. 18, 1864.
Ditch Bayou, Ia., June 6, 1864. (See Lake Chicot.)
Dobbin's Ferry, or La Vergne, Tenn., Dec. 9, 1862. 35th Ind.; 51st Ohio; 8th and 21st Ky.; 7th Ind. Battery. Union, 5 killed, 48 wounded.
Dog Walk, Ky., Oct. 9, 1862. (See Lawrenceburg.)
Donaldsonville, La., June 28, 1863. 28th Me. Inf.; Convalescents, assisted by U. S. vessels "Princess Royal" and "Winona." Confed., 39 killed, 112 wounded, 150 missing.
Donaldsonville, or Kock's Plantation, La., July 13, 1863. Portions of Weitzel's and Grover's Div., 19th Corps.
Donaldsonville, La., Feb. 8, 1864. 4th Wis. Cav.
Donaldsonville, La., Aug. 5, 1864. 11th N. Y. Cav.
Doniphan and Black River, Mo., Sept. 17 to 20, 1864. One company, 3d Mo. Militia Cav.
Doubtful Cañon, Ariz., May 4, 1864. Detachment of 5th Cal. Inf.; 1st Cal. Cav. Union, 1 killed, 6 wounded; Confed., 10 killed, 20 wounded.
Douglass Landing, Pine Bluff, Ark., Feb. 22, 1865. 11th Ill. Cav. Union, 40 wounded; Confed., 26 wounded.
Dover, Mo., Oct. 20, 1864.
Dover, Tenn., Feb. 14 to 16, 1862. (See Ft. Donelson.)
Dover Road, N. C., April 28, 1863. Troops under Brig.-Gen. Palmer.
Downer's Bridge, Va., May 20, 1864. 5th N. Y. Cav.
Drainesville, Va., Nov. 26, 1861. 1st Pa. Cav. Confed., 2 killed.
Drainesville, Va., Dec. 20, 1861. 1st 6th, 9th, 10th, and 12th Pa. Reserve Corps; 1st Pa. Artil.; 1st Pa. Cav. Union, 7 killed, 61 wounded; Confed., 43 killed, 143 wounded.
Drainesville, Va., Feb. 22, 1864. Detachment of 2d Mass. Cav. Union, 10 killed, 7 wounded, 57 captured; Confed., 2 killed, 4 wounded.
Draft Riots in N. Y. City, N. Y., July 13 to 15, 1863. Over 1,000 Rioters killed and wounded.

Dresden, Ky., May 5, 1862. (See Lockridge Mills.)
Dresden, Tenn., May 5, 1862.
Dripping Springs, Ark., Dec. 28 and 29, 1862.
Driver's Gap, Ala., May 1, 1863. (See Sand Mountain.)
Droop Mountain, Va., Nov. 6, 1863. 10th W. Va.; 28th Ohio; 14th Pa. Cav.; 2d and 5th W. Va. Cav.; Battery B, W. Va. Art. Union, 31 killed, 94 wounded; Confed., 50 killed, 250 wounded, 100 missing.
Drewry's Bluff, Va., May 12 to 16, and May 20, 1864. (See Ft. Darling.)
Dry Creek, Va., Aug. 29, 1863. (See Bottom's Bridge.)
Dry Fork Creek, or Dry Forks, Mo., July 5, 1861. (See Carthage.)
Dry Forks, Cheat River, W. Va., Jan. 8, 1862. One company, 2d W. Va. Cav. Union, 6 wounded; Confed., 6 killed.
Dry Wood, or Ft. Scott, Mo., Sept. 2, 1861. 5th and 6th Kan.; one company, 9th Kan. Cav.; 1st Kan. Battery. Union, 4 killed, 9 wounded.
Dry Wood, or Ft. Scott, Mo., Nov. 10, 1862, and Nov. 29, 1864.
Duck Creek, S. C., Feb. 16, 1865.
Duck River Island, Tenn., April 26, 1863. Ellett's Miss. Ram Fleet.
Dug Gap, Alpine Gap, and Steven's Gap, or Davis' Cross Roads, Ga., Sept. 11, 1863. Advance of Army of the Cumberland.
Dug Gap, Ga., May 7, 1864. (See Mill Creek.)
Dug Springs, Mo., Aug. 2, 1861. 1st Iowa; 3d Mo.; five Batteries of Mo. Light Art. Union, 4 killed, 37 wounded; Confed., 40 killed, 44 wounded.
Dukedom, Ky., Feb. 28, 1864. 7th Tenn. Cav.
Dumfries, Va., Dec. 19, 1862. (See Occoquan.)
Dumfries, Va., Dec. 27, 1862. 5th, 7th, and 66th Ohio; 12th Ill. Cav.; 1st Md. Cav.; 6th Me. Battery. Union, 3 killed, 8 wounded; Confed., 25 killed, 40 wounded.

Dumfries, Va., March 2, 1863.
Dunbar's Plantation, La. April 15, 1863. 2d Ill. Cav. Union, 1 killed, 2 wounded.
Duncan's Run, Va., March 15, 1865.
Dunksburg, near Sedalia, Mo., Dec. 4, 1861. Citizens repulse raiders. Confed., 7 killed, 10 wounded.
Dunn's Bayou, Red River, La., May 5, 1864. 56th Ohio on board U. S. Gunboat "Signal," Steamer "Covington," and transport "Warner." Union, 35 killed, 65 wounded, 150 missing.
Dunn's Lake, Fla., Feb. 5, 1865. Detachment of 17th Conn. Inf.
Durhamville, Tenn., Sept. 17, 1862. Detachment of 52d Ind. Inf. Union, 1 killed, 10 wounded; Confed., 8 killed, 10 wounded.
Dutch Gap, Va., Aug. 13, 1864.
Dutch Gap, Va., Aug. 24, and Sept. 7, 1864. 4th U. S. Colored Troops.
Dutch Gap, Va., Nov. 17, 1864.
Dutch Mills, Ark., April 14, 1864. 6th Kan. Cav. (Steele's Raid.)
Dutton's Hill, or Somerset, Ky., March 30, 1863. 1st Ky. Cav.; 7th Ohio Cav.; 44th and 45th Ohio Mounted Inf. Union, 10 killed, 25 wounded; Confed., 290 killed, wounded and missing.
Duvall's Bluff and Des Arcs, Ark., Jan. 16, 1863. 24th Ind. Inf., assisted by U. S. Gunboat "De Kalb."
Duvall's Bluff, Ark., Dec. 12, 1863. 8th Mo. Cav.
Duvall's Bluff, Ark., Aug. 21 and Sept. 6, 1864. Mo. Cav.
Duvall's Mills, Va., Dec. 1, 1864. (See Stony Creek Sta.)
Dyersburg, Tenn., Jan. 30, 1863. 22d Ohio Inf.

EAGLEVILLE, Tenn., March 2, 1863. 15th, 16th, 18th, and 19th U. S. Inf.
East Pascagoula, Miss., April 9, 1863. 74th U. S. Colored Troops.
East Point, Ga., Sept. 5, 1864.

East Point, Miss., Oct. 10, 1864. 61st U. S. Colored Troops. Union, 16 killed, 20 wounded.
Eastport, Miss., Nov. 11, 1864.
Ebenezer Creek, Cypress Swamp, Ga., Dec. 7, 1864. 9th Mich. and 9th Ohio Cav.
Ebenezer Church, Ala., April 1, 1865. (See Bogler's Creek.)
Eden Sta., Ga., Dec. 7 to 9, 1864. (See Ogeechee River.)
Edgefield Junction, Tenn., Aug. 20, 1862. Detachment of 59th Ind. Inf.
Edgefield, Tenn., Nov. 15, 1862.
Edisto Island, S. C., April 18, 1862. 55th Pa. and 3d N. H., assisted by U. S. Steamer "Crusader." Union, 3 wounded.
Edward's Ferry, Md., July —, 1861.
Edward's Ferry, Va., June 17, 1861. Portion of 1st Pa. Union, 1 killed, 4 wounded ; Confed., 15 killed.
Edward's Ferry, Va., Oct. 21, 1861. (See Ball's Bluff.)
Edward's Sta., Miss., May 16, 1863. (See Champion Hills.)
Eel River, Cal., May 3, 1863.
Egypt Sta., Miss., Dec. 28, 1864. 4th and 11th Ill. Cav.; 7th Ind.; 4th and 10th Mo.; 2d Wis.; 2d N. J.; 1st Miss. and 3d U. S. Colored Cav. Union, 23 killed, 88 wounded; Confed., 500 captured. Confed., Brig.-Gen. Gholson killed.
Elizabethtown, Ark., Oct. 1, 1863.
Elizabethtown, Ky., Dec., 27, 1862. 91st Ill. Union, 500 captured. (Morgan's Raid.)
Elizabethtown, Ky., Dec. 16 and 24, 1864. 1st Wis. Cav.
Elliott's Mills, or Camp Crittenden, Mo., Sept. 22, 1861. 7th Iowa Inf. Union, 1 killed, 5 wounded.
Elk Creek, Ind. Ter., July 17, 1863. (See Honey Springs.)
Elk Creek, Nev., Aug. 15, 1864.
Elk Fork, Tenn., Dec. 28, 1862. 6th and 10th Ky. Cav. Confed., 36 killed, 175 wounded, 51 missing.
Elkhorn Tavern, Ark., March 8, 1862. (See Pea Ridge.)
Elkhorn Tavern, Ark., Oct. 16, 1862.

Elkin's Ford, Ark., April 4 to 6, 1864. 43d Ind.; 29th and 36th Iowa; 1st Iowa Cav.; Battery E, 2d Mo. Light Artil. Union, 5 killed, 33 wounded; Confed., 18 killed, 30 wounded.
Elk River, Tenn., July 2, 1863. Cav., Army of the Cumberland.
Elk River, Tenn., July 14, 1863. 14th Corps. Union, 10 killed, 30 wounded; Confed., 60 killed, 24 wounded, 100 missing.
Elk Shute, Mo., Aug. 3 and 4, 1864. Troops under Col. Burris.
Elkton, Ky., Dec. 12, 1864. 1st Cav. Div. under Gen. McCook.
Elkton Sta., near Athens, Ala., May 9, 1862. Company E, 37th Ind. Inf. Union, 5 killed, 43 captured; Confed., 13 killed.
Elk Water, W. Va., Sept. 11, 1861. 3d Ohio; 15th and 17th Ind.
Ellison's Mills, Va., June 26, 1862. (See Mechanicsville and Seven Days' Retreat.)
Ellistown, Miss., June 16 and 21, 1864.
Eltham's Landing, Va., May 7, 1862. (See West Point.)
Eminence, Mo., June 17, 1862.
Enterprise, Mo., Aug. 7, 1864.
Eudora Church, Ark., May 9, 1864.
Evacuation of Ft. Wagner and Battery Gregg, Morris Island, S. C., Sept. 7, 1863. Troops under Gen. Gilmore, assisted by Naval Fleet.
Evacuation of Corinth, Miss., May 30, 1862. (See Corinth.)
Evlington Heights, Va., July 3, 1862. (See Haxal's Pass.)
Exp. to Jacksonville, Fla., March 29, 1863. 8th Me.; 6th Conn.; 33d U. S. Colored Troops. (Including Skirmish at Baldwin.)
Exp. up Steele's Bayou and at Deer Creek, Miss., March 16 to 22, 1863. 2d Div., 15th Corps, assisted by Gunboat Fleet.
Exp. up the Yazoo River, Miss., Feb. 1 to March 8, 1864. 11th Ill.; 47th U. S. Colored Troops and part of Porter's Fleet of Gunboats. Union, 35 killed, 121 wounded · Confed., 35 killed, 90 wounded.

Exp. from Vicksburg to Jackson, Miss., July 3 to 9, 1864. 1st Div., 17th Corps. Union, 150 wounded; Confed., 200 wounded.

Exp. from Vicksburg to Meridian, Miss., Feb. 3 to March 5, 1864. (Including engagements at Champion Hills,Raymond,Clinton,Jackson,Decatur, Chuncky Sta., occupation of Meridian, Lauderdale Springs and Merion, Miss.) Veatch's and A. J. Smith's Div., 16th Corps; Leggett's and Crocker's Divs., 17th Corps; 5th and 11th Ill.; 4th Iowa; 10th Mo. and Foster's Cav. Union, 56 killed, 138 wounded, 105 missing; Confed., 503 killed and wounded, 212 captured.

Exp. to Hamilton, N. C., Dec. 9 to 12, 1864. (Including engagements at Foster's Bridge, Dec. 10, and Butler's Bridge, Dec. 12.) 27th Mass.; 9th N. J. Inf.; N. C. Cav.; 3d N. Y. Art.

Exp. up the Chowan River, N. C., July 28 and 29, 1864. Troops assisting U. S. Steamer " Whitehead."

Exp. to western part of N. C., Dec. 9, 1864, to Jan. 14, 1865. 3d N. C. Inf.

Exp. to western part of N. C., Jan. 29 to Feb. 11, 1865. 3d N. C. Inf.

Explosion of Ammunition, City Point, Va., Aug. 9, 1864. (See City Point.)

Explosion of Magazine, Ft. Fisher, N. C., Jan. 16, 1865. (See Ft. Fisher.)

Ezra Chapel, Ga., July 28, 1864. (Hood's Sortie at Atlanta.) Army of the Tenn. Union, 100 killed, 600 wounded; Confed., 4,642 killed, wounded and missing.

F AIRBURN, Ga., Aug. 18, 1864. Cav., Army of the Cumberland.

Fairfax, Va., near Rapidan R. R. Bridge, July 13, 1862. 1st Md. Cav.

Fairfax, Va., June 27, 1863. 11th N. Y. Cav.

Fairfax C. H., Va., June 1, 1861. Co. B, 2d U. S. Cav. Union, 1 killed, 4 wounded; Confed., 1 killed, 14 wounded.

Fairfax C. H., Va., March 8, 1863. Brig.-Gen. Stoughton and 33 men captured by Moseby.

Fairfax Sta., Va., Sept. 17, 1864. 13th and 16th N. Y. Cav.

Fairfield, Pa., July 3, 1863. 6th U. S. Cav.

Fairfield, Pa., July 5, 1863. Cav., Army of Potomac.

Fairfield, Tenn., June 29, 1863.

Fair Gardens, or French Broad, or Kelley's Ford, near Severisville, Tenn., Jan. 27, 1864. Sturgis's Cav. Union, 100 killed and wounded; Confed., 65 killed, 100 captured.

Fairmount, W. Va., April 29, 1863. Detachments of 106th N. Y.; 6th W. Va. and Va. Militia. Union, 1 killed, 6 wounded; Confed., 100 killed and wounded.

Fair Oaks, Va., May 31 and June 1, 1862. (See Seven Pines.)

Fair Oaks, Va., Oct. 27 to 28, 1864. 10th and 18th Corps; Kautz's Cav. Union, 120 killed, 783 wounded, 400 missing; Confed., 60 killed, 311 wounded, 80 missing.

Falling Waters, or Haynesville, or Martinsburg, Md., July 2, 1861. 1st Wis.; 11th Pa. Union, 8 killed, 15 wounded; Confed., 31 killed, 50 wounded.

Falling Waters, Md., July 7, 1863. Detachments of 60th, 78th, 102d, 137th, 149th N. Y. Inf., under Lieut.-Col. Redington.

Falling Waters, Md., July 14, 1863. 3d Cav. Div., Army of the Potomac. Union, 29 killed, 36 wounded; Confed., 125 killed and wounded, 1,500 prisoners. Confed., Maj.-Gen. Pettigrew killed.

Fall of Petersburg, Va., April 2, 1865. 2d, 6th, 9th, and 24th Corps. Union, 124 killed, 706 wounded; Confed., 3,000 killed and wounded, 5,500 captured.

Falmouth, Va., April 18th, 1862. 2d N. Y. Cav. Union, 5 killed, 16 wounded; Confed., 19 captured.

Farmington, Miss., May 3, 1862. 10th, 16th, 22d, 27th, 42d, 51st Ill.; Yates'

LIST OF BATTLES AND ENGAGEMENTS.

Sharpshooters; 10th and 16th Mich.; 2d Mich. Cav. and Battery C, 1st Ill. Art. Union, 2 killed, 12 wounded; Confed., 30 killed.

Farmington, Miss., May 9, 1862. Part of the Army of the Miss.

Farmington, Miss., May 26 and 28, 1862.

Farmington, Tenn., Oct. 7, 1863. (See Shelbyville Pike.)

Farmville, Va., April 7, 1865. 2d Corps, Army of the Potomac. Union, 655 killed and wounded.

Farr's Mills, Ark., July 14, 1864. One company, 4th Ark. Cav. Union, 1 killed, 7 wounded; Confed., 4 killed, 6 wounded.

Fayette, Miss., Nov. 22 and Dec. 22, 1863, and Oct. 3, 1864.

Fayette, Mo., Oct. 7, 1862, and July 1 and Nov. 18, 1864.

Fayette, Mo., Sept. 24, 1864. 9th Mo. Militia Cav. Union, 3 killed, 5 wounded; Confed., 6 killed, 30 wounded.

Fayetteville, Ark., July 15, 1862. Detachment of Cav. under Maj. W. H. Miller. Confed., 150 captured.

Fayetteville, Ark., Oct. 24, 27, and 28, 1862. (See Cross Hollows.)

Fayetteville, Ark., Dec. 7, 1862. (See Prairie Grove.)

Fayetteville, Ark., April 18, 1863. 1st Ark. Inf.; 1st Ark. Cav.

Fayetteville, Ark., May 19, 1864. 6th Kan. Cav.

Fayetteville, Ark., June 24 and Aug. 28, 1864.

Fayetteville, Ark., Oct. 28, 1864. 1st Ark. Cav.

Fayetteville, N. C., March 13, 1865. (See Silver Run.)

Fayetteville, Tenn., Nov. 1, 1863. 4th Ind. Cav.

Fayetteville, W. Va., Sept. 10, 1862. 34th and 37th Ohio; 4th W. Va. Union, 13 killed, 80 wounded.

Fayetteville and White Sulphur Springs, or Little Washington, Va., Nov. 15, 1862. 1st and 2d Brigade of Sturgis' Div., 9th Corps; Cav., Army of Potomac.

Fayetteville, Va., May 17 to 20, 1863. 12th and 21st Ohio Inf.; 2d W. Va. Cav.

Federal Point, N. C., Feb. 11, 1865. (See Sugar Loaf Battery.)

Ferry's Landing, Ark., Sept. 7, 1863.

Fiker's Ferry, Ala., April 8, 1865.

Fillmore, Va., Oct. 4, 1864.

Fish Bayou, La., June 5, 1864.

Fish Creek, Nev., Jan. 22, 1866.

Fisher's Hill, near Strasburg, Va., Aug. 15, 1864. 6th and 8th Corps; 1st Cav. Div., Army of Potomac. Union, 30 wounded.

Fisher's Hill, or Woodstock, Va., Sept. 22, 1864. (See, also, Winchester and Fisher's Hill.) 6th Corps; 8th Corps; 1st and 2d Divs., 19th Corps; 1st and 2d Cav. Divs., Army of Potomac.

Fisher's Hill, Va., Oct. 9, 1864. (See Tom's Brook.)

Fishing Creek, Ky., Jan. 19 and 20, 1862. (See Mill Springs.)

Fishing Creek, Hartford, Ky., May 25, 1863.

Fish Springs, Tenn., Jan. 23, 1863.

Fitzhugh's Crossing, Rappahannock River, April 29 and 30, 1863. 1st Corps, Army of Potomac.

Fitzhugh's Woods, Ark., April 1, 1864. (See Augusta.)

Five Forks, Va., April 1, 1865. Cav. Div., Army of the James; 5th Corps; and 1st, 2d, and 3d Cav. Divs., Army of Potomac. Union, 124 killed, 706 wounded; Confed., 3,000 killed and wounded, 5,500 captured.

Five Mile Creek, Ala., March 31, 1865. (See Montevallo.)

Five Points, Va., Jan. 1, 1864. (See Rectortown.)

Flat Lick Fords, Ky., Feb. 14, 1862. 49th Ind.; 6th Ky. Cav. Confed., 4 killed, 4 wounded.

Flat Rock Bridge, Va., May 14, 1864.

Flat Shoals, Ga., July 28, 1864. Portion of Garrad's Cav. (Stoneman's Raid.)

Flint Creek, Ark., March 6, 1864. 14th Kan. Cav.

Flint Hill, Va., Sept. 1, 1862.

Flint River, Ga., Sept. 1, 1864.
Flock's Mills, Md., Aug. 1, 1864. (See Cumberland.)
Florence, Ala., May 27, 1863. Brigade of Cav. under Col. Comyar; 10th Mo. Cav.
Florence, Ala., Jan. 26, 1864. Troops under Col. Miller; 72d Ind. Inf.
Florence, Ala., April 13, 1864. Detachment of 9th Ohio Cav.
Florence, Ala., Oct. 6, 1864. 60th Ill. Inf.; 3d and 6th Tenn. Cav.
Florence, Ky., Sept. 17, 1862. Detachment of 10th Ky. Cav.
Florence, Mo., July 10, 1863.
Florence, S. C., March 3, 1865. Detachment of Mounted Inf. from Sherman's Army.
Florida, Mo., May 22, 1862. Detachment of 3d Iowa Cav. Union, 2 wounded.
Florida, or Bole's Farm, Mo., July 23, 1862. Two companies, 3d Iowa Cav. Union, 22 wounded; Confed., 3 killed.
Florida, Mo., July 24, 1862.
Flowing Springs, Va., Aug. 21, 1864. (See Summit Point.)
Floyd's Fork, Ky., Oct. 1, 1862. 34th Ill.; 77th Pa.; 4th Ind. Cav.
Forsyth, Mo., July 22, 1861. 1st Iowa; 2d Kan.; Stanley Dragoons and Totten's Battery. Union, 3 wounded; Confed., 5 killed, 10 wounded.
Forsyth, Mo., Aug. 2, 1862. (See Ozark.)
Fort Abercrombie, Dak. Ter., Sept. 3 to 6, and 23 to 25, 1862. (Indian Fight.)
Fort Adams, La., Oct 5, 1864. 2d Wis. and 3d U. S. Colored Cav.
Fort Anderson, Paducah, Ky., March 25, 1864. 122d Ill.; 16th Ky. Cav.; 8th U. S. Colored Artil., assisted by U. S. steamers "Peosta" and "Pawpaw." Union, 14 killed, 46 wounded; Confed., 10 killed, 40 wounded. Confed. Brig.-Gen. Thompson killed.
Fort Anderson, Town Creek, and Wilmington, N. C., Feb. 18 to 22, 1865. 23d and 24th Corps, assisted by Porter's Gunboats. Union, 40 killed, 204 wounded; Confed., 70 killed, 400 wounded, 375 missing.

Fort Barrancas, Fla., Jan. 8, 1861. 1st U. S. Artil. First Union gun fired.
Fort Beauregard, La., Sept. 4, 1863.
Fort Bisland, La., April 12, 1863. (See Irish Bend.)
Fort Blair, Waldron, Ark., Oct. 6, 1863. Detachment of 3d Wis. Cav.
Fort Blakely, Ala. (Siege), March 31 to April 9, 1865. 13th and 16th Corps Military Div. of the Miss. Union, 629 killed, wounded, and missing; Confed., 2,900 killed, wounded, and missing.
Fort Blound, Ind. Ter., May 20, 1863. (See Fort Gibson.)
Fort Blunt, Ind. Ter., March 27 to June 19, 1863.
Fort Brady, or Fort Burnham, or Bogg's Mills, Va., Jan. 24, 1865. U. S. Colored Troops and Heavy Artil., Army of the James.
Fort Brown Road, Texas, Dec. 14, 1862.
Fort Burnham, Va., Dec. 10, 1864. Portion of the Army of the James.
Fort Burnham, Va., Jan. 24, 1865. (See Fort Brady.)
Fort Cobb, Ind. Ter., Oct. 21, 1862. Loyal Indians.
Fort Cottonwood, Nev., Aug. 28, 1864. 7th Iowa Cav. (Indian Fight.)
Fort Cottonwood, Nev., Sept. 18, 1864. 7th Iowa Cav.
Fort Craig, New Mexico, Aug. 23 and Sept. 6, 1861.
Fort Craig, or Valverde, New Mexico, Feb. 21, 1862. 1st New Mexico Cav.; 2d Col. Cav.; detachments of 1st, 2d, and 5th New Mexico and of the 5th, 7th, and 10th U. S. Inf., together with Hall's and MacRae's Batteries. Union, 62 killed, 140 wounded; Confed., 150 wounded.
Fort Craig, New Mexico, May 23, 1862. 3d U. S. Cav. Union, 3 wounded.
Fort Darling, Drewry's Bluff, Va., May 12 to 16, 1864. 10th and 18th Corps. (Including losses at Wierbottom Church, Proctor's Creek and Palmer's Creek.) Union, 422 killed, 2,389 wounded, 210 missing; Confed., 400 killed, 2,000 wounded, 100 missing.

LIST OF BATTLES AND ENGAGEMENTS. 141

Fort Davidson, or Pilot Knob, or Ironton, Mo., Sept. 26 and 27, 1864. 47th and 50th Mo.; 14th Iowa; 2d and 3d Mo. Cav.; Battery H, 2d Mo. Light Artil. (Price's Invasion.)
Fort De Russy, La., March 14, 1864. Detachments of 16th and 17th Corps, assisted by Porter's Miss. Squadron. Union, 7 killed, 41 wounded; Confed., 5 killed, 4 wounded, 260 prisoners.
Fort Donelson, Tenn., Feb. 14 to 16, 1862. 17th and 25th Ky.; 11th, 25th, 31st, and 44th Ind.; 2d, 7th, 12th, and 14th Iowa; 1st Neb.; 58th and 76th Ohio; 8th and 13th Mo.; 8th Wis.; 8th, 9th, 11th, 12th, 17th, 18th, 20th, 28th, 29th, 30th, 31st, 41st, 45th, 46th, 48th, 49th, 57th, and 58th Ill.; Batteries B and D, 1st Ill. Artil.; D and E, 2d Ill. Artil.; four companies Ill. Cav.; Birge Sharpshooters and seven U. S. Gunboats. Brig.-Gen. U. S. Grant, commanding. Union, 446 killed, 1,735 wounded, 150 missing; Confed., 231 killed, 1,007 wounded, 13,829 prisoners. Union, Maj.-Gen. John A. Logan wounded.
Fort Donelson, Tenn., Aug. 25, 1862. 71st Ohio and 5th Iowa Cav.
Fort Donelson, or Cumberland Iron Works, Tenn., Feb. 3, 1863. 83d Ill.; 2d Ill. Artil. and one Battalion, 5th Iowa Cav. Union, 16 killed, 60 wounded, 50 missing; Confed., 140 killed, 400 wounded, 130 missing.
Fort Donelson, Tenn., Oct. 11, 1864. Portion of the 4th U. S. Colored Heavy Artil.
Fort Esperanza, Tex., Nov. 30, 1862.
Fort Esperanza, Tex., Nov. 27 to 29, 1863. 8th and 18th Ind.; 33d and 99th Ill.; 23d and 34th Iowa; 13th and 15th Me.; 7th Mich.; Company F, 1st Mo. Battery and a portion of 1st and 2d Divs., 13th Corps.
Fort Fillmore, New Mexico, July 27, 1861. 7th U. S. Inf. and U. S. Mounted Rifles. Union, 420 captured.
Fort Fillmore, New Mexico, Aug. 7, 1862. Cal. Troops under Gen. Canby.
Fort Fisher, N. C., Dec. 25, 1864. 10th Corps and North Atlantic Squadron. Union, 8 killed, 38 wounded; Confed., 3 killed, 65 wounded, 280 prisoners.
Fort Fisher, N. C., Jan. 13 to 15, 1865. Captured after three days' bombardment by fleet and assault by Troops. 2d Div. and 2d Brigade, 1st Div., 24th Corps; 3d Div., 25th Corps, together with sailors and marines from the Atlantic Blockading Squadron. Union, 184 killed, 749 wounded; Confed., 400 killed and wounded, 2,083 captured.
Fort Gaines, Ala., Aug. 2 to 23, 1864.
Fort Gibson, Ind. Ter., Oct. 5, 1862, and Feb. 28, 1863.
Fort Gibson and Fort Blunt, Ind. Ter., May 20 and 25, 1863. 6th Kan. and 3d Wis. Cav.; 1st, 2d, and 3d Kan. Indian Home Guards.
Fort Gibson, Ind. Ter., Sept. 16 to 18, 1864. 79th U. S. Colored Troops and 2d Kan. Cav. Union, 38 killed, 48 wounded.
Fort Gibson, Ind. Ter., Sept. —, 1865.
Fort Gilmore, Va., Sept. 29, 1864. (See New Market Heights.)
Fort Grant, Ariz. Ter., Jan. 21, 1866.
Fort Gregg, Va., April 2, 1865.
Fort Halleck, Dak. Ter., Feb. 20, 1863, and July 4, 1865.
Fort Halleck, Ind. Ter., July 7, 1863. (See Grand Pass.)
Fort Harrison, Va., Sept. 29, 1864. (See New Market Heights.)
Fort Hatteras, N. C., July 28 and 29, 1861. 9th, 20th, and 99th N. Y., assisted by Com. Stringham's Fleet. Union, 1 killed, 2 wounded; Confed., 5 killed, 51 wounded, 715 prisoners.
Fort Hell, Va., Sept. 28 and Nov. 5, 1864. (See Ft. Sedgwick.)
Fort Hill, Miss., June 25 and 28, 1863. (See Vicksburg.)
Fort Hinman, Ark. Post, Ark., Jan. 11, 1863. 13th Corps, Maj.-Gen. McClernand; 15th Corps, Maj.-Gen. Sherman, assisted by Gunboats of

the Miss. Squadron. Union, 129 killed, 831 wounded; Confed., 100 killed, 400 wounded, 5,000 prisoners.
Fort Johnson, S. C., June 16, 1862. (See Secessionville.)
Fort Johnson, James Island, S. C., July 2, 1864. Troops of the Department of the South. Union, 19 killed, 97 wounded, 135 missing.
Fort Jones, Ky., Feb. 18, 1865. 12th U. S. Colored Heavy Art.
Fort Kelly, W. Va., Nov. 28, 1864. Union, 700 missing.
Fort Larned, Kan., May 22, 1865.
Fort Leavenworth, Kan., Oct. 20 to 26, 1864.
Fort Lyons, or Sand Creek, Ind. Ter., Dec. 9, 1864. 1st Col. Cav. Massacre of 500 Indians.
Fort Lyons, Va., June 9, 1863.
Fort Macon, N. C., April 25 and 26, 1862. Bombarded by six U. S. Steamers on the 25th and surrendered to Gen. Park's Div. of Inf. on the 26th.
Fort McAllister, Ga., Dec. 13, 1864. 2d Div., 15th Corps. Union, 24 killed, 110 wounded; Confed., 250 missing.
Fort McCook, Ala., Aug. 27, 1862. 33d Ohio Inf. and detachment of Cav.
Fort Morgan, Ala., Aug. 5 to 23, 1864.
Fort Myers, Fla., Feb. 20, 1865.
Fort Pemberton, Miss., March 13 to April 5, 1863. 13th Corps, Brig.-Gen. Ross; 17th Corps, Brig.-Gen. Quinby, assisted by U. S. Gunboats "Chillicothe" and " De Kalb."
Fort Pickens, Fla., Jan. 13, 1861. U. S. Regulars.
Fort Pickens, Fla., Nov. 23, 1861. Companies C and E, 3d U. S. Inf.; Companies G and L, 6th N. Y.; Batteries A, F and L, 1st U. S. Art.; C, H and K, 2d U. S. Art. Union, 5 killed, 7 wounded; Confed., 5 killed, 23 wounded.
Fort Pillow, Tenn., March 16, 1864.
Fort Pillow, Tenn., April 12, 1864. 6th U. S. Colored Heavy Art.; Battery F, 2d U. S. Light Art.; Bradford's Battalion, 13th Tenn. Cav. Union,

350 killed, 60 wounded, 164 missing; Confed., 80 killed and wounded.
Fort Pocohontas, Va., Aug. —, 1864.
Fort Pulaski, Ga., April 10, 1862. 6th and 7th Conn.; 3d R. I.; 46th and 48th N. Y.; 8th Me.; 15th U. S. Inf., assisted by the crew of U. S. Steamer "Wabash." Union, 1 killed; Confed., 4 wounded, 360 prisoners.
Fort Rice, Dak. Ter., Sept. 27, 1864, and July 28 and 30, 1865.
Fort Ridgeley, Minn., Aug. 20 and 22, 1862. Companies B and C, 5th Minn. Inf.; Renville Rangers. (Indian Fight.)
Fort Sanders, Knoxville, Tenn., Nov. 29, 1863. Army of the Ohio. Repulse of Confed. Assault during the Siege of Knoxville.
Fort Scott, Kan., Sept. 1 and 3, 1861, and Oct. 22 and 28, 1864. [Wood.)
Fort Scott, Mo., Sept. 2, 1861. (See Dry
Fort Sedgwick, or Fort Hell, Jerusalem Plank Road, Va., Sept. 28, 1864. 3d Div., 9th Corps.
Fort Sedgwick, or Fort Hell, Va., Nov. 5, 1864. 2d and 3d Corps.
Fort Smith, Ark., May 15, 1863, July 29 to 31, Sept. 1 and 11, and Dec. 24, 1864.
Fort Smith, Ark., Aug. 31 and Sept. 1, 1863. (See Devil's Backbone.)
Fort Smith, Ark., July 27, 1864. (See Mazzard Prairie.)
Fort Smith, Ark., Aug. 24 and 27, 1864. 11th U. S. Colored Troops.
Fort Stedman (in front of Petersburg), Va., March 25, 1865. 1st and 3d Divs., 9th Corps. Union, 68 killed, 337 wounded, 506 missing. Confed., 800 killed and wounded. 1,881 missing. In the assault of the 2d and 6th Corps. Union, 103 killed, 864 wounded, 209 missing; Confed., 834 captured.
Fort Stevens, Washington, D. C., July 12, 1864. 22d Corps; 1st and 2d Divs., 6th Corps; Marines; Home Guards; Citizens; Convalescents. Union, 54 killed, 318 wounded; Confed., 500 killed and wounded.

Fort Strong, N. C., Feb. 21, 1865. Gen. Terry's Troops, assisted by the Navy.
Fort Sumner, New Mexico, Jan. 4, 1864. Company "B," 2d Cal. Inf.; Apache Indians; Citizens. (Indian Fight.)
Fort Sumter, S. C., April 12 and 13, 1861. 1st U. S. Artil., Battery E.
Fort Sumter, S. C., April 15, 1861. Union, 1 killed, 3 wounded by explosion of cannon in firing salute to the U. S. Flag.
Fort Taylor, Fla., Aug. 21, 1864.
Fort Taylor, West Point, Ga., April 16, 1865. 2d Brigade, 1st Cav. Div., Military Div. of the Miss. (Wilson's Raid.)
Fort Wagner (Siege of Fort Wagner), Morris Island, S. C., July 10 to Sept. 6, 1863. Attack and bombardment by Troops of the Dep't of the South, under Maj.-Gen. Gilmore, and U. S. Navy under Admiral Dahlgren. Union, 1,757 killed, wounded, and missing; Confed., 561 killed, wounded, and missing.
Fort Wagner, S. C., July 11, 1863. Assault on the Fort. 7th Conn.; 76 Pa.; 9th Mo.; 3d N. H.; 48th and 100th N. Y.
Fort Wagner, S. C., July 18, 1863. Second Assault. 54th Mass.; 6th Conn.; 48th and 100th N. Y.; 3d and 7th N. H.; 76th Pa.; 9th Me.; 62d and 67th Ohio.
Forty Hills, or Hankinson's Ferry, Miss., May 3, 1863. 7th Div., 17th Corps.
Foster's Bridge, N. C., Dec. 10, 1864.
Foster's Exp. to Goldsboro, N. C., Dec. 12 to 18, 1862. (See Goldsboro.)
Fouch La Faix Mountain, Ark., Nov. 11, 1863.
Fourteen Mile Creek, Ind. Ter., Oct. 30, 1863.
Fourteen Mile Creek, Miss. May 12, 1863, 13th Corps and 15th Corps.
Fox Creek, Mo., March 7, 1862. 4th Mo. Cav. Union, 5 wounded.
Frankfort, Ky., June 10, 1864.
Frankfort, Va., Nov. 26, 1862. (See Cold Knob Mountains.)

Franklin, La., May 25, 1863. 4th Mass. and other troops not reported.
Franklin, Miss., Jan. 2, 1865. 4th and 11th Ill. Cav.; 3d U. S. Colored Cav. Union, 4 killed, 9 wounded; Confed., 26 killed, 30 wounded.
Franklin, Mo., Oct. 13, 1862.
Franklin, Mo., Oct. 1, 1864. Mo. Militia.
Franklin, Tenn., Dec. 12, 1862. Stanley's Cav. Div., Army of the Cumberland.
Franklin, Tenn., Feb. 1, 1863.
Franklin, Tenn., March 9, 1863. 125th Ohio Inf.
Franklin and Little Harpeth, Tenn., March 25, 1863. 4th and 6th Ky. Cav.; 9th Pa. Cav.; 2d Mich. Cav. Union, 4 killed, 19 wounded, 40 missing.
Franklin and Harpeth River, Tenn., April 10, 1863. 40th Ohio and a part of Granger's Cav. Union, 100 killed and wounded; Confed., 19 killed, 35 wounded, 83 missing.
Franklin, Tenn., April 27, 1863. Cav. under Col. Walkins.
Franklin, Tenn., June 4, 1863. 35th Ind.; 4th, 6th and 7th Ky.; 9th Pa. and 2d Mich. Cav. Union, 25 killed and wounded; Confed., 200 killed and wounded.
Franklin, Tenn., Nov. 29 and 30, 1864, 4th, 23d and Cav. Corps. Union, 189 killed; 1033 wounded; 1004 missing. Confed. killed 1750, five generals slain; wounded and captured 4500, seven generals.
Franklin, Tenn., Dec. 17, 1864. Wilson's Cav. Confed., 1,800 wounded, sick captured.
Franklin, Va., Oct. 3, 1862. Troops under Gen. Spear, assisted by three U. S. Steamers.
Franklin, Va., Oct. 31, 1862.
Franklin, Va., Dec. 2, 1862. 11th Pa. Cav.
Franklin Creek, or Franklin, Miss., Dec. 18, 1864. Troops of 3d Corps.
Franklin's Crossing, Rappahannock River, Va., June 5, 1863. 26th N. J.; 5th Ver.; 15th and 50th N. Y. Engineers, supported by 6th Corps. Union, 6 killed, 35 wounded.

Frazier's Farm, Va., June 30, 1862. (See White Oak Swamp, also Seven Days' Retreat.)
Frederick, Md., Sept. 12, 1862. Advance Troops, Army of Potomac.
Frederick City, Md., July 7, 1864. (See Solomon's Gap.)
Fredericksburg, Mo., July 17, 1864. 2d Col. Cav.
Fredericksburg, Va., Nov. 9, 1862. 1st Ind. Cav.
Fredericksburg, Va., Dec. 11 to 16, 1862. (Main battle on Dec. 13.) Army of Potomac, Maj.-Gen. Burnside; 2d Corps, Maj.-Gen. Couch; 9th Corps, Maj.-Gen. Wilcox; Right Grand Div., Maj.-Gen. Sumner; 5th Corps, Maj.-Gen. Reynolds; 6th Corps, Maj.-Gen. W. S. Smith; Left Grand Div., Maj.-Gen. Franklin; 5th Corps, Maj.-Gen. Butterfield; 3d Corps, Maj.-Gen. Stoneman; Centre Grand Div., Maj.-Gen. Hooker. Union, 1,108 killed, 9,028 wounded, 2,145 missing; Confed., 579 killed, 3,870 wounded, 127 missing. Union, Brig.-Gens. Jackson and Bayard killed; Brig.-Gens. Givens and Vinton, wounded. Confed., Brig.-Gen. Cobb killed; Gen. Gregg wounded.
Fredericksburg, Va., May 1 to 4, 1863. (See Chancellorsville.)
Fredericksburg Road, Va., May 8 to 18, 1864. (See Spottsylvania C. H.)
Fredericksburg Road, Va., May 16 to 20, 1864. Tyler's Div., 5th Corps, Army of Potomac.
Fredericktown and Ironton, Mo., Oct. 17 to 21, 1861. 17th, 20th, 21st, 23d, and 28th Ill.; 8th Wis.; 1st Ind. Cav.; Company A, 1st Mo. Light Artil. Union, 6 killed, 60 wounded; Confed., 200 wounded.
Freeman's Ford, Va., Aug. 24, 1862. (See Lee Springs.)
Freemont's Orchard, Col., April 12, 1864. Two companies, 1st Col. Cav.
French Broad, Tenn., Jan. 27, 1864. (See Fair Gardens.)
French Point, Mo., May 15, 1863.

Frog Bayou, Ark., July 1, 1864.
Front of Petersburg, Va. (See Petersburg.)
Front Royal, Va., May 23, 1862. 1st Md.; detachments of 29th Pa.; Mape's Pioneers; 5th N. Y. Cav. and 1st Pa. Artil. Union, 32 killed, 122 wounded, 750 missing.
Front Royal, Va., May 30, 1862. 1st R. I. Cav. Union, 5 killed, 8 wounded; Confed., 156 captured.
Front Royal, Va., Aug. 15, 16, 1864. (See Crooked Run.)
Front Royal Pike, Va., Sept. 21, 1864. 2d Div., Cav. Corps, Army of Potomac.
Frying Pan, Va., June 4, 1863. Detachment of the 5th Mich. Cav.
Fry Mountain, Ky., Nov. 9, 1861. (See Piketown.)
Fulton, Ga., Oct. 13, 1864.
Fulton, Mo., July 17, 1861. Four hundred of 3d Mo. Reserves. Union, 1 killed, 15 wounded.
Funkstown, Md., July 12 and 13, 1863. Portion of Army of Potomac.

G AINES' Mills, or Cold Harbor, or Chickahominy, Va., June 27 and 28, 1862. 5th Corps, reinforced by Meagher's and French's Brigades, 1st Div., 2d Corps. (See also Seven Days' Retreat.)
Gaines' Mills, Salem Church, and Hawes' Shop, Va., June 2, 1864. Engagements by the Cav. Army of Potomac.
Gainesville, Fla., Feb. 14, 1864. 40th Mass. Inf.
Gainesville, Fla., Aug. 17, 1864. 75th Ohio Mounted Inf. Union, 16 killed, 30 wounded, 102 missing.
Gainesville, Va., Aug. 28 and 29, 1862. (See Groveton.)
Gallatin, Tenn., Aug. 12, 1862. 2d Ind.; 4th and 5th Ky.; 1st Pa. Cav. Union, 30 killed, 50 wounded, 200 captured; Confed., 6 killed, 18 wounded. (Morgan's Raid.)
Gallatin, Tenn., Aug. 13, 1862. 13th

and 16th Ohio; 11th Mich. Confeds. driven from town with slight loss.
Gallatin, Tenn., Sept. 9, 1862.
Gallatin, Tenn., Oct. 1, 1862. 1st Tenn. Cav.
Galveston, Tex., Jan. 1, 1863. Three companies, 42d Mass. Inf., assisted by six U. S. Gunboats. Union, 600 killed, wounded, and missing; Confed., 50 killed and wounded.
Galveston, Tex., June 2, 1865.
Garrettsburg, Ky., Nov. 6, 1862. 8th Ky. Cav. Confed., 17 killed, 85 wounded.
Gaucha Mountain, Cal., July 22, 1865.
Gauley Bridge, W. Va., Nov. 10, 1861. 11th Ohio; 7th Ky. Cav. Union, 2 killed, 16 wounded.
Geiger Lake, Ky., Sept. 3, 1862. 8th Ky. Cav.
Georgia Landing, La., Oct. 27, 1862. (See Labadieville.)
Germantown, Tenn., June 25, 1862. 56th Ohio. Union, 10 killed.
Germantown, Tenn., Jan. 27 and April 1, 1863.
Gettysburg, Pa., July 1 to 3, 1863. Army of Potomac., Maj.-Gen. Geo. G. Meade; 1st Corps, Maj.-Gen. Reynolds; 2d Corps, Maj.-Gen. Hancock; 3d Corps, Maj.-Gen. Sickles; 5th Corps, Maj.-Gen. Sykes; 6th Corps, Maj.-Gen. Sedgwick; 11th Corps, Maj.-Gen. Howard; 12th Corps, Maj.-Gen. Slocum; Cav. Corps, Maj.-Gen. Pleasanton. Union, 2,834 killed, 13,700 wounded, 6,643 missing; Confed., 3,500 killed, 14,500 wounded, 13,621 missing. Union, Maj.-Gen. Reynolds, Brig.-Gens. Weed, Zook, and Farnsworth killed; Maj.-Gens. Sickles and Hancock, Brig.-Gens. Paul, Rowley, Gibbons, and Barlow wounded. Confed., Maj.-Gen. Pender, Brig.-Gens. Gurnett, Barksdale, and Semmes killed; Maj.-Gens. Hood, Trimble, and Heth, Brig.-Gens. Kemper, Scales, Anderson, Hampton, Jones, Jenkins, Pettigrew, and Posey wounded. Numbers engaged: Army of Potomac, Inf., 80,000; Cav., 10,000; Artil., 5,000—with 327 guns—Total, 95,000. Army of Northern Va.: Inf., 90,000; Cav., 10,000; Artil., 5,000—with over 250 guns. Total, 105,000.
Ghent, Ky., Aug. 29, 1864. 117th U. S. Colored Troops.
Gila River, New Mexico, Nov. 5, 1863.
Glade Springs, Va., Dec. 15, 1864. 12th Ky. Cav. (Stoneman's Raid.)
Gladesville, Round Gap, Va., Oct. 2, 1864. 1st Ky. Cav.; 3d Ky. Mounted Inf.
Glasgow, Ky., Oct. 5, 1862. 20th Ky. Inf.
Glasgow, Ky., Dec. 24, 1862. Five Companies 2d Mich. Cav. Union, 1 killed, 1 wounded; Confed., 3 killed, 3 wounded.
Glasgow, Ky., Oct. 5, 1863. 37th Ky. Mounted Inf. Union, 3 wounded, 100 missing; Confed., 13 wounded.
Glasgow, Ky., March 25, 1865.
Glasgow, Mo., Oct. 15, 1864. 42d Mo. and detachments of 17th Ill., 9th Mo. Militia, and 13th Mo. Cav.; 66th U. S. Colored Troops. (Price's Invasion.)
Glass Bridge, Tenn., Sept. 2, 1864.
Glendale, Ala., Feb. 22, 1863.
Glendale, near Corinth, Miss., May 8, 1862. 7th Ill. Cav.; 3d Mich. Cav. Union, 1 killed, 4 wounded; Confed., 30 killed and wounded.
Glendale, Miss., April 14, 1863.
Glendale, Va., June 30, 1862. (See White Oak Swamp, also Seven Days' Retreat.)
Glendennin's Raid, Va., May 20 to 28, 1863. (See Clendennin's Raid.)
Glorietta, New Mexico, March 26 to 28, 1862. (See Apache Cañon.)
Gloucester, Va., Nov. 17, 1862. 104th Pa. Inf. Union, 1 killed, 3 wounded.
Gloucester C. H. and Ware River, Va., April 8 and 9, 1863. Troops assisted by U. S. Steamer, "Commodore Morris."
Gloucester Point, Va., Feb. 10, 1863.
Golding's Farm, Va., June 28, 1862. 33d and 49th N. Y.; 7th Me. and 3d N. Y. Battery.

Goldsboro, N. C., Dec. 12 to 18, 1862. (Foster's Expedition to Goldsboro.) 1st, 2d, and 3d Brigades, 1st Div. and Wessell's Brigade of Peck's Div., Dep't of N. C. Union, 90 killed, 478 wounded; Confed., 71 killed, 268 wounded, 400 missing.
Goldsboro, N. C., Dec. 17, 1862. 9th N. J.; 3d, 17th, 23d, 24th, and 45th Mass.; 3d N. Y. Cav.; 3d and 23d N. Y. Battery.
Goldsboro, N. C., March 21, 1865. Troops under Gen. Schofield.
Golgotha, Ga., June 16, 1864. (See Kenesaw Mountain.)
Goodrich's Landing, La., June 30, 1863, March 24 and July 16, 1864.
Good's Landing, Miss., Dec. 16 to 25, 1864.
Goose Creek, Va., Oct. 22, 1861.
Goose Creek, or Leesburg Road, Va., Sept. 17, 1862. Kilpatrick's Cav. Brigade.
Gov. Moore's Plantation, La., May 2. 1864. Detachments of 83d Ohio and 3d R. I. Cav. Union, 2 killed, 10 wounded.
Grafton, W. Va., Aug. 13, 1861. One Company 4th W. Va. Inf.
Grafton, W. Va., Dec. 1, 1861.
Grahamsville, S. C., Nov. 30, 1864. (See Honey Hill.)
Granby, Mo., Sept. 24, 1862.
Grand Coteau or Bayou Bordeaux, or Carrion Crow Bayou, La., Nov. 3, 1863. 3d and 4th Divs., 13th Corps. Union, 26 killed, 124 wounded, 576 missing; Confed., 60 killed, 320 wounded, 65 missing.
Grand Gulf, Miss., April 1, 1863. Troops assisted by three U. S. Steamers.
Grand Gulf., Miss., Jan. 16 to 18, 1864. Cav. and Inf. of the Miss. Marine Brigade.
Grand Gulf, Port Gibson, Miss., July 16 and 17, 1864. 72d and 76th Ill.; 2d Wis.Cav.; 53d U.S. Colored Troops.
Grand Haze, Ark., July 4, 1862. 13th Ill. Cav.
Grand Lake, Ark., June 16, 1863.
Grand Pass, Fort Halleck, Ind. Ter., July 7, 1863. 9th Kan. (Indian Fight.)

Grand Prairie, near Aberdeen, Ark., July 6, 1862. 24th Ind. Inf. Union, 1 killed, 21 wounded; Confed., 84 killed and wounded.
Grand Prairie, Mo., Oct. 24, 1862. Two battalions, Mo. Militia Cav. Union, 3 wounded; Confed., 8 killed, 20 wounded.
Grand River, Mo., Nov. 30, 1861.
Grand River, Mo., Aug. 10 to 13, 1862. (Including engagements at Lee's Ford, Charriton River, Walnut Creek, Compton Ferry, Switzler's Mills, and Yellow Creek.) 9th Mo. Militia. Union, 100 killed and wounded.
Grant's Creek, N. C., April 12, 1865. (Stoneman's Raid.)
Grass Lick, W. Va., April 23, 1862. 3d Md. and Potomac Home Guards. Union, 3 killed.
Grassy Lick, Va., May 9 and 10, 1864. (See Cloyd's Mountain.)
Gravel Hill, Va., Aug. 14, 1864. Gregg's Cav. Union, 3 killed, 18 wounded.
Gravelly Run, Va., March 29, 1865. (See Quaker Road.)
Graves' House, Ga., May 17 and 18, 1864. (See Adairsville.)
Graysville, Ga., Sept. 10, 1863. Cav., Army of the Cumberland.
Greasy Creek, Ky., May 11, 1863. (See Horseshoe Bend.)
Great Bear Creek, Ala., April 17, 1863. (See Bear Creek.)
Great Bethel, Va., June 10, 1861. 1st, 2d, 3d, 5th, and 7th N. Y.; 4th Mass., detachment of 2d U. S. Artil. Union, 16 killed, 34 wounded; Confed., 1 killed, 7 wounded.
Great Bethel, Va., April 4, 1862. Advance of 3d Corps, Army of Potomac. Union, 4 killed, 10 wounded.
Great Cacapon Bridge, Va., Jan. 4, 1862. (See Bath.)
Great Falls, Va., July 7, 1861. 8th N. Y. Inf. Union, 2 killed; Confed., 12 killed.
Green Brier, W. Va., Oct. 3, 1861. 24th, 25th, and 32d Ohio; 7th, 9th, 13th, 14th, 15th, and 17th Ind.; Battery G, 4th U. S. Artil.; Battery A, 1st

Mich. Artil. Union, 8 killed, 32 wounded; Confed., 100 killed, 75 wounded.
Greencastle, Pa., June 20, 1863.
Greenfield, Ark., Oct. 22, 1861.
Greenleaf Prairie, Ind. Ter., June 16 and Nov. 12, 1863.
Greenland Gap, W. Va., April 25, 1863. Detachments of 23d Ill. and 14th W. Va.
Greenland Gap Road, near Moorefield, W. Va., June 6, 1864. 22d Pa. Cav.
Green River Bridge, or Tebb's Bend, Ky., July 4, 1863. Five companies, 25th Mich. Inf. (Morgan's Raid.)
Green's Chapel, Ky., Dec. 25, 1862. Detachments of 4th and 5th Ind. Cav. Union, 1 killed; Confed., 9 killed, 22 wounded.
Green Springs, or Green Springs Depot, W. Va., Aug. 2, 1864. 153d Ohio. Union, 1 killed, 5 wounded, 90 missing; Confed., 5 killed, 22 wounded.
Greenville, Miss., May 20 to 27, 1864.
Greenville, Mo., July 26, 1862. 3d and 12th Mo. Militia Cav. Union, 2 killed, 5 wounded.
Greenville, N. C., Nov. 25, 1863. 12th N. Y. Cav.; 1st N. C. Inf.; 24th N. Y. Battery.
Greenville, N.C., Dec. 30, 1863. Detachment of 12th N. Y.; 23d N. Y. Battery; and 1st N. C. Inf.
Greenville, Tenn., Sept. 4, 1864. 9th and 13th Tenn., and 10th Mich. Cav. Union, 6 wounded; Confed., 10 killed, 60 wounded, 75 missing. Confed., Gen. John Morgan killed.
Greenville, Tenn., Oct. 12, 1864.
Greenville Road, Ky., Nov. 5, 1862. 8th Ky. Cav.
Greenville Road, N. C., May 31, 1862. 3d N. Y. Cav.
Greenville Springs Road, La., Sept. 19 and Oct. 5, 1863.
Greenwich, Va., May 30, 1863. 1st Vt.; 5th N. Y., and 7th Mich. Cav.
Gregory's Farm, S. C., Dec. 6 and 9, 1864. (See Deveaux Neck.)
Grenada, Miss., Aug. 13, 1863. 9th Ill.; 2d Iowa Cav.; 3d Mich. Cav.; 3d, 4th, 9th, 11th Ill. Cav.

Greysville, Ga., Nov. 27, 1863. (See Ringgold.)
Grier's Farm, Ga., June 21, 1864.
Grierson's Exp. from La Grange, Tenn., to Baton Rouge, La., April 17 to May 2, 1863. 6th and 7th Ill. Cav.; 2d Iowa Cav. Confed., 100 killed and wounded, 500 prisoners.
Griswoldville, Ga., Nov. 22, 1864. Walcott's Brigade, 1st Div., 15th Corps, and 1st Brigade, 3d Div., Cav. Union, 10 killed, 52 wounded; Confed., 50 killed, 200 wounded, 400 missing.
Grosse Tete Bayou, La., Feb. 19, 1864. 4th Wis. Cav. Union, 2 wounded; Confed., 4 killed, 6 wounded.
Grosse Tete Bayou, La., March 30, 1864. Detachment of 118th Inf.
Ground Squirrel Church Bridge, South Anna, Va., May 10, 1864. 1st Div., Cav. Corps, Army of Potomac. (Sheridan's Raid.)
Grouse Creek, Cal., May 23, 1864.
Groveton and Gainesville, Va., Aug. 28 and 29, 1862. 1st Corps, Maj.-Gen. Seigel; 3d Corps, Maj.-Gen. McDowell, Army of Va.; Hooker's and Kearney's Div., 3d Corps and Reynold's Div., 1st Corps, Army of Potomac; 9th Corps, Maj.-Gen. Reno. Union, 7,000 killed, wounded, and missing; Confed., 7,000 killed, wounded, and missing.
Guerilla Warfare, Mo., July 20 to Sept. 20, 1862. Gen. Schofield's Command with Porter's and Poindexter's Guerillas. Union, 77 killed, 156 wounded, 347 missing; Confed., 506 killed, 1,800 wounded, 560 missing.
Gum Slough, Ark., March 16, 1863.
Gum Swamp, N. C., May 22, 1863. 58th Pa.; 5th, 25th, 27th, 46th Mass., and Bogg's Battery.
Gunboats on James River, Va., Oct. 22, 1864. Confed. Gunboats attack Union Battery.
Gunter's Bridge, S. C., Feb. 14, 1865. 3d Cav. Div., Sherman's Army.
Guntown, Miss., May 4, 1863.
Guntown, Miss., June 10, 1864. (See Brice's Cross Roads.)

Gurley Farm, Va., June 25, 1864.
Guyandotte, W. Va., Nov. 10, 1861. Recruits of 9th W. Va. Union, 7 killed, 20 wounded; Confed., 3 killed, 10 wounded.
Guy's Gap and Shelbyville, Tenn., June 27, 1863. Cav. Div., Army of the Cumberland, supported by Granger's Div.

H AGAR'S Mountain and Middleton, Md., July 7, 1864. 8th Ill. Cav. and Alexander's Baltimore Battery.
Hagerstown, Md., July 6, 1863. 3d Cav. Div., Army of Potomac.
Hagerstown, Md., July 11, 1863. Cav., Army of Potomac.
Hagerstown, Pleasant Valley, Md., July 5, 1864. 1st Md. Cav. and Potomac Home Guards. Union, 2 killed, 6 wounded. [1863.
Haguewood Prairie, Tenn., Sept. 26, Haguewood Sta., Ark., Sept. 27, 1863. (See Moffet's Station.)
Haines' Bluff, Miss., Jan. 1 and May 18, 1863. Attack by troops and fleet.
Half-moon Battery, Sugar-loaf Hill, N. C., Jan. 19, 1865. Parts of 24th and 25th Corps, Army of the James.
Half Mount, Ky., April 14, 1864. 14th Ky. and Inf.
Hall Island, S. C., Nov. 24, 1863.
Hall's Ferry, Miss., May 13, 1863. 2d Ill. Cav. Confed., 12 killed.
Hallsville, Mo., Dec. 28, 1861. (See Mount Zion.)
Halltown, Va., July 15, 1863. 16th Pa. and 1st Me. Cav. Union, 25 killed and wounded; Confed., 20 killed and wounded.
Halltown, Va., Aug. 24 to 27, 1864. Portion of 8th Corps, Army of W. Va. Union, 39 killed, 178 wounded; Confed., 130 killed and wounded.
Hamburg, Tenn., May 30, 1863.
Hamburg Landing, Ala., May 29, 1863.
Hamilton, N. C., July 9, 1862. 9th N. Y. and Gunboats "Perry," "Ceres," and "Shawseen." Union, 1 killed, 20 wounded.

Hamilton, Va., March 21, 1865. 12th Pa. Cav.
Hammack's Mills, W. Va., July 3, 1864. 153d Ohio National Guard. Union, 3 killed, 7 wounded.
Hampton, Va., Aug. 7, 1861. 20th N. Y. Confed., 3 killed, 6 wounded.
Hampton Roads, Va., March 9, 1862. 20th Ind.; 7th and 11th N. Y., together with Gunboats "Monitor," "Minnesota," "Congress," and "Cumberland." Union, 261 killed, 108 wounded; Confed., 7 killed, 17 wounded.
Hancock, Va., Jan. 4, 1862. (See Bath.)
Hanging Rock, W. Va., Sept. 23, 1861. (See Romney.)
Hankinson's Ferry, Miss., May 3, 1863. (See Forty Hills.)
Hanover, Pa., June 30, 1863. 3d Div. Cav. Corps, Army of Potomac. Union, 12 killed, 43 wounded; Confed., 75 wounded, 60 missing.
Hanover C. H., Va., May 27, 1862. 12th, 13th, 14th, 17th, 25th, and 44th N. Y.; 62d and 83d Pa.; 16th Mich.; 9th and 22d Mass.; 5th Mass. Art.; 2d Me. Art.; Battery F. 5th U. S. Art.; 1st U. S. Sharpshooters. Union, 53 killed, 344 wounded; Confed., 200 killed and wounded, 730 prisoners.
Hanover C. H., Va., May 30, 1864. 3d Div., Cav. Corps, Army of Potomac. (Including loss at Ashland, May 30.) Union, 26 killed, 130 wounded.
Hanoverton, Hawe's Shop, and Salem Church, Va., May 27 and 28, 1864. 1st and 2d Divs., Cav. Corps. Army of Potomac, under Maj.-Gen. Sheridan. Union, 25 killed, 119 wounded, 200 missing; Confed., 475 killed, wounded, and missing.
Hardy Co., W. Va., Jan. 5, 1863.
Harney Lake Valley, Ore., April 7, 1864. 1st Ore. Cav.
Harney Lake Valley, Ore., Sept. 23, 1865.
Harper's Farm, Va., April 6, 1865. (See Sailor's Creek.)
Harper's Ferry, Va., April 18 and Oct. 11, 1861.

LIST OF BATTLES AND ENGAGEMENTS. 149

Harper's Ferry, Va., May 28, 1862. (See Charlestown.)
Harper's Ferry, Va., Sept. 12 to 15, 1862. 39th, 111th, 115th, 125th, and 126th N. Y.; 12th N. Y. Militia; 32d, 60th, and 82d Ohio; 9th Ver.; 65th Ill.; 15th Ind.; 1st and 3d Md. Home Brigade; 8th N. Y. Cav.; 12th Ill. Cav.; 1st Md. Cav.; Phillips', Graham's, Pott's, and Rigby's Batteries. Union, 80 killed, 120 wounded, 11,583 missing and captured. Confed., 500 killed and wounded.
Harper's Ferry, Va., Oct. 5, 1863.
Harper's Ferry Bridge, Va., July 7, 1863. Potomac Home Brigade; 1st Mass. Heavy Artil.
Harpeth River, Tenn., March 2 and 4, 1863. (See Petersburg.)
Harpeth River, Tenn., April 10, 1863. (See Franklin.)
Harris' Farm, Va., Feb. 6, 1864.
Harrison, Mo., Sept. 29 and 30, 1864. (See Leesburg.)
Harrisonburg, Va., June 6, 1862. 1st N. J. Cav.; 1st Pa. Rifles; 8th W. Va. and 60th Ohio Inf. Union, 63 missing; Confed., 17 killed, 50 wounded. Confed., Brig.-Gen. Ashby killed.
Harrison's Field, Ga., Dec. 9, 1864.
Harrison's Island, Va., Oct. 21, 1861. (See Ball's Bluff.)
Harrison's Landing, Va., July 2, 3, and 30, 1862.
Harrisonville and Cartersville, Mo., July 18 and 19, 1861. Van Horne's Battalion and Cass Co. Home Guards. Union, 1 killed; Confed., 14 killed.
Harrisonville, Mo., July 26, 1861. Mo. Home Guards; 5th Kan. Cav.
Harrisonville, Mo., Nov. 3, 1862. 5th and 6th Mo. Cav. Union, 10 killed, 3 wounded; Con., 6 killed, 20 wnd.
Harrisville, Miss., July 13 and 14, '64.
Harrisonville, Mo., Oct. 24, 1863.
Harrodsburg, Ky., Oct. 10, 1862. Union Troops under Lieut.-Col. Boyle and 9th Ky. Cav. Confed., 1,600 captured.

Harrodsburg, Ky., Oct. 21, 1864. 5th U. S. Colored Cav.
Hartford, Ky., May 25, 1863. (See Fishing Creek.)
Hartsville, or Wood's Fork, Mo., Jan. 11, 1863. 21st Iowa; 99th Ill.; 3d Iowa Cav.; 3d Mo. Cav.; Battery L, 2d Mo. Artil. Union, 7 killed, 64 wounded; Confed., 300 killed and wounded. Confed., Brig.-Gen. McDonald killed.
Hartsville, Mo., May 23, 1863.
Hartsville, Tenn., Dec. 7, 1862. 106th and 108th Ohio; 104th Ill.; 2d Ind. Cav.; 11th Ky. Cav.; 13th Ind. Battery. Union, 55 killed, 1,800 captured; Confed., 21 killed, 114 wounded.
Hartwood Church, Va., Nov. 28, 1862. 3d Pa. Cav. Union, 4 killed, 9 wounded, 200 missing.
Hartwood Church, Va., Feb. 25, 1863. Brig.-Gen. Averill's Cav. Brigade.
Hatcher's Run, or Boydton Road, or Vaughn Road, or Burgess' Farm, Va., Oct. 27, 1864. Gregg's Cav.; 2d and 3d Divs., 2d Corps; 5th and 9th Corps. Union, 156 killed, 1,047 wounded, 699 missing; Confed., 200 killed, 600 wounded, 200 missing.
Hatcher's Run, Va., Dec. 8 and 9, 1864. 1st Div., 2d Corps; 3d and 13th Pa. Cav.; 6th Ohio Cav. Union, 125 killed and wounded.
Hatcher's Run, Va., Feb. 5 to 7, 1865. (See Dabney's Mills.)
Hatcher's Run, Va., March 25, 1865.
Hatchie River, Miss., Oct. 5, 1862. (See Big Hatchie River, or Metamora.)
Hatchie River, Miss., Aug. 10, 1864.
Hawes' Shop, Totoptomoy Creek, or Salem Church, Va., May 28, 1864. 1st and 2d Divs. Cav., Army of Potomac.
Hawes' Shop, Va., June 2, 1864. (See Gaines' Mills.)
Hawk's Nest, W. Va., Aug. 20, 1861. Union, 3 wounded; Confed., 1 killed, 3 wounded.
Haxal's, or Evlington Heights, Va., July 3, 1862. 14th Ind.; 7th W.Va.; 4th and 8th Ohio. Union, 8 killed,

32 wounded; Confed., 100 killed and wounded.
Haymarket, Va., Oct. 18, 1862. Detachment of 6th Iowa Cav. Union, 1 killed, 6 wounded, 32 captured.
Haymarket, Va., Oct. 19, 1863.
Hayne's Bluff, Miss., Feb. 3 and April —, 1864.
Haynesville, Md., July 2, 1861. (See Falling Waters.)
Hazel Bottom, Mo., Oct. 14, 1862.
Hazel River, Va., Oct. 6, 1863.
Hedgeville, Va., Oct. 22, 1862. 4th Pa. Cav.
Hedgeville, Va., Oct. 15, 1863. Detachment of 1st N. Y. and 12th Pa. Cav., also, 116 Ohio Inf.
Helena, Ark., Aug. 11 to 14, 1862. 2d Wis. Cav.
Helena, Ark., Sept. 20, 1862. 4th Iowa Cav.
Helena, Ark., Oct. 11, 1862, and Aug. 2, 1864.
Helena, Ark., Oct. 18, 1862. Detachment of 43d Ind. Inf.
Helena, Ark., Dec. 5, 1862. 30th Iowa; 29th Wis. Confed., 8 killed.
Helena, and Clarendon Road, Ark., Jan. 15, 1863. 2d Wis. Cav.
Helena, Ark., May 25, 1863. (See Polk's Plantation.)
Helena, Ark., July 4, 1863. Maj.-Gen. Prentiss' Div., 16th Corps, assisted by U. S. Gunboat "Tyler." Union, 57 killed, 117 wounded, 32 missing; Confed., 173 killed, 687 wounded, 776 missing.
Henderson, Ky., July 21, 1864.
Henderson, Ky., Sept. 25, 1864. 118th U. S. Colored Troops.
Henderson Hills, or Bayou Rapids, La., March 21, 1864. Detachments of 16th Corps and Cav. Div., 19th Corps. Union, 1 wounded; Confed., 8 killed, 250 captured.
Henderson's Mill, Tenn., Oct. 11, 1863. 5th Ind. Cav. Union, 11 wounded; Confed., 30 killed and wounded.
Hendricks, Miss., Sept. 15, 1863. 10th Mo. Cav.
Henrytown, Mo., Oct. 13, 1861. (See West Glaize.)

Henry Co., Ky., Nov. 9, 1862. 14th Ky. Cav.
Hermitage, Mo., Nov. 2, 1864.
Hernando, Miss., April 18, 1863. 2d Brigade, Cav. Div.; detachments of Inf. and Artil. from the 16th Corps.
Hernando, Miss., May 28, 1863.
Hernando, Miss., June 20, 1863. 5th Ohio; 2d Ill., and 1st Mo. Cav.
Hiampom Valley, Cal., Oct. 10, 1863.
Hickory Grove, Mo., Aug. 23, 1862.
Hickory Grove, Mo., Sept. 19, 1862. 6th Kan. Cav.
Hickory Hills, S. C., Feb. 1, 1865.
Hicksford, Va., Dec. 9, 1864. (See Bellefield.)
High Bridge, Appomattox River, Va., April 6, 1865. Portion of 24th Corps. Union, 10 killed, 31 wounded, 1,000 missing and captured.
Hillsboro, Ala., April 17, 1863. (See Bear Creek.)
Hillsboro, or Sunshine Church, Ga., July 31, 1864. Cav. of the Army of the Cumberland. (Stoneman's Raid.)
Hillsboro, Ky., Oct. 8, 1861. Ky. Home Guards. Union, 3 killed, 2 wounded; Confed., 11 killed, 29 wounded.
Hillsborough, Miss., Feb. 10, 1864.
Hill's Plantation, Ark., July 7, 1862. (See Bayou Caché.)
Hill's Plantation, Miss., June 22, 1863. Detachment of 4th Iowa Cav. Union, 4 killed, 10 wounded, 28 missing.
Hill's Point, Va., April 18, 1863. (See Battery Huger.)
Hodgeville, Ky., Oct. 23, 1861. Detachment of 6th Ind. Inf. Union, 3 wounded; Confed., 3 killed, 5 wounded.
Holland House, Va., May 15 and 16, 1863. (See Carrsville.)
Hollow Tree Gap, Tenn., Dec. 17, 1864. 5th and 7th Cav. Divs., Gen. Thomas' Army.
Holly River, W. Va., April 17, 1863. 10th W. Va. Inf. Union, 3 wounded; Confed., 2 killed.
Holly Springs, Miss., Nov. 12, 1862. (See Lamar.)
Holly Springs, Miss., Nov. 28, 1862, April 17, 1863, and Aug. 1 and 8, 1864.

Holly Springs, Miss., Dec. 20, 1862. 2d Ill. Cav.; 8th Wis. Inf. Union, 1,000 captured.
Holly Springs, Miss., May 24, 1864. 4th Mo. Cav. Union, 1 killed, 2 wounded.
Holly Springs, Miss., Aug. 27 and 28, 1864. 14th Iowa; 11th U. S. Colored Artil.; 10th Mo. Cav. Union, 1 killed, 2 wounded.
Holston River, near Knoxville, Tenn., Nov. 15, 1863. 11th Ky.; 45th Ohio; 37th Ky. Mounted Inf.
Holston River, Tenn., Feb. 20, 1864. 4th Tenn. Inf. Union, 2 killed, 3 wounded; Confed., 5 killed, 10 wounded.
Honey Hill, Broad River, or Grahamsville, S. C., Nov. 30, 1864. 25th Ohio; 56th and 155th N. Y.; 26th, 32d, 35th, and 102d U. S. Colored Troops; 54th and 55th Mass. Colored Troops. Union, 66 killed, 645 wounded.
Honey Springs, Ind. Ter., July 17, 1863. 2d, 6th, and 9th Kan. Cav.; 2d and 3d Kan. Battery; 2d and 3d Kan. Indian Home Guards. Union, 17 killed, 60 wounded; Confed., 150 killed, 400 wounded.
Honey Springs, Kan., Aug. 22, 1863.
Hoover's Gap, Tenn., June 24, 1863. 17th and 72d Ind.; 123d Ill.; 98th Ill. Mounted Inf.; 18th Ind. Battery.
Hopkinsville, Ky., Nov. 6, 1862.
Hopkinsville, Ky., Dec. 12 to 16, 1864. 2d and 3d Brigade, McCooke's 1st Cav. Div.
Hornersville, Mo., Sept. 20, 1862.
Hornsboro, S. C., March 3, 1865.
Horse Creek, Dak. Ter., June 14, 1865.
Horse Creek, Mo., Sept. 17, 1863.
Horsehead Creek, Ark., Feb. 17, 1864.
Horse Landing, Fla., May 23, 1864. 35th U. S. Colored Troops captured on board U. S. Tug "Columbine."
Horse-shoe Bend, or Greasy Creek, Ky., May 11, 1863. Detachment under Col. R. T. Jacobs. Union, 10 killed, 20 wounded, 40 missing; Confed., 100 killed, wounded, and missing.

Horton's Mills, near Newberne, N. C., April 27, 1862. 103d N. Y. Inf. Union, 1 killed, 6 wounded; Confed., 3 wounded. [Mo. Cav.
Hot Springs, Ark., Feb. 4, 1864. 3d Howard Co., Mo., Aug. 28, 1862. 4th Mo. Militia Cav.
Howard Co., Mo., Aug. 28, 1864. Company E, 4th Mo. Militia Cav.
Howell's Ferry, Ga., July 1, 1864.
Howe's Ford, or Weaver's Store, Ky., April 28, 1863. 1st Ky. Cav.
Hudnot's Plantation, La., May 1, 1864. Cav. of 19th Corps.
Hudson, Mo., Dec. 21, 1861. Detachment of 7th Mo. Cav. Union, 5 wounded; Confed., 10 killed.
Hudsonville, Miss., Nov. 8, 1862. 7th Kan. Cav.; 2d Iowa Cav. Confed., 16 killed, 185 captured.
Hudsonville, Miss., June 21, 1863.
Huff's Ferry, Tenn., Nov. 14, 1863. 111th Ohio; 107th Ill.; 11th and 13th Ky.; 23d Mich.; 24th Mich. Battery. Union, 100 killed and wounded.
Humonsville, Mo., March 26, 1862. Company B, 8th Mo. Militia Cav. Union, 5 wounded; Confed., 15 wounded.
Humonsville, Mo., Aug. 12, 1862, and Oct. 16 and 17, 1863.
Humboldt, Tenn., Dec. 20, 1862.
Hunnewell, Mo., Jan. 3, 1862. Four Companies, 10th Mo. Cav.
Hunter's Mills, Va., Nov. 26, 1861. 3d Pa. Cav.
Huntersville, Va., Jan. 4, 1862. Detachments of 23d Ohio, 2d W. Va., 1st Ind. Cav. Union, 1 wounded; Confed., 1 killed, 7 wounded.
Hunterstown, Pa., July 2, 1863.
Huntsville, Ala., April 11, 1862. 3d Div., Army of the Ohio. Confed., 200 prisoners.
Huntsville, Ala., Oct. 1, 1864. Detachments of 12th and 13th Ind. Cav.
Huntsville, Tenn., Nov. 11, 1862. Tenn. Home Guards.
Hurricane Bridge, W. Va., March 28, 1863. Four Companies, 13th W. Va. Inf.

Hurricane Creek, Ark., Oct. 23, 1864.
Hurricane Creek, Miss., Aug. 14, 16, and 22, 1864. Cav. and Inf., 16th Corps.
Hurricane Creek, Miss., Oct. 23, 1864, 1st Iowa and 9th Kan. Cav.
Hutchinson, Minn., Sept. 3 and 4, 1862. (Indian Fight.)

ILLINOIS Creek, Ark., Dec. 7, 1862. (See Prairie Grove.)
Independence, Mo., June 17, 1861. Mo. Inf.
Independence, or Little Blue, Mo., Nov. 26, 1861. 7th Kan. Cav.
Independence, Mo., Feb. 18, 1862. 2d Ohio Cav. Union, 1 killed, 3 wounded; Confed., 4 killed, 5 wounded.
Independence, or Little Santa Fé, Mo., March 22, 1862. 2d Kan. Inf. Union, 1 killed, 2 wounded; Confed., 7 killed.
Independence, Mo., Aug. 11, 1862. 7th Mo. Cav. Union, 14 killed, 18 wounded, 312 missing.
Independence, Mo., Feb. 3 and 8, 1863. 5th Mo. Militia Cav.
Independence, Mo., March 23 and April 23 and 24, 1863; Feb. 19 and March 4, 1864.
Independence, Mo., Oct. 22 and 26, 1864. 2d Col.; 5th, 7th, 11th, 15th, and 16th Kan. Cav.; Kan. Militia; 1st, 2d, 4th, 6th, 7th, 8th, and 9th Mo. Militia Cav.; 13th Mo.; 3d Iowa and 17th Ill. Cav. (Price's Invasion.)
Indian Bay, Ark., Feb. 16, 1864.
Indian Bay, Ark., April 13, 1864. 56th U. S. Colored Troops.
Indian City Village, La., Aug. 6, 1864. (See Placquemine.)
Indian Ridge, La., April 12 to 14, 1863. (See Irish Bend.)
Indiantown, or Sandy Swamp, N. C., Dec. 18, 1863. 36th U. S. Colored Troops; 2d N. C. Inf.; 5th U. S. Colored Troops.

Indian Village, Dak. Ter., March 27, 1863.
Indian Village, Placquemine Bayou, La., Jan. 27, 1863. 1st La. Cav.
Ingham's Mills, near Byhalia, Miss., Oct. 12, 1863. 2d Cav. Brigade of 16th Corps.
Ingham's Plantation, Miss., Oct. 10, 1863. 2d Wis. Cav.
Irish Bend and Bisland, or Indian Ridge and Centreville, or Bayou Teché, La., April 12 and 14, 1863. 19th Corps (Grover's Div.) at Irish Bend; Emery's and Weitzel's Divs. at Bisland. Union, 350 killed, wounded, and missing; Confed., 400 wounded, 2,000 missing and captured.
Iron Bridge, Ind. Ter., June 19, 1864.
Iron County, Mo., Sept. 11, 1862.
Ironton, Mo., Oct. 17 to 21, 1861. (See Fredericktown.)
Ironton, Mo., Sept. 26 and 27, 1864. (See Pilot Knob, or Ft. Davidson.)
Irvine, Ky., July 30, 1863. 14th Ky. Cav. Union, 4 killed, 5 wounded; Confed., 7 killed, 18 wounded.
Irwinsville, Ga., May 10, 1865. 1st Wis. and 4th Mich. Cav. Capture of Jefferson Davis.
Island Ford, Va., July 18, 1864. (See Snicker's Ferry.)
Island Mound, Mo., Oct. 29, 1862. (See Butler.)
Island No. 76, Miss., Jan. 20, 1864. Battery E, 2d Colored Light Artil.
Island No. 10, Tenn., April 8, 1862. Maj.-Gen. Pope's Command and Navy under Flag Officer A. H. Foote. Confed., 17 killed, 3,000 prisoners.
Island No. 10, Tenn., Oct. 17, 1862, and Oct. 16, 1863.
Isle of Wight C. H., Va., Dec. 24, 1862. Detachment of 2d N. Y. Mounted Rifles.
Issequena County, Miss., July 10 and Aug. 17, 1864.
Iuka, Miss., Sept., 19 and 20, 1862. (Skirmishing from the 13th to 19th.) Stanley's and Hamilton's Divs., Army of the Miss., under Maj.-Gen. Rosecrans. Union, 144 killed, 598

LIST OF BATTLES AND ENGAGEMENTS. 153

wounded; Confed., 263 killed, 692 wounded, 561 captured. Confed., Brig.-Gens. Little and Whitfield wounded.
Iuka, Miss., July 7 to 9, and July 14, 1863. 10th Mo. and 7th Kan. Cav.
Ivy Ford, Ark., Jan. 19, 1864. (See Branchville.)
Ivy Ford, Ark., Jan. 8, 1865. 79th U. S. Colored Troops.
Ivy Hills, Miss., Feb. 22, 1864. (See Okalona.)
Ivy Mountain, Ky., Nov. 9, 1861. (See Piketown.)

JACINTO, Miss., Aug. 13, 1863.
Jackson, Ark., Aug. 3, 1862, and April 26, 1863.
Jackson, La., Aug. 3, 1863. 73d, 75th, and 78th U. S. Colored Troops. Union, 2 killed, 2 wounded, 27 missing.
Jackson, La., Oct. 5, 1864. 23d Wis.; 1st Tenn and 1st La. Cav.; 2d and 4th Mass. Battery. Union, 4 killed, 10 wounded.
Jackson, La., Nov. 21, 1864. (See Liberty.)
Jackson, Miss., May 14, 1863. 15th Corps, Maj.-Gen. Sherman; 17th Corps, Maj.-Gen. McPherson. Union, 40 killed, 240 wounded; Confed., 450 killed and wounded.
Jackson, Miss., July 9 to 16, 1863. (Including engagements at Rienzi, Bolton Depot, Canton, and Clinton.) 9th, 13th, 15th, and part of 16th Corps. Union, 100 killed, 800 wounded, 100 missing; Confed., 71 killed, 504 wounded, 764 missing.
Jackson, Miss., Feb. 5, 1864. (See Clinton.)
Jackson, Miss., July 5 to 8, 1864. 2d Wis.; 5th and 11th Ill.; 3d U. S. Colored Cav.; 46th, 76th, and 79th Ill. Inf.
Jackson, Mo., April 9, 1862, and April 27, 1863.
Jackson, or Salem Cemetery, or Lexington, Tenn., Dec. 18, 1862. 43d and 61st Ill.; 11th Ill. Cav.; 5th Ohio Cav.
Jackson, Tenn., July 13, 1863. 3d Mich.; 3d Iowa; 9th Ill. and 1st Tenn. Cav.
Jacksboro', Big Creek Gap, Tenn., March 10, 1862. 2d Tenn. Inf. Union, 2 wounded; Confed., 2 killed, 4 wounded.
Jackson Co., Mo., June 2, 1862, and April 5, 1863.
Jackson Cross Roads, La., June 20, 1863. Detachments of 52d Mass. Inf.; 6th and 7th Ill., and 2d R. I. Cav.; a Battery of Artil.
Jacksonport, Ark., Dec. 23, 1863. 3d Mo. Cav.
Jacksonport, Ark., April 24, 1864. 1st Neb. Cav.
Jacksonport, Ark., Aug. 26, 1864.
Jackson's Ford, Ala., July 14, 1864. (See Ten Islands.)
Jacksonville, Fla., March 29, 1863. (Including Skirmish at Baldwin.) 8th Me.; 6th Conn.; 33d U. S. Colored Troops.
Jacksonville, Fla., Feb. 5 to April 14, 1864. Exp. of the Army under Gen. Gilmore and Navy under Admiral Dahlgren.
Jacksonville, Fla., May 1 and 28, 1864. 7th U. S. Colored Troops. Union, 1 killed.
Jacksonville, Fla., April 4, 1865.
Jack's Shop, or Madison C. H., Va., Sept. 22, 1863. (See Madison C. H.)
Jack's Shop, near Gordonsville, Va., Dec. 23, 1864. 1st Cav. Div., Army of Potomac; 2d Cav. Div., Army of W. Va.
James City, or Robertson's Run, Va., Oct. 10, 1863. Pleasonton's Cav. Union, 10 killed, 40 wounded.
James Island, S. C., June 8, 1862. Recon. of Troops, together with eight U. S. Gunboats.
James Island, S. C., June 10, 1862. Union, 3 killed, 13 wounded; Confed., 17 killed, 30 wounded.
James Island, S. C., June 13, 1862. Union, 3 killed, 19 wounded; Confed., 19 killed, 6 wounded.

James Island, S. C., July 16, 1863. (See Secessionville.)
James Island, S. C., May 21, 1864.
James Island, S. C., July 1, 2, 5, and 7, 1864. Troops of the Dep't of the South.
James Island, S. C., Feb. 10, 1865. Gen. Schimmelfennig's Div. of Maj.-Gen. Gilmore's Command, Dep't of the South. Union, 20 killed, 76 wounded; Confed., 20 killed, 70 wounded.
James Island, S. C., Feb. 18, 1865. Evacuated by the Confederates.
James and Nansemond Rivers, Va., April 14 and 15, 1864. Exp. of Troops, supported by U. S. Gunboats.
Jarrett's Sta., Weldon R. R., Va., May 9, 1864. 11th Pa. Cav.; 8th N. Y. Battery. (Kautz's Raid.)
Jasper, Sweden's Cove, Tenn., June 4, 1862. 79th Pa.; 5th Ky. and 7th Pa. Cav.; 1st Ohio Battery. Union, 2 killed, 7 wounded; Confed., 20 killed, 20 wounded. [1863.
Jasper Co., Mo., June 10, and Oct. 5,
Jenkin's Ferry, Ark., April 15, 1864.
Jenkin's Ferry, Saline River, Ark., April 30, 1864. 77th Ohio; 4th, 18th, 29th, 33d, 36th, and 40th Iowa; 1st Ark.; 12th Kan.; 9th and 27th Wis.; 43d Ill. Inf.; 79th and 83d U. S. Colored Troops; Battery A, 3d Ill., and 2d Ind. Battery; 1st Iowa; 2d, 6th, and 14th Kan.; 1st and 2d Mo.; 13th Ill. Cav. and 3d Cav. Div., 17th Corps. (Steele's Exp.) Union, 200 killed, 955 wounded; Confed., 300 killed, 800 wounded.
Jenkin's Ferry, Ark., May 4, 1864.
Jenk's Bridge, Ga., Dec. 7 to 9, 1864. (See Ogeechee River, or Eden Station.)
Jennie's Creek, or Paintsville, Ky., Jan. 7, 1862. Four companies 1st W. Va. Cav. Union, 3 killed, 1 wounded; Confed., 6 killed, 14 wounded.
Jefferson, Tenn., Dec. 30, 1862. 2d Brigade, 1st Div., Thomas' Corps. Union, 20 killed, 40 wounded; Confed., 15 killed, 50 wounded.

Jefferson, Va., Nov. 14, 1863.
Jefferson City, Mo., Oct. 7, 1864. (See Moreau Bottom.)
Jefferson City, Mo., Nov. 3, 1864.
Jeffersonton, Va., Oct. 12, 1863. 2d Cav. Div., Army of Potomac. Union, 12 killed, 80 wounded, 400 missing.
Jeffersonville, or Abb's Valley, Va., May 8, 1864. Cav. of the Army of W. Va.
Jeff Thompson's Surrender, Ark., May 11, 1865. (See Thompson's Surrender.)
Jericho Ford, Va., May 23 to 27, 1864. (See North Anna River.)
Jerusalem Plank Road, Va., June 22 and 23, 1864. (See Weldon R. R.)
Jerusalem Plank Road, Va., Sept. 28, 1864. (See Fort Hell.)
Jettersville, Va., April 5, 1865. (See Amelia Springs.)
John Day's River, Ore., July 12, 1864.
John Day's River, Ore., April 16, 1865. (See South Fork.)
John's Island, S. C., July 5 to 7, 1864. Maj.-Gen. Foster's Troops, Dep't of the South. Union, 16 killed, 82 wounded; Confed., 20 killed, 80 wounded.
Johnson Co., Mo., July 16, 1864.
Johnson's Depot, Tenn., Sept. 22, 1863. 8th Tenn. Inf.
Johnson's Mills, Tenn., Feb. 22, 1864. Detachment of 24 men of 5th Tenn. Cav. captured and massacred by Ferguson's Guerillas.
Johnsonville, Tenn., Sept. 25, 1864. 13th U. S. Colored Troops.
Johnsonville, Tenn., Nov. 4 and 5, 1864. 12th Wis.; 12th U. S. Colored Troops: 11th Tenn. Cav.
Johnston's Surrender, N. C. April 26. 1865. Armies of the Tenn., Ga. and Ohio, under Maj.-Gen. W. T. Sherman. Confed., 29,924 captured.
Johnstown, Mo., Nov. 24, 1861. Mo. Home Guards.
Jonesboro', Ark., Aug. 3, 1862. 1st Wis. Cav.
Jonesboro'. Ga., Aug. 19 and 20, 1864. 2d Cav. Div., Army of the Cumberland.

Jonesboro', Ga., Aug. 31 and Sept. 1, 1864. 15th, 16th, 17th, and Davis' Cav. Divs. of the 14th Corps. Union, 1,149 killed and wounded; Confed., 2,000 killed, wounded, and missing. Confed., Brig.-Gens. Anderson, Cummings, and Patten killed.
Jonesboro', Ga., Sept. 7, 1864.
Jonesboro', Ga., Nov. 16, 1864. (See Lovejoy Sta.)
Jonesboro', Mo., Aug. 21 and 22, 1861. Mo. Home Guards.
Jonesboro', Mo., Oct. 12 and 13, 1863. (See Merrill's Crossing.)
Jones' Bridge, Va., June 23, 1864. Torbett's and Gregg's Cav. Divs.; 28th U. S. Colored Troops.
Jones' Cross Roads, Miss., May 3, 1863.
Jones' Ford, Black River, Miss., July 6, 1863. 6th Iowa and 48th Ill.
Jones' Ford, Tenn., July 2, 1863.
Jones' Hay Sta. and Ashley Sta., Ark., Aug. 24, 1864. 9th Iowa and 8th and 11th Mo. Cav. Union, 5 killed, 41 wounded; Confed., 60 wounded.
Jones' Plantation, Ga., Nov. 27 to 29, 1864.
Jones' Surrender, Fla., May 10, 1865. (See Tallahassee.)
Jonesville, Va., Jan. 3, 1864. Detachment of 16th Ill. Cav.; 22d Ohio Battery. Union, 12 killed, 48 wounded, 300 missing; Confed., 4 killed, 12 wounded.
Jornado Del Nuerto, New Mexico, June 16, 1863. One company of 1st New Mexico Cav.
Joy's Farm, Miss., Feb. 22, 1864.
Joy's Ford, Ark., Jan. 8, 1865.
Julesburg, Ind. Ter., Jan. 7, 1865. One company of 7th Iowa Cav. (Indian Fight.)
Jumpertown, Miss., Nov. 5, 1862.

K ANAWHA Gap, W. Va., Sept. 25, 1861.
Kansas City, Mo., Nov. 22, 1864.
Kautz's Raid, Va., May 4 to 12, 1864. From Suffolk, Wall's Bridge, Stony Creek Sta., Jarrett's Sta., White's Bridge to City Point, Va. 5th and 16th Pa.; 3d N. Y.; 1st D. C. Cav.; 8th N. Y. Battery. Union, 10 killed, wounded, and missing; Confed., 20 wounded, 50 prisoners.
Kautz's Raid on R. R., Va., May 12 to 17, 1864. (Petersburg & Lynchburg R. R.) Union, 6 killed, 28 wounded.
Kearnstown, Mo., March 23, 1864.
Kearnstown, Va., March 23, 1862. (See Winchester.)
Kearneysville, Va., Aug. 25, 1864. (See Smithfield.)
Keytesville, Mo., May —, 1862.
Keller's Bridge, Ky., June 10, 1864. (See Cynthiana.)
Kelley's Ford, Tenn., Jan. 27, 1864. (See Fair Gardens.)
Kelley's Ford, Rappahannock River, Va., Aug. 21, 1862. Cav. of the Army of Va.
Kelley's Ford, Va., March 17, 1863. 1st and 5th U. S. Regulars; 3d, 4th, and 16th Pa.; 1st R. I.; 6th Ohio; 4th N. Y. Cav.; 6th N. Y. Battery. Union, 9 killed, 35 wounded; Confed., 11 killed, 88 wounded.
Kelley's Ford, Va., Aug. 1 to 3, 1863. (See Rappahannock Sta.)
Kelley's Ford, Va., Nov. 7, 1863. 1st U. S. Sharpshooters; 40th N. Y.; 1st and 20th Ind.; 3d and 5th Mich.; 110th Pa., supported by the remainder of 3d Corps. Union, 70 killed and wounded; Confed., 5 killed, 59 wounded, 295 missing.
Kelley's Island, Va., June 26, 1861. (See Patterson Creek.)
Kelley's Store, Va., Jan. 30, 1863. (See Deserted House.)
Kenesaw Mountain, or Lost Mountain, or Big Shanty, or Marietta, or Nose's Creek, Ga., June 9 to 30, 1864. (Including engagements at Pine Mountain, June 14; Pine Knob, June 19; Golgotha, June 19; Culp's House, June 22; general assault, June 27; McApee's Cross Roads, Lattamore's Mills, or Noon-day Creek and Powder Springs.) 4th, 14th, and 20th Corps, Army of the Cumber-

land, Maj.-Gen. Thomas; 15th, 16th, and 17th Corps, Army of the Tenn., Maj.-Gen. McPherson; 23d Corps, Maj.-Gen. Schofield; Army of the Miss., Maj.-Gen. W. T. Sherman. Union, 1,370 killed, 6,500 wounded, 800 missing; Confed., 1,100 killed and wounded, 3,500 missing. Union, Brig.-Gens. Harker and McCooke, killed; Confed., Lieut.-Gen. L. Polk killed.

Kernstown, Va., July 23, 1864. Cav. of the Army of W. Va.

Kernstown, Va., Nov. 11, 1864.

Kettle Run, Va., Aug. 27, 1862. Maj.-Gen. Hooker's Div. of 3d Corps Army of Potomac. Union, 300 killed and wounded; Confed., 300 killed and wounded.

Keysville, Cal., April 19, 1863.

Keytesville, Mo., Feb. 17 and 26, 1862. 6th Mo. Cav. Union, 2 killed, 1 wounded; Confed., 4 killed.

Kilpatrick's Raid, Va., Feb. 28 to March 4, 1864. (From Stevensburg to Richmond, Va.) Kilpatrick's Cav., Army of Potomac. Union, 330 killed, wounded, and captured; Confed., 308 killed, wounded, and captured.

Kilpatrick's Raid on the Atlanta R. R., Ga., Aug. 18 to 22. 1864. Kilpatrick's Cav. Union, 400 wounded.

Kincaeds, Tenn., Nov. 6, 1863.

Kinderhook, Tenn., Aug. 11, 1862. Detachment of 3d Ky. and 1st Tenn. Cav. Union, 3 killed; Confed., 7 killed.

King and Queen C. H., Va., June 24, 1864.

King George Co., Va., Aug. 24, 1863. 3d Div., Cav. Corps, Army of Potomac. [8th Pa. Cav.

King George C. H., Va., Dec. 2, 1862.

King's Creek, Miss., July 9, 1864.

King's Court, Tenn., Dec. 13, 1864. 8th, 9th, and 13th Tenn. Cav. (Stoneman's Raid.)

King's River, Carroll Co., Ark., April 16, 1864. 2d Ark. Cav.

King's School House, Va., June 25, 1862. (See Oak Grove.)

Kingston, Ga., May 18, 1864. (See Rome.)

Kingston, Ga., May 24, 1864. 50th Ohio and 14th Ky. Inf.; 2d Ky. Cav.

Kingston, Ga., Oct. 12, 1864.

Kinston, N. C., Dec. 14, 1862. 1st, 2d, and 3d Brigades, 1st Div. and Wessell's Brigade of Peck's Div., Dep't of N. C. Union, 40 killed, 120 wounded; Confed., 50 killed, 75 wounded, 400 missing.

Kinston, N. C., March 14, 1865. Troops under Gen. Schofield.

Kingston, Tenn., Nov. 26, 1863. Cav., Army of the Ohio.

Kingston, Tenn., Aug. 26, 1864.

Kingsville, Mo., June 12, 1864. Portion of 1st Mo. Militia Cav.

Kirby Smith's Surrender, May 26, 1865. (See Smith's Surrender.)

Kirksville, Mo., Aug. 5 and 6, 1862. Mo. State Militia. Union, 28 killed, 60 wounded; Confed., 128 killed, 200 wounded.

Kirksville, Mo., Aug. 26, 1862. 1st Mo. Militia.

Knob Gap, Tenn., Dec. 26, 1862. (See Nolensville.)

Knobnoster, Mo., Jan. 22, 1862. 2d Mo. Cav.

Knoxville, Tenn., Sept. 10, 1863. Occupied by Army of the Ohio, Maj.-Gen. Burnside. (See, also, Siege of Knoxville.)

Kock's Plantation, Ga., July 13, 1863. (See Donaldsonville.)

Kossuth, Miss., Aug. 26, 1862. (See Rienzi.)

L ABADIESVILLE, or Thibodeauxville, or Georgia Landing, La., Oct. 27, 1862. 8th N. H.; 12th and 13th Conn.; 78th N. Y. Inf.; 1st La. Cav.; 1st Me. Battery.

Lacy, Ark., May 19, 1862.

Lacy's Springs, Va., Sept. 20, 1864. Custer's Cav., Army of Potomac.

Ladiga, Ala., Oct. 30, 1864. Gerrod's Cav. Div., Army of the Cumberland.

Lafayette, Ga., June 10 and 24, 1864.

Lafayette, Tenn., Dec. 25, 1863. 117th Ill. Inf.
Lafayette, Tenn., June 9, 1864. 9th Kan. Cav.
Lafayette, Tenn., June 24, 1864.
Lafayette Co., Mo., June 14, 1864.
La Fourché Crossing, or Thibodeaux, La., June 20 and 21, 1863. Detachments of 2d Conn.; 176th N. Y.; 26th, 42d, and 47th Mass, and 21st Ind. Inf. Union, 8 killed, 40 wounded; Confed., 53 killed, 150 wounded.
La Grange, Ark., Sept. 6, 1862. 1st Mo. Cav.
La Grange, Ark., Oct. 11, 1862. Detachment of 4th Iowa Cav. Union, 4 killed, 13 wounded.
La Grange, Ark., Nov. 7, 1862. (See Marianna.)
La Grange, Ark., Dec. 30, 1862.
La Grange, Ark., Jan. 3, 1863. Portion of Washburn's Cav. Regiment.
La Grange, Ark., May 1, 1863. 3d Iowa Cav. Union, 3 killed, 9 wounded, 30 missing.
La Grange, Tenn., Nov. 11, 1862. (See Lebanon.)
La Grange, Tenn., July 16, 1863.
Lake Chicot, or Old River Lake, or Ditch Bayou, Fish Bayou, Columbia, Ark., June 6, 1864. 16th Corps. Union, 40 killed, 70 wounded; Confed., 100 killed and wounded.
Lake Chicot, Ark., July 6 and 7, 1864.
Lake City, Fla., Feb. 12, 1864. 40th Mass. Inf.; Independent Battalion, Mass. Cav.
Lake Providence, La., Feb. 10, 1863. (See Old River.)
Lake Providence, La., May 27, 1863. 47th U. S. Colored Troops. Union, 1 killed, 1 wounded.
Lake Providence, La., June 10 and 29, 1863.
Lake Village, Ark., Feb. 10, 1864.
Lamar and Holly Springs, Miss., Nov. 12, 1862. 2d Ill.; 3d Mich.; 2d Iowa, and 7th Kan. Cav.
Lamar, Mo., Aug. 24, 1862. (See Coon Creek.)
Lamar, Mo., Nov. 5, 1862. 8th Mo. Inf.; 8th Mo. Militia Cav.

Lamb's Ferry, Tenn., Dec. 25, 1864. (See Pulaski.)
Lamonica Springs, N. Mex., Sept. 4, 1865.
Lancaster, Ky., Oct. 14, 1862. (See Stanford.)
Lancaster, Mo., Nov. 24, 1861. 21st Mo. Inf.
Lane Prairie, near Rolla, Mo., July 26, 1861. Mo. Home Guards. Union, 3 wounded; Confed., 1 killed, 3 wounded.
Lane's Prairie, Mo., May 26, 1864. Two companies 2d Wis. Cav.
Languelle Ferry, Ark., Aug. 3, 1862. 1st Wis. Cav. Union, 17 killed, 38 wounded.
Lattamore's Mills, Ga., June 20, 1864. (See Kenesaw Mountain.)
Lauderdale Springs, Miss., Feb. 15, 1864. 3d Wis. Inf. and Ind. Troops. (Exp. to Meridian.)
Laurel Hill, Va., May 8 to 18, 1864. (See Spottsylvania C. H.)
Laurel Hill, Va., Sept. 28 to 30, 1864. (See New Market Heights.)
Laurel Hill, Va., Oct. 7, 1864.
Laurel Hill, or Bealington, W. Va., July 8, 1861. 14th Ohio and 9th Ind. Inf. Union, 2 killed, 6 wounded.
La Vergne, Tenn., Oct. 7, 1862. Palmer's Brigade. Union, 5 killed, 9 wounded; Confed., 80 killed and wounded, 175 missing.
La Vergne, Tenn., Nov. 27, 1862.
La Vergne, Tenn., Dec. 9, 1862. (See Dobbin's Ferry.)
La Vergne, Tenn., Jan. 1, 1863. 1st Mich. Engineers.
La Vergne, Tenn., Sept. 1, 1864. 1st and 4th Tenn.; 2d Mich.; 1st Wis.; 8th Iowa; 2d and 8th Ind.; 6th Ky. Cav. (Rousseau's pursuit of Wheeler, Sept. 1 to 8.)
Lawrence, Kan., July 27, 1863.
Lawrence, Kan., Aug. 21, 1863. Quantrell's Plunder and Massacre. 140 citizens killed, 24 wounded; Confed., 40 killed.
Lawrenceburg, or Dog Walk, Ky., Oct. 9, 1862. 1st and 49th Ohio Inf.;

15th and 19th U. S. Inf.; 9th Ky. Cav.; 5th U. S. Artil.

Lawrenceburg, Ohio, July 14, 1863. 105th Ind. Minutemen. (Morgan's Raid.)

Lawrenceburg, Tenn., Nov. 4, 1863. 14th Mich. Mounted Inf.

Lawrenceburg, Campbellville, and Lynnville, Tenn., Nov. 22, 1864. Hatch's Cav. Union, 75 killed and wounded; Confed., 50 killed and wounded.

Lawrenceburg, Tenn., Nov. 27 and Dec. 22, 1864.

Lay's Ferry, Ga., May 15, 1864. Portion of 16th Corps, Army of the Tenn.

Lead's Cross Roads, Ga., Nov. 1, 1864.

Leatherwood, Ky., Nov. 6, 1862. Captain Powell's Command.

Lebanon, Ala., Feb. 3 and 6, 1864. Portion of troops of Army of the Cumberland.

Lebanon, Ky., July 12, 1863. 28th Ky. and Lebanon Home Guards. (Morgan's Raid.) Union, 2 killed, 65 prisoners.

Lebanon, Ky., July 5, 1863. 20th Ky. Vols. Union, 9 killed, 15 wounded, 400 missing; Confed., 3 killed, 6 wounded.

Lebanon, Ky., July 30, 1864. One Company, 12th Ohio Cav. Confed., 6 killed.

Lebanon, Mo., March 12, 1862. Confed., 13 killed, 5 wounded.

Lebanon, Tenn., May 5, 1862. 1st, 4th, and 5th Ky. Cav.; detachment of 7th Pa. Cav. Union, 6 killed, 25 wounded; Confed., 66 prisoners.

Lebanon, or La Grange, Tenn., Nov. 11, 1862. 1st Ky. and 4th Mich. Cav.

Lebanon, Tenn., Dec. 6, 1862. 93d Ohio Inf.

Lebanon, Tenn., Feb. 8, 1863.

Leesburg and Harrison, Mo., Sept. 29 and 30, 1864. 14th Iowa; 2d Mo. Militia Cav.; Battery H, 2d Mo. Light Artil. (Price's Invasion.)

Leesburg, Mo., Oct. 1 and 28, 1864.

Leesburg, Va., Oct. 21, 1861. (See Ball's Bluff.)

Leesburg Road, Va., Sept. 17, 1862. (See Goose Creek.)

Lee's Creek, Ark., Aug. 1, 1864.

Lee's Ford, Mo., Aug. 10 to 13, 1862. (See Grand River.)

Lee's Mills, Va., April 16, 1862. 3d, 4th and 6th Ver. Inf.; 3d N. Y. Battery; Battery of 5th U. S. Artil. Union, 35 killed, 129 wounded; Confed., 20 killed, 75 wounded, 50 captured.

Lee's Mills, near Ring's Sta., Va., July 12, 1864. 2d Div., Gregg's Cav., Army of Potomac. Union, 3 killed, 13 wounded; Confed., 25 killed and wounded.

Lee's Mills, Va., July 30, 1864. Davis' Cav. Union, 2 killed, 11 wounded.

Lee Springs and Freeman's Ford, Va., Aug. 24, 1862. Army of Va.

Lee's Surrender at Appomattox, Va., April 9, 1865. Armies of the Potomac and James, under Maj.-Gen. U. S. Grant. Confed., 26,000 prisoners.

Leesville, Mo., March 19, 1862.

Leetown, Ark., March 7, 1862. (See Pea Ridge.)

Leetown, Va., July 3, 1864. 10th W. Va.; 1st N. Y. Cav. Union, 3 killed, 12 wounded.

Leetown, Va., Aug. 25, 1864.

Legare's Point, S. C., June 3, 1863. 28th Mass.; 100th Pa. Union, 5 wounded.

Leighton, Ala., April 24, 1863.

Leiper's Ferry, Tenn., Oct. 28, 1863. 11th and 37th Ky.; 112th Ill. Inf. Union, 2 killed, 5 wounded.

Leland's Point, Ark., May 27, 1864.

Lenoirs, Tenn., Nov. 15, 1863. Cav. and Inf., Army of the Ohio.

Lett's Tan Yard, near Chickamauga, Ga., Sept. 13, 1863. Wilder's Brigade of Mounted Inf. Union, 50 killed and wounded; Confed., 10 killed, 40 wounded.

Lewinsville, Va., Sept. 11, 1861. 19th Ind.; 3d Ver.; 65th N. Y.; 79th N. Y. Militia. Union, 6 killed, 8 wounded.

Lewisburg, Ark., Jan. 17, 1864. Detachment of 2d Ark. Cav

Lewisburg, Va., May 23, 1862. 36th and 44th Ohio; 2d W. Va. Cav. Union, 14 killed, 60 wounded; Confed., 40 killed, 66 wounded, 100 captured.

Lexington, Ky., Oct. 17, 1862. Detachment of 3d and 4th Ohio. Cav. Union, 4 killed, 24 wounded, 350 missing.

Lexington, Ky., July 28, 1863. (See Richmond.)

Lexington, Ky., June 10, 1864. 4th Ky. Cav.

Lexington, Mo., Aug. 29, 1861. Mo. Home Guards. Confed., 8 killed.

Lexington, Mo., Sept. 12 to 20, 1861. 23d Ill.; 8th, 25th, and 27th Mo.; 13th and 14th Mo. Home Guards; 1st Ill. Cav.; Berry's and Van Horne's Mo. Cav. Union, 42 killed, 108 wounded, 1,624 missing and captured; Confed., 25 killed, 75 wounded.

Lexington, Mo., March 12, 1862. 1st Iowa Cav. Union, 1 killed, 1 wounded; Confed., 9 killed, 3 wounded.

Lexington, Mo., Oct. 17, 1862, and Feb. 22, 1864.

Lexington, Mo., June 14, 1864. Detachment of 1st Mo. Cav. Union, 8 killed, 1 wounded.

Lexington, Mo., Oct. 19 and 21, 1864. 5th, 11th, 15th, and 16th Kan. Cav.; 3d Wis. Cav.

Lexington, Tenn., Dec. 18, 1862. 11th Ill.; 5th Ohio, and 2d Tenn. Cav. Union, 7 killed, 10 wounded, 124 missing. Confed., 7 killed, 28 wounded.

Lexington, Tenn., June 29, 1863.

Lexington, W. Va., June 10 and 11, 1864. 2d Div., Army of W. Va. Union, 6 killed, 18 wounded.

Liberty and Jackson, La., Nov. 21, 1864. 4th Wis. Cav.; 1st Wis. Battery.

Liberty and Sibley's Landing, Mo., Oct. 6, 1862. 5th Mo. Militia Cav.

Liberty, Va., June 20, 1864. Cav. Div., Army of W. Va.

Liberty Creek, La., Nov. 15, 1864. (See Clinton.)

Liberty Gap, or Beech Grove, Tenn., June 25, 1863. 20th Corps, Maj.-Gen. McCooke, Army of the Cumberland. (Rosecrans' Campaign.)

Liberty Mills, Va., Oct. 15, 1863. (See McLean Ford.)

Liberty P. O., and Occupation of Camden, Ark., April 15 and 16, 1864. 29th Iowa; 50th Ind.; 9th Wis. Union, 255 killed and wounded.

Lick Creek, Ark., Jan. 12, 1863. 2d Wis. Cav.

Lick Creek, Miss., April 26, 1862. Advance of Gen. A. J. Smith's Troops.

Lick Creek, Tenn., April 24, 1862.

Licking, Mo., May 4, 1862. 24th Mo. and 5th Mo. Militia Cav. Union, 1 killed, 2 wounded.

Limestone Sta., near Telford, Tenn., Sept. 5, 1863. Five Companies, 100th Ohio Inf. Union, 12 killed, 20 wounded, 240 missing; Confed., 6 killed, 10 wounded.

Linden, Tenn., May 12, 1863. 6th Tenn. Cav.

Linden, Va., May 15, 1862. One Company, 28th Pa. Inf. Union, 1 killed, 3 wounded, 14 missing.

Linn Creek, Mo., Oct. 15, 1861. 13th Ill. Inf.; 6th Mo. Cav. Confed., 63 killed, 40 wounded.

Linn Creek, Va., Feb. 8, 1862. Detachment of 5th W. Va. Inf. Union, 1 killed, 1 wounded; Confed., 8 killed, 7 wounded.

Liscomb's Hill, Cal., June 6, 1862.

Little Bear Creek, Ala., Nov. 28, 1862. Part of 2d Div., 16th Corps.

Little Bear Creek, Ala., Dec. 12, 1862. 52d Ill. Inf. Union, 1 killed, 2 wounded; Confed., 11 killed, 30 wounded.

Little Bethel Ch., Tenn., Feb. 13, 1862.

Little Black River, Mo., May 20, 1863.

Little Blue, Dak. Ter., Aug. 12, 1864. Detachment of 7th Iowa Cav.

Little Blue, Mo., Nov. 11, 1861. 110 men of 7th Kan. Cav. Union, 7 killed, 9 wounded.

Little Blue, or Independence, Mo., Nov. 26, 1861. 7th Kan. Cav Union, 1 killed, 1 wounded.

Little Blue, Mo., July 6, 1864. 2d Col. Cav. Union, 8 killed, 1 wounded.
Little Blue, Mo., Oct. 21, 1864. 2d Col.; 3d Wis.; 5th, 11th, 15th, and 16th Kan. Cav.; one Brigade of Kan. Militia; 2d and 5th Mo. Militia; two Battalions 2d Mo. Artil. (Price's Invasion.)
Little Blue River, Mo., April 12, 1862. Confed., 5 killed.
Little Cacapon, Va., April 10, 1864. Company K, 54th Pa. Inf.
Little Creek, N. C., Nov. 3, 1862. (See Rawle's Mills.)
Little Harpeth, Tenn., March 25, 1863. (See Franklin.)
Little Lermio, Col., Aug. 5, 1865.
Little Mo. River, Ark., Jan. 25, 1864.
Little Mo. River, Ark., April 4 to 6, 1864. (See Elkin's Ford.)
Little Mo. River, Dak. Ter., Aug. 8, 1864. (See Two Hills.)
Little Osage River, Kan., Oct. 25, 1864. (See Mine Creek.)
Little Pond, Tenn., Aug. 30, 1862. (See McMinnville.)
Little Red River, Ark., June 5, 1862.
Little Red River, Ark., June 25, 1862. 4th Iowa Cav. Union, 2 wounded.
Little River, Tenn., Oct. 20, 1864. Cav. and portion of 15th Corps.
Little Rock, Ark., Sept. 10, 1863. Maj.-Gen. Steele's Troops and Davidson's Cav.
Little Rock, Ark., April 26, 1864.
Little Rock, Ark., May 28, 1864. 57th U. S. Colored Troops.
Little Rock Landing, Tenn., April 26, 1863.
Little Rock Road, Ark., April 2, 1863. One Company, 5th Kan. Cav.
Little Salkahatchie, S. C., Feb. 5, 1865.
Little Santa Fé, Mo., Nov. 6, 1861. 4th Mo.; 5th Kan. Cav.; Kowald's Mo. Battery. Union, 2 killed, 6 wounded.
Little Santa Fé, Mo., Nov. 20, 1861.
Little Santa Fé, Mo., March 23, 1862. (See Independence.)
Little Washington, Va., Nov. 15, 1862. (See Fayetteville.)
Liverpool Heights, Miss., Feb. 3, 1864.

11th Ill. Inf.; 47th U. S. Colored Troops.
Livingston, Miss., March 27, 1864.
Lockridge Mills, or Dresden, Ky., May 5, 1862. 5th Iowa Cav. Union, 4 killed, 16 wounded, 68 missing.
Lock's Ford, Opequan, Va., Sept. 13, 1864. 2d Brigade, 3d Div., Cav. Corps, Army of the Middle Military Div. Union, 2 killed, 18 wounded; Confed., 181 captured.
Locust Grove, Ind. Ter., July 3, 1862.
Locust Grove, Va., Nov. 26 to 28, 1863. (See Mine Run.)
Logan's Cross Roads, Ky., Jan. 19 and 20, 1862. (See Mill Springs.)
London Lane, Ala., April 25, 1863.
Lone Jack, Mo., Aug. 11, 15, and 16, 1862. Mo. Militia Cav. Union, 60 killed, 100 wounded; Confed., 110 killed and wounded.
Lone Jack, Mo., Nov. 1, 1864.
Long Prairie, Ark., Aug. 24, 1864. (See Jones' Hay Sta.)
Longview and Mount Elba, Ark., March 26 and 30, 1864. 28th Wis.; 5th Kan. Cav.; 7th Mo. Cav. Union, 4 killed, 18 wounded; Confed., 12 killed, 35 wounded, 300 captured.
Lookout Mountain, Tenn., Nov. 24, 1863. (See Chattanooga and Orchard Knob.)
Lookout Sta., Mo., Aug. 20, 1861. Union, 1 killed, 6 wounded.
Lost Creek, Mo., Aug. 15, 1862.
Lost Mountain, Ga., June 9 to 30, 1864. (See Kenesaw Mountain.)
Lotspeach Farm, Mo., July 8, 1862. One Company, 1st Iowa Cav.
Lotus Steamer, Ark., Jan. 17, 1865.
Loudon Creek, Tenn., Nov. 15, 1863. 111th Ohio Inf. Union, 4 killed, 12 wounded; Confed., 6 killed, 10 wounded.
Loudon Heights, Va., Jan. 10, 1864. 1st Md., Potomac Home Brigade.
Louisa C. H., Va., May 1, 1863.
Louisville, Ga., Dec. 1, 1864. Two Companies. 1st Me. Cav. (Stoneman's Raid.)
Louisville, Tenn., Nov. 28, 1863. 6th Ill. Cav.

LIST OF BATTLES AND ENGAGEMENTS. 161

Lovejoy Sta., Ga., July 29 and 30, 1864. Cav., Army of the Cumberland. (McCooke's Raid.)
Lovejoy Sta., Ga., Aug. 20, 1864. Cav., Army of the Cumberland. (Kilpatrick's Raid.)
Lovejoy Sta., Ga., Sept. 2 to 6, 1864. 23d Corps, Army of the Ohio; 4th Corps, Army of the Cumberland.
Lovejoy Sta. and Bear Creek Sta., Jonesboro', Ga., Nov. 16, 1864. Kilpatrick's Cav. Confed., 50 captured.
Lovettsville, Va., Aug. 8, 1861. 19th N. Y. Inf. Confed., 1 killed, 5 wounded.
Lovettsville, Va., Oct. 21, 1862. Detachment of Gen. Geary's Brigade.
Low Creek, W. Va., June 21, 1863.
Lowndesboro', Ala., April 10, 1865. 2d Brigade, 1st Cav. Div., Military Div. of the Miss. (Wilson's Raid.)
Lowtonville, S. C., Feb. 5, 1865.
Lucas Bend, Ky., Dec. 26, 1861. Stewart's Cav. Confed., 4 killed.
Lumkin's Mills, Miss., Nov. 29 and 30, 1862. (See Waterford.)
Luna Landing, Ark., Feb. 22, 1864. 1st Miss. Marine Brigade.
Lundy's Lane, Ala., April 17, 1863. (See Bear Creek.)
Luray, Va., June 30 and July 12, 1862. Detachment of Cav. of Brig.-Gen. Crawford's Command.
Luray, Va., Sept. 24, 1864. 1st Div. Cav. Corps, Army of Potomac.
Lynchburg, Va., June 17 and 18, 1864. Sullivan's and Crook's Div., together with Averill's and Duffie's Cav., Army of W. Va. Union, 100 killed, 500 wounded, 100 missing; Confed., 200 killed and wounded.
Lynch's Creek, S. C., Feb. 26, 1865. Advance of 15th Corps.
Lynnville, Tenn., Nov. 24, 1864. (See Campbellville.)
Lynnville, Tenn., Dec. 23, 1864. Cav. of Gen. Thomas' Army.

M ACON, Ga., July 30, 1864. Cav., Army of the Cumberland. (Stoneman's Raid.)

Macon, Ga., Nov. 20, 1864. 10th Ohio Cav.; 9th Pa. Cav.; 92d Ill. Mounted Inf.; 10th Wis. Battery.
Macon, Ga., Nov. 24, 1864.
Macon, Ga., April 20, 1865. 2d Div., Wilson's Cav.Corps. (Wilson's Raid.)
Macon, Mo., Feb. 12, 1865.
Madeline Plains, Cal., Nov. 17, 1862.
Madison, Ark., April 4, 1863. 3d Iowa Cav.
Madison C. H., Va., Sept. 21, 1863.
Madison C. H., Va., Sept. 22, 1863. (See Jack's Shop.)
Madison C. H., Va., Dec. 20, 1864. Mich. Cav. Brigade; 1st Cav. Div., Army of Potomac.
Madison Sta., Ala., May 17, 1864. 3d Div., 15th Corps, Army of the Tenn.
Madison Sta., Ala., Nov. 26, 1864. 101st U. S. Colored Troops.
Madisonville, Ky., Aug. 26, 1862. Lieut.-Col. Porter's Cav.
Madisonville, Ky., Oct. 5, 1862. 4th Ind. Cav.
Madisonville, La., Jan. 7, 1864.
Mad River, Cal., July 11, 1863.
Magnolia, Tenn., Jan. 7, 1865.
Magnolia Hills, Miss., May 1, 1863. (See Port Gibson.)
Malhuer River, Ore., July 9, 1865.
Malvern Hill, or Crew's Farm, Va., July 1, 1862. 2d, 3d, 4th, 5th, and 6th Corps. (See, also, Seven Days' Retreat.)
Malvern Hill, Va., Aug. 5, 1862. Portion of Hooker's Div.; 3d Corps; Richardson's Div., 2d Corps, and Cav., Army of Potomac. Union, 3 killed, 11 wounded; Confed., 100 captured.
Malvern Hill, Va., June 15, 1864. (See Samaria Church.)
Malvern Hill, Va., July 27 and 28, 1864. (See Deep Bottom.)
Manassas, Va., July 21, 1861. (See Bull Run.)
Manassas, Va., Aug. 30, 1862. (See 2d Bull Run.)
Manassas Gap, Va., Nov. 5, 1862. Cav. Brigade under Gen. Averill.
Manassas Gap, Va., July 21, 1863. 1st, 2d, and 5th U. S. Cav.

Manassas Gap, Va., July 23, 1863. (See Wapping Heights.)
Manassas Junction, Va., Oct. 24, 1862.
Manchester, Tenn., Aug. 29, 1862. Two Companies, 18th Ohio; one Company, 9th Mich. Inf. Confed., 100 killed and wounded.
Manchester, Tenn., March 17, 1864. 5th Tenn. Cav. Confed., 21 killed.
Mansfield, La., April 8, 1864. (See Sabine Cross Roads.)
Mansura, Avoyelle's Prairie, Moreauville, or Marksville, La., May 14 to 16, 1864. 3d Div., 16th Corps; Portion of Cav. Div., 9th Corps. (Red River Exp.)
Maplesville, Ala., April 1, 1865. (See Bogler's Creek.)
Marshfield, Mo., Oct. 20, 1862. 10th Ill. Cav.
Matthew's C. H., Va., Dec. 12, 1862. Detachments of N. Y. Independent Battalion and 6th N. Y. Cav., assisted by seamen from the U. S. Steamer "Mahaska."
Maria des Cygnes, Kan., Aug. 31, 1863.
Maria des Cygnes, Kan., Oct. 25, 1864. (See Mine Creek.)
Marianna, Fla., Sept. 27, 1864. 7th Vt.; 82d U. S. Colored Troops; 2d Me. Cav. Union, 32 wounded; Confed., 81 missing.
Marianna, or La Grange, Ark., Nov. 7, 1862. 3d and 4th Iowa Inf.; 9th Ill. Cav. Union, 3 killed, 20 wounded; Confed., 50 killed and wounded.
Marie County, Mo., May 6, 1864.
Marietta, Ga., June 9 to 30, 1864. (See Kenesaw Mountain.)
Marietta, Ga., July 3 to 4, 1864.
Marietta. Miss., Aug. 31, 1862.
Marion, Miss., Feb. 17,'64. Portion of 17th Corps. Expedit'n to Meridian.
Marion, Ark., Jan. 14, 1863.
Marion and Wytheville, Va., Dec. 16, 1864. 8th, 9th, and 13th Tenn. Cav. (Stoneman's Raid.)
Marion, Va., Dec. 18, 1864. Cav., Army of the Ohio. (Stoneman's Raid.)
Marion County, Fla., March 10, 1865.
Markham, Va., Nov. 5, 1862. (See Barbee's Cross Roads.)

Mark's Mills, Ark., April 5, 1864.
Mark's Mills, Ark., April 25, 1864. 36th Iowa; 77th Ohio; 43d Ind.; Battery E, 2d Mo. Light Artil.; 7th Mo. Cav.; 1st Ind. Cav. Union, 100 killed, 250 wounded, 100 missing; Confed., 110 killed, 228 wounded, 40 missing.
Marksville, La., May 14 to 16, 1864. (See Mansura.)
Marrowbone, or Burkesville, Ky., July 2, 1863. 1st and 9th Ky. Cav.; 24th Ind. Battery. (Morgan's Raid in Ky., Ohio, and Ind., July 1 to 26.)
Marshall, Mo., July 28, 1863. 4th Mo. Militia Cav.
Marshall, Mo., Oct. 12 and 13, 1863. (See Merrill's Crossing.)
Marshfield, Mo., Feb. 14, 1862. 6th Mo. and 3d Ill. Cav.
Marshfield, Mo., Oct. 20, 1862. 10th Ill. Cav.
Martinsburg, Md., July 2, 1861. (See Falling Waters.)
Martinsburg, Mo., July 17, 1861. One Company 1st Mo. Reserves. Union, 1 killed, 1 wounded.
Martinsburg, Va., Sept. 6, 1862. Troops under Brig.-Gen. White.
Martinsburg, Va., June 14, 1863. 106th N. Y.; 126th Ohio and W. Va. Battery. Union, 200 missing; Confed., 1 killed, 2 wounded.
Martinsburg, Va., Aug. 19, 1864. One Company, Averill's Cav. Union, 25 killed and wounded.
Martinsburg, Va., Sept. 18, 1864.
Martin's Creek, Ark., Jan. 7, 1864.
Maryland Heights, Va., May 28-30 and Sept. 12-13,'62. (See Harpers Ferry.)
Maryland Heights, Va., July 4 to 7, 1864. (See Bolivar Heights.)
Marysville, Tenn., Nov. 14, 1863. 11th Ky. Cav. Union, 100 killed and wounded.
Mason's Bridge, S. C., Dec. 6 to 9, 1864. (See Deveaux Neck.)
Mason's Neck, Occoquan, Va., Feb. 24, 1862. 37th N. Y. Inf. Union, 2 killed, 1 wounded.
Massacre at Centralia, Mo., Sept. 27, 1864. (See Centralia.)

Massacre on North Mo. River, Mo., Sept. 27, 1864. Furloughed soldiers.
Massacre on Steamer "Sam Gaty," Mo., March 30, 1863. (See Sibley's Landing.)
Matagorda Bay, Tex., Dec. 29 and 30, 1863. Three Companies, 13th Me. Inf., assisting Naval Forces.
Matapony, or Thornburg, Va., Aug. 6, 1862. Detachment of King's Div. Union, 1 killed, 12 wounded, 72 missing.
Matote, Cal., May 26, 1864.
Matthias' Point, Va., July 29, 1861. Troops assisted U. S. Steamer "Freeborn."
Mayfield, Ky., Jan. 12, 1864. 58th Ill. Inf. Union, 1 killed, 1 wounded; Confed., 2 killed.
Marye's Heights, Va., May 3, 1863.
Maysville, Ala., Aug. 28, 1863. 4th Ky. Cav.
Maysville, Ala., Oct. 13, 1863. 1st Div., Cav. Corps, Army of the Cumberland.
Maysville, Ark., Oct. 22, 1862. (See Old Fort Wayne.)
Mazzard Prairie, Fort Smith, Ark., July 27, 1864. 200 men, 6th Kan. Cav. Union, 12 killed, 17 wounded, 152 captured; Confed., 12 killed, 20 wounded.
McAfee's Cross Roads, Ga., June 12, 1864. (See Kenesaw Mountain.)
McConnellsburg, Pa., June 24, 1863. 12th Pa. Cav.
McConnellsburg, Pa., June 29, 1863. 1st N. Y. Cav.
McCooke's Raid to Lovejoy Sta., Ga., July 26 to 31, 1864. 1st Wis.; 5th and 8th Iowa; 2d and 8th Ind.; 1st and 4th Tenn.; 4th Ky. Cav. Union, 100 killed and wounded, 500 missing.
McCullough's Store, Mo., July 26 and Aug. 3, 1861.
McDonald County, Mo., Aug. 5, 1864.
McDowell, or Bull Pasture, Va., May 8, 1862. 25th, 32d, 75th, and 82d Ohio; 3d W. Va.; 1st W. Va. Cav.; 1st Conn. Cav.; 1st Ind. Battery. Union, 28 killed, 225 wounded; Confed., 100 killed, 200 wounded.
McGuire's Ferry, Ark., Sept. 23, 1862.
McKay's Point, S. C., Dec. 22, 1864.
McLean's Ford, or Liberty Mills, Va., Oct. 15, 1863. N. J. Brigade of 3d Corps, Army of Potomac. Union, 2 killed, 25 wounded; Confed., 60 killed and wounded.
McMinnville, Tenn., July 6, 1862, and Sept. 28, 1863.
McMinnville, or Little Pond, Tenn., Aug. 30, 1862. 26th Ohio; 17th and 58th Ind.; 8th Ind. Battery. Confed., 1 killed, 20 wounded.
McMinnville, Tenn., April 20, 1863. 1st Brigade of Cav., Army of the Cumberland.
McMinnville, Tenn., Oct. 3, 1863. 4th Tenn. Inf. Union, 7 killed, 31 wounded, 350 missing; Confed., 23 killed and wounded.
Meadow Bluff, W. Va., Dec. 12, 1863. (See Big Sewell.)
Meadow Bridge, Va., May 12, 1864. 1st and 3d Divs., Cav. Corps, Army of Potomac. (Sheridan's Raid.)
Mechanicsburg, Miss., May 29, 1863.
Mechanicsburg and Sartoria, Miss., June 4, 1863. 5th Ill. Cav.; 8th Wis. Inf.
Mechanicsburg, Miss., June 7, 1863.
Mechanicsburg, Miss., May 24, 1863.
Mechanicsburg, Miss., May 29, 1863. Part of 17th Corps, under Maj.-Gen. F. P. Blair.
Mechanicsville, or Ellison's Mills, Va., June 26, 1862. 5th Corps and McCall's Div., 1st Corps. (See, also, Seven Days' Retreat.)
Medalia, Minn., April 16, 1863. 18 Soldiers, 7th Minn. Inf. (Indian Fight.)
Medley, near Williamsport, W. Va., Jan. 29, 1864. 1st and 14th W. Va.; 23d Ill.; 2d Md.; Potomac Home Brigade; 4th W. Va. Cav.; Ringgold Cav. Union, 10 killed, 7 wounded; Confed., 100 wounded.
Medoc, Mo., Aug. 23, 1861.
Medon Sta., or Toon's Sta., Tenn., Aug. 31, 1862. 45th Ill.; 7th Mo. Union, 3 killed, 13 wounded, 43 missing.
Meffleton Lodge, Ark., June 29, 1864.

Memphis, Mo., July 18, 1862. 9th and 11th Mo. State Militia; 2d Mo. Cav. Union, 13 killed, 35 wounded; Confed, 23 killed.
Memphis, Tenn., May 2, 1864. 7th Kan. Cav.
Memphis, Tenn., Aug. 21, 1864. Detachments of 8th Iowa, 108th and 113th Ill., 39th, 40th, and 41st Wis., 61st U. S. Colored Troops, 3d and 4th Iowa Cav., Battery G, 1st Mo. Light Artil. Union, 30 killed, 100 wounded; Confed., 100 killed and wounded.
Memphis, Tenn., Oct. 4, 1864. One Company 7th Ind. Cav.
Memphis, Tenn., Dec. 14, 1864. 4th Iowa Cav. Union, 3 killed, 6 wounded.
Meridian, Miss., Feb. 9 to 19, 1864. Troops under Gen. Sherman.
Merrill's Crossing to Lamine Crossing, or Marshall, Arrow Rock, Black Water, and Jonesboro, Mo., Oct. 12 and 13, 1863. 1st, 4th, and 7th Mo. Militia Cav.; 1st Mo. Militia Battery; Mo. enrolled Militia.
Merriweather's Ferry, Tenn., Aug. 15, 1862. One Company 2d Ill. Cav. Union, 3 killed, 6 wounded; Confed., 20 killed.
Messenger's Bridge, Miss., Oct. 5, 1863.
Messenger's Ferry, Miss., July 1 and 2, 1863. (See Black River.)
Messilla, New Mexico, Aug. 3, 1861. 7th U. S. Inf. and U. S. Mounted Rifles. Union, 3 killed, 6 wounded; Confed., 12 killed.
Metamora, Miss., Oct. 5, 1862. (See Big Hatchie River.)
Metley's Ford, Tenn., Nov. 4, 1863. Cav., Army of Ohio.
Mexico, Mo., July 15, 1861.
Mezeal River, Cal., May 29, 1864.
Michel's Creek, Miss., May 5, 1863.
Middleburg, Miss., Dec. 24, 1862. 115 men, 12th Mich. Inf. Union, 9 wounded; Confed., 9 killed, 11 wounded.
Middleburg, Tenn., Sept. 21, 1862.
Middleburg, Va., March 28, 1862. 28th Pa. Inf.
Middleburg, Va., June 19, 1863. 1st Me.; 2d, 4th, and 10th N. Y.; 4th and 16th Pa.; 6th Ohio Cav.
Middle Creek and Prestonburg, Ky., Jan. 10, 1862. 40th and 42d Ohio; 14th and 22d Ky. Inf. Union, 2 killed, 25 wounded; Confed., 40 killed.
Middle Creek Fork, or Buckhannon, W. Va., July 6, 1861. One Company 3d Ohio. Union, 1 killed, 6 wounded. Confed., 6 killed.
Middleton, Md., July 7, 1864. (See Hagar's Mountain, or Solomon's Gap.)
Middleton, Tenn., Jan. 5, 1863. Cav., Army of the Cumberland.
Middleton, Tenn., Jan. 31, 1863. 2d and 3d Tenn. Cav.
Middleton, Tenn., May 21, 1863. 4th Mich.; 3d Ind.; 7th Pa.; 3d and 4th Ohio and 4th U. S. Cav.; 39th Ind. Mounted Inf.
Middleton, Shelbyville Pike, Tenn., June 24, 1863. 1st Cav. Div., Army of the Cumberland.
Middleton, Tenn., Jan. 14, 1863. 35th Ohio Inf.
Middletown, Va., March 7, 1862, and Nov. 12, 1864.
Middletown, Va., May 24, 1862. 48th Pa.; 28th N. Y. Inf.; 1st Me. and 1st Vt. Cav. One Battery, N. Y. Artil.
Middletown, Va., June 11th, 1863. 13th Pa. Cav.; 87th Pa. Inf.; Battery L, 5th U. S. Artil. Confed., 8 killed, 42 wounded.
Middletown, Va., Oct. 19, 1864. (See Cedar Creek.)
Middle Yager, Cal., June 28, 1863.
Milford, or Shawnee Mound, or Black Water, Mo., Dec. 18, 1861. 27th Ohio; 8th, 12th, 22d, and 24th Ind.; 31st Kan.; 1st Iowa Cav.; detachment of U. S. Cav.; 2 batteries, 1st Mo. Light Artil. Union, 2 killed, 8 wounded. Confed., 1,300 captured.
Milford, Va., July 2, 1862. 1st Me. Cav.
Milford, Va., Dec. 2, 1862.
Milford Sta., Va., May 20, 1864. 1st Cav. Div., Army of Potomac.

Mill Creek, and Dug Gap, Ga., May 7, 1864. 20th Corps, Army of the Cumberland.
Mill Creek, Mo., April 24, 1863.
Mill Creek, Tenn., Nov. 27, 1862.
Mill Creek, Tenn., Dec. 2 and 3, 1864. (See Block House No. 2.)
Mill Creek Gap., Ga., May 5 to 9, 1864. (See Rocky-face Ridge.)
Mill Creek Mills, W. Va., Oct. 26, 1861. (See Romney.)
Mill Creek Valley, W. Va., Nov. 13, 1863.
Millen Grove, Ga., Dec. 1, 1864. 1st Ky. and 8th Ind. Cav.
Milliken's Bend, La., Aug. 18, 1862. (See Capture of steamer "Fairplay.")
Milliken's Bend, or Ashland, La., June 6 to 8, 1863. 5th U. S. Colored Heavy Artil.; 23d Iowa Inf.; 49th and 51st U. S. Colored Troops, assisted by U. S. Steamers "Choctaw" and "Lexington." Union, 154 killed, 223 wounded, 115 missing; Confed., 125 killed, 400 wounded, 200 missing. (No quarter given to the Union Troops.)
Mill Point, W. Va., Nov. 5, 1863. 14th Pa. and 3d W. Va. Cav.
Mill Springs, or Logan's Cross Roads, Beech Grove, Somerset, and Fishing Creek, Ky., Jan. 19 and 20, 1862. 9th Ohio; 2d Minn.; 4th Ky.; 10th Ind.; 1st Ky. Cav. Union, 38 killed, 104 wounded; Confed., 190 killed, 160 wounded. Confed., Gen. Zollikoffer killed.
Millsville, or Wentzville, Mo., July 16, 1861. 8th Mo. Inf. Union, 7 killed, 1 wounded; Confed., 7 killed.
Milltown Bluff, S. C., July 10, 1863.
Millwood, Va., Dec. 17, 1864.
Milton, Black Water, Fla., Oct. 26, 1864. 19th Iowa Inf.; 2d Me. Cav.
Milton, Tenn., Feb. 18, 1863, 2d Mich. and 3d Ohio Cav. March 20, 1863, 80th and 123rd Ill.,105th O., 101 Ind.
Mine Creek, Miria des Cygnes, and Little Osage River, Kan., Oct. 25, 1864. Pleasanton's and Curtis' Cav.
Mineral Point, Mo., Sept. 27, 1864.

Mine Run, Va., Nov. 26 to 28, 1863. (Including engagements at Raccoon's Ford and Bartlett's Mills, or Locust Grove, on the 26th, also, Robertson's Tavern, or Payne's Tavern, on the 27th, and New Hope, or Orange Grove, on the 28th.) 1st, 2d, 3d, 5th, and 6th Corps; 1st and 2d Cav. Divs., Army of Potomac. Union, 100 killed, 400 wounded; Confed., 100 killed, 400 wounded.
Mine Explosion at Petersburg, Va., July 30, 1864. 9th Corps, supported by 18th Corps, with 2d and 5th Corps as Reserves. Union, 419 killed, 1,679 wounded, 1,910 missing; Confed., 1,200 killed, wounded, and missing.
Mingo Swamp, Mo., Feb. 3, 1863. 12th Mo. Militia.
Mint's Raid, Ga., Oct. 18, 1864.
Missionary Ridge, Tenn., Nov. 25, 1863. (See Orchard Knob, or Chattanooga.)
Mission Ridge, Tenn., Dec. 31, 1862.
Mississippi City, Miss., March 8, 1862. 26th Mass. Inf.
Mississippi Springs, Miss., May 13, 1863.
Missouri River, Dak. Ter., July 30, 1863. 6th Minn. Inf.; 1st Minn. Cav.; 3d Minn. Battery. (Indian Fight.)
Mitchell's Creek, Fla., Dec. 17, 1864. 82d U. S. Colored Troops.
Mitchell's Sta., Va., Aug. 9, 1862. (See Cedar Mountain.)
Mobile, Ala., Dec. 22, 1864.
Mobile, Ala., April 8, 9, and 12, 1865. Troops under Gen. R. S. Canby and Naval Forces.
Mobile Bay, Ala., Aug. 22 and 23, 1864. Troops and Naval Forces attack Ft. Morgan, Mobile Point.
Mobile Bay, Ala., April 11, 1865. Capture of Fts. Huger and Tracy by troops and Naval Forces.
Moccasin Gap, Va., Dec. 24, 1864. 8th Tenn. Cav. (Stoneman's Raid.)
Moffett's Sta., or Haguewood Sta., Ark., Sept. 27, 1863. Detachment of 1st Ark. Inf. Union, 2 killed, 2 wounded; Confed., 5 killed, 20 wounded.

Monaqua Springs, Mo., March 25, 1862.
Monday's Hollow, Mo., Oct. 13, 1861. (See West Glaze.)
Monetis Bluff, Cane River, La., April 23-4, 1864. Portion of 13th, 17th, and 19th Corps. (Including loss at Cloutierville, April 24.) Union, 350 killed and wounded; Confed., 400 killed and wounded.
Monocacy, Md., July 9, 1864. 1st and 2d Brigades, 3d Div., 6th Corps; detachment of 8th Corps. Union, 90 killed, 579 wounded, 1,290 missing; Confed., 400 wounded.
Monroe Co., Mo., Sept. 16 and Oct. 4, 1862.
Monroe Cross-roads, N. C., March 10, 1865. Kilpatrick's Cav. Div.
Monroe Sta., Mo., July 9 and 10, 1861. 16th Ill.; 3d Iowa; Mo. Home Guards. Union, 3 killed; Confed., 4 killed, 20 wounded, 75 prisoners.
Montevallo, Mo., April 14, 1862. Two Companies, 1st Iowa Cav. Union, 2 killed, 6 wounded; Confed., 2 killed, 10 wounded.
Montevallo, or Church in the Woods, Mo., Aug. 6, 1862. 3d Wis. Cav. Union, 1 wounded, 3 missing.
Monterey, Owen Co., Ky., June 11, 1862. Capt. Blood's Mounted Provost Guards; 13th Ind. Battery. Union, 2 killed; Confed., 100 captured.
Monterey, Tenn., April 28, 1862. 2d Iowa Cav. Union, 1 killed, 3 wounded; Confed., 5 killed.
Monterey, Tenn., May 13, 1862. Part of Brig.-Gen. M. L. Smith's Brigade. Union, 2 wounded; Confed., 2 killed, 3 wounded.
Monterey, Va., April 12, 1862. 75th Ohio Inf.; 1st W. Va. Cav. Union, 3 wounded.
Monterey Gap, and Smithsburg, Md., July 4, 1863. Kilpatrick's Cav. Union, 30 killed and wounded; Confed., 30 killed and wounded, 100 prisoners. (Loss including Fairfield, Pa., July 5.)
Montevallo, Ala., March 13, 1865.
Montevallo and Six Mile Creek, Ala.,

March 30 and 31, 1865. Advance Cav.
Montgomery, Ala., April 12 and 13, 1865. 2d Brigade, 1st Cav. Div., Military Div. of the Miss. (Wilson's Raid.)
Montgomery, Ga., July 18, 1864. (See Chewa Sta.)
Monticello, Ark., Jan. 16, 1864.
Monticello, Ark., March 18, 1864. 4th Mo. Cav.
Monticello, Ky., May 1, 1863. 2d Tenn.; 1st Ky.; 2d and 7th Ohio Cav.; 112th Ill. Mounted Inf.; 45th Ohio Inf.
Monticello and Rocky Gap, Ky., June 9, 1863. 2d and 7th Ohio Cav.; 1st Ky. Cav.; 45th Ohio and 2d Tenn. Mounted Inf. Union, 4 killed, 26 wounded; Confed., 20 killed, 80 wounded.
Moorefield, or South Fork, W. Va., Nov. 9, 1862. 23d Ill.; 1st N. Y. Cav.; Ringgold and Washington Cav.
Moorefield, W. Va., Jan. 3, 1863. 116th Ohio Inf.
Moorefield, W. Va., Sept. 5, 1863. 1st W. Va. Inf.
Moorefield, W. Va., Sept. 11, 1863.
Moorefield, W. Va., Feb, 4, 1864. 23d Ill. Inf.; portion of the Troops of the Dep't of W. Va.
Moorefield, W. Va., Aug. 7, 1864. 14th Pa.; 8th Ohio; 1st and 3d W. Va., and 1st N. Y. Cav. Union, 9 killed, 22 wounded; Confed., 100 killed and wounded, 400 missing.
Moore's Bluff, Miss., Sept. 29, 1864.
Moore's Mills, Mo., July 24, 1862.
Moore's Mills, Mo., July 28 and 29, 1862. 9th Mo.; 3d Iowa Cav.; 2d Mo. Cav.; 3d Ind. Battery. Union, 19 killed, 21 wounded; Confed., 30 killed, 100 wounded.
Moreau Bottom, near Jefferson City, Mo., Oct. 7, 1864. Mo. Militia Cav., Inf., and Artil. (Price's Invasion.)
Moresburg, Tenn., Dec. 10, 1863. Cav., Army of the Ohio.
Morgan County, Tenn., Feb. 2, 1862.
Morganfield, Ky., Aug. 31, 1862.

Morgan's Mills, Spring River, Ark., Feb. 9, 1864. Detachment of 4th Ark.; 11th Mo. Cav. and 1st Neb. Cav. Union. 1 killed, 4 wounded; Confed., 65 killed and wounded.
Morgan's Raid into Ky., Ind., and Ohio, July 1 to 26, 1863. (Including skirmishes at Burkesville, Columbia, Green River Bridge, Lebanon, and Brandenburg, Ky.; Corydon and Vernon, Ind. Pursued and captured by Brig.-Gens. Hobson and Shackleford's Cav. Capture of the larger part on Buffington Island, Ohio, and final capture at New Lisbon, Ohio, July 26.) Union, 33 killed, 97 wounded, 805 missing; Confed., 795 killed and wounded, 4,104 captured.
Morgansville, Ky., Sept. 2, 1862. 8th Ky. Cav. and Union Troops under Col. Shackleford.
Morgantown, Ky., Oct. 29, 1861. (See Woodbury.)
Morgantown, Ky., Oct. 24, 1862.
Morganzia, La., Sept. 29, 1863. 19th Iowa; 26th Ind. Union, 14 killed, 40 wounded, 400 missing. (See, also, Sterling's Plantation.)
Morganzia, La., May 18 and 30, and Nov. 23, 1864.
Morning Sun, Tenn., July 1, 1862. 57th Ohio. Union, 4 wounded; Confed., 11 killed, 26 wounded.
Moro Bottom and Moro Creek, Ark., April 25 and 26, 1864. 33d and 40th Iowa; 5th Kan.; 2d and 4th Mo.; and 1st Iowa Cav. Union, 5 killed, 14 wounded.
Moreauville, La., May 14 to 16, 1864. (See Mansura.)
Morris Island, S. C., July 10, 1863.
Morris Mills, W. Va., July 31, 1863.
Morristown, Mo., Sept. 17, 1861. 5th 6th, and 9th Kan. Cav.; 1st Kan. Battery. Union, 2 killed, 6 wounded; Confed., 7 killed.
Morristown, Tenn., Dec. 1, 1861.
Morristown, Tenn., Dec. 10, 1863. Cav. Army of the Ohio.
Morristown, Tenn., Oct. 28, 1864. Gen. Gillem's Cav. Union, 8 killed, 42 wounded; Confed., 240 missing.

Morristown, Tenn., Nov. 13, 1864. (See Bull's Gap.)
Morton, Miss., Feb. 7 and 8, 1864. Cav. of Gen. Sherman's Forces. (Exp. to Meridian.)
Morton's Ford, Va., May 27, 1863.
Morton's Ford, Va., Feb. 6, 1864. Portion of 2d Corps. Union, 10 killed, 201 wounded; Confed., 100 missing.
Mosby's surrender, Va., April 17, 1865. (See Berryville.)
Moscow, Ark., April 13, 1864. 18th Iowa; 6th Kan. Cav.; 2d Ind. Battery. Union, 5 killed, 17 wounded; Confed., 30 killed and wounded.
Moscow, Tenn., Feb. 18 and Dec. 2 and 3, 1863.
Moscow, Tenn., Nov. 4, 1863. Cav. Brigade, 16th Corps.
Moscow, Tenn., June 15, 1864. 55th U. S. Colored Troops.
Moscow Sta., or Wolf River Bridge, Miss., Dec. 4, 1863. Cav. Div., 16th Corps.
Moses Creek, Ga., Oct. 3, 1864.
Mossy Creek, Tenn., Dec. 29, 1863. (See Talbot's Sta.)
Mossy Creek, Tenn., Jan. 13, 1864. McCooke's Cav. Confed., 14 killed.
Mossy Creek Sta., Tenn., Dec. 24, 1863.
Moulton, Ala., May 28 and 29, 1864. 1st, 3d, and 4th Ohio Cav.
Mound Plantation, La., June 29, 1863.
Mountain Fork, Ark., Feb. 4, 1864.
Mountain Grove, Mo., March 9, 1862. 10th Mo. Cav. Union, 10 killed, 2 wounded.
Mountain Home, Mo., Oct. 17, 1862.
Mountain Run, Va., Nov. 27, 1863.
Mountain Store and Big Piney, Mo., July 25 and 26, 1862. Three Companies, 3d Mo. Cav.; Battery L, 2d Mo. Artil. Confed., 5 killed.
Mountain Store, Mo., May 26, 1863.
Mount Carmel, Tenn., Nov. 29, 1864. (See Spring Hill.)
Mount Clio, S. C., Feb. 26, 1865. Detachment of Mounted Men under Capt. Duncan.
Mount Crawford, Va., June 5, 1864. (See Piedmont.)

Mount Crawford, Va., Feb. 28, 1865. 3d Brigade, 3d Cav. Div., Army of Potomac. (Sheridan's Raid.)

Mount Elba, Ark., March 30, 1864. 7th Mo. and 5th Kan. Cav.; 28th Wis. Inf.

Mount Elba Ferry, Ark., April 26, 1864.

Mount Ivy, or Ivy Hills, Miss., Feb. 22, 1864. (See Okalona.)

Mount Jackson, Va., May 23, 1862, and Nov. 22, 1864.

Mount Jackson, Va., Nov. 17, 1863. 1st N. Y. Cav. Union, 2 killed, 3 wounded; Confed., 27 missing.

Mount Olive, N. C., March 19, 1865.

Mount Olive, Va., Oct. 9, 1864.

Mount Pleasant, Ala., April 1, 1865. Portion of Cav., Gen. Canby's Forces.

Mount Pleasant, Miss., May 21, 1864. 4th Mo. Cav. Union, 2 killed, 1 wounded.

Mount Pleasant Landing, La., May 15, 1864. 67th U. S. Colored Troops. Union, 3 killed, 5 wounded.

Mount Sterling, Ky., July 29, 1862. 18th Ky. Inf. and Home Guards.

Mount Sterling, Ky., March 22, 1863. 10th Ky. Cav. Union, 4 killed, 10 wounded; Confed., 8 killed, 13 wounded.

Mount Sterling, Ky., June 9, 1864. Burbridge's Cav. Union, 35 killed, 150 wounded; Confed., 50 killed, 200 wounded, 250 captured.

Mount Tabor Church, N. C., July 26, 1863. (See Pattacassey Creek.)

Mount Vernon, Ark., May 11, 1863. 5th Kan. Cav.; 5th Ill. Cav.

Mount Vernon, Mo., Sept. 30, 1864.

Mount Washington, Ky., Oct. 2, 1862. Advance Troops, Army of the Ohio.

Mount Zion and Hallsville, Mo., Dec. 28, 1861. Birge's Sharpshooters and 3d Mo. Cav. Union, 5 killed, 63 wounded; Confed., 25 killed, 150 wounded.

Mount Zion Church, Va., July 6, 1864. 2d Mass. Cav.

Mouth of Monocacy River, Md., Oct. 11, 1862. 3d and 4th Me. Inf.

Mud Creek, Ala., Jan. 5, 1865.

Mud Creek, Ga., June 18, 1864.

Muddy Run, near Culpepper, Va., Nov. 8, 1863. 1st Div., Cav., Army of Potomac. Union, 4 killed, 25 wounded.

Mud Springs, Ind. Ter., Feb. 8, 1865. (Indian Fight.)

Mulberry Gap, or Wyerman's Mills, Tenn., Feb. 22, 1864. 9th Tenn Cav. Union, 13 killed and wounded, 256 captured.

Muldraugh's Hill, Ky., Dec. 28, 1862. 6th Ind. Cav.

Mumford's Sta., Blue Mount, Ala., April 13, 1865. 1st Brigade, 1st Cav. Div., Military Div. of the Miss. (Wilson's Raid.)

Munfordville, Ky., Dec. 17, 1861. (See Rowlett's Sta.)

Munfordville, Ky., Sept. 14 to 16, 1862. 18th U. S. Inf.; 28th and 33d Ky.; 17th, 50th, 60th, 67th, 68th, 74th, 78th, and 89th Ind.; Conkle's Battery, 13th Ind. Artil.; and Louisville Provost Guard. Union, 50 killed, 3,566 captured and missing; Confed., 714 killed and wounded.

Munfordville, Ky., Sept. 21, 1862. 3d Ohio Cav.

Munson's Hill, Va., Aug. 31, 1861. Two Companies 23d N. Y. Inf. Union, 2 killed, 2 wounded.

Munson's Hill, or Camp Advance, Va., Sept. 29, 1861. 69th Pa., through mistake, fired into the 71st Pa., killing 9, wounding 25.

Murfreesboro', Tenn., July 13, 1862. 9th Mich.; 3d Minn.; 4th Ky. Cav.; 7th Pa. Cav.; 1st Ky. Battery. Un'on, 33 killed, 62 wounded, 800 missing; Confed., 50 killed, 100 wounded.

Murfreesboro', or Stone River, Tenn., Dec. 31, 1862, to Jan. 2, 1863. Army of the Cumberland, Maj.-Gen. Rosecrans; Right Wing, McCooke's Corps; Centre, Thomas' Corps; Left Wing, Crittenden's Corps. Union, 1,533 killed, 7,245 wounded, 2,800 missing; Confed., 14,560 killed, wounded, and missing. Union Brig.-Gen. Sill killed; Brig.-Gen.

Kirke wounded; Confed.,Brig.-Gens. Raines and Hanson killed; Brig.-Gens. Chalmers and Davis wounded.
Murfreesboro', Tenn., Jan. 26, 1863. Detachment of 10th Mich. Vols.
Murfreesboro',Shelbyville,Tenn.,June 6, 1863. 2d and 8th Ind. Cav.
Murfreesboro', Tenn., Sept. 3, 1864. 100th U. S. Colored Troops.
Murfreesboro', or Cedars, Tenn., Dec. 5 to 8, 1864. Gen. Rosseau's Troops. Union, 30 killed, 175 wounded; Confed., 197 missing.
Murfreesboro', Tenn., Dec. 15, 1864. Gen. Rosseau's Troops.
Murfreesboro', Tenn., Dec. 24, 1864. 12th U. S. Colored Troops.
Murfreesboro' Road, Tenn., Oct. 4, 1863. 2d Ky. Cav. and Wilder's Brigade of Mounted Inf.
Muscle Shoals, Raccoon Ford, Ala., Oct. 30, 1864. 1st Brigade, 1st Cav. Div., Army of the Cumberland.
Mustang Island, Aranzas Pass, Tex., Nov. 17, 1863. 13th and 14th Me.; 34th Iowa; 18th Ind.; Battery F, 1st Mo. Artil., assisted by U. S. Steamer "Monongahela."
Myrestown, Va., Nov. 18, 1864. Detachment of 91st Ohio. Union, 60 killed and wounded; Confed., 10 killed and wounded.

NAMOZIN Church and Willicomack, Va., April 3, 1865. 3d Cav. Div., Army of Potomac.
Nansemond, Va., April 14, 1863.
Nansemond River, Va., May 1, 1863. (See South Quay Bridge.)
Nansemond River, Va., May 3, 1863. Gen. J. J. Peck's Troops.
Nansemond River, Va., April 14 and 15, 1864. (See James River.)
Narrows, Ga., Oct. 11, 1864. Garrard's Cav. Div., Army of the Cumberland.
Nashville, Tenn., March 8, 1862. 1st Wis. Inf.; 4th Ohio Cav. Union, 1 killed, 2 wounded; Confed., 4 killed.
Nashville, Tenn., July 21, 1862. 2d Ky. Inf.

Nashville,Tenn., Oct. 20, 1862. Troops under Col. J. F. Miller.
Nashville, Tenn., Nov. 5, 1863. 16th and 51st Ill.; 69th Ohio; 14th Mich.; 5th Tenn. Cav.; 7th Pa. Cav. Union, 26 wounded; Confed., 23 captured.
Nashville, Tenn., May 24, 1864. 15th U. S. Colored Troops. Union, 4 killed, 8 wounded.
Nashville, Tenn., Dec. 1 to 14, 1864. (Skirmishing in front of Nashville.) 4th, 23d, and 1st and 2d Divs., 16th Corps; Wilson's Cav. Union, 16 killed, 100 wounded.
Nashville, or Brentwood, Overton's Hills, Tenn., Dec. 15 and 16, 1864. 4th Corps; 1st and 3d Div., 16th Corps; 23d Corps; Wilson's Cav.; detachments of Colored Troops; Convalescents. Union, 400 killed, 1,740 wounded; Confed., 4,462 missing.
Natchez, Miss., Nov. 11, 1863. 58th U. S. Colored Troops.
Natchez, Miss., Dec. 7 and 10, 1863. One Company, 4th Iowa Cav.
Natchitoches, La., March 31, 1864. Cav. of 19th Corps. (Red River Exp.)
Natchitoches, La., April 19, 1864. 4th Brigade, Cav. Div., 19th Corps.
Natchitoches, La., May 5, 1864.
Natural Bridge, Fla., March 6, 1865. 2d and 99th U. S. Colored Troops. Union, 22 killed, 46 wounded.
Nauvoo, Ala., Jan. 2, 1865. 15th Pa. and detachments of 2d Tenn. and 10th,12th,and 13th Ind. Cav. (Capture and destruction of Hood's supply and pontoon train.)
Near Pine Bluff, Ark., Sept. 9, 1864.
Near Point Washington, Fla., Feb. 9, 1864.
Nelson's Farm, Va., June 30, 1862. (See White Oak Swamp, also, Seven Days' Retreat.)
Neosho, Mo., April 26, 1862. 1st Mo. Cav. Union, 3 killed, 3 wounded; Confed., 30 wounded, 62 prisoners.
Neosho, Mo., May 31, 1862. 10th Ill. Cav.; 14th Mo. Militia Cav. Union, 2 killed, 3 wounded.

Neosho, Mo., Sept. 1 to 4, and Dec. 15, 1862; March 2, and Nov. 5, 1863; June 3 and Nov. 10, 1864.

Neosho, Mo., Oct. 4, 1863. Three Companies, 6th Mo. Militia Cav. Union, 1 killed, 14 wounded, 43 missing.

Neuse River, N. C., April 10, 1865. Advance of Gen. Sherman's Army.

New Albany, Miss., April 19, 1863. 7th Ill. Cav.

New Albany, Miss., Oct. 5, 1863, and July 10, 1864.

Newark, Mo., Aug. 1, 1862. 73 men, 11th Mo. State Militia. Union, 4 killed, 4 wounded, 60 captured; Confed., 73 killed and wounded.

New Baltimore, Salem, and Thoroughfare Gap, Va., Nov. 5, 1862. Cav. Brigade, Army of Potomac.

Newbern, N. C., March 14, 1862. 51st N. Y.; 8th, 10th, and 11th Conn.; 21st, 23d, 24th, 25th, and 27th Mass.; 9th N. J.; 51st Pa.; 4th and 5th R. I. Union, 91 killed, 466 wounded; Confed., 64 killed, 106 wounded, 413 captured.

Newbern, N. C., May 22, 1862. Company I, 17th Mass. Inf. Union, 3 killed, 8 wounded.

Newbern, or Bachelor's Creek, N. C., Nov. 11, 1862.

Newbern, N. C., Feb. 27, 1863. Detachment of 3d N. Y. Cav.

Newbern, N. C., March 14, 1863. Troops of Depts. of Va. and N. C., supported by Naval Forces.

Newbern, N. C., Feb. 1 to 3, 1864. (See Bachelor Creek.)

Newbern, N. C., Feb. 29, and May 5 and 6, 1864.

New Bridge, Va., May 24, 1862. 4th Mich. Inf. Union, 1 killed, 10 wounded; Confed., 60 killed and wounded, 27 captured.

New Cider Mills, Tenn., Nov. 29, 1864.

New Creek, W. Va., June 17, 1861. Local Militia.

New Creek, W. Va., Aug. 4, 1864.

New Creek Valley, W. Va., Feb. 1, 1864. Detachment of Inf.

New Hope, Ky., July 11, 1862. 33d Ohio Inf.

New Hope, or Orange Grove, Va., Nov. 28, 1863. (See Mine Run.)

New Hope Church, Ga., May 25 to June 4, 1864. (See Dallas.)

New Kent C. H., Va., May 9, 1862. (See Slatersville.)

New Kent C. H., Va., March 2, 1864.

New Lisbon, Ohio, July 26, 1863. Portion of Gen. Shackleford's Cav. Surrender of Morgan and his Raiders.

New Madrid, Mo., March 3, 1862. 5th Iowa; 59th Ind.; 39th and 63d Ohio; 2d Mich. Cav.; 7th Ill. Cav. Union, 1 killed, 3 wounded.

New Madrid, Mo., March 13, 1862. 10th and 16th Ill.; 27th, 39th, 43d, and 63d Ohio; 3d Mich. Cav.; 1st U. S. Inf.; Bissell's Mo. Engineers. Union, 50 wounded; Confed., 100 wounded.

New Madrid, Mo., Aug. 7, 1863. One Company 24th Mo. Inf. Union, 1 killed, 1 wounded.

New Madrid Bend, Tenn., Oct. 22, 1863. 32d Iowa Inf.

New Market, Va., May 15, 1864. Maj.-Gen. Sigel's Command, Army of W. Va. Union, 120 killed, 560 wounded, 240 missing; Confed., 85 killed, 320 wounded.

New Market, Va., July 27 and 28, 1864. (See Deep Bottom.)

New Market, or New Market Heights, Va., Oct. 7, 1864. 3d Div., Custer's Cav. (See, also, Darbytown Roads.)

New Market Bridge, near Newport News, Va., Dec. 22, 1861. 20th N. Y. Inf. Union, 6 wounded; Confed., 10 killed, 20 wounded.

New Market Cross Ronds, Va., June 30, 1862. (See White Oak Swamp, also, Seven Days' Retreat.)

New Market Heights, Va., June 24, 1864.

New Market Heights, or Chapin's Farm, Laurel Hill, Forts Harrison and Gilmore, Va., Sept. 28 to 30, 1864. 10th Corps; 18th Corps and Kautz's Cav. Union, 400 killed, 2,029 wounded; Confed., 2,000 killed and wounded.

LIST OF BATTLES AND ENGAGEMENTS. 171

Newman, Ga., July 30 and 31, 1864. Cav., Army of the Cumberland. (McCooke's Raid.)
Newport Barracks, N. C., Feb. 1 to 3, 1864. (See Bachelor Creek.)
Newport News, Va., July 5, 1861. One Company, 9th N. Y. Inf. Union, 6 wounded; Confed., 3 wounded.
New Providence, Tenn., Sept. 6, 1862.
New River, La., Feb. 9, 1864.
New River Bridge, Va., May 9 and 10, 1864. (See Cloyd's Mountain.)
Newton, La., Oct. 4, 1863.
Newton Co., Mo., Feb. 10, 1863.
Newtonia, Mo., Aug. 5 and Oct. 4, 5 and 7, 1862, and Sept. 27, 1863.
Newtonia, Mo., Sept. 13, 1862. 3d and 6th Mo. Militia Cav.
Newtonia, Mo., Sept. 30, 1862. 1st Brigade, Army of Kan.; 4th Brigade, Mo. Militia Cav. Union, 50 killed, 80 wounded, 115 missing; Confed., 220 killed, 280 wounded.
Newtonia, Mo., Oct. 28 to 30, 1864. Col. Blunt's Cav. Confed., 250 wounded.
Newtown, Va., May 24, 1862. 28th N. Y.; 2d Mass.; 29th Pa.; 27th Ind.; 3d Wis.; two battalions of Artil.
Newtown, Ninevah, and Cedar Springs, Va., Nov. 12, 1864. Merritt's, Custer's, and Powell's Cav. Union, 84 wounded, 100 missing; Confed., 150 missing.
Newulm, Minn., Aug. 25 and 26, 1862. (Indian Fight.)
New York City, N. Y., July 13 to 15, 1863. Draft Riots. Over 1,000 rioters killed and wounded.
Nickajack Creek, or Smyrna, Vining Sta., Ga., July 2 to 5, 1864. Army of the Cumberland and Army of the Tenn., under Maj.-Gen. Sherman. Union, 60 killed, 310 wounded; Confed., 100 killed and wounded.
Nickajack Trace, Ga., April 23, 1864. Detachment of 92d Ill. Inf. Union, 5 killed, 9 wounded, 22 prisoners.
Ninevah, Va., Nov. 12, 1864. (See Newtown.)
Niobrara, Neb., Dec. 4, 1863. One Company, 7th Iowa Cav.

Nolansville, Md., Sept. 9, 1862. 3d Ind. and 8th Ill. Cav.
Nolensville, or Knob Gap, Tenn., Dec. 26, 1362. 2d Brigade, 1st Div., McCooke's Corps.
Nolensville, Tenn., Feb. 15, 1863. Detachment of 2d Minn. Inf.
Noonday Creek, Ga., June 20, 1864. (See Kenesaw Mountain.)
Norfolk, Va., May 10, 1862. 10th, 20th, and 99th N. Y.; 1st Del.; 58th Pa.; 20th Ind.; 16th Mass.; 1st N. Y. Mounted Rifles; Battery D, 4th U. S. Artil. (Surrender of Norfolk.)
North Anna, Va., May 9, 1864. (See Beaver Dam Sta.)
North Anna River, Va., July 23, 1862. 2d N. Y. and 3d Ind. Cav.
North Anna River, or Taylor's Bridge, or Jericho Ford, Totopotomoy Crk., Va., May 23 to 27, 1864. 2d, 5th, and 9th Corps, Army of Potomac, under Maj.-Gen. Meade. Union, 223 killed, 1,460 wounded, 290 missing; Confed., 2,000 killed and wounded.
Northeast River, N. C., Jan. 17, 1863. (See Pollocksville.)
North Fork, Shenandoah, Va., March 6, 1865. Part of Sheridan's Cav., under Col. Thompson.
North Mountain, Va., July 3, 1864. Detachment of 135th Ohio National Guards.
Northport, Ala., April 3, 1865. 1st Brigade; 1st Cav. Div., Military Div. of the Miss. (Wilson's Raid.)
North Shenandoah, Va., Oct. 5. 1864. 8th Ohio Cav.
Nose's Creek, Ga., June 17, 1864.
Nose's Creek, Ga., Oct. 1 to 3, 1864. (See Sweetwater.)
Nottaway Creek, Va., May 9, 1864. (See White's Bridge.)
Nottaway, C. H., Va., June 23, 1864. 3d Cav. Div., Army of Potomac. (Wilson's Raid.)
Nueces River, Tex., Aug. 10, 1862. Texas Loyalists. Union, 40 killed; Confed., 8 killed, 14 wounded.
Ny River, Va., May 8 to 18, 1864. (See Spottsylvania C. H.)

OAK Grove, or King's School House, or The Orchards, Va., June 25, 1862. Hooker's and Kearney's Divs., 3d Corps; Palmer's Brigade, 4th Corps, and part of Richardson's Div., 2d Corps. Union, 51 killed, 401 wounded, 64 missing; Confed., 65 killed, 465 wounded, 11 missing.
Oak Grove, Va., Oct. 15, 1863.
Oak Hills, Mo., Aug. 10, 1861. (See Wilson's Creek.)
Oakland, Miss., Dec. 3 and 8, 1862. 1st Ind. Cav.
Oak Woods, Va., Nov. 25, 1863.
Ocean Pond, Fla., Feb. 20, 1864. (See Olustee.)
Occoquan, Va., March 5, 1862. Detachment of 63d Pa. Inf. Union, 2 killed, 2 wounded.
Occoquan, Va., Dec. 19, 1862. Detachment of 12th Army Corps.
Occoquan, Va., Dec. 28, 1862. 2d and 17th Pa. Cav.
Occoquan Bridge, Va., Jan. 29, 1862. Detachments of 37th N. Y.; 1st N. J. Cav. Union, 1 killed, 4 wounded; Confed., 10 killed.
Occoquan Creek, Va., Nov. 12, 1861. Detachment of 1st N. Y. Cav. Union, 3 killed, 1 wounded.
Occupation of Atlanta, Ga., Sept. 2, 1864. 20th Corps. Confed, 200 captured.
Occupation of Camden, Ark., April 15 and 16, 1864. (See Liberty P. O.)
Offett's Knob, Mo., April 28, 1864. 1st Mo. Militia Cav.
Ogeechee River, or Jenk's Bridge, or Eden Sta., or Poole's Sta., Ga., Dec. 7 to 9, 1864. 15th and 17th Corps, Army of the Military Div. of the Miss.
Okalona, Ark., April 3, 1864. 27th Wis.; 40th Iowa; 77 Ohio; 43d Ill.; 1st Mo. Cav.; 13th Ill. Cav. Union, 16 killed, 74 wounded; Confed., 75 killed and wounded. (Steele's Exp.)
Okalona and Mount Ivy, or Ivy Hills, Miss., Feb. 22, 1864. Smith's and Grierson's Cav. Divs.
Old Church, Va., June 13, 1862. 5th U. S. Cav. Confed., 1 killed.

Old Church, Va., May 30, 1864. Torbett's Cav., Army of Potomac. Union, 16 killed, 74 wounded.
Old Church, Va., June 10 and 11, 1864. 3d Div., Cav. Corps, Army of Potomac.
Old Fort Wayne, or Maysville, Ark., Oct. 22, 1862. 1st Div., Army of the Frontier.
Old Oaks, La., May 18, 1864. (See Bayou de Glaize.)
Old Randolph, Mo., Sept. 14, 1861.
Old River, Lake Providence, La., Feb. 10, 1863. Detachments from 1st Kan., 17th and 95th Ill., 16th Wis. Inf., and 3d La. Cav.
Old River, La., May 22, 1864. 6th Mo. Cav.
Old River Lake, Ark., June 5 and 6, 1864.
Olive Branch, La., March 6, 1865. 4th Wis. Cav. Union, 3 killed, 2 wounded.
Olive Hill, Ky., Oct. 2, 1862. Ky. Home Guards.
Olustee, or Ocean Pond and Silver Lake, Fla., Feb. 20, 1864. 47th, 48th, and 115th N. Y.; 7th Conn.; 7th N. H.; 40th Mass.; 8th and 54th U. S. Colored Troops; 1st N. C. Colored Troops; 1st Mass. Cav.; 1st and 3d U. S. Artil.; 3d R. I. Artil. Union, 193 killed, 1,175 wounded, 460 missing; Confed., 100 killed, 400 wounded.
Oostenaula, Ga., May 13 to 16, 1864. (See Resaca.)
Opelousas, La., Oct. 21, 1863. Franklin's Div. of Gen. Bank's Troops.
Opequan, Va., Sept. 13, 1864. (See Lock's Ford.)
Opequan, Winchester, or Belle Grove, Va., Sept. 19, 1864. 8th Corps and 2d Cav. Div., Army of W. Va.; 6th Corps and 1st and 3d Cav. Divs., Army of Potomac; 1st and 2d Divs., 19th Corps, Army of the Middle Military Div. Union, 653 killed, 3,719 wounded, 618 missing; Confed., 5,500 killed, wounded, and missing.
Operations at Mine Run, Va., Nov. 26 to 28, 1863. (See Mine Run.)

Orangeburg, North Edisto River, S. C., Feb. 12, 1865. 17th Corps, Army of the Tenn.
Orange C. H., Va., July 25, 1862. Detachment from Gen. Gibson's Div.
Orange C. H., Va., Aug. 2, 1862. 5th N. Y. Cav.; 1st Vt. Cav. Union, 4 killed, 12 wounded; Confed., 11 killed, 52 captured.
Orange Grove, Va., Nov. 28, 1863. (See New Hope, also Mine Run.)
Orchard Knob, Tenn., Nov. 23, 1863. (See Chattanooga.)
Oregon County, Mo., Oct. 23, 1863, and March 19, 1864.
Oregon Mountains, Oregon, Jan. 28, 1864. 1st Cal. Cav.
Orleans, Ind., July 17, 1863. Ind. Home Guards. (Morgan's Raid.)
Osage, or Island Mounds, Mo., Oct. 29, 1862. (See Butler.)
Osage Mission, Kan., Sept. 26, 1864.
Osage River, Mo., Oct. 6, 1864. (See Prince's Place.)
Osceola, Ark., Aug. 2 and 4, 1864. 2d and 3d Mo. Militia; 1st and 6th Mo. Cav.
Osceola, Mo., Sept. 21 and 22, 1861. (See Papinsville.)
Osceola, Mo., May 27, 1862. 1st Iowa Cav. Union, 3 killed, 2 wounded.
Otter Creek, near Liberty, Va., June 16, 1864. Hunter's Command, in advance of Army of W. Va. Union, 3 killed, 15 wounded.
Overall's Creek, Tenn., Dec. 4, 1864. (See Block House No. 7.)
Overton's Hills, Tenn., Dec. 15 and 16, 1864. (See Nashville.)
Owensboro', Ky., Aug. 27, 1864. 108th U. S. Colored Troops.
Owensboro, Ky., Sept. 19 and 20, 1862. Ind. Home Guards; 14th Ky. Cav.
Owensburg, N. C., April 6, 1865.
Owen's Cross Roads, S. C., Feb. 2, 1865.
Owen's River, Cal., April 9, 1862. 2d Cal. Cav. Union, 1 killed, 2 wounded.
Owen's Valley, Cal., March 3, 1863. 2d Cal. Cav.
Owen's Valley, Cal., March 19 and April 10, 1863.

Oxford, Miss., Dec. 3, 1862. Cav. Brigade, under Col. Hatch.
Oxford, Miss., Aug. 12, 19, 22 and 23, 1864.
Oxford Bend, Ark., Oct. 28, 1862. (See Cross Hollows.)
Oxford Hill, Miss., Aug. 21 and 22, 1864. (See College Hill.)
Ox Hill, Va., Sept. 1, 1862. (See Chantilly.)
Ozark, Ark., Oct. 29, 1863.
Ozark, or Forsythe, Mo., Aug. 2, 1862. 14th Mo. State Militia. Union, 1 wounded; Confed., 3 killed, 7 wounded.
Ozark, Mo., Dec. 2, 1862. 3d and 9th Mo. Cav.
Ozark, Mo., July 14 and 15, 1864. 14th Kan. Cav.

P ADUCAH, Ky., March 25, 1864. (See Fort Anderson.)
Paint Rock R. R. Bridge, Tenn., April 28, 1862. 10th Wis. Inf. Dec. 31, 1864. 13th Wis. Inf.
Paintsville, Ky., Jan. 7, 1862. (See Jennie's Creek.)
Paintsville, Ky., April 13, 1864. Ky. Inf.
Palmer's Creek, Va., May 12 to 16, 1864. (See Fort Darling.)
Palmetto Ranch, Texas, May 13, 1865. 34th Ind.; 62d U. S. Colored Troops; 2d Texas Cav. Union, 118 killed and wounded.
Palmyra, Mo., Nov. 18, 1861. Detachment of 2d Mo. Cav. Confed., 3 killed, 5 wounded.
Palmyra, Tenn., Nov. 13, 1863. Detachment of Mounted Inf.
Palo Alto, Miss., April 21 and 22, 1863. 2d Iowa Cav.
Panther Creek, Mo., Aug. 8, 1862. 1st Mo. Militia Cav. Union, 1 killed, 4 wounded.
Panther Gap and Buffalo Gap, W. Va., June 3 to 6, 1864. Hayes' Brigade, 2d Div., Army of W. Va. Union, 25 killed and wounded; Confed., 25 killed and wounded.

Panther Springs, Tenn., March 5, 1864. One Company, 3d Tenn. Inf. Union, 2 killed, 8 wounded, 22 captured. Confed., 30 wounded.

Papinsville, Kan., Sept. 5, 1861.

Papinsville, or Osceola, Mo., Sept. 21 and 22, 1861. 5th, 6th, and 9th Kan. Cav. Union, 17 killed.

Paris, Ky., July 30, 1862. 9th Pa. Cav. Confed., 27 killed, 39 wounded.

Paris, Ky., March 11 and July 29, 1863.

Paris, Tenn., March 11, 1862. Detachments of 5th Iowa and 1st Neb. Cav.; Battery K, 1st Mo. Artil. Union, 5 killed, 5 wounded; Confed., 10 wounded.

Paris, Tenn., April 10, 1862, and Sept. 13, 1863.

Parker's Cross Roads, or Red Mound, Tenn., Dec. 30, 1862. 18th, 106th, 119th, and 122d Ill.; 27th, 39th, and 63d Ohio; 50th Ind.; 39th Iowa; 7th Tenn.; 7th Wis. Battery. Union, 23 killed, 139 wounded, 58 missing; Confed., 50 killed, 150 wounded, 300 missing.

Parkersville, Mo., July 18, 1861. (See Harrisonville.)

Parkersville, Mo., Dec. 6, 1862.

Pass Christian, Miss., April 4, 1862. 9th Conn. and 6th Mass. Artil.

Pastasquotank, N. C., Aug. 18, 1863. 1st N. Y. Mounted Rifles; 11th Pa. Cav.

Pass Manchas, La., March 20, 1864.

Pattacassey Creek, or Mount Tabor Church, N. C., July 26, 1863. Brig.-Gen. Heckman's Troops. Union, 3 killed, 17 wounded.

Patten, Mo., July 26, 1862. Mo. Militia.

Patterson, Mo., April 20, 1863. 3d Mo. Militia Cav. Union, 12 killed, 7 wounded, 41 missing.

Patterson Creek, or Kelly's Island, Va., June 26, 1861. 11th Ind. Inf. Union, 1 killed, 1 wounded; Confed., 7 killed, 2 wounded.

Patterson Creek, W. Va., Feb. 3, 1864.

Pattersonville, Atchafalaya River, La., March 28, 1863. Detachment of 12th Conn. and 160th N. Y. on board the U. S. Gunboat "Diana." Union, 4 killed, 14 wounded, 99 missing.

Pawnee Forks, Kan., Nov. 25, 1864. One Company, 1st Col. Cav.

Pawnee Reservation, Ind. Ter., June 20, 1863. 2d Neb. Cav.

Paw Paw Fur'ce, W. Va., Nov. 6, '62.

Payne's Plantation, Miss., Aug. 18, 1863.

Payne's Tavern, Va., Nov. 27, 1863. (See Robertson's Tavern, also Mine Run, Nov. 26.)

Peach Orchard or Allen's Farm, Va., June 29, 1862. Richardson's and Sedgwick's Divs., 2d Corps. (See, also, Seven Days' Retreat.)

Peach Tree Creek (Hood's 1st Sortie), Ga., July 20, 1864. 4th, 14th, and 20th Corps, under Maj.-Gen. Geo. H. Thomas. Union, 300 killed, 1,410 wounded; Confed., 1,113 killed, 2,500 wounded, 1,183 missing; Confed., Brig.-Gens. Featherstone, Long, Pettis, and Stevens killed.

Pea Ridge, Ark., March 6 to 8, 1862. (Including engagements at Bentonville, March 6; Leetown, March 7; Elkhorn Tavern, March 8.) 25th, 35th, 36th, 37th, 44th, and 59th Ill.; 2d, 3d, 12th, 15th, 17th, 24th, and Phelp's, Mo.; 8th, 18th, and 22d Ind.; 4th and 9th Iowa; 3d Iowa Cav.; 3d and 15th Ill. Cav.; 1st, 4th, 5th, and 6th Mo. Cav.; Batteries D and F, 2d Mo. Light Artil.; 2d Ohio Battery; 1st Ind. Battery; Battery A, 2d Ill. Artil. Union, 203 killed, 972 wounded, 174 missing; Confed., 1,100 killed, 2,500 wounded, 1,600 captured and missing. Union, Brig.-Gen. Aspoth and Acting Brig.-Gen. Carr wounded; Confed., Brig.-Gen. McCullough and Acting Brig.-Gen. McIntosh killed.

Pea Ridge, Mo., Feb. 17, 1862. (See Sugar Creek.)

Pea Vine Creek, Ga., Nov. 27, 1863. (See Ringgold.)

Pechacho Pass, Dak. Ter., April 15, 1862. 1st Cal. Cav. Union, 3 killed, 3 wounded.

Penbescott Bayou, near Osceola, Ark., April 8, 1864. Battery I, 2d Mo. Light Artil.
Pendleton, Mo., Oct. 29, 1864.
Pensacola, Fla., Nov. 23, 1861. (See Fort Pickens.)
Pensacola, Fla., April 2, 1864. One Company, 14th N. Y. Cav.
Peralto, New Mexico, April 15, 1862. 4th and 5th New Mexico Inf.
Perry County, Ark., Nov. 9, 1862.
Perryville, Ark., Aug. 26, 1863. 6th Mo. Militia; 3d Wis. and 2d Kan. Cav.; 2d Ind. Battery.
Perryville, or Chapin Hill, Ky., Oct. 8, 1862. 1st Corps, Army of the Ohio, Maj.-Gen. McCooke; 3d Corps, Brig.-Gen. Gilbert. Union, 916 killed, 2,943 wounded, 489 missing; Confed., 2,500 killed, wounded, and missing; Union, Brig.-Gens. J. S. Jackson and Terrill killed; Confed., Brig.-Gens. Claberne, Wood, and Brown wounded.
Perryville, Ind. Ter., Aug. 26, 1863.
Petersburg, Chapel Hill, and Harpeth River, Tenn., March 2 and 4, 1863. 1st Tenn. Cav.
Petersburg, Va., June 10, 1864, to April 2, 1865. (Siege of Petersburg.)
Petersburg, Va., June 10, 1864. Portion of 10th Corps and Kautz's Cav. Union, 20 killed, 67 wounded.
Petersburg, Va., June 15 to 19, 1864. 10th and 18th Corps, Army of the James, Maj.-Gen. B. F. Buttler; 2d, 5th, 6th, and 9th Corps, Army of the James, Maj.-Gen. Geo. G. Meade. Union, 1,298 killed, 7,474 wounded, 1,814 missing. (Losses include those at Baylor's Farm, June 15; Walthal, June 16, and Weirbottom Church, June 16.)
Petersburg, Va., June 20 to 30, 1864. (Trenches in front of Petersburg.) 5th and 9th Corps, Army of Potomac; 10th and 18th Corps, Army of the James. Union, 112 killed, 506 wounded, 800 missing; Union, Gens. Chamberlin and Egan wounded.
Petersburg, Va., July 1 to 31, 1864. (In front of Petersburg, including Deep Bottom, New Market, and Malvern Hill on the 27th, and Mine Explosion on the 30th.) 2d, 5th, 9th, 10th, and 18th Corps. Union, 898 killed, 4,060 wounded, 3,110 missing. Confed. loss at Deep Bottom, 400 killed, 600 wounded, 200 missing.
Petersburg, Va., July 30, 1864. (Mine Explosion.) 9th Corps, supported by 18th Corps. Union, 419 killed, 1,679 wounded, 1,910 missing; Confed., 1,200 killed, wounded, and missing. .
Petersburg, Va., Aug. 1 to 31, 1864. (In front of Petersburg.) 2d, 5th, 9th, and 18th Corps. Union, 87 killed, 484 wounded.
Petersburg, Va., Sept. 1 to Oct. 30, 1864. (In front of Petersburg.) Army of Potomac. Union, 170 killed, 822 wounded, 812 missing; Confed., 1,000 missing.
Petersburg, Va., Dec. 1 to 31, 1864. (In front of Petersburg.) Army of Potomac. Union, 40 killed, 329 wounded.
Petersburg, Va., March 25, 1865. 2d and 6th Corps. Union, 103 killed, 864 wounded, 209 missing; Confed., 834 killed, wounded, and missing.
Petersburg, Va., April 2, 1865. (Fall of Petersburg.) 2d, 6th, 9th, and 24th Corps. Union, 296 killed, 2,565 wounded, 500 missing; Confed., 3,000 prisoners.
Petersburg, W. Va., Sept. 7, 1861. Three Companies, 4th Ohio Inf.
Petersburg, W. Va., Jan. 8, 1864.
Petit Jean, Arkansas River, Ark., July 12, 1864. One Company, 3d Ark. Cav.
Philadelphia, Tenn., Oct. 20 and 22, 1863. 45th Ohio Mounted Inf.; 1st, 11th, and 12th Ky. Cav.; 24th Ind. Battery. Union, 20 killed, 80 wounded, 354 missing; Confed., 15 killed, 82 wounded, 111 missing.
Philadelphia, Tenn., Oct. 26, 1863.
Phillippi, W. Va., June 3, 1861. 1st W. Va.; 14th and 16th Ohio; 7th and 9th Ind. Union, 2 wounded; Confed., 16 wounded.

Phillip's Creek, Miss., May 21, 1862. 2d Div., Army of the Tenn. Union, 3 wounded.
Philomont, Va., Nov. 1, 1862. Pleasanton's Cav.
Pickett's Mills, Ga., May 27, 1864. 4th Corps.
Piedmont, or Mount Crawford, Va., June 5, 1864. Portion of Army of W. Va., under Maj.-Gen. Hunter. Union, 130 killed, 650 wounded; Confed., 460 killed, 1,450 wounded, 1,060 missing. Confed., Gen. W. E. Jones killed.
Piedmont Sta., Va., May 16, 1863. W. Va. and Pa. Cav.
Pierce's Point, Black Water, Fla., Oct. 18, 1864. 19th Iowa Inf.; 2d Me. and 1st Fla. Cav.
Pierson's Farm, Va., June 16, 1864. 36th U. S. Colored Troops.
Pigeon-Roost Creek, Miss., May 14, 1863.
Piketown, or Ivy Mountain, or Fry Mountain, Ky., Nov. 9, 1861. 2d, 21st, 33d, and 59th Ohio; 16th Ky. Union, 4 killed, 26 wounded; Confed., 18 killed, 45 wounded, 200 captured.
Pikesville, Ark., June 25 to 29, 1864. (See Clarendon.)
Pikeville, Ky., April 15, 1863. 39th Ky. Mounted Inf.
Pilot Knob, or Ironton, Fort Davidson, Mo., Sept. 26 and 27, 1864. (See Fort Davidson.)
Pilot Knob, Mo., Oct. 26, 1864.
Pinal Creek, Ariz. Ter., Aug. 1 and 5, 1864.
Pinckney Island, S. C., Aug. 21, 1862. Union, 3 killed, 3 wounded.
Pine Barren Creek, Ala., Dec. 17 to 19, 1864. 82d and 97th U. S. Colored Troops.
Pine Barren Creek, or Bluff Springs, Ala., March 25, 1865. Advance of Gen. Stelle's Forces. [18, 1864.
Pine Barren Fork, Fla., Dec. 17 and
Pine Bluff, Ark., Oct. 25, 1863. 5th Kan. and 1st Ind. Cav. Union, 11 killed, 27 wounded. Confed., 53 killed, 164 wounded.

Pine Bluff, Ark., Jan. 19, 1864. (See Branchville.)
Pine Bluff, Ark., May 1, 21, and June 27, 1864.
Pine Bluff, Ark., June 21, 1864. 27th Wis. Inf.
Pine Bluff, Ark., July 2, 1864. 64th U. S. Colored Troops. Union, 6 killed.
Pine Bluff, Ark., Sept. 14, 1864. (Near Pine Bluff.) Two Companies, 1st Ind. Cav.
Pine Bluff, Ark., Feb. 22, 1865. (See Douglass Landing.)
Pine Bluff,Tennessee River,Tenn.,Aug. 19, 1864. Detachment of Company B, 83d Ill. Mounted Inf. Union, 8 killed and mutilated by guerillas.
Pine Forrest, Nevada, Nov. 17, 1865.
Pine Knob, Ga., June 19, 1864. (See Kenesaw Mountain.)
Pine Mountain, Ga., June 14, 1864. (See Kenesaw Mountain.)
Pineville, Mo., Nov. 19, 1862.
Pineville, Mo., Aug. 13, 1863. 6th Mo. Military Cav. Confed., 65 wounded.
Pine Factory, Tenn., Nov. 3, 1863. (See Centreville.)
Piney Woods, La., April 2, 1864. (See Crump's Hill.)
Pink Hill, Mo., June 11, 1862.
Pinos Altos, Ariz. Ter., Feb. 27, 1864.
Pinos Altos Mines, Ariz. Ter., Jan. 29, 1863. One Company, 1st Cal. Inf.
Pittman's Ferry, Ark., July 20, 1862. 13th Ill. Cav.
Pittman's Ferry, Ark., Nov. 25, 1862.
Pittman's Ferry, Mo., Oct. 27, 1862. 23d Iowa; 24th and 25th Mo.; 1st Mo. Militia; 12th Mo. Cav.
Pittsburg Landing, Tenn., March 2, 1862. 32d Ill. and U. S. Gunboats "Lexington" and "Pilot." Union, 5 killed, 5 wounded; Confed., 20 killed, 200 wounded.
Pittsburg Landing, Tenn., April 6 and 7, 1862. (See Shiloh.)
Placquemine, La., June 18, 1863, and June 28, 1864.
Placquemine Bayou, La., Jan. 27, 1863. (See Indian Village.)
Placquemine, or Indian City Village, La., Aug. 6, 1864. 4th Wis. Cav.;

14th R. I. Heavy Artil. Union, 2 killed.
Plain's Store, La., May 21, 1863. 1st Div., Auger's 19th Corps.
Plain's Store, La., April 7, 1864. Detachment of 118th Ill.; 21st N. Y. Battery; 3d Ill. Cav.
Plantersville, Ala., April 1, 1865. (See Bogler's Creek.)
Platte Bridge, Dak., June 3 and July 26, 1865.
Platte City, Mo., Sept. 14, 1861, and July 3, 1864.
Plattsburg, Mo., Oct. 27, 1861. Confed., 8 killed, 12 captured.
Pleasant Grove, La., April 8, 1864. (See Sabine Cross Roads.)
Pleasant Hill, or Pleasant Hill Landing, or Blair's Landing, Red River, La., April 12, 1864. 17th Corps and U. S. Gunboats "Osage" and "Lexington." Union, 7 wounded; Confed., 200 killed and wounded.
Pleasant Hill, Mo., July 8, 1862.
Pleasant Hill, Mo., July 11, 1862. 1st Iowa Cav.; Mo. Militia. Union, 10 killed, 19 wounded; Confed., 6 killed, 5 wounded.
Pleasant Hill, Mo., May 28, 1864. 2d Col. Cav.
Pleasant Hills, La., April 9, 1864. 1st and 3d Divs., 16th Corps; 1st Div., 19th Corps; Cav. Div., 16th Corps. (Red River Exp.) Union, 100 killed, 700 wounded, 300 missing; Confed., 2,000 killed, wounded, and missing.
Pleasant Ridge, Ala., April 6, 1865.
Pleasant Valley, Md., July 5, 1864. (See Hagerstown.)
Plenitude, Miss., July 10, 1864.
Plymouth, N. C., Sept. 2, 1862. 1st N. C. Inf.; Company F, 9th N. Y. Inf.
Plymouth, N. C., Nov. 26, 1863, and April 1, 1864.
Plymouth, N. C., April 17 to 20, 1864. 85th N. Y.; 103d Pa.; 16th Conn.; U. S. Steamers "Miami" and "Southfield." (Loss including Forts Gray, Wessels, and Williams.) Union, 20 killed, 80 wounded, 1,500 missing; Confed., 500 killed, wounded, and missing.
Pocahontas, Ark., Aug. 22, 1863.
Pocahontas, Mo., Feb. 10, 1864.
Pocotaligo, S. C., May 29, 1862. 50th Pa.; 79th N. Y.; 8th Mich.; 1st Mass. Cav. Union, 2 killed, 9 wounded.
Pocotaligo, or Yemassee, S. C., Oct. 22, 1862. 47th, 55th, and 76th Pa.; 48th N. Y.; 6th and 7th Conn.; 3d and 4th N. H.; 3d R. I.; 1st N. Y. Engineers; 1st Mass. Cav.; Batteries D and M, 1st U. S. Artil.; Battery E, 3d U. S. Artil. Union, 43 killed, 258 wounded; Confed., 14 killed, 102 wounded.
Pocotaligo, S. C., Jan. 14 to 16, 1865. 17th Corps, Army of the Tenn. Union, 25 wounded.
Point Lick and Big Hill Road, Ky., Oct. 23, 1862. Cav. under Col. McCooke.
Point Lookout, Va., May 13, 1864. Detachment of 36th U. S. Colored Troops, assisted by seamen.
Point of Rocks, Kan., Jan. 20, 1865.
Point of Rocks, Md., Aug. 5, 1861. 28th N. Y. Inf. Confed., 3 killed, 2 wounded.
Point of Rocks, Md., June 9, 1864. 2d U. S. Colored Cav. Union, 2 killed.
Point of Rocks, Md., July 4, 1864. Md. Potomac Home Brigade.
Point Pleasant, La., June 25, 1864. 64th U. S. Colored Troops.
Point Pleasant, Mo., April 6 and 7, 1862.
Point Pleasant, W. Va., March 30, 1863. One Company, 13th W. Va. Inf. Union, 1 killed, 3 wounded; Confed., 20 killed, 25 wounded.
Point Washington, Fla., Feb. 9, 1864. (Near Point Washington.) Detachment of 7th Vt. Vols.
Poison Springs, near Camden, Ark., April 18, 1864. 18th Iowa; 79th U. S. Colored Troops; 6th Kan. Cav. Union, 113 killed, 88 wounded, 68 missing. (Steele's Campaign.)
Polk's Plantation, near Helena, Ark., May 25, 1863. 3d Iowa and 5th Kan. Cav.

Pollocksville, N. C., April 14, 1862. 103d N. Y. Inf. Confed , 7 wounded.
Pollocksville and Northeast River, N. C., Jan. 17, 1863. 3d N. Y. Cav.
Ponchatoula, La., Sept. 14, 1862. 12th Me.; 26th Mass.; 13th Conn.
Ponchatoula, La., March 24, 1863. 127th, 165th N. Y.; 9th Conn.; 14th and 24th Me.; 6th Mich. Union, 6 wounded; Confed., 3 killed, 11 wounded.
Ponchatoula, La., May 13, 1863. Col. Davis' Command. [Ky. Inf.
Pond Creek, Ky., May 16, 1864. 39th
Pond Spring, Ala., Dec. 29, 1864. 15th Pa.; detachments of 2d Tenn., 12th and 13th Ind. Cav.
Pontotoc, Miss., July 11, 1864. 8th Wis.; 5th Minn. and 11th Mo. Inf.; 2d Iowa Cav. (Exp. to Tupelo.)
Poole Sta., Ga., Dec. 7 to 9, 1864. (See Ogeechee River, also, Eden Sta.)
Poolesville, Md., Sept. 7, 1862. 3d Ind. and 8th Ill. Cav. Union, 2 killed, 6 wounded; Confed., 3 killed, 6 wounded.
Pope's Campaign in Va., Aug. 23 to Sept. 1, 1862. Army of Va. Union, 7,000 killed, wounded, and missing; Confed., 1,500 killed, 8,000 wounded and missing.
Poplar Springs Church, or Preble's Farm, Va., Sept. 30 and Oct. 1, 1864. 1st Div., 5th Corps; 2d Div., 9th Corps. Union, 141 killed, 788 wounded, 1,756 missing; Confed., 800 wounded, 100 missing. (See, also, Preble's Farm.)
Po River, Va., May 10, 1864.
Port Conway, Va., Sept. 19, 1863.
Port Gibson or Thompson's Hill and Magnolia Hill, Miss., May 1, 1863. 13th Corps, Maj.-Gen. McClernand; 3d Div., 17th Corps, Maj.-Gen. McPherson; Maj.-Gen. U. S. Grant, Commanding. Union, 130 killed, 718 wounded; Confed., 1,150 killed and wounded, 500 missing. Confed.. Brig.-Gen. Tracey killed. (Including skirmishes at Bayou Pierre.) The first engagement in Grant's Campaign against Vicksburg.

Port Gibson, Miss., Dec. 26, 1863. Miss. Marine Brigade of Inf. and Cav.
Port Gibson, Miss., July 7 and 15, and Oct. 1, 1864.
Port Hudson, La., March 14, 1863. Troops under Gen. Banks, assisting U. S. Fleet under Admiral Farragut. Union, 65 wounded.
Port Hudson, La., May 21, 1863. (See Plain's Store.)
Port Hudson, La., May 27 to July 9, 1863. (Siege of Port Hudson.) Gens. Weitzel's, Grover's, Paine's, Auger's, and Dwight's Divs., 19th Corps; Gen. Bank's Army of the Gulf and Naval Forces under Admiral Farragut. Union, 500 killed, 2,500 wounded; Confed., 100 killed, 700 wounded, 6,408 prisoners. Union, Brig.-Gens. Sherman and Paine wounded.
Port Hudson, La., June 11 and 14, 1863. Army of the Gulf.
Port Hudson, La., April 7, 1864. (Near Port Hudson.) Detachments of 118th Ill., 3d Ill. Cav., 21st N. Y. Battery. Union, 1 killed, 4 wounded.
Port Republic, Va., June 9, 1862. 5th, 7th, 29th, and 66th Ohio; 84th and 110th Pa.; 7th Ind.; 1st W. Va., Battery E, 4th U. S. Artil.; Batteries A and L, 1st Ohio Artil. Union, 67 killed, 361 wounded, 574 missing; Confed., 88 killed, 535 wounded, 34 missing.
Port Republic, Va., Sept. 1, 1864.
Port Royal, or Port Royal Ferry, Coosaw River. S. C., Jan. 1, 1862. 3d Mich.; 47th, 48th, and 79th N. Y.; 50th Pa. Union, 1 killed, 10 wounded.
Port Walthal, or Walthal, Va., June 16 and 17, 1864. 1st Div., 10th Corps. (Siege of Petersburg.)
Porter's House, Va., Jan. 29, 1862.
Potosi, Mo., Aug. 10, 1861. Mo. Home Guards. Union, 1 killed; Confed., 2 killed, 3 wounded.
Pound Gap, Ky., April 19, 1864. 45th Ky. Inf.
Pound Gap, or Sounding Gap, Cum-

berland Mountain, Tenn., March 16, 1862. Detachments of 22d Ky., 40th and 42d Ohio Inf. and 1st Ohio Cav.
Pound Gap Exp., Tenn., July 6, 1863. 10th Ky. and 1st Ohio Cav.
Powder River, Dak. Ter., Sept. 5 to 11, 1865.
Powder Mills, Mo., Oct. 3, 1864.
Powder Springs, Ga., June 20, 1864. (See Kenesaw Mountain.)
Powder Springs Creek, Ga., Oct. 1 to 3, 1864. (See Sweetwater.)
Powell's River Bridge, Tenn., Feb. 22, 1864. Two Companies 24th Ky. Inf.
Powhatan, Va., June 25, 1865. 1st U. S. Colored Cav.
Prairie Chapel, Mo. Sept. 4, 1862.
Prairie De'Ann, Ark., April 10 to 13, 1864. 1st Ark.; 18th, 29th, 33d, 36th, and 40th Iowa; 50th Ind.; 43d Ill.; 27th Wis.; 12th Kan. Inf.; 2d and 3d Mo. Cav.; 13th Ill. Cav.; 2d, 6th, and 14th Kan. Cav.; 1st Iowa Cav.; Battery A, 3d Ill. Artil.; 2d Ind. Artil. (Steele's Exp.) Union, 100 killed and wounded; Confed., 50 killed and wounded.
Prairie Grove, or Fayetteville and Ill. Creek, Ark., Dec. 7, 1862. 1st, 2d, and 3d Divs., Army of the Frontier. Union, 167 killed, 798 wounded, 183 missing; Confed., 300 killed, 1,200 wounded and missing.
Prairie Sta., Miss., Feb. 21, 1863. 2d Iowa Cav.
Prairie Sta., Miss., Feb. 20, 1864. (Smith's Raid.)
Preble's Farm, Poplar Springs Church, Va., Sept. 30 and Oct. 1, 1864. 1st Div., 5th Corps; 2d Div., 9th Corps. (See, also, Poplar Springs Church.)
Prentiss and Bolivar, Miss., Sept. 20. 1862. 33d Ill. Inf., assisted by U. S. Transport and U. S. Ram "Queen of the West."
Prestonburg, Ky., Jan. 10, 1862. (See Middle Creek.)
Price's Invasion of Mo., Sept. 24 to Oct. 28, 1864. (Including 15 engagements.) Mo. Militia Cav.; Gen. A. J. Smith's Cav.; Cav., Army of the Border; Kan. Militia. Union, 170 killed, 336 wounded.
Prince George C. H., Va., Jan. 21 and Nov. 2, 1864.
Prince's Place, Osage River, Mo., Oct. 6, 1864. 1st, 7th, and 9th Mo. Militia Cav. (Price's Invasion.)
Princeton, Ark., Dec. 6 and 8, 1863.
Princeton, Ark., April 29, 1864. 40th Iowa; 43d Ill.; 6th Kan. Cav.; 3d Ill. Battery.
Princeton, Ark., Oct. 23, 1864. 3d Mo. Cav.
Princeton, Ky., June 10, 1864.
Princeton, W. Va., May 15 to 18, 1862. Gen. J. D. Cox's Div. Union, 30 killed, 70 wounded; Confed., 2 killed, 14 wounded.
Princeton, W. Va., May 6, 1864. Advance of Gen. Crooke's Troops.
Pritchard's Mills, or Darnestown, Md., Sept. 15, 1861. 28th Pa.; 13th Mass. Union, 1 killed; Confed., 8 killed, 75 wounded.
Proctor's Creek, Va., May 12 to 16, 1864. (See Fort Darling.)
Pueblo Colorado, N. Mex., Aug. 18, 1863. Three Companies, 1st N. Mex. Cav.
Pulaski, Ala., July 15, 1863. 3d Ohio and 5th Tenn. Cav. Confed., 3 killed, 50 missing.
Pulaski, Tenn., May 4, 1862.
Pulaski, Tenn., May 13, 1864. 111th U. S. Colored Troops.
Pulaski, Tenn., Sept. 26 and 27, 1864. Gen. Rousseau's Cav.
Pulaski, Lamb's Ferry, Anthony's Hill, and Sugar Creek, Tenn., Dec. 25, 1864. Cav. Gen. Thomas' Army.
Pumpkinvine Creek, Ga., May 25 to June 4, 1864. (See Dallas.)
Putnam, Mo., Sept. 1, 1862.
Putnam's Ferry, near Doniphan, Mo., April 2, 1862. 21st and 38th Ill.; 5th Ill. Cav.; 16th Ohio Battery; Col. Carlin's Brigade. Confed., 3 killed.
Pyramid Lake, Nev., May 14, 1865.

QUAKER Bridge, or Comfort, N. C., July 6, 1863. 17th, 23d, and 27th Mass.; 9th N. J.; 81st and 158th N. Y.; Beleger's and Angel's Batteries.
Quaker Road, Gravelly Run, Va., March 29, 1865. Warren's 5th Corps; Griffin's 1st Div., Army of Potomac. Union, 55 killed, 306 wounded; Confed., 135 killed, 400 wounded, 100 missing.
Quinatown, or Deep Creek. N.C., Feb. 5, 1864. Detachment of 14th Ill. Cav. Union, 3 killed, 6 wounded; Confed., 50 captured, including Maj.-Gen. Vance.
Quantrell's Attack at Baxter Springs, Ark., Oct. 6, 1863. (See Baxter Springs.)
Quantrell's Plunder of Lawrence, Kan., Aug. 21, 1863. (See Lawrence.)
Queen's Hill, Miss., Feb. 4, 1864.
Quicksand Creek, Ky., April 6, 1864. Company I, 14th Ky. Inf. Confed., 10 killed, 7 wounded.
Quincy, Mo., Nov. 1, 1864.

RACCOON Ford, Ala., Oct. 30, 1864. (See Muscle Shoales.)
Raccoon Ford, Rapidan Sta., Va., Sept. 14 and 19, 1863. Cav. Corps, Army of Potomac.
Raccoon Ford, Va., Nov. 26, 1863. (See Mine Run.)
Raceland, near Algiers, La., June 22, 1862. 8th Vt. Inf. Union, 3 killed, 8 wounded.
Raid to Rocky Mount and Tar River, N. C., July 18 to 21, 1863. (Potter's Raid.) 3d and 12th N. Y. Cav.; 1st N. C. Cav. Union, 60 wounded.
Raid to Gordonsville, Va., Dec. 8 to 28, 1864. Merritt's and Custer's Cav. Union, 43 wounded.
Raleigh, N. C., April 7 and 13, 1865.
Randolph Co., Mo., May 8, 1864.
Rapidan, Va., Oct. 10, 1863. Buford's Cav. Union, 20 wounded.
Rapidan, Va., Oct. 17, 1863. 1st Div. Cav. Corps, Army of Potomac.
Rapidan, Va., Feb. 3, 1864.
Rapidan, Va., March 1, 1864. (See Standardsville.)
Rapidan Sta., Va., May 1, 1863. Averill's Cav. Div., Army of Potomac. (Stoneman's Raid.)
Rapidan Sta., Va., Sept. 14 and 19, 1863. (See Raccoon Ford.)
Rappahannock Bridge, Va., Nov. 8, 1862. Cav. Brigade, under Gen. Bayard.
Rappahannock Bridge, Va., Oct. 24, 1863. (See Bealton.)
Rappahannock Crossing, Va., Oct. 22, 1863. (See Beverly Ford.)
Rappahannock River, Va., Aug. 21, 1862. (See Kelly's Ford.)
Rappahannock River, Va., Aug. 23, 1862. (See Waterloo Bridge.)
Rappahannock River, Va., April 1, 1864. (Near Rappahannock River.) Detachment of 1st Conn. Cav.
Rappahannock Sta., Kelly's Ford, and Brandy Sta., Va., Aug. 1 to 3, 1863. Brig.-Gen. Buford's Cav. Union, 16 killed, 134 wounded.
Rappahannock Sta., Va., Nov. 7, 1863. 5th Wis.; 5th and 6th Me.; 49th and 119th Pa.; 121st N. Y., supported by balance of 6th Corps and portion of 5th Corps. Union, 370 killed and wounded; Confed., 11 killed, 98 wounded, 1,629 missing.
Rawle's Mills, or Little Creek, Williamstown, N. C., Nov. 3, 1862. 24th and 44th Mass.; 9th N. J.; N. Y. and Me. Batteries.
Raymond, Miss., May 12, 1863. 17th Corps, Maj.-Gen. McPherson. Union, 69 killed, 341 wounded; Confed., 969 killed and wounded. Confed., Gen. Tilgh. killed.
Raymond, Miss., Feb. 4, 1864. (See Champion Hills.)
Raytown, Mo., June 23, 1863. 7th Mo. Cav. Union, 1 killed, 1 wounded.
Readyville, or Round Hill, Tenn., Aug. 28, 1862. 10th Brigade, Army of the Ohio. Union, 5 wounded.
Readyville, Tenn., Sept. 7, 1864. Detachment of 9th Pa. Cav.
Ream's Sta., Va., June 22, 1864. Kautz's Cav., Army of the James; 3d Cav. Div., Army of Potomac.

LIST OF BATTLES AND ENGAGEMENTS.   181

Ream's Sta., Va., June 29, 1864. Wilson's Cav.
Ream's Sta., Va., Aug. 25, 1864. 2d Corps and Gregg's Cav. Union, 127 killed, 546 wounded, 1,759 missing; Confed., 1,500 killed and wounded.
Recon. to Strasburg, Va., Oct. 13, 1864. Maj.-Gens. Emery's and Cooke's Troops. Union, 30 killed, 144 wounded, 40 missing.
Recon. on Charles City Cross Roads, Va., Oct. 1, 1864. (See Charles City Cross Roads.)
Recon. on Corinth Road, Miss., April 8, 1862. (See Corinth Road.)
Recon. to Boydton Road, Va., Oct. 8, 1864.
Recon. by 5th and 9th Corps, Army of Potomac. (See, also, Boydton Plank Road.)
Recon. to Hatcher's Run, Va., Dec. 8 and 9, 1864. (See Hatcher's Run.)
Recon. on Darbytown Road, Oct. 13, 1864. 1st and 3d Divs., 10th Corps; Cav., Army of the James.
Rector's Farm, Ark., Dec. 19, 1864.
Rectortown, or Five Points, Va., Jan. 1, 1864. 1st Md. Cav.; Potomac Home Brigade.
Red Bone, Miss., April 21, 1864. 2d Wis. Cav. Union, 1 killed, 6 wounded.
Red Bend, Ky., Aug. 24, 1862.
Red Bend Church, Mo., Sept. 25, 1863. 2d Wis. Cav.
Red Clay, Ga., May 3, 1864. 1st Div. McCooke's Cav. Union, 10 killed and wounded.
Red Hill, Ala., Jan. 14, 1865. 15th Pa. Cav.
Red House, W. Va., July 12, 1861. (See Barboursville.)
Red Mound, Tenn., Dec. 30, 1862. (See Parker's Cross Roads.)
Red Oaks, Ga., Aug. 19 and 20, 1864. Cav., Army of the Cumberland. (Kilpatrick's Raid.)
Red Oaks, Ga., Aug. 28, 1864.
Redoubt before Yorktown, Va., April 26, 1862. (See Yorktown.)
Red River Exp., March 7 to May 16, 1864. Troops under Gen. Banks, supported by Naval Forces under Ad. Porter.
Redwood, Cal., Aug. 4, 1863.
Redwood, Minn., Aug. 18, 1862. One Company, 5th Minn. Inf. massacred by Indians.
Redwood Creek, Cal., July 7, 1863. One Company, 1st Battalion, Cal. Mountaineers. (Indian Fight.)
Reed's Mountain, Ark., Dec. 5, 1862. 2d Kan. Cav.
Reedy Creek, W. Va., May 13, 1862. Gen. Kelly's Command.
Renick, Randolph Co., Mo., Nov. 1, 1861. Union, 14 wounded.
Rensey's Ferry, Mo., May 31, 1862.
Rerock, Ariz. Ter., March 24, 1865. 1st New Mexico Cav.
Resaca, or Sugar Valley, or Oostenaula, Ga., May 13 to 16, 1864. 4th, 14th, 20th, and Cav. Corps, Army of the Cumberland, Maj.-Gen. Thomas; 15th and 16th Corps, Army of the Tenn., Maj.-Gen. McPherson; 20th Corps, Army of the Ohio, Maj.-Gen. Schofield. Union, 600 killed, 2,147 wounded; Confed., 300 killed, 1,500 wounded, 1,000 missing. Confed., Brig.-Gen. Wadkins killed.
Resaca, Ga., Oct. 12, 1864. Garrison under Col. Weaver.
Reynold's Plantation, Ga., Nov. 27 to 29, 1864. (See Waynesboro.)
Reynold's Sta., Tenn., Aug. 27, 1862.
Rhea's Mills, Ark., Nov. 7, 1862. 3d Ark. Indian Home Guards.
Rheatown, Tenn., Oct. 11, 1863. 2d Brigade, Cav. Div., Army of the Ohio.
Richfield, Mo., May 19, 1863. 25th Mo. Inf.
Richland, Ark., May 3, 1864. 2d Ark. Cav. Union, 20 killed.
Richland, Tenn., Oct. 23, 1862.
Richland, Tenn., Sept. 26, 1864. 111th U. S. Colored Troops.
Richmond, Ky., Aug. 30, 1862. 12th, 16th, 55th, 66th, 69th, and 71st Ind.; 95th Ohio; 18th Ky.; 6th and 7th Ky. Cav.; Batteries D and G, Mich. Artil. Union, 200 killed, 700 wounded, 4,000 missing; Confed., 250 killed, 500 wounded.

Richmond and Lexington, Ky., July 28, 1863.
Richmond, or Roundaway Bayou, La., March 30, 1863. 69th Ind. Inf.; detachment of 2d Ill. Cav.
Richmond, La., June 15, 1863. Gen. Mower's Brigade and Elliott's Miss. Marine Brigade.
Richmond, Miss., June 14, 1863.
Richmond, Va., Sept. 29 and 30, and Oct. 28 and 29, 1864, and March 30 to April 3, 1865.
Richmond, Va., April 3, 1865. (Fall of Richmond.) Confed., 6,000 prisoners.
Richmond & Petersburg R. R., near Fort Walthal and Chester Sta., Va., May 6 and 7, 1864. Portion of 10th and 18th Corps. Union, 48 killed, 256 wounded; Confed., 50 killed, 200 wounded.
Rich Mountain, W. Va., July 11, 1861. 8th, 10th, and 13th Ind.; 19th Ohio. Union, 11 killed, 35 wounded; Confed., 60 killed, 140 wounded, 100 prisoners.
Rickett's Hill, Tenn., Aug. 6, 1862.
Rickett's Hill, Tenn., Sept. 7, 1862. (See Clarksville.)
Riddle's Shop, Va., June 13, 1864. (See White Oak Swamp Bridge.)
Rienzi, Miss., Aug. 19, and Sept. 9 and 18, 1862.
Rienzi and Kossuth, Miss., Aug. 26, 1862. 2d Iowa Cav.; 7th Kan. Cav. Union, 5 killed, 12 wounded.
Rincon de Mascaras, N. Mex., Dec. 11, 1863.
Ringgold, Ga., Sept. 11, 1863. Advance of 21st Corps. Union, 8 killed, 19 wounded; Confed., 3 killed, 18 missing.
Ringgold, Greysville, Peavine Creek, and Taylor's Bridge, Ga., Nov. 27, 1863. Geary's Div., 12th Corps; Johnson's Div., 14th Corps; Osterhouse's Div., 15th Corps. Union, 68 killed, 151 wounded; Confed., 50 killed, 200 wounded, 230 missing.
Rio De Los Animos, N. Mex., July 19, 1863.
Rio Hondo, N. Mex., July 18, 1863.
One Company, 1st N. Mex. Cav. (Indian Fight.)
Rio Verde, Ariz. Ter., Oct. 13, 1865.
Ripley, Miss., July 7, 1863.
Ripley, Miss., Dec. 1, 1863. 2d Brigade, Cav. Div., Army of the Tenn.
Ripley, Miss., June 7, 1864. Cav. Advance of Sturgis' Troops. (Exp. to Guntown, June 5 to 10.)
Ripley, Miss., June 11, 1864. 3d and 4th Iowa; 2d N. J.; 4th Mo. Cav.
Ripley, Miss., July 7, 1864. 2d Iowa Cav.
Ripley, Tenn., Jan. 8, 1863. 2d Ill. Cav.
Ripley, Va., Dec. 19, 1861.
River's Bridge, Salkahatchie, S. C., Feb. 3 to 9, 1865. (Including engagements at Hickory Hill, Owen Cross Roads, Lowtonville, Duck Creek, and Whiphy's Swamp.) 15th and 17th Corps.
Roach's or Brooke's Plantation, near Snydersville, Miss., March 31, 1864. 3d U. S. Colored Cav.
Roanoke, Mo., Sept. 6, 1862.
Roanoke Island, N. C., Feb. 7 and 8, 1862. 21st, 23d, 24th, 25th, and 27th Mass.; 10th Conn.; 9th, 51st, and 53d N. Y.; 9th N. J.; 51st Pa.; 4th and 5th R. I., assisted by a large Naval Force. Union, 35 killed, 200 wounded; Confed., 16 killed, 39 wounded, 2,527 captured.
Roan's Tanyard, Mo., Jan. 8, 1862. (See Silver Creek.)
Robertson's Run, Va., Oct. 10, 1863. (See James City.)
Robertson's Tavern, or Payne's Tavern, Va., Nov. 27, 1863. (See Mine Run.)
Robinson's Ford, Va., Sept. 16, 1863.
Robinson's Mills, Miss., Oct. 17, 1863.
Rocheport, Mo., June 1, 1863. 1st Mo. Enrolled Militia; 9th Mo. Militia Cav.
Rocheport, Mo., June 18, 1863.
Rock Cañon, Nev., Feb. 15, 1866.
Rock Castle, Ky., Oct. 21, 1861. (See Wildcat.)
Rock Creek, Dak., July 1, 1865.
Rockford, Tenn., Dec. 14, 1863. 1st Ky. Cav.; 45th Ohio Mounted Inf. Union, 25 wounded.

Rock House, W. Va., Feb. 12, 1864. 14th Ky. Confed., 12 killed, 4 wounded.
Rockingham, N. C., March 7, 1865. Kilpatrick's Cav.
Rockport, Ark., March 25, 1864.
Rockport, Mo., Sept. 23, 1864. 3d Mo. Militia Cav.
Rockville, Md., Sept. 22, 1863. 11th N. Y. Cav. Confed., 34 killed and wounded.
Rocky Bluff, Mo., Aug. 7, 1862.
Rocky Creek Church, Ga., Dec. 2, 1864. 3d Ky. and 5th Ohio.
Rocky Crossing, Miss., June 20, 1863. 5th Ohio Cav.; 9th Ill. Mounted Inf. Union, 7 killed, 28 wounded, 30 missing.
Rocky Face Ridge, Ga., Feb. 25 to 27, 1864. (See Buzzard Roost.)
Rocky Face Ridge, Ga., May 5 to 9, 1864. (Including Tunnel Hill, Mill Creek Gap, Buzzard Roost, Snake Creek Gap, and Dalton.) Army of the Cumberland, Maj.-Gen. Thomas; Army of the Tenn., Maj.-Gen. McPherson; Army of the Miss., Maj.-Gen. Sherman. Union, 200 killed, 637 wounded; Confed., 600 killed and wounded.
Rocky Gap, Ky., June 9, 1863. (See Monticello.)
Rocky Gap, near White Sulphur Springs, Va., Aug. 26, 1863. 3d and 8th W. Va.; 14th Pa. Cav.; 2d and 3d W. Va. Cav. Union, 16 killed, 113 wounded; Confed., 156 killed and wounded.
Rodman's Point, near Washington, N. C., April 4, 1863. Troops under Gen. Foster.
Rodney and Port Gibson, Miss., Dec. 17 to 26, 1863. 1st Miss. Marine Brigade. Union, 2 killed.
Rodney, Miss., March 4, 1864. Cav. and Inf. of Miss. Marine Brigade.
Rodney, Miss., Aug. 1, 1864.
Rogersville, Ala., May 13, 1862. 1st Wis.; 38th Ind. and detachment of Cav.
Rogersville, Tenn., Nov. 6, 1863. 7th Ohio Cav.; 2d Tenn. Mounted Inf.; 2d Ill. Battery. Union, 5 killed, 12 wounded, 650 missing; Confed., 10 killed, 20 wounded.
Rogersville, Tenn., Aug. 22, 1864.
Rolla, Mo., Aug. 1, 1864. 5th Mo. Militia Cav.
Rolla, Mo., Nov. 1, 1864.
Rolling Fork, Miss., Nov. 22, 1864. 3d U. S. Colored Cav.
Rolling Prairie, Ark., Jan. 23, 1864. 11th Mo. Cav. Union, 11 killed.
Rolling Prairie, Ark., Feb. 4, 1864. 8th Mo. Militia Cav.
Rome, Ga., May 18, 1864. 2d Div., 14th Corps and Cav., Army of the Cumberland.
Rome, Ga., Oct. 13, 1864.
Rome Cross Roads, Ga., May 16, 1864. 16th Corps, Army of the Tenn.
Romney, W. Va., June 11, 1861. 11th Ind. Union, 1 wounded; Confed., 2 killed, 1 wounded.
Romney, or Hanging Rock, W. Va., Sept. 23, 1861. 4th and 8th Ohio. Union, 3 killed, 50 wounded; Confed., 35 killed.
Romney, or Mill Creek Mills, W. Va., Oct. 26, 1861. 4th and 8th Ohio; 7th W. Va.; Md. Inf.; 2d Regiment, Potomac Home Guards; Ringgold Cav. Union, 2 killed, 15 wounded; Confed., 20 killed, 15 wounded, 50 captured.
Romney, W. Va., Feb. 16, 1863. (Near Romney.) Detachment of 116th and 122d Ohio. Union, 72 wounded and captured.
Rood's Hill, Va., May 14, 1864. Portion of the Army of W. Va.
Rood's Hill, Va., Nov. 22, 1864. 1st and 3d Divs., Cav. Corps, Army of Potomac; 2d Cav. Div., Army of W. Va. Union, 18 killed, 52 wounded.
Rosecran's Campaign in Tenn., June 23 to 30, 1863. (From Murfreesboro' to Tullahoma, including engagements at Middleton, Hoover's Gap, Beech Grove, Liberty Gap, and Gray's Gap.) Army of the Cumberland; 14th, 20th, and 21st Corps; Granger's Reserve Corps and Stan-

ley's Cav. Union, 85 killed, 462 wounded; Confed., 1,634 killed, wounded, and captured.
Roseville, Ark., Nov. 12, 1863. Two Companies, 2d Kan. Cav.
Roseville, Ark., March 29 and April 15, 1864.
Roseville, Ark., April 5, 1864. Detachments of the 2d and 6th Kan. Cav., in engagement with Guerrillas. Union, 19 killed, 11 wounded; Confed., 15 killed, 25 wounded, 11 captured.
Roseville, Mo., April 16, 1864.
Roseville Creek, Ark., March 20, 1864.
Ross Landing, Grand Lake, Ark., Feb. 14, 1864. 51st U. S. Colored Troops.
Roundaway Bayou, La., March 30, 1863. (See Richmond.)
Round Hill, Ark., July 7, 1862. (See Bayou Caché.)
Round Hill, Tenn., Aug. 28, 1862. (See Readyville.)
Rousseau's Campaign in Tenn., June 23 to 30, 1863. Troops under Gen. Rousseau.
Rousseau's Pursuit of Wheeler, Tenn., Sept. 1 to 8, 1864. Rousseau's Cav.; 1st and 4th Tenn.; 2d Mich.; 1st Wis.; 8th Iowa; 2d and 8th Ind.; 6th Ky. Union, 10 killed, 30 wounded; Confed., 300 killed, wounded, and captured.
Rousseau's Raid in Ala. and Ga., July 11 to 22, 1864. (Including engagements at Ten Islands and Stone's Ferry, Ala., also, Auburn and Chewa Sta., Ga.) 8th Ind.; 5th Iowa; 9th Ohio; 2d Ky. and 4th Tenn. Cav.; Battery E. 1st Mich. Artil. Union, 3 killed, 30 wounded; Confed., 95 killed and wounded.
Rover, Tenn., Jan. 31, 1863. 4th Ohio Cav. Confed., 12 killed, wounded, 300 captured.
Rover, Tenn., June 23, 1863.
Rowanty Creek, Va., Feb. 5 to 7, 1865. (See Dabney's Mills.)
Rowlett's Sta., or Munfordville, or Woodsonville, Ky., Dec. 17, 1861. 32d Ind. Union, 10 killed, 22 wounded; Confed., 33 killed, 50 wounded.

Ruckersville, Miss., Oct. 6, 1862.
Rural Hills, Tenn., Feb. 18, 1862. 8th Ky. Cav. Confed., 16 killed.
Rush Creek, Ind. Ter., Feb. 9, 1865. 11th Ohio and 7th Iowa Cav. (Indian Fight.)
Russell's House, before Corinth, Miss., May 17, 1862. Gen. Smith's Brigade, 5th Div., Army of the Tenn.
Russellville, Ky., July 29, 1862. 7th Ind.; Ky. Home Guards. Union, 1 wounded.
Russellville, Ky., Sept. 30, 1862. 17th Ky. and Troops under Col. Harrison.
Russellville, Mo., Oct. 9, 1864.
Russellville, Tenn., July 1, 1862. 1st Ohio Cav.
Rutherford's Creek, Tenn., March 10, 1863. 4th Cav. Brigade under Col. Minty.
Rutherford's Creek, Tenn., Dec. 19, 1864. Cav. of Gen. Thomas' Army.

SABINE Cross Roads, or Mansfield, and Pleasant Grove, La., April 8, 1864. Portion of 13th, 16th, and 19th Corps; Cav. Div., Army of the Dep't of the Gulf. Union, 300 killed, 1,600 wounded, 2,100 missing; Confed., 600 killed, 2,400 wounded, 500 missing. Union, Maj.-Gen. Franklin and Brig.-Gen. Ransom wounded; Confed., Maj.-Gen. Moulton and Brig.-Gen. Parsons killed.
Sabine Pass, Tex., Sept. 8, 1863. Portion of 19th Corps, under Gen. Franklin, assisted by Naval Force.
Sabine Pass, Tex., May 25, 1865. Surrender of Confed. Forces.
Sacramento, Ky., Dec. 28, 1861. 3d Ky. Cav. Union, 1 killed, 8 wounded; Confed., 30 killed.
Sacramento Mountains, N. Mex., Aug. 25, 1864. 1st N. Mex. Cav.
Sacramento Mountains, N. Mex., July 1, 1865.
Sage Creek, Dak. Ter., April 21, 1865.
Sailor's Creek, or Harper's Farm, and Deatonsville, Va., April 6, 1865. 2d and 6th Corps and Sheridan's Cav.

LIST OF BATTLES AND ENGAGEMENTS. 185

Union, 166 killed, 1,014 wounded; Confed., 1,000 killed and wounded, 6,000 prisoners.
Salem, or Spring River, Ark., March 18, 1862. Detachments of 6th Mo. and 3d Iowa Cav. Union, 5 killed, 10 wounded; Confed., 100 killed, wounded, and missing.
Salem, Miss., Oct. 8, 1863. Cav. under Cols. McCrellis and Phillips.
Salem, Miss., June 11, 1864.
Salem, Mo., Dec. 3, 1861. Detachment of 10th Mo. Cav.; 13th Ill. Cav. Union, 6 killed, 10 wounded; Confed., 16 killed, 20 wounded.
Salem, Mo., July 6 and Aug. 9, 1862.
Salem, N. C., April 3, 1865. Cav. under Col. Palmer. (Stoneman's Raid.)
Salem, Va., Nov. 5, 1862. (See New Baltimore.)
Salem, Va., June 21, 1864. Averill's Cav. Union, 6 killed, 10 wounded; Confed., 10 killed and wounded.
Salem Cemetery, Tenn., Dec. 18, 1862. (See Jackson.)
Salem Church, Va., May 28, 1864. (See Hawe's Shop.)
Salem Church, Va., June 2, 1864. (See Gaines' Mills, also, Cold Harbor.)
Salem Heights, Va., May 3 and 4, 1863. (See Chancellorsville.)
Salem Pike, near Murfreesboro', Tenn., March 21, 1863. 3d Tenn. Cav.
Saline, Ind. Ter., Dec. 2, 1862.
Saline Co., Mo., July 30, 1863. 1st and 4th Mo. Enrolled Militia.
Saline River, Ark., May 4, 1864, and May 10, 1865.
Salisbury, N. C., April 12, 1865. (See Grant's Creek.)
Salisbury, Tenn., Aug. 11, 1862. 11th Ill. Cav.
Salisbury, Tenn., April 16, 1863.
Salisbury, Tenn., Dec. 3, 1863. 2d Brigade, Cav. Div., 16th Corps.
Salkahatchie, S. C., Feb. 3 to 9, 1865. (See River's Bridge.)
Salkahatchie River, S. C., Feb. 6, 1865.
Salt Lake, Va., Oct. 14, 1863. 6th W. Va. Inf.
Salt Springs, Ga., Oct. 1, 1864.
Saltville, Va., Oct. 2, 1864. 11th and 13th Ky.; 12th Ohio; 11th Mich.; 5th and 6th U. S. Colored Cav.; 26th, 30th, 35th, 37th, 40th, and 45th Ky. Mounted Inf. Union, 54 killed, 190 wounded, 104 missing; Confed., 18 killed, 71 wounded, 21 missing.
Saltville, Va., Dec. 20, 1864. Gillem's and Burbridge's Cav.
Salyersville, Ky., Nov. 30, 1863. 14th Ky. Inf.
Samaria Church, Malvern Hill, Va., June 15, 1864. 3d Div., Cav. Corps, Army of Potomac. Union, 25 killed, 3 wounded; Confed., 100 killed and wounded.
Samaria Church, Va., June 24, 1864. 1st and 2d Divs., Cav. Corps, Army of Potomac.
Sam Jones' Surrender, Fla., May 10, 1865. (See Tallahassee.)
San Andras Mountain, N. Mex., July 1, 1865.
San Carlos River, Cal., May 27, 1864. Company K, 5th Cal. Cav.
Sand Creek, Ind. Ter., Dec. 9, 1864. (See Ft. Lyons.)
Sandersville, or Buffalo Creek, Ga., Nov. 26, 1864. 3d Brigade, 1st Div., 20th Corps. Union, 100 missing; Confed., 100 missing.
Sand Mountain and Black Warrior Creek, or Driver's Gap and Crooked Creek, Ala., May 1, 1863. (Streight's Raid.)
Sand Mountain, Ala., April 30, 1865.
Sandy Swamp, N. C., Dec. 18, 1863.
Sandster's Sta., Va., Dec. 15, 1863. 159th N. Y.
Santa Fé, Mo., July 24 and 25, 1862. 3d Iowa Cav. Union, 2 killed, 13 wounded.
Santa Rosa, Fla., Oct. 9, 1861. 6th N. Y.; Company A, 1st U. S. Artil.; Company H, 2d U. S. Artil.; Companies C and E, 3d U. S. Inf. Union, 14 killed, 29 wounded; Confed., 350 wounded.
Saratoga, Tenn., Oct. 26, 1861. 9th Ill. Union, 4 wounded; Confed., 8 killed, 17 wounded.
Sartoria, Miss., June 4, 1863. (See Mechanicsburg.)

Sauk Centre, Minn., Sept. 10, 1862.
Saulsbury, Miss., July 2, 1864. 3d Iowa Cav.
Saunders, Fla., May 19, 1864. (See Welaka.)
Savage Sta., Va., June 29, 1862. 2d and 6th Corps. (See, also, Seven Days' Retreat.)
Savannah, Ga., Dec. 10 to 21, 1864. (See Siege of Savannah.)
Savannah, Tenn., April 16, 1862. Confed., 5 killed, 65 wounded.
Scarytown, W. Va., July 17, 1861. 2d Ky.; 12th and 21st Ohio; 1st Ohio Battery. Union, 9 killed, 38 wounded.
Scatterville, Ark., July 10, 1862. Detachment of 1st Wis. Cav.
Scatterville, Ark., Aug. 3, 1862.
Scottsboro', Ala., Jan. 8, 1865. Detachment of 101st U. S. Colored Troops.
Scott's Farm, Ark., Feb. 12, 1864. (See Caddo Gap.)
Scott's Ford, Mo., Oct. 14, 1863.
Scott's Mills Road, Tenn., Jan. 27, 1864. 13th Ky. and 23d Mich.
Scottsville, Ala., April 2. 1865. 2d Brigade, 1st Cav. Div., Military Div. of the Miss. (Wilson's Raid.)
Serougesville and La Vergne, Tenn., Nov. 27, 1862. 5th Brigade, Sill's Div., Army of the Ohio.
Scullyville, Ind. Ter., April 16, 1864. 3d Kan. Indian Home Guards.
Seabrook's Point, S. C., June 1, 1862.
Searcy, Ark., June 3, 1864. Detachment of 3d Mo. Cav.
Searcy, Ark., July 4, 1864. Detachment of 3d Ark. Cav.
Searcy, Ark., Sept. 6 and 13, 1864. Detachment of 9th Iowa Cav.
Searcy Landing, Little Red River, Ark., May 19, 1862. Detachments of 3d and 17th Mo. Inf.; 4th Mo. Cav.; Battery B., 1st Mo. Light Artil. Union, 18 killed, 27 wounded; Confed, 150 killed, wounded, and missing.
Secessionville, or Fort Johnson, James Island, S. C., June 16, 1862. 46th, 47th, and 79th N. Y.; 3d R. I.; 3d N. H.; 45th, 97th, and 100th Pa.;

6th and 7th Conn.; 8th Mich.; 28th Mass.; 1st N. Y. Engineers; 1st Conn. Artil.; Battery E, 3d U. S. Artil.; Battery I, 3d R. I. Artil.; Company H, 1st Mass. Cav. Union, 85 killed, 472 wounded, 128 missing; Confed., 51 killed, 144 wounded.
Secessionville, James Island, S. C., July 16, 1863. Troops under Gen. Terry, assisting U. S. Steamer " Com. McDonough."
Second Assault on Fort Wagner, S. C., July 18, 1863. (See Fort Wagner.)
Second Assault on Port Hudson, La., June 14, 1863. (See Port Hudson.)
Second Assault on Vicksburg, Miss., May 20, 1863. (See Vicksburg.)
Section 37, N. & N. W. R. R., Tenn., Nov. 24. 1864.
Sedalia, Mo., April 9, 1863.
Sedalia, Mo., Oct. 15, 1864. 1st and 7th Mo. Militia Cav. (Price's Invasion.)
Selma, Ala., April 2, 1865. 2d Cav. Div., Military Div. of the Miss. (Wilson's Raid.)
Senatobia, Miss., May 25, 1863. 3d Ill. Cav.
Seneca, Md., June 11, 1863. 6th Mich. Cav.
Seneca Sta., Buffalo Creek, Ind. Ter., Sept. 14, 1863. 1st Ark.
Seven Days' Retreat, Va., June 26 to July 1, 1862. (Including engagements at Mechanicsville, or Ellison's Mills, on the 26th ; Gaine's Mills, or Cold Harbor and Chickahominy, on the 27th ; Peach Orchard and Savage Sta., on the 29th ; White Oak Swamp, or Charles City Cross Roads, Glendale, Nelson's Farm, Frazier's Farm, Turkey Bend and New Market Cross Roads, on the 30th; and Malvern Hill, on July 1st.) Army of Potomac, Maj.-Gen. Geo. B. McClellan commanding. Union, 1st Corps, Brig.-Gen. McCall's Div., 253 killed, 1,240 wounded, 1,581 missing; 2d Corps, Maj.-Gen. E. V. Sumner, 187 killed, 1,076 wounded, 848 missing ; 3d Corps, Maj.-Gen. Heintzelman, 189 killed, 1,051 wounded, 833 missing; 4th Corps, Maj.-Gen. E. D. Keyes,

69 killed, 507 wounded, 201 missing; 5th Corps, Maj.-Gen. Fitz-John Porter, 620 killed, 2,460 wounded, 1,198 missing; 6th Corps, Maj.-Gen. Franklin, 245 killed, 1,313 wounded, 1,179 missing; Cav., Brig.-Gen. Stoneman, 19 killed, 60 wounded, 97 missing; Engineer Corps, 2 wounded, 21 missing; Total, 1,582 killed, 7,709 wounded, 5,958 missing. Maj.-Gen. Sumner, Brig.-Gens. Meade, Brookes, and Burns wounded; Confed., Maj.-Gen. Hager's Div., 187 killed, 803 wounded, 360 missing; Maj.-Gen. Magruder's Div., 258 killed, 1,495 wounded, 30 missing; Maj.-Gen. Longstreet's Div., 763 killed, 3,929 wounded, 239 missing; Maj.-Gen. Hill's Div., 619 killed, 3,251 wounded; Maj.-Gen. Jackson's Div., 966 killed, 4,417 wounded, 63 missing; Maj.-Gen. Holme's Div., 2 killed, 52 wounded; Maj.-Gen. Stuart's Cav., 15 killed, 30 wounded, 60 missing; Artil., Brig.-Gen. Pendleton, 10 killed, 34 wounded; Total, 2,820 killed, 14,011 wounded, 752 missing. Brig.-Gen. Griffith killed, and Brig.-Gens. Anderson, Featherstone, and Pender wounded.

Seven Pines and Fair Oaks, Va., May 31 and June 1, 1862. 2d, 3d, and 4th Corps, Army of Potomac. Union, 890 killed, 3,627 wounded, 1,222 missing; Confed., 2,800 killed, 3,897 wounded, 1,300 missing. Union, Brig.-Gens. Howard, Naglee, and Wessells wounded; Confed., Brig.-Gen. Hatton killed, and Gen. J. E. Johnson and Brig.-Gen. Rhoads wounded; Brig.-Gen. Pettigrew captured.

Shady Springs, W. Va., Aug. 28, 1862, and July 14, 1863. 2d W. Va. Cav.

Shanghai, Mo., Sept. 27, 1861.

Shanghai, Mo., Oct. 13, 1861. (See West Glaize.)

Shannon Hill, Va., May 4, 1863. 5th N. Y. Cav. (Stoneman's Raid.)

Sharon, Miss., Feb. 27, 1864.

Sharpsburg, Md., Sept. 17, 1862. (See Antietam.)

Shawnee Mound, Mo., Dec. 18, 1861. (See Milford.)

Shawneetown, Kan., June 6, 1863.

Shelbina, Mo., Sept. 4, 1861. 3d Iowa.

Shelbourne, Mo., Sept. 15, 1862. Mo. Militia.

Shelby Depot, Tenn., Oct. 23, 1862. 55th Ill.

Shelbyville, Tenn., June 6, 1863. (See Murfreesboro'.)

Shelbyville, Tenn., June 27, 1863. (See Guy's Gap.)

Shelbyville Pike, Tenn., June 4, 1863.

Shelbyville Pike, Tenn., June 24, 1863. (See Middleton.)

Shelbyville Pike, Tenn., Oct. 7, 1863. (Near Farmington.) 1st, 2d, and 4th Ohio; 2d Ky. Cav.; Wilder's Brigade of Mounted Inf. (See, also, Farmington.)

Shell's Mills, Ark., Oct. 10, 1862.

Shepherdstown, Va., Sept. 20, 1862. (See Blackford's Ford.)

Shepherdstown, Va., Oct. 1, 1862. 8th Ill.; 8th Pa.; 3d Ind. Cav.; Pennington's Battery. Union, 12 wounded; Confed., 60 killed.

Shepherdstown, Va., July 16, 1863. 1st, 4th, and 16th Pa.; 10 N. Y. and 1st Me. Cav. Confed., 25 killed, 75 wounded.

Shepherdstown, Va., Aug. 25, 1864. (See Smithfield.)

Shepherdsville, Ky., Sept. 21, 1862. Col. Grangers' Command.

Sheridan's Cav. Raid in Va., May 9 to 13, 1864. (Including engagements at Beaver Dam Sta., South Anna Bridge, Ashland, and Yellow Tavern.) Union, 50 killed, 174 wounded, 200 missing; Confed., Maj.-Gens. J. E. B. Stuart killed and J. B. Gordon wounded.

Sheridan's Raid in Va., Feb. 27 to March 25, 1865, 1st and 3d Divs., Cav. Corps, Army of Potomac. Union, 35 killed and wounded; Confed., 1,667 captured.

Sherwood, Mo., May 18, 1863. 29th U. S. Colored Troops; Detachment of 2d Kan. Artil.

Shiloh, or Pittsburg Landing, Tenn.,

April 6 and 7, 1862. Army of
Western Tenn., Maj.-Gen. U. S.
Grant commanding. 1st Div., Maj.-
Gen. McClernand; 2d Div., Maj.-
Gen. C. F. Smith; 3d Div., Brig.-
Gen. Wallace; 4th Div., Brig.-
Gen. Hurlburt; 5th Div., Brig.-Gen.
Sherman; 6th Div., Brig.-Gen. Prentiss. Army of the Ohio, Maj.-Gen.
D. C. Buell commanding. 2d Div.,
Brig.-Gen. Cooke; 4th Div., Brig.-
Gen. Nelson; 5th Div., Brig.-Gen.
Crittenden and 21st Brigade of the
6th Div., assisted by U. S. Gunboats
"Tyler" and "Lexington." Union,
1,735 killed, 7,882 wounded, 3,956
captured; Confed., 1,728 killed,
8,012 wounded, 959 captured. Union,
Brig.-Gens. Sherman and Wallace
wounded, and Brig.-Gen. Prentiss
captured. Confed., Maj.-Gen. A. S.
Johnson, Commander-in-Chief, and
Brig.-Gen. Gladdin killed. Maj.-
Gen. Cheatham, and Brig.-Gens.
Clarke, B. R. Johnson, and Bowen
wounded.

Ship's Gap, Taylor's Bridge, Ga., Oct. 16, 1864. 1st Div., 15th Corps.

Shirley's Fork, Spring River, Mo., Sept. 20, 1862. 2d Kan. Indian Home Guards.

Shoal Creek, Ala., Nov. 9, 1864. 5th Cav. Div., Army of the Cumberland.

Sibley's Landing, Mo., Oct. 6, 1862. (See Liberty.)

Sibley's Landing, Mo., March 30, 1863. Massacre on Steamer "Sam Gaty," Mo. Militia, Citizens, and Contrabands.

Siege of Atlanta, Ga., July 28 to Sept. 2, 1864. Armies of the Cumberland, Tenn. and Ohio, under Maj.-Gen. W. T. Sherman.

Siege of Corinth, Miss., Apr. 30 to May 30, '62. Maj.-Gen. Halleck's Army.

Siege of Fort Wagner, Morris Island, S. C., July 10 to Sept. 6, 1863. (See Fort Wagner.)

Siege of Knoxville, Tenn., Nov. 17 to Dec. 4, 1863. Army of the Ohio, Maj.-Gen. Burnside commanding.

Siege of Mobile, Ala., March 26 to April 9, 1865. (Including Spanish Fort and Fort Blakely.) 13th and 16th Corps, assisted by Naval Force. Union, 213 killed, 1,211 wounded; Confed., 500 killed and wounded, 2,952 missing and captured.

Siege of Petersburg, Va., June 15, 1864, to April 2, 1865. 10th and 28th Corps, Army of the James; 2d, 5th, 6th, and 9th Corps, Army of Potomac.

Siege of Port Hudson, La., May 27 to July 9, 1863. Portion of 19th Corps, Gen. Bank's Army of the Gulf, and Naval Forces under Admiral Farragut. Union, 500 killed, 2,500 wounded; Confed., 100 killed, 700 wounded, 6,408 prisoners.

Siege of Savannah, Ga., Dec. 10 to 21, 1864. 14th, 15th, 17th, and 20th Corps of Sherman's Army. Union, 200 wounded; Confed., 800 missing.

Siege of Suffolk, Va., April 12 to May 4, 1863. Army of Va.; Army of dep't of N. C. Union, 44 killed, 200 wounded; Confed., 500 killed and wounded, 400 captured.

Siege of Vicksburg, Miss., May 18 to July 4, 1863. 13th Corps, 15th Corps, and 17th Corps, under Maj.-Gen. U. S. Grant, assisted by Gunboat Fleet under Admiral Porter, afterward three Divs. of the 16th Corps, two Divs. of the 9th Corps and Maj.-Gen. Herron's Div. were added. (Including Assault on Fort Hill, May 19 and the General Assault, May 20, in which Confed. Brig.-Gen. Green was killed.) Union, 545 killed, 3,688 wounded, 303 missing; Confed., 31,277 killed, wounded, and prisoners.

Siege of Washington, N. C., March 30 to April 16, 1863. Troops under Maj.-Gen. Foster assisted by Naval Force.

Siege of Yorktown, Va., April 5 to May 3, 1862. 2d, 3d, and 4th Corps, Army of Potomac.

Silver Creek, Ala., Nov. 9, 1864.

Silver Creek, Ga., Oct., 13, 1864.

LIST OF BATTLES AND ENGAGEMENTS. 189

Silver Creek, or Roan's Tanyard, or Sugar Creek, Mo., Jan. 8, 1862. Detachments of 1st and 2d Mo.; 4th Ohio and 1st Iowa Cav. Union, 5 killed, 6 wounded; Confed., 80 wounded.
Silver Lake, Fla., Feb. 20, 1864. (See Olustee.)
Silver Run, Fayetteville, N. C.. March 13, 1865. Advance of 14th and 17th Corps.
Simmsport, La., May 18, 1864. (See Bayou de Glaize.)
Simmsport, La., Oct. 6, 1864.
Simpsonville, Ky., Jan. 25, 1865. 5th U. S. Colored Cav.
Sinking Creek, Va., Nov. 26, 1862. (See Cold Knob Mountain.)
Sinkpole Woods, Mo., March 23, 1862.
Sipsey Swamp, Ala., April 6, 1865. 1st Cav. Brigade, 1st Div., Military Div. of the Miss. (Wilson's Raid.)
Six Mile Creek, Ala., March 31, 1865. (See Montevallo.)
Six Mile House, Weldon R. R., Va., Aug. 18 to 21, 1864. 5th and 9th Corps; Kautz's Cav. and Gregg's Cav. Union, 212 killed, 1,155 wounded, 3,176 missing; Confed., 2,000 wounded, 2,000 missing. Confed., Brig.-Gens. Saunders and Lamar killed, and Brig.-Gens. Claigman, Barton, Finnegan, and Anderson wounded.
Skeet, or Swan's Headquarters, N. C., March 4, 1863. 3d N. Y. Cav.
Skull Valley, Ariz. Ter., May 26, 1865.
Slatersville, or New Kent C. H., Va., May 9, 1862. 98th Pa.; 2d R. I.; 6th U. S. Cav. Union, 4 killed, 3 wounded; Confed., 10 killed, 14 wounded.
Slaughter Mountain, Va., Aug. 9, 1862. (See Cedar Mountain.)
Slaughterville, Ky., Sept. 3, 1862. Foster's Cav. Confed., 3 killed, 2 wounded, 25 captured.
Smithfield, Ky., Jan. 5, 1865. 6th U. S. Colored Troops.
Smithfield, Va., Feb. 13, 1863. 12th Pa. Cav.
Smithfield, Va., Sept. 15, 1863. Detachments of 1st N. Y. and 12th Pa. Cav.

Smithfield, Va., Feb. 1, 1864. Detachments of 99th N. Y., 21st Conn., 20th N. Y. Cav., 3d Pa. Artil. and Marines from U. S. Gunboats "Minnesota" and "Smith Briggs." Union, 90 missing.
Smithfield, or Cherry Grove, Va., April 14, 1864. 9th N. J.; 23d and 25th Mass.; 118th N. Y. Union, 5 wounded; Confed., 6 wounded.
Smithfield and Shepherdstown, or Kearneysville, Va., Aug. 25, 1864. Merritt's and Milton's Cav., Army of Potomac. Union, 20 killed, 61 wounded, 100 missing; Confed., 300 killed and wounded.
Smithfield, Va., Aug. 29, 1864. 3d Div., 6th Corps and Torbett's Cav. Union, 10 killed, 90 wounded; Confed., 200 killed and wounded.
Smithsburg, Md., July 4, 1863. (See Monterey Gap.)
Smith's Exp. from La Grange, Tenn., to Tupelo, Miss., July 5 to 18, 1864. 1st and 3d Divs., 16th Corps; One Brigade, U. S. Colored Troops and Grierson's Cav. Union, 85 killed, 567 wounded; Confed., 110 killed, 600 wounded.
Smith's Farm, N. C., March 16, 1865. (See Averasboro'.)
Smith's Raid from Germantown,Tenn., to Miss., Feb. 10 to 25, 1864. 4th Mo.; 2d N. J.; 19th Pa.; 2d Iowa; 2d, 3d, 6th, 7th, 9th, and 11th Ill.; 3d Tenn.; 4th U. S. and 5th Ky. Cav., and 72d Ind. Mounted Inf. (Smith's and Grierson's Cav.) Union, 43 killed, 267 wounded; Confed., 50 wounded, 300 captured.
Smith's Sta., Ind. Ter., May 12, 1864. 1st Neb. Cav.
Smith's Surrender, May 26, 1865. Surrender of Kirby Smith to Maj.-Gen. Canby's Command. Confed., 20,000 prisoners.
Smithville, Ark., June 18, 1862. Union, 2 killed, 4 wounded; Confed., 4 wounded, 15 prisoners.
Smoky Hill, Col., May 16, 1864. One Company, 1st Col. Cav. McLain's Colored Battery.

Smoky Hill Crossing, Kan., Aug. 16, 1864. Detachments of 7th Iowa and U. S. Cav.
Smyrna, Ga., July 2 to 5, 1864. (See Nickajack Creek.)
Snaggy Point, La., May 3, 1864. (See City Belle.)
Snake Creek Gap, Ga., May 8, 1864. 15th Corps, Army of the Tenn.
Snake Creek Gap, Ga., Oct. 15, 1864. Portion of Army of the Tenn.
Snia Hills, Mo., April 29 and May 21, 1864. 2d Col. Cav.
Snicker's Gap, Va., Nov. 2, 1862. Batteries of 2d Corps, Army of Potomac.
Snicker's Gap, Va., July 17, 1864. Army of W. Va.
Snicker's Gap, Va., Aug. 13, 1864. (Near Snicker's Gap.) 144th and 149th Ohio. Union, 14 killed, 10 wounded, 200 missing; Confed., 2 killed, 3 wounded.
Snicker's Gap Pike, Va., Aug. 19, 1864. Detachment of 5th Mich. Cav. Union, 30 killed, 3 wounded. The wounded and all prisoners put to death by Mosby's Guerrillas.
Snicker's Ferry and Berryville, Va., Nov. 30, 1862. 1st Cav. Brigade, Staehl's Div.
Snicker's Ferry, Island Ford, Shenandoah River, Va., July 18, 1864. Army of W. Va.; portion of the 6th Corps.
Snow Hill, Tenn., April 2 and 3, 1863. (See Woodbury.)
Snyder's Bluff, Miss., April 30, 1863. Portion of the 15th Corps.
Snydersville, Miss., March 31, 1864. (Near Snydersville.) 3d U. S. Colored Cav. Union, 16 killed, 3 wounded; Confed., 3 killed, 7 wounded.
Soldier's Grove, Cal., Sept. 26, 1864.
Solomon's Gap, and Middleton, Frederick City, Md., July 7, 1864. 8th Ill. Cav.; Potomac Home Brigade and Alexander's Baltimore Battery. Union, 5 killed, 20 wounded.
Somerset, Ky., Jan. 19 and 20, 1862. (See Mill Springs.)

Somerset, Ky., March 30, 1863. (See Dutton's Hill.)
Somerville, Tenn., Jan. 3, 1863.
Somerville, Tenn., March 29, 1863. 6th Ill. Cav. Union, 9 killed, 29 wounded.
Somerville Heights, Va., May 7, 1862. 13th Ind. Union, 2 killed, 7 wounded, 24 missing.
Sounding Gap, Tenn., March 16, 1862. (See Pound Gap.)
South Anna, near Hanover C. H., Va., June 26, 1863. 2d Mass.; 12th Ill. Inf.; 11th Pa. Cav.
South Anna Bridge, Va., May 9 to 13, 1864.
South Anna River, Va., March 15, 1865. 5th U. S. Cav.
South Branch, Edisto River, S. C., Feb. 9, 1865. (See Binnaker's Bridge.)
South Branch of the Watonwan, Minn., April 16, 1863. (See Medalia.)
South Fork, Fla., Feb. 9 and 10, 1864. (See Barber's Place.)
South Fork, Jno. Day's River, Ore., April 16, 1865. One Company, 1st Ore. Cav.
South Fork, W. Va., Nov. 9, 1862. (See Moorefield.)
South Mills, N. C., April 19, 1862. (See Camden.)
South Mountain, Md., Sept. 14, 1862. (See Turner's Gap.)
South Quay, Va., April 17, 1863. 99th and 130th N. Y.
South Quay Bridge, Nansemond River, Va., May 1, 1863. 99th N. Y. Inf.
South Tunnel, Tenn., Oct. 10, 1864. 40th U. S. Colored Troops.
South Union, Ky., May 13, 1863.
Southwest Creek, N. C., Dec. 13, 1862. 8th N. J.; 85th Pa.; 3d N. Y. Cav.; 3d N. Y. Artil.
Southwest Mountain, Va., Aug. 9, 1862. (See Cedar Mountain.)
Spanish Fort, Ala., March 26 to April 8, 1865. 13th and 16th Corps, assisted by Naval Fleet. Union, 100 killed, 695 wounded; Confed., 552 killed, wounded, and missing.
Spanish Fork Cañon, Utah Ter., April 15, 1863. 2d Cal. Cav. (Indian Fight.)

Sparta, Tenn., Aug. 4, 1862. Detachments of 4th Ky. and 7th Ind. Cav.
Sparta, Tenn., Aug. 9, 1863. Cav., Army of the Cumberland. Union, 6 killed, 25 wounded.
Sparta, Tenn., Nov. 26, 1863. 1st Tenn. and 9th Pa. Cav. Confed., 1 killed, 2 wounded.
Sperryville, Va., July 5, 1862. 1st Me. Cav.
Spoonville, Terrenoire Creek, Ark., April 2, 1864. 29th Iowa; 9th Wis.; 50th Ind.; 1st Mo. Cav. (Steele's Exp.) Union, 10 killed, 35 wounded; Confed., 100 killed and wounded.
Sporting Hill, near Harrisburg, Pa., June 30, 1863. 22d and 37th N. Y. Militia and Lander's Battery.
Spottsylvania, Va., May 8 to 18, 1864. (Including Fredericksburg Road, Laurel Hill, and Ny River.) Army of Potomac, Maj.-Gen. Meade commanding; 2d Corps, Maj.-Gen. Hancock; 5th Corps, Maj.-Gen. Warren; 6th Corps, Maj.-Gen. Wright; 9th Corps, Maj.-Gen. Burnside, and Sheridan's Cav. Union, 4,177 killed, 19,687 wounded, 2,577 missing; Confed., 1,000 killed, 5,000 wounded, 3,000 missing. Union, Maj.-Gen. Sedgwick and Brig.-Gens. Rice, Owens, and Stevenson killed; Brig.-Gens. Robertson, Bartlett, Morris, and Baxter wounded. Confed., Gens. Daniels and Perrin killed; Hayes and Walker wounded, and Maj.-Gen. E. Johnson and Brig.-Gen. Stewart captured.
Spottsylvania C. H., Va., April 30, 1863. 6th N. Y. Cav. Union, 58 killed and wounded.
Spring Creek, Ind. Ter., June 6, 1863.
Spring Creek, Mo., Aug. 23, 1862.
Springfield, near Texas, Ky., Oct. 6, 1862. Advance of 3d Corps.
Springfield, Mo., Aug. 10, 1861. (See Wilson's Creek.)
Springfield, Mo., Oct. 5, 1861, and Dec. 16, 1863.
Springfield, or Zagoni's Charge, Mo.,

Oct. 25, 1861. Fremont's Body Guards and White's Prairie Scalps. Union, 18 killed, 37 wounded; Confed., 106 killed.
Springfield, Mo., Feb. 13, 1862.
Springfield, Mo., Jan. 7 and 8, 1863. Mo. Militia; Convalescents and Citizens. Union, 14 killed, 144 wounded; Confed., 40 killed, 200 wounded and missing; Union, Brig.-Gen. Browne wounded.
Springfield, W. Va., Feb. 3, 1864. Cav. under Col. Thompson.
Springfield Landing, La., July 2, 1863. 2d R. I. Cav.
Spring Hill, Mo., Oct. 27, 1861. One Company, 7th Mo. Cav. Union, 5 wounded.
Spring Hill, Tenn., March 4 and 5, 1863. (See Thompson's Station.)
Spring Hill, or Mount Carmel, Tenn., Nov. 29, 1864. 4th Corps and Cav.
Spring Hill, Va., Dec. 10, 1864.
Spring River, Ark., March 18, 1862. (See Salem.)
Spring River, Ark., Feb. 9, 1864. (See Morgan's Mills.)
Spring River, Mo., Sept. 1, 1862.
Spring River, Mo., Feb. 19, 1863. One Company, 9th Kan. Inf.
Stahel's Recon. in Va., Nov. 30, 1862.
Stanardsville and Burton's Ford, Rapidan, Va., March 1, 1864. 1st, 2d, 5th, and 6th U. S.; 6th Pa.; 1st N. Y.; 1st N. J. Cav. Union, 10 wounded; Confed., 30 captured.
Stanford, or Lancaster, Ky., Oct. 14, 1862. Advance Troops of Army of the Ohio.
State Creek, near Mount Sterling, Ky., June 11, 1863. 1st Tenn. and 14th Ky. Cav.
Statesboro, Ga., Dec. 4, 1864. Detachment of 15th Corps.
St. Augustine, Fla., Dec. 30, 1863. 10th Conn. and 24th Mass. Union, 4 killed.
Staunton Bridge, Va., June 24, 1864. 3d Div., Cav. Corps, and Kautz's Cav. (Wilson's Raid.)
Staunton Road, Va., June 1 and 2, 1862. (See Strasburg.)

St. Catherine's Creek, near Natchez, Miss., July 28, 1863. Detachment of 72d Ill. Inf.
St. Charles, White River, Ark., June 17, 1862. 43d and 46th Ind., assisted by U. S. Gunboats "Lexington," "Mound City," "Connestoga," and "St. Louis." Union, 105 killed, 30 wounded; Confed., 155 killed, wounded, and captured.
St. Charles, Ark., June 25 to 29, 1864. (See Clarendon.)
St. Francis County, Mo., April 8, 1863. Detachment of Cav. and one Company, 4th Iowa Cav., under Maj. Winslow.
St. Francois River, Mo., April 30 and May 1, 1863. (See Chalk Bluff.)
St. George's Creek, Ohio, July 19, 1863. (See Buffington Island.)
St. John's Bluff, Fla., Oct. 3, 1862. Troops under Gen. Branan, assisted by Naval Force.
St. John's River, Fla., May 23, 1864. (See Horse Landing.)
St. Louis, Mo., May 10, 1861. (Camp Jackson.) 1st, 3d, and 4th Mo. Reserve Corps; 3d Mo. Inf. Confed., 639 prisoners.
St. Louis, Mo., May 10, 1861. 5th Mo. Reserve Corps attacked by Rioters.
St. Mary's Church, Va., June 7, 1864.
St. Mary's River, Fla., Feb. 9 and 10, 1864. (See Barber's Place.)
St. Mary's Trestle, Fla., July 26, 1864. 75th Ohio Mounted Inf.
Steamer "Clara Bell," Carrolton Landing, Carolina Bend, Miss., July 24, 1864. 6th Mich. Artil.
Sterling's Plantation, La., Dec. 12, 1863. Battery E, 1st Mo. Artil. Union, 3 killed, 3 wounded.
Sterling's Plantation, near Morganzia, La., Sept. 29, 1863. 19th Iowa and 26th Ind.
Stevensburg, Va., Nov. 7, 1863. 3d Cav. Div., Army of Potomac.
Steven's Gap, Ga., Sept. 11, 1863. (See Dug Gap.)
Stevenson, Ala., Aug. 31, 1862.
Stevenson's Depot, Va., July 20, 1864. (See Winchester.)

Stewart's Creek, Tenn., Dec. 29, 1862. 3d Ky. (Advance of Crittenden's Corps.)
Stewart's Creek, Tenn., Jan. 1, 1863. 10th Ohio Inf.; 3d Ohio Cav.
Stewart's Plantation, Ark., June 27, 1862. (See Village Creek.)
Stockade at Stone River, Tenn., Oct. 5, 1863. One Company, 19th Mich. Union, 6 wounded, 44 captured.
Stockton, Mo., Aug. 9, 1862. Mo. State Militia. Confed., 13 killed, 36 wounded.
Stoneman's Cav. Raid in Va., April 27 to May 8, 1863. Cav. Corps, Army of Potomac.
Stoneman's Raid, Macon, Ga., July 26 to 31, 1864. Stoneman's & Garrard's Cav. Union, 100 killed and wounded, 900 missing.
Stoneman's Raid from Bean's Sta., Tenn., to Saltville, Va., Dec. 12 to 21, 1864. (Including Engagements at Abingdon, Glade Springs, and Marion.) Union, 20 killed, 123 wounded; Confed., 8 killed, 126 wounded, 500 missing.
Stoneman's Raid into Southwestern Va. and N. C., March 20 to April 6, 1865. Palmer's, Browne's, and Miller's Cav. Brigades.
Stone River, or Murfreesboro, Tenn., Dec. 31, 1862, to Jan. 2, 1863. Army of the Cumberland, Maj.-Gen. Rosecrans commanding. Right Wing, McCooke's Corps; Centre, Thomas' Corps; Left Wing, Crittenden's Corps. Union, 1,533 killed, 7,245 wounded, 2,800 missing; Confed., 14,560 killed, wounded, and missing. Union, Brig.-Gens. Sill killed, and Kirke wounded; Confed., Brig.-Gens. Raines and Hanson killed, and Brig.-Gens. Chalmers and Davis wounded.
Stone's Farm, Ark., April 5, 1864. 26 men of 6th Kan. Cav. in engagement with Guerrillas. 11, including Assistant Surgeon Fairchild, captured and massacred.
Stone's Ferry, Tallapoosa River, Ala., July 15, 1864.

LIST OF BATTLES AND ENGAGEMENTS. 193

Stony Creek, Va., June 28, 1864. Gen. Wilson's Cav.
Stony Creek Sta., Weldon R. R., Va., May 7, 1864. 5th and 11th Pa.; 3d N. Y. and 1st D. C. Cav.; 8th N. Y. Battery. (Kautz's Raid.)
Stony Creek Sta., Va, Oct., 11, 1864. 13th Pa. Cav.
Stony Creek Sta. and Duvall's Mills, Weldon R. R., Va., Dec. 1, 1864. Gregg's Cav. Union, 40 wounded; Confed., 175 captured.
Stony Lake, Dak. Ter., July 28, 1863. 1st Minn. Cav.; 3d Minn. Battery; 6th, 7th, and 10th Minn. Inf. (Sioux Indian Fight.)
Stony Point, Ark., May 20, 1864.
Stono River, S. C., July 1 to 10, 1864. Forces under Gen. Schimmelfennig, assisted by Naval Forces.
Strasburg, Va., March 27, 1862. Portion of Gen. Bank's Command.
Strasburg and Staunton Road, Va., June 1 and 2, 1862. 8th W. Va; 60th Ohio; 1st N. J. Cav. and 1st Pa. Cav. Union, 2 wounded.
Strasburg, Va., Oct. 9, 1864. (See Tomm's Brook.)
Strasburg, Va., Oct. 13, 1864. Recon. by 1st and 2d Divs., 19th Corps, and 1st and 2d Divs., Army of W. Va.
Strasburg Road, Va., Feb. 26, 1863. 13th Pa. and 1st N. Y. Cav.
Strasburg Road, Va., April 22, 1863. 3d W. Va. Cav.
Strawberry Plains, Tenn., Jan. 10, 1864. Detachment of Cav.
Strawberry Plains, Deep Bottom Run, Va., Aug. 14 to 18, 1864. 2d Cav. Div. and 2d Corps, Army of Potomac; 10th Corps, Army of the James. Union, 400 killed, 1,755 wounded, 1,400 missing; Confed., 1,000 wounded.
Streight's Raid from Tuscombia, Ala., to Rome, Ga., April 27 to May 3, 1863. (Including skirmishes at Day's Gap, April 30, Black Warrior Creek, May 1, and Blount's Farm, May 2.) 3d Ohio; 51st and 73d Ind.; 80th Ill. Mounted Inf.; two Companies 1st Ala. Cav. Union, 12 killed, 69

wounded, 1,466 missing and captured.
St. Stephens, S. C., March 1, 1865.
Stumptown, Mo., Aug. 2, 1863.
Sturgeon, Mo., Sept. 22, 1862. Maj. Hunt's Command.
St. Vrain's Old Fort, New Mexico, Nov. 25, 1864. One Company 1st New Mex. Cav.
Suffolk, Va., Dec. 28, 1862. Reconnoitering Forces.
Suffolk, Va., April 4, 1863.
Suffolk, Va., May 4, 1863. Troops of Dep'ts of Va. and N. C. (Siege raised.)
Suffolk, Va., May 15 and 16, 1863. (See Carrsville.)
Suffolk, Va., March 9, 1864. 2d U. S. Colored Cav. Union, 8 killed, 1 wounded; Confed., 25 wounded.
Sugar Creek, Ark., Oct. 17, 1862.
Sugar Creek, Mo., Jan. 8, 1862. (See Silver Creek.)
Sugar Creek, or Pea Ridge, Mo., Feb. 17, 1862. 1st and 6th Mo.; 3d Ill. Cav. Union, 5 killed, 9 wounded.
Sugar Creek, near Pulaski, Tenn., Oct. 9, 1863. 3d Brigade, 2d Cav. Div.
Sugar Creek, Tenn., Dec. 25 and 26, 1864. (See Pulaski.)
Sugar Loaf Battery, Federal Point, N. C., Feb. 11, 1865. 2d Div. and 1st Brigade, 1st Div., 24th Corps; 3d Div., 25th Corps. Union, 14 killed, 114 wounded.
Sugar Loaf Hill, N. C., Jan. 19, 1865. (See Half Moon Battery.)
Sugar Loaf Mountain, Md., Sept. 10, 1862. 6th U. S. Cav.
Sugar Valley, Ga., May 13 to 16, 1864. (See Resaca.)
Sulphur Branch Trestle, Ala., Sept. 25, 1864. 111th U. S. Colored Troops; 9th Ind. Cav.
Sulphur Springs, Ala., Jan. 25, 1864.
Sulphur Springs, Va., Aug. 25, 1862. Army of Virginia.
Sulphur Springs, Va., Nov. 8, 1862.
Sulphur Springs, Va., Oct. 12, 1863. (See Culpeper.)
Sulphur Springs Bridge and Whiteport, Va., Aug. 11, 1864. 1st and 3d

Divs. and Reserve Cav. Brigade, Army of Potomac.
Summerville, Miss., Nov. 26, 1862. 7th Ill. Cav. Confed., 28 captured.
Summerville, Tenn., Dec. 24 and 25 1863. (See Boliver.)
Summerville, Va., Feb. 9, 1863. Cav. under Major Knox.
Summerville Ford, Va., Sept. 16, 1864.
Summerville, W. Va., Aug. 26, 1861. (See Cross Lanes.)
Summit Point, Va., Oct. 27, 1863.
Summit Point, Berryville and Flowing Springs, Va., Aug. 21, 1864. 6th Corps and Merritt's and Wilson's Cav. Union, 600 killed and wounded; Confed., 400 killed and wounded.
Sumterville, S. C., March 23, 1865.
Sumterville, S. C., April 9, 1865. Troops of the Dep't of the South.
Sunnyside Landing, Ark., June 7, 1864.
Sunshine Church, Ga., July 31, 1864. (See Hillsboro'.)
Supply Train, Tenn., Oct. 23, 1863. 79th Ind.
Sutherland Sta., Va., April 2, 1865.
Sutton, Va., Sept. 23, 1862. 10th W. Va.
Suwano Gap, N. C., April 23, 1865. Gillem's Cav.
Swallow's Bluff, Tenn., Sept. 30, 1863. 7th Kan and 7th Ill. Cav.
Swan Lake, Ark., April 23, 1864. 5th Kan Cav.
Swan's Quarters, or Swan's Headquarters, N. C., March 4, 1863. (See Skeet.)
Sweden's Cove, Tenn., June 4, 1862. (See Jasper.)
Sweetwater, Nose's Creek and Powder Springs Creek, Ga., Oct. 1 to 3, 1864. Kilpatrick's Cav., Army of the Cumberland.
Sweetwater, Tenn., Oct. 24, 1863. Cav., Army of the Ohio.
Swift ·Creek, S. C., April 19, 1865. Troops of the Dep't of the South.
Swift Creek, or Arrowfield Church, Va., May 9 and 10, 1864. 10th and 18th Corps, Army of the James. Union, 90 killed, 400 wounded; Confed., 500 missing.

Swift Creek Bridge, N. C., June 27, 1862.
Switzler's Mills, Mo., Aug. 10, 1862. (See Grand River.)
Sycamore Church, near Petersburg, Va., Aug. 3, 1862. 3d Pa. Cav.; 5th U. S. Cav. Union, 2 wounded; Confed., 6 wounded.
Sycamore Church, Va., Sept. 16, 1864. 1st D. C. and 13th Pa. Cav. Union, 400 killed, wounded, and captured; Confed., 50 killed and wounded.
Sykestown, Mo., March 1, 1862. 10th Ill. and 7th Ill. Cav.
Sylamore, Ark., May 28 and 29, 1862. 10th Mo. and 3d Iowa Cav.
Sylvan Grove, Ga., Nov. 26, 1864. 8th Ind. and 7th Ky. Cav.
Syracuse, Mo., Oct. 14, 1863.

TABERVILLE, Ark., July 20, 1862.
Taberville, Ark., Aug. 11, 1862. 1st Mo. and 3d Wis. Cav.
Taberville, Mo., Aug. 2, 1862. (See Clear Creek.)
Table Mountain, Nev., May 20, 1865.
Tah-Kah-O-Kuty, Dak., July 28, 1864. 8th Minn. Mounted Inf.; 6th and 7th Iowa; Dak. Militia Cav.; Brackett's Minn. Cav. (Indian Fight.)
Tahlequah, Ind. Ter., March 30, 1863. 3d Kan. Indian Home Guards.
Talbot's Ferry, Ark., April 19, 1862. 4th Iowa Cav. Union, 1 killed; Confed., 3 killed.
Talbot's Sta. and Mossy Creek, Tenn., Dec. 29, 1863. 1st Brigade, 2d Div., 23d Corps; 1st Tenn. Cav.; 1st Wis. Cav.; 2d and 4th Ind. Cav.; 24th Ind. Battery.
Tallahatchie, Miss., June 18, 1862.
Tallahatchie, Miss., Oct. 13, 1863. (See Wyatt.)
Tallahatchie River, Miss., Aug. 7 to 9, 1864. Cav. and Inf., 16th Corps.
Tallahassee, Fla., May 10, 1865. Surrender of Sam Jones' Command to Troops under Gen. McCooke. Confed., 8,000 prisoners.
Talladega, Ala., April 22, 1865. 1st

Brigade, 1st Cav. Div., Military Div. of the Miss. (Wilson's Raid.)
Tanner's Bridge, near Rome, Ga., May 15, 1864. 2d Cav. Div., Army of the Cumberland. Union, 2 killed, 16 wounded.
Taylor's Bridge, Ga., Oct. 16, 1864. (See Ship's Gap.)
Taylor's Bridge, Va., May 25 to 27, 1864.
Taylor's Ford, Waukauga River, Tenn., Nov. 10, 1861. Loyal Citizens.
Taylor's Hole Creek, N. C., March 15, 1865. Kilpatrick's Cav.
Taylor's Ridge, Ga., Nov. 27, 1863. (See Ringgold.)
Taylor's Surrender., Tenn., May 4, 1865. Confed. loss 10,000.
Taylorsville, Ky., April 18, 1865.
Taylorsville, South Anna River, Va., Feb. 29, 1864. 6th N. Y. Cav. (Kilpatrick's Raid.)
Tazeville, Tenn., Aug. 6, 1862. 16th and 42d Ohio; 14th and 22d Ky.; 4th Wis. Battery. Union, 3 killed, 23 wounded, 50 missing; Confed., 9 killed, 40 wounded.
Tazeville, Tenn., Jan. 24, 1864. 34th Ky.; 116th and 118th Ind.; 11th Tenn. Cav.; 11th Mich. Battery.
Tebb's Bend, Ky., July 4, 1863. (See Green River Bridge.)
Ten Islands, or Jackson's Ford, Coosa River, Ala., July 14, 1864. 8th Ind. and 5th Iowa Cav. (Rousseau's Raid.)
Ten Miles from Columbus, Ky., Jan. 18, 1865. Tenn. Cav.
Terrapin Creek, Ala., Oct. 30, 1864. (See Ladij's.)
Terre Noire Creek, Ark., April 2, 1864. (See Spoonville.)
Terrisville, Cosby Creek, Tenn., Jan. 14, 1864. Detachments of 15th Pa. and 10th Ohio Cav.
Texas Co., Mo., Sept. 12, 1863. 5th Mo. Militia Cav.
The Cedars, Tenn., Dec. 5 to 8, 1864. (See Murfreesboro'.)
The Island, Mo., March 30, 1863. 3d Wis. Cav.
The Orchards, Va., June 25, 1862. (See Oak Grove.)

Thibodeaux, La., June 20 and 21, 1863. (See La Fourché Crossing.)
Thibodeauxville, La., Oct. 27, 1862. (See Labadiesville.)
Thomas' Place, Cal., June 28, 1864.
Thomas' Ranch, Cal., Nov. 12, 1863.
Thomas' Sta., Ga., Nov. 27 to 29, 1864.
Thomas' Waynesboro'.)
Thomas' Sta., Ga., Dec. 3, 1864. 92d Ill. Mounted Inf. Union, 2 killed, 1 wounded.
Thompson Cove, Tenn., Oct. 3, 1863. 1st Brigade, 2d Div. Cav.; Wilder's Brigade of Mounted Inf.
Thompson's Hill, Miss., May 1, 1863. (See Port Gibson.)
Thompson's Sta., or Spring Hill, and Unionville, Tenn., March 4 and 5, 1863. 33d and 85th Ind.; 22d Wis.; 19th Mich.; 124th Ohio; 18th Ohio Battery; 2d Mich. Cav.; 9th Pa. Cav.; 4th Ky. Cav. Union, 100 killed, 300 wounded, 1,306 captured; Confed., 150 killed, 450 wounded.
Thompson's Surrender, Ark., May 11, 1865. (See Chalk Bluff.)
Thornburg, Va., Aug. 6, 1862. (See Matapony.)
Thorn Hill, Ala., Jan. 3, 1865. 15th Pa., and detachments of 10th, 12th, and 13th Ind., and 2d Tenn. Cav.
Thoroughfare Gap, Va., April 2, 1862. 28th Pa.
Thoroughfare Gap, Va., Oct. 17, 1862. Detachment of Cav.
Thoroughfare Gap, Va., Nov. 5, 1862. (See New Baltimore.)
Tickfaw River, Miss., May 1, 1863. 7th Ill. Cav.
Tillafinny River, S. C., Dec. 6 to 9, 1864.
Tilton, Ga., Oct. 13, 1864.
Tilton, Tenn., May 13, 1864.
Timber Hill, Ind. Ter., Nov. 19, 1864.
Tiptonville, Tenn., April 7, 1862.
Tobbert's Ferry, Ark., March 20, 1865.
Tobosofkee, Ga., April 20, 1865. 17th Ind. Mounted Inf. (Wilson's Raid.)
Todd's Tavern, Va., May 8, 1864. 2d Div., Cav. Corps, Army of Potomac. Union, 40 killed, 150 wounded; Confed., 30 killed, 150 wounded.

Tompkinsville, Ky., July 9, 1862. One
Regiment, Pa. Cav. Union, 4 killed,
6 wounded; Confed., 10 killed and
wounded.
Tompkinsville, Ky., April 22, 1863.
Tomm's Brook, or Fisher's Hill, Strasburg, and Woodstock, Va., Oct. 9,
1864. Merritt's, Custer's, and Corbett's Cav. Union, 9 killed, 67
wounded; Confed., 100 killed and
wounded, 180 missing.
Tongue River, Dak., Aug. 29, 1865.
Toon's Sta., Miss., Aug. 31, 1862. (See
Medon.)
Torpedo Explosion, N. C., May 26,
1864. (See Bachelor's Creek.)
Totopotomoy, Va., May 29 to 31, 1864.
2d and 5th Corps, Army of Potomac.
Totopotomoy Creek, Va., May 23 to 27,
1864. (See North Anna River.)
Town Creek, Ala., April 27 and 28,
1863. Portion of 16th Corps.
Town Creek, N. C., Feb. 20, 1865. 3d
Div., 23d Corps, Army of the Ohio.
Township, Fla., Jan. 26, 1863. 32d U.
S. Colored Troops.
Tracy City, Tenn., Jan. 20, 1864. Detachment of 20th Conn. Union, 2
killed.
Training Post, Ark., Oct. 24, 1864.
Tranter's Creek, N. C., June 5, 1862.
24th Mass.; Company I, 3d N. Y.
Cav.; Marine Artil. Union, 7 killed,
11 wounded.
Treadwell's Plantation, Miss., Oct. 20,
1863.
Trenches in front of Petersburg, Va.,
June 20 to Dec. 31, 1864. (See Petersburg.)
Trenton, Ark., Oct. 14, 1862.
Trenton, N. C., Dec. 12, 1862. 3d N.
Y. Cav.
Trenton, Tenn., Aug. 7, 1862. 2d Ill.
Cav. Confed., 30 killed, 20 wounded.
Trenton, Tenn., Dec. 20, 1862. Detachments of 122d Ill.; 7th Tenn.
Cav. and Convalescents. Union, 1
killed, 250 prisoners; Confed., 17
killed, 50 wounded.
Trenton Bridge, N. C., May 14, 1862.
17th, 25th, and 27th Mass.; Battery
B, 3d N. Y. Artil.; two Companies,
3d N. Y. Cav.

Trevillian Sta., Central R. R., Va.,
June 11 and 12, 1864. Sheridan's
Cav. Union, 85 killed, 490 wounded,
160 missing; Confed., 370 missing.
Trinity, Ala., July 24, 1862. Company
E, 31st Ohio. Union, 2 killed, 11
wounded; Con., 12 killed, 30 wnd.
Trinity, La., Sept 1, 1863.
Trinity River, Cal., Nov. 13, 1863. Two
Companies, 1st Battalion Cal.
Mounted Inf. Union, 2 wounded.
Trion, Ala., April 1, 1865. 1st Brigade,
1st Div., Cav. Corps, Military Div.
of the Miss. (Wilson's Raid.)
Triplett's Bridge, Ky., June 16, 1863.
15th Mich.; 10th and 14th Ky. Cav.;
7th and 9th Mich. Cav.; 11th Mich.
Battery. Union, 15 killed, 30
wounded.
Triune, Tenn., June 9, 1863. Gen.
Mitchell's Cav. Div.
Try Mountain, Ky., Nov. 9, 1861. (See
Piketown.)
Tule Rosa Valley, Cal., Feb. 26, 1863.
Tulifing Cross Roads, S. C., Dec. 6, 7,
and 9, 1864. Troops under Gen.
Hatch, assisted by Naval Force under
Com. Preble.
Tulip, Ark., Oct. 10, 1863.
Tullahoma, Tenn., July 1, 1863. Gen.
Rosecrans' Army.
Tullahoma, Tenn., Oct. 23, 1863. 70th
Ind.
Tunica Bend (near Tunica Bend), Red
River, La., April 22, 1864. Three
Companies, 3d R. I. Cav. Union, 2
killed, 17 wounded.
Tunnel Hill, Ga., Jan. 28, 1864. Part
of 14th Corps. Union, 2 wounded;
Confed., 32 wounded.
Tunnel Hill, Ga., Feb. 25 to 27, 1864.
(See Buzzard Roost.)
Tunnel Hill, Ga., May 7, 1864. 4th
Corps and Cav. Army of the Cumberland.
Tunnel Hill, Miss., Feb. 13, 1864. Cav.
of Gen. Sherman's Troops.
Tunnel Mountain, Miss., Feb. 7, 1864.
Tupelo, Miss., May 6, 1863. 10th Mo.
and 7th Kan. Cav.
Tupelo, Miss., July 13 to 15, 1864. 1st
and 3d Divs., 16th Corps; one Bri-

LIST OF BATTLES AND ENGAGEMENTS. 197

gade of Colored Troops, and Cav. (Including engagements at Harrisburg, July 13, and Old Town Creek, July 15.) Union, 85 killed, 453 wounded; Confed., 700 killed, wounded, and missing.
Tupelo, Miss., July 25, 1864.
Turkey Bend, Va., June 30, 1862. (See White Oak Swamp, also Seven Days' Retreat.)
Turkey Island Bridge, Va., July 20, 1862. 8th Pa. Cav.
Turman's Ferry, Ky., Jan. 9, 1864. 39th Ky.
Turn-back Creek, Mo., April 26, 1862. 5th Kan. Cav. Union, 1 killed.
Turner's Gap, and Crampton's Gap, or South Mountain, Md., Sept. 14, 1862. 1st Corps, Maj.-Gen. Hooker; 6th Corps, Maj.-Gen. Franklin; 9th Corps, Maj.-Gen. Reno. Union, 443 killed, 1,806 wounded; Confed., 500 killed, 2,343 wounded, 1,500 captured. Union, Maj.-Gen. Reno killed. Confed., Brig.-Gen. Garland killed.
Turnstall Sta., Va., June 14, 1862. Union, 4 killed, 8 wounded.
Turnstall Sta., Va., May 4, 1863. 12th Ill. Cav. (Stoneman's Raid.)
Turnstall Sta., Va., March 3, 1864. 7th Mich. and 1st Vt. Cav. (Kilpatrick's Raid.)
Tuscahoma, Miss., May 15, 1863.
Tuscaloosa, Ala., April 4, 1865. 1st Brigade, 1st Cav. Div., Military Div. of the Miss. (Wilson's Raid.)
Tuscumbia, Ala., Feb. 22, 1863. Cav. Brigade under Col. Cornyn.
Tuscumbia, Ala., April 24, 1863. 2d Div., 16th Corps.
Tuscumbia, Ala., Oct. 26, 1863. (See Cane Creek.)
Tuscumbia Creek, Miss., May 30, 1862. Cav., Army of the Miss.
Tuscumbia River, Ala., Oct. 5, 1862.
Twelve Miles from Yazoo City, Miss., Dec. 1, 1864. Detachment of 2d Wis. Cav. Union, 5 killed, 9 wounded, 25 missing.
Two Hills, Bad Lands, Little Mo. River, Dak. Ter., Aug. 8, 1864. 8th Minn. Inf.; 2d Minn.; 6th and 7th Iowa; Dak. Militia and Brackett's Minn. Cav.
Tyree Springs, Tenn., Nov. 7 and 8, 1862.

UNION, Miss., Feb. 21 and 22, 1864. Union, Va., Nov. 3, 1862. Pleasanton's Cav.
Union Church, Miss., April 28, 1863. 6th Ill. Cav. (Grierson's Expedition.)
Union Church, Va., June 8, 1862. (See Cross Keys.)
Union City, Ky., March 24, 1864. 7th Tenn. Cav., 450 men captured by Forrest. [2d Ill. Cav.
Union City, Tenn., March 30, 1862.
Union City, Tenn., July 10, 1863. 4th Mo. Cav.; Cav. of Army of Tenn.
Union City, Tenn., Nov. 19, 1863. 2d Ill. Cav. Union, 1 killed; Confed., 11 killed, 53 captured.
Union Mills, Mo., Aug. 20, 1862. 1st Mo. Cav.; 13th Ill. Cav. Union, 4 killed, 3 wounded; Confed., 1 killed.
Union Sta., Tenn., Nov. 1 to 4, 1864. 10th Mo. Cav. Union, 2 killed, 2 wounded, 26 missing.
Unionville, Tenn., March 4 and 5, 1863. (See Thompson's Sta.)
University Place, Tenn., July 4, 1863. 6th Ky. Cav.
Upper Mo. River, Ark., Oct. 10, 1862. (Indian Fight.)
Upperville, Va., Nov. 3, 1862. Cav. Advance, Army of Potomac.
Upperville, Va., June 21, 1863. Pleasanton's Cav. Union, 94 wounded; Confed., 20 killed, 100 wounded, 60 missing.
Upperville, Va., Sept. 25, 1863. 1st Md. Potomac Home Brigade.
Upton Hill, Ky., Oct. 12, 1861. 39th Ind. Inf. Confed., 5 killed, 3 wounded.
Urbana, Va., May 12 and 13, 1864. Detachment of Troops assisting Potomac Flotilla.
Utoy Creek, Ga., Aug. 5 and 6, 1864. Armies of the Cumberland, Tenn., and Ohio.

VACHE GRASS, Ark., Sept. 26, 1864.
14th Kan. Cav.
Valley Sta., Col., Jan. 15, 1865.
Valverde, N. Mex., Feb. 21, 1862. (See Fort Craig.)
Van Buren, Ark., Dec. 21, 1862.
Van Buren, Ark., Dec. 28, 1862. (See Dripping Springs.)
Van Buren, Ark., Aug. 11, 1864. 2d and 6th Kan. Cav.
Van Buren Co., Ark., March 25, 1864.
Vance's Store, Ark., Oct. 2, 1863.
Van Wert, Ga., Oct. 10, 1864.
Varnell's Sta., Ga., May 9, 1864. 1st Div., McCooke's Cav. Union, 4 killed, 25 wounded.
Vaughn, Miss., May 12, 1864. 11th, 72d, and 76th Ill.
Vaughn Road, Va., Oct. 27, 1864. (See Hatcher's Run.)
Vaughn Road, Va., Feb. 5 to 7, 1865. (See Dabney's Mills.)
Vaught's Hill, near Milton, Tenn., March 20, 1863. 105th Ohio; 101st Ind.; 80th and 123d Ill.; 1st Tenn. Cav.; 9th Ind. Battery. Union, 7 killed, 48 wounded; Confed., 63 killed, 300 wounded.
Vera Cruz, Ark., Nov. 3, 1864. One Company, 46th Mo. Inf.
Vermillion Bayou, La., April 17, 1863. (See Bayou Vermillion.)
Vermillion Bayou, La., Oct. 10, 1863. 1st Brigade, 1st Div., 19th Corps.
Vermillion Bayou, La., Nov. 30, 1863.
Vernon, Ind., July 12, 1863. Ind. Minute Men. (Morgan's Raid.)
Verona, Miss., Dec. 25, 1864. 7th Ind. Cav.
Vicksburg, Miss., Dec. 29, 1862. Gen. Sherman's Troops, supported by Gunboats.
Vicksburg, Miss., May 18 to July 4, 1863. (See Siege of Vicksburg.)
Vicksburg, Miss., May 19, 1863. First Assault by Gen. Grant's Troops.
Vicksburg, Miss., May 20, 1863. Second Assault by the Army of the Tenn.
Vicksburg, Miss., June 25 and 28, 1863. Fort Hill attacked.
Vicksburg, Miss., July 4, 1863. Surrender of Vicksburg.
Vicksburg, Miss., Aug. 27, 1863. 5th U. S. Heavy Artil.
Vicksburg, Miss., Feb. 13, 1864. 52d U. S. Colored Troops.
Vicksburg, Miss., July 4, 1864. 48th U. S. Colored Troops. Union, 1 killed, 7 wounded.
Vidalia, La., Sept. 14, 1863. 3d Mo. Inf. Union, 2 killed, 4 wounded; Confed., 6 killed, 11 wounded.
Vidalia, La., Feb. 7, 1864. 30th Mo.; 6th U. S. Colored Heavy Artil.; 64th U. S. Colored Troops. Confed., 6 killed, 10 wounded.
Vidalia, La., July 22, 1864. 6th U. S. Colored Heavy Artil.
Vienna, Va., June 17, 1861. 1st Ohio. Union, 5 killed, 6 wounded; Confed., 6 killed.
Vienna, Va., Dec. 3, 1861. Detachment of 3d Pa. Cav. Union, all captured; Confed., 1 killed.
Vienna, Va., Sept. 2, 1862. 1st Minn. Inf. Union, 1 killed, 6 wounded.
Village Creek, or Stuart's Plantation, Ark., June 27, 1862. 9th Ill. Cav. Union, 2 killed, 30 wounded.
Vincent's Cross Roads, or Bay Springs, Miss., Oct. 26, 1863. 1st Ala. Cav. Union, 14 killed, 25 wounded.
Vinegar Hill, Morris Island, S. C., Aug. 26, 1863. 7th Conn.; 76th Pa.; 9th Me.; 3d N. H.; 48th and 100th N. Y.
Vining Sta., Ga., July 2 to 5, 1864. (See Nickajack Creek.)

WACHITA Indian Agency, Tex., Feb. 10, 1863. Loyal Delawares and Shawnees.
Waddell's Farm, near Village Creek, Ark., June 12, 1862. Detachment of 9th Ill. Cav. Union, 12 wounded; Confed., 28 killed and wounded.
Waddell's Farm, Ark., June 27, 1862. Detachment of 3d Iowa Cav.
Wadesburg, Mo., Dec. 24, 1861. Mo. Home Guards. Union, 2 wounded.
Waldron, Ark., Sept. 11, 1863. 14th Kan. Cav.

LIST OF BATTLES AND ENGAGEMENTS. 199

Waldon, Ark., Oct. 6, 1863. (See Fort Blair.)
Waldron, Ark., Dec. 30, 1863. 2d Kan. Cav. Union, 2 killed, 6 wounded.
Waldron, Ark., Feb. 1, 1864. 2d Kan. Cav.
Walker's Ford, Clinch River, W. Va., Dec. 2, 1863. 65th, 116th, 118th Ind.; 21st Ohio Battery; 5th Ind. Cav.; 14th Ill. Cav. Union, 9 killed, 39 wounded; Confed., 25 killed, 50 wounded.
Walkersville, Mo., April 2, 1862.
Walkersville, Mo., April 14, 1862. 2d Mo. Militia Cav. Union, 2 killed, 3 wounded.
Walkertown, Va., March 2, 1864 (near Walkertown), 2d N. Y. Cav. (Kilpatrick's Raid.)
Wallace's Ferry, Big Creek, Ark., July 26, 1864. 15th Ill. Cav.; 60th and 56th U. S. Colored Troops; Company E, 2d U. S. Colored Artil. Union, 16 killed, 32 wounded; Confed., 150 wounded.
Wall Bridge, Va., May 5, 1864. Cav. Div., Army of the James. (Kautz's Raid.)
Wall Hill, Miss., Feb. 12, 1864.
Walnut Creek, Mo., Aug. 8, 1862.
Walnut Creek, Mo., Aug. 10 to 13, 1862. (See Grand River.)
Walnut Grove Church, Ga., June 24, 1863.
Walthall, Va., June 16, 1864. 1st Div., 10th Corps, Army of the James.
Wapping Heights, or Manassas Gap, Va., July 23, 1863. 3d Corps, Army of Potomac.
Wardensville, Va., May 28, 1862. 3d Md. Potomac Home Brigade; 3d Ind. Cav. Confed., 2 killed, 3 wounded.
Warm Springs, Fort McRae, New Mexico, June 20, 1863. Detachment of 1st New Mexico Cav.
Warm Springs, N. C., Nov. 26, 1863.
Warm Springs, Tenn., Aug. 19, 1863.
Warrensburg, Mo., Oct. 18, 1861.
Warrensburg, or Briar, Mo., March 26, 1862. 60 men, of 7th Mo. Militia Cav. Union, 1 killed, 22 wounded; Confed., 9 killed, 17 wounded.
Warrensburg, Mo., March 28, 1862. 1st Ill. Cav. Union, 3 killed, 1 wounded; Confed., 15 killed.
Warrensburg, Mo., April 8, 1862.
Warrensburg, Mo., June 17, 1862. 7th Mo. Militia Cav. Union, 2 killed, 2 wounded.
Warrensburg, Mo., May 28, 1864.
Warrenton, Va., Jan. 15, 1862.
Warrenton Junction, Va., Sept. 26, 1862. Cav. under Col. McLean.
Warrenton Junction, Va., May 3, 1863. 1st W. Va. Cav.; 5th N. Y. Cav. Union, 1 killed, 16 wounded; Confed., 15 wounded.
Warrenton Junc., Va., May 14, 1863.
Warrenton, Miss., May 19, 1862.
Warrenton Springs, Va., Oct. 12 and 13, 1863. (See Culpeper.)
Warsaw, Mo., Oct. 16, 1861.
Warsaw, Mo., April 8, 17, and 28, 1862.
Warsaw, Mo., Oct. 8, 1863. 7th Mo. Militia Cav.
Warsaw, N. C., April 6, 1865.
Wartrace, Tenn., Oct. 5, 1863. 5th Iowa Cav.
Washington, N. C., May 31, 1862. (Near Washington.) 3d N. Y. Cav. Union, 1 wounded; Confed., 3 killed, 2 wounded.
Washington, N. C., Sept. 6, 1862. 1st N. C.; 24th Mass.; 3d N. Y. Cav., assisted by U. S. Gunboat "Picket." Union, 8 killed, 36 wounded; Confed., 30 killed, 100 wounded.
Washington, N. C., March 30 to April 4, 1863. Maj.-Gen. Foster's Command.
Washington, N. C., Nov. 1, 1863.
Waterford and Lumkin's Mills, Miss., Nov. 29 and 30, 1862. Advance Cav. of Gen. Grant's Army.
Waterford, Miss., Aug. 16 and 17, 1864.
Waterford, Va., Aug. 7, 1863. Detachments of 1st Conn. and 6th Mich. Cav.
Waterloo, La., Oct. 20, 1864.
Waterloo Bridge, Rappahannock River, Va., Aug. 23, 1862. Army of Virginia.

LIST OF BATTLES AND ENGAGEMENTS.

Waterproof, La., Feb. 14 and 15, 1864. 49th U. S. Colored Troops, assisted by U. S. Gunboat "Forest Rose." Union, 8 killed, 14 wounded; Confed., 15 killed.

Waterproof, La., April 20, 1864. 63d U. S. Colored Troops.

Water Valley, Miss., Dec. 4, 1862. 1st and 2d Cav. Brigade, under Cols. Hatch and Lee.

Waugh's Farm, near Batesville, Ark., Feb. 19, 1864. 11th Mo. Cav. and 4th Ark. Inf.

Wauhatchie, Tenn., Oct. 27, 1863. 11th Corps and 2d Div., 12th Corps. Union, 76 killed, 339 wounded. Confed., 300 killed, 1,200 wounded.

Wautauga Bridge and Carter's Sta., Tenn., Dec. 30, 1862. 7th Ohio Cav.; 9th Pa. Cav. Union, 1 killed, 2 wounded; Confed., 7 killed, 15 wounded, 273 missing.

Wautauga Bridge, or Carter's Sta., Tenn., April 25 and 26, 1864. 10th Mich. Cav. Union, 3 killed, 9 wounded.

Waverly, Tenn., Oct. 23, 1862. 83d Ill. Inf. Union, 1 killed, 2 wounded; Confed., 40 killed and wounded.

Waverly, Tenn., April 10, 1863. One Company, 5th Ohio Cav.

Wayne County, Mo., April 26, 1864.

Wayne C. H., W. Va., Aug. 27, 1861. 5th W. Va. Inf.

Waynesboro, Thomas' Sta., and Buckhead Creek, or Reynold's Plantation, and Brown's Cross Roads, Ga., Nov. 27 to 29, 1864. 3d Cav. Div. Military Div. of the Miss.

Waynesboro and Brier Creek, Ga., Dec. 4, 1864. 3d Cav. Div., Military Div. of the Miss.

Waynesboro, Va., Sept. 28, 1864. 3d Div., Cav. Corps, Army of Potomac.

Waynesboro, Va., Oct. 2, 1864. Portion of Custer's and Merritt's Cav. Union, 50 killed and wounded.

Waynesboro, Va., March 2, 1865. 3d Div., Cav. Corps, Army of Potomac. (Sheridan's Raid.)

Waynesville, Mo., Aug. 25, 1863. Detachment of 5th Mo. Militia Cav.

Weaver's Store, Ky., April 28, 1863. (See Howe's Ford.)

Weber's Falls, Ind. Ter., April 11 and 26, 1863.

Weber's Falls, Ind. Ter., Sept. 9, 1863. 2d Col. Cav.

Weber's Falls, Ind. Ter., Oct. 12, 1863.

Welaka and Saunders, Fla., May 19, 1864. Detachment of 17th Conn. Inf.

Weldon R. R., or Williams' Farm, or Jerusalem Plank Road, or Davis' Farm, Va., June 22 and 23, 1864. 2d, 6th, and 1st Div., 5th Corps, Army of Potomac. Union, 604 killed, 2,494 wounded, 2.217 missing; Confed., 300 wounded, 200 missing.

Weldon R. R., Va., Aug. 18 to 21, 1864. (See Six Mile House.)

Weldon R. R. Exp., Va., Dec. 7 to 11, 1864. 5th Corps, 3d Div. of 2d Corps and 2d Div. Cav. Corps, Army of Potomac. Union, 100 wounded.

Wellington, Mo., July 8, 1864.

Wentzville, Mo., July 16, 1861. (See Millsville.)

West Branch, Va., April 14, 1863.

West Glaize, or Henrytown, Monday's Hollow, and Shanghai, Mo., Oct. 13, 1861. 6th and 10th Mo. Cav.; Fremont's Cav. Confed., 62 killed.

West Liberty, Ky., Oct. 23, 1861. 2d Ohio; 1st and Loughlin's Ohio Cav.; 1st Ohio Artil. Union, 2 wounded; Confed., 10 killed, 5 wounded.

Westminster, Md., June 29, 1863. Detachment of 1st Delaware Cav. Union, 2 killed, 7 wounded; Confed, 3 killed, 15 wounded.

Weston, W. Va., Aug. 31, 1862. Two Companies 6th W. Va. Inf.

West Plains, Mo., Feb. 18, 1862.

West Point, White River, Ark., Aug. 14, 1863. 32d Iowa Inf., assisted by U. S. Gunboats "Lexington," "Cricket," and "Mariner." Union, 2 killed, 7 wounded.

West Point, Ark., June 16, 1864. 9th Iowa Cav.

West Point, Ark., July 28, 1864. 11th Mo. Cav.

West Point, Ark., Aug. 5, 1864.
West Point, Ga., April 16, 1865. (See Fort Taylor.) [Smith's Raid.
West Point, Miss., Feb. 21, 1864.
West Point, Mo., Oct. 15, 1861.
West Point, White River, Ark., Aug. 14, 1863. 32d Iowa, assisted by U. S. Gunboats "Lexington," "Cricket," and "Mariner." Union, 2 killed, 7 wounded.
West Point, Mo., Oct. 26, 1864.
West Point, or Eltham's Landing, Va., May 7, 1862. 16th, 31st, and 32d N. Y.; 95th and 96th Pa.; 5th Me.; 1st Mass. Artil.; Battery D, 2d U. S. Artil. Union, 49 killed, 104 wounded, 41 missing.
West Point R. R., Ga , July 18, 1864. (See Chewa Sta.)
Westport, Mo., June 17, 1863. Two Companies 9th Kan. Inf. Union, 14 killed, 6 wounded.
Westport, Big Blue, Mo., Oct 23, 1864. Mo. Militia Cav.; Gen. A. J Smith's Cav.; Cav. and Inf., any of the Border. (Price's Invasion.)
West Prairie, Mo., July 23, 1862.
Weyer's Cave, Va., Sept. 27, 1864. 2d Cav. Div., Army of W. Va.
Whiphy's Swamp, S. C., Feb. 10, 1865.
Whistler Sta., Ala., April 13, 1865. 3d Div., 13th Corps, Army of W. Miss.
White County, Ark., Feb. 9, 1864. (See Morgan's Mills.)
White County, Tenn., Jan. 16, 1864.
Whitehall, N. C., Dec. 16, 1862. 9th N. J.; 17th, 23d, 24th, and 45th Mass.; 3d N. Y. Cav.; 3d and 23d N. Y. Batteries.
White House, Va., June 20, 1864. Brigade under Gen. Abercrombie.
White House Landing, Va., June 21, 1864. Portions of 1st and 2d Divs., Cav. Corps, Army of Potomac.
Whitemarsh, or Wilmington Island, Ga., April 16, 1862. 8th Mich. Inf. and one Battery, R. I. Light Artil. Union, 10 killed, 35 wounded; Confed., 5 killed, 7 wounded.
White Mountains, Dak., Nov. 25, 1862.
White Oak Creek, Ark., April 14 and Aug. 11, 1864.
White Oak Ridge, near Hickman, Ky., Aug. 19, 1862. 2d Ill. Cav. Union, 2 wounded; Confed., 4 killed.
White Oak Road, Va., March 31, 1865. (See Boydton Road.)
White Oak Swamp, or Glendale, Charles City Cross Roads, Nelson's Farm, Frazier's Farm, Turkey Bend, and New Market Cross Roads, Va., June 30, 1862. 2d Corps; 3d Corps; 4th Corps; 5th Corps; 6th Corps; McCall's Div. of 1st Corps. (See, also, Seven Days' Retreat.)
White Oak Swamp Bridge, Va., Aug. 4, 1862. 3d Pa. Cav. Confed., 10 wounded, 28 captured.
White Oak Swamp Bridge, Charles City Cross Roads, or Riddle's Shop, Va., June 13, 1864. Wilson's and Crawford's Cav. Union, 50 killed, 250 wounded.
White Post, Va., June 13, 1864. 6th W. Va. Cav.
Wh.te Post, Va., Aug. 11, 1864. (See Sulphur Springs Bridge.)
White Post, Va., Dec. 6, 1864. 50 men, 21st N. Y. Cav. Union, 30 wounded.
White River, Ark., May 6, 1862, and April 26, 1863.
White River, Ark., June 22, 1864. Three Companies, 12th Iowa and U. S. Gunboat "Lexington." Union, 2 killed, 4 wounded; Confed., 2 killed, 3 wounded.
White River, Ark., Oct. 22, 1864. 53d U. S. Colored Troops.
White River, Mo., Aug. 4, 1862, and April 17, 1863.
White River, Dak.. June 17, 1865.
White Sulphur Springs, Va., Nov. 15, 1862. (See Fayetteville.)
White Sulphur Springs, Va., Oct. 12 and 13, 1863. (See Culpeper.)
White's Bridge, Nottaway Creek, Va., May 9, 1864. 3d N. Y.; 8th N. Y. Battery; 1st D. C. Cav. (Kautz's Raid.)
White's Ford, Va., Sept. 21, 1863. Cav. Army of Potomac.
Whiteside, Black Creek, Fla., July 27, 1864. 35th U. S. Colored Troops.

Whitestone Hill, Dak. Ter., Sept. 3 to 5, 1863. 2d Neb.; 6th Iowa and one Company, 7th Iowa Cav. (Indian Fight.)
White Water, Mo., April 24, 1863. 1st Wis. Cav. Union, 2 killed, 6 wounded.
Whitlen's Mill, Ark., Oct. 8, 1864.
Whittaker's Mills, near Williamsburg, Va., April 11, 1863. 5th Pa. Cav.
Wier Bottom Church, Va., May 12 to 16, 1864. (See Fort Darling, or Drewry's Bluff.)
Wier Bottom Church, or Wier Bottom Creek, Va., June 16, 1864. 2d Div., 10th Corps, Army of the James.
Wild Cat, or Rock Castle, Ky., Oct. 21, 1861. 33d Ind.; 14th and 17th Ohio; 1st Ky. Cav., and 1st Ohio Battery.
Wilderness, Va., May 5 to 7, 1864. Army of Potomac, Maj.-Gen. Meade commanding. 2d Corps, Maj.-Gen. Hancock; 5th Corps, Maj.-Gen. Warren; 6th Corps, Maj.-Gen. Sedgwick; 9th Corps, Maj.-Gen. Burnside; Sheridan's Cav. Union, 5,597 killed, 21,463 wounded, 10,677 missing; Confed., 2,000 killed, 6,000 wounded, 3,400 missing. Union, Brig.-Gens. Wadsworth, Hayes, and Webb killed; Confed., Gens. Jones and Pickett killed, and Gens. Longstreet, Pegram, Stafford, Hunter, and Jennings wounded.
Wilcox's Bridge, Wise's Fork, N. C., March 8 to 10, 1865. Palmer's, Carter's, and Ruger's Divs. Union, 80 killed, 421 wounded, 600 missing; Confed., 1,500 killed, wounded, and missing.
Williston, S. C., Feb. 8, 1865.
Wilkinson's Pike, Tenn., Dec. 7, 1864.
Williams' Bridge, Amite River, La., June 27, 1862. 21st Ind. Union, 2 killed, 4 wounded; Confed., 4 killed.
Williamsburg, Ky., Oct. 28, 1862. 7th Ky. Inf.
Williamsburg, Va., May 5, 1862. 3d and 4th Corps, Army of Potomac. Union, 456 killed, 1,400 wounded, 372 missing; Confed., 1,000 killed, wounded, and missing.

Williamsburg, Va., July 11, 1862. Confed., 3 killed.
Williamsburg, Va., Sept. 9, 1862, Feb. 7 and March 29, 1863. 5th Pa. Cav.
Williamsburg, Va., March 4, 1864.
Williamsburg Road, Va., June 18, 1862. 16th Mass. Union, 7 killed, 57 wounded; Confed., 5 killed, 9 wounded.
Williams' Farm, Va., June 22, 1864. (See Weldon R. R.)
Williamsport, Md., Sept. 20, 1862. Couch's Div., Army of Potomac.
Williamsport, Md., July 6, 1863. 3d Cav. Div., Army of Potomac.
Williamsport, Tenn., Aug. 11, 1862. Gen. Nagley's Troops.
Willicomack, Va., April 3, 1865. (See Namozin Church.)
Willis' Church, Va., June 29, 1862. Cav. Advance of Casey's Div., 4th Corps. Confed., 2 killed, 15 wounded, 46 captured.
Willmarsh Island, S. C., Feb. 22, 1864. 85th Pa. and 4th N. H.
Willow Creek, Cal., Nov. 17, 1863. 1st Cal. Battalion, Mounted Inf.
Willow Springs, Dak. Ter., Aug. 12, 1865.
Will's Valley, Ga., Sept. 7, 1863.
Wilmington, N. C., Feb. 23, 1865. 2d and 3d Divs., 23d Corps, and a portion of the 24th Corps.
Wilmington Island, Ga., April 16, 1862. (See Whitemarsh.)
Wilson's Creek, near Boston, Ky., June 13, 1863. Ky. Provost Guard.
Wilson's Creek, or Springfield, and Oak Hill, Mo., Aug. 10, 1861. 6th and 10th Mo. Cav.; 2d Kan. Mounted Inf.; one Company, 1st U. S. Cav.; 1st Iowa; 1st Kan.; 1st, 2d, 3d, and 5th Mo.; detachments of 1st and 2d U. S. Inf.; Mo. Home Guards; 1st Mo. Light Artil.; Battery F, 2d U. S. Artil. Union, 223 killed, 721 wounded, 291 missing; Confed., 265 killed, 800 wounded, 30 missing. Union, Brig.-Gen. Lyon killed.
Wilson's Farm, La., April 7, 1864. Advance Cav. of 19th Corps. Union, 14 killed, 39 wounded; Confed., 15 killed, 40 wounded, 100 captured.

Wilson's Landing, Va., June 11, 1864. 1st U. S. Colored Cav.
Wilson's Raid on the Weldon R. R., Va., June 22 to 30, 1864. Kautz's and Wilson's Cav. Union, 92 killed, 317 wounded, 734 missing; Confed., 365 killed and wounded.
Wilson's Raid from Chickasaw, Ala., to Macon, Ga., March 22 to April 24, 1865. 1st and 2d Brigades, 1st Div.; 1st and 2d Brigades, 2d Div.; 1st and 2d Brigades, 4th Div.; Cav. Corps; Military Div. of the Miss. (Six engagements.) Union, 63 killed, 345 wounded, 63 missing; Confed.; 22 killed, 38 wounded, 6,766 captured.
Wilson's Wharf Landing, Va., May 24, 1864. 1st D. C. Cav.; 10th U. S. Colored Cav.; Battery B, U. S. Colored Artil. Union, 2 killed, 24 wounded; Confed., 20 killed, 100 wounded.
Winchester, Tenn., Sept. 14, 1863.
Winchester, or Kearnstown, Va., March 23, 1862. 1st W. Va.; 84th and 110th Pa.; 5th, 7th, 8th, 29th, 62d, and 67th Ohio; 7th, 13th, and 14th Ind.; 30th Ill.; 1st Ohio Cav.; 1st Mich. Cav.; 1st W. Va., Artil.; 1st Ohio Artil.; Company E, 4th U. S. Artil. Union, 103 killed, 440 wounded, 24 missing; Confed., 80 killed, 342 wounded, 269 captured.
Winchester, Va., May 25, 1862. 2d Mass.; 29th and 46th Pa.; 27th Ind.; 3d Wis.; 28th N. Y.; 5th Conn.; Battery N, 1st N. Y. Artil.; 1st Ver. Cav.; 1st Mich. Cav.; 5th N. Y. Cav. Union, 38 killed, 155 wounded, 711 missing.
Winchester, Va., May 19, 1863. Detachment of Milroy's Cav.
Winchester, Va., June 13 and 15, 1863. 2d, 67th and 87th Pa.; 18th Conn.; 12th W. Va.; 110th, 116th, 122d, and 123d Ohio; 3d, 5th, and 6th Md.; 12th and 13th Pa. Cav.; 1st N. Y. Cav.; 1st and 3d W. Va. Cav.; Battery L, 5th U. S. Artil.; 1st W. Va. Battery; Baltimore Battery; One Company, 14th Mass. heavy Artil.

Union, 3,000 killed, wounded, and missing; Confed., 850 killed, wounded, and missing.
Winchester, or Stevenson's Depot, and Carter's Farm, Va., July 20, 1864. 2d Cav. Div., Army of W. Va.
Winchester, Va., July 23, 1864. (See Kernstown.)
Winchester, Va., Aug. 17, 1864. N. J. Brigade, 6th Corps; Wilson's Cav. Union, 50 wounded, 250 missing.
Winchester, Va., Sept. 19, 1864. (See Opequan.)
Winnsboro, S. C., Feb. 21, 1865.
Wireman's Shoals, Big Sandy River, Ky., Dec. 4, 1862. 39th Ky. Inf.
Wirt C. H., W. Va., Nov. 19, 1861. Detachment of 1st W. Va. Cav.
Wise's Fork, N. C., March 8 to 10, 1865. (See Wilcox's Bridge.)
Wittsburg, Ark., June 6, 1864.
Wolf Creek Bridge, near Memphis, Miss., Sept. 23, 1862. 57th Ohio Inf.
Wolf River, Tenn., April 8, 1864. Gen. Grierson's Cav.
Wolf River Bridge, Miss., Dec. 4, 1863. (See Moscow Sta.)
Woodbury and Morgantown, Ky., Oct. 29, 1861. 17th Ky. Inf.; 3d Ky. Cav. Union, 1 wounded.
Woodbury, Tenn., Jan. 24, 1863. 2d Div. of Crittenden's Corps. Union, 2 killed, 1 wounded; Confed., 35 killed, 100 missing.
Woodbury and Snow Hill, Tenn., April 2, and 3, 1863. 3d and 4th Ohio Cav. Union, 1 killed, 8 wounded.
Wood's Fork, Mo., Jan. 11, 1863. (See Hartsville.)
Wood Lake, Minn., Sept. 23, 1862. (See Yellow Medicine.)
Woodsonville, Ky., Dec. 17, 1861. (See Rowlett's Sta.)
Woodstock, Va., May 20 and June 2, 1862.
Woodstock, Va., Sept. 22, 1864. (See Fisher's Hill.)
Woodstock, Va., Oct. 9, 1864. (See Tomm's Brook.)
Woodville, Miss., Oct. 6, 1864.
Woodville, Tenn., Oct. 21, 1862. 2d Ill. Cav.

13

Wormley's Gap, Va., Aug. 29, 1864. 96th Ohio and detachment under Capt. Blazer.
Worthington, W. Va., Sept. 2, 1861.
Wright County, Mo., July 22, 1864.
Wyatt, Tallahatchie, Miss., Oct. 13, 1863. 2d Brigade, Cav. Div., 16th Corps.
Wyatt, Miss., Feb. 5, 1864. 114th Ill. Inf.
Wyerman's Mills, Tenn., Feb. 22, 1864. (See Mulberry Gap.)
Wyoming, C. H., W. Va., Aug. 11, 1862. Detachment of 37th Ohio Inf. Union, 2 killed.
Wytheville, Va., July 18, 1863. 34th Ohio Inf.; 1st and 2d W. Va. Cav. Union, 17 killed, 61 wounded; Confed., 75 killed, 125 missing.
Wytheville, Va., Dec. 16, 1864. (See Marion.)
Wytheville, Va., April 3, 1865. 16th Pa. Cav. (Stoneman's Raid.)

YATES' Ford, Ky., Aug. 31, 1862. 94th Ohio Inf. Union, 3 killed, 10 wounded.
Yazoo City, Miss., July 13, 1863. Maj.-Gen. Herron's Div., assisted by 3 Gunboats; Confed., 250 captured.
Yazoo City, Miss., Dec. 27 and Oct. 31, 1862, May 13, 1864, and March 15, 1865.
Yazoo City, Miss., Dec. 1, 1864. (See Twelve Miles from Yazoo City.)
Yazoo City Exp., Miss., May 4 to 13, 1864. (Including engagements at Benton and Vaughn.) 11th, 72d, and 76th Ill. Inf.; 5th Ill. Cav.; 3d U. S. Colored Cav.; 7th Ohio Battery. Union, 5 killed, 20 wounded.
Yazoo Exp., Miss., Feb. 28, 1864. 3d U. S. Colored Cav. and 1st Miss. Inf.
Yazoo Pass, Miss., Feb. 16 to 20, 1863. 5th Ill. Cav.
Yellow Bayou, La., May 10, 1864.
Yellow Bayou, La., May 18 and 19, 1864. (See Bayou De Glaize.)
Yellow Creek, Mo., Aug. 10 to 13, 1862. (See Grand River.)
Yellow Medicine, or Wood Lake, Minn., Sept. 23, 1862. 3d, 6th, and 7th Minn.; Renville Guards.
Yellow Tavern, near Richmond, Va., May 11, 1864. 1st and 3d Divs., Cav. Corps, Army of Potomac. (Sheridan's Raid.)
Yellow Tavern, Weldon R. R., Va., Oct. 1 to 5, 1864. 3d Div., 2d Corps, Army of Potomac.
Yellville, Ark., June 25, 1862, and March 10, 1863.
Yemassee, S. C., Oct. 22, 1862. (See Pocotaligo.)
Yorktown, Va., April 5 to May 3, 1862. (Siege of Yorktown.) 2d, 3d, and 4th Corps, Army of Potomac.
Yorktown, Va., April 11, 1862. 12th N. Y.; 57th and 63d Pa. Union, 2 killed, 8 wounded.
Yorktown, Va. (in front of Yorktown), April 26, 1862. Three Companies 1st Mass. Inf. Union, 3 killed, 16 wounded.
Young's Cross Roads, N. C., July 26, 1862. 9th N. J. Inf.; 3d N. Y. Cav. Union, 7 wounded; Confed., 4 killed, 18 wounded.

ZAGONI'S Charge, Mo., Oct. 25, 1861. (See Springfield.)
Zollicoffer, Tenn., Sept. 24, 1863. 3d Brigade, Cav. Div., Army of the Ohio.
Zuni, near Black Water, Va., Dec. 12, 1862. Gen. Terry's Brigade.

Naval Engagements.

ABACO, N. C., Aug. 16, 1863. (Near Abaco.) U. S. Str. "Rhode Island," captures C o n f e d. Str. "Cronstadt."
Acquia Creek, Va., May 29, 1861. Potomac Flotilla cannonades Confed. Batteries.
Acquia Creek, Va., May 31, 1861. Bombardment of Confed. Batteries by U. S. Strs. "Resolute," "Anacostia," and "Freeborn."
Acquia Creek, Va., June 1, 1861. Potomac Flotilla and U. S. Str. "Pawnee" engage Confed. Batteries.
Acquia Creek, Va., July 7, 1861. U. S. Str. "Pocahontas" attacks Confed. Str. "George Hayes."
Acquia Creek, Va., March 16, 1862. U. S. Strs. "Anacostia" and "Yankee" engage Confed. Batteries.
Albemarle Sound and Roanoke River, N. C., May 5, 1864. U. S. Gunboats "Ceres," "Commodore Hull," "Mattabesett," "Sassacus," "Seymour," "Wyalusing," "Miami," and "Whitehead" attack Confed. Ram "Albemarle." Union, 5 killed, 26 wounded; Confed., 57 captured.
Alexandria, Red River, La., May 7, 1863. Seized by Admiral Porter's Forces.
Apalachicola, Fla., April 3, 1862. Occupied by a Force from U. S. Strs. "Mercedita" and "Sagamore."
Apalachicola River, Fla., Oct. 15, 1862. Recon. by a Naval Force.
Appomattox River, Va., June 26, 1862. Naval Exp. under Capt. Rodgers.

Aranzas Pass, Texas, Nov. 17, 1863. (See Mustang Island.)
Arkansas Post, Ark., Jan. 10 and 11, 1863. (See Fort Hindman.)
Ashepoo River, S. C., May 25 to 27, 1864. U. S. Strs. "Com. McDonough," "E. D. Hale," and "Dai Ching" co-operate with Gen. Birney's Troops. Transport "Boston" lost.
Ashland, La., June 6 to 8, 1863. (See Milliken's Bend.)
Atchafalaya River, La., Nov. 5, 1862. U. S. Strs. "Diana," "Estrella," "Kingsman," and "Calhoun" engage Confed. Str. "Cotton" and Confed. Batteries.
Atchafalaya River, La., March 28, 1863. (See Pattersonville.)
Atchafalaya River, near Simmsport, La., June 8, 1864. Confed. Battery captured by U. S. Str. "Chillicothe" and other vessels.
At Sea, April 21, 1861. U. S. Vessel "Saratoga" captures the "Nightingale," with 961 slaves aboard.
At Sea, June 3, 1861. U. S. Brig "Perry" captures Confed. Privateer "Savannah."
At Sea, Nov. 12, 1861. U. S. Bark "W. G. Anderson" captures Confed. Privateer "Beauregard."
At Sea, July 25, 1863. U. S. Str. "Iroquois" captures C o n f e d. Strs. "Merrimac" and "Lizzie."
At Sea, Dec. 24, 1864. U. S. Transport "North America" sailing from New Orleans to N. Y., sprang a leak and sank, with 225 sick and wounded soldiers aboard.

LIST OF NAVAL ENGAGEMENTS.

Augusta, Ky., Sept. 27, 1862. Captured by U. S. Str. "Kensington."
Aylett's, Mattapony River, Va., June 4 and 5, 1863. Exp. by U. S. Str. "Com. Morris" and Troops.

BAHAMA Channel, Nov. 8, 1861. U. S. Str. "San Jacinto" seizes Mason and Slidell from Str. "Trent."
Bahia, Brazil, Oct. 7, 1864. (In harbor of Bahia.) U. S. Str. "Wachusett" captures Confed. Str. "Florida."
Battery Gregg, S. C., Sept. 2, 1863. (See Fort Gregg.)
Battery Gregg, S. C., Sept. 6 and 7, 1863. (See Fort Wagner.)
Baton Rouge, La., May 9, 1862. Occupied by U. S. Str. "Iroquois."
Baton Rouge, La., Aug. 5, 1872. U. S. Strs. "Essex," "Kineo," and "Katahdin," under Com. Porter, supported by Troops under Gen. Williams.
Bayou Sara, Miss., April 6, 1863. Exp. by U. S. Strs. "Hartford," "Switzerland," and "Albatross."
Bayou Teché, La., Nov. 3, 1862. Attack by U. S. Gunboats "Kinsman," "Estrella," "St. Mary," "Calhoun," and "Diana."
Bayou Teché, La., Jan. 14, 1863. U. S. Gunboats "Calhoun," "Diana," "Kinsman," and "Estrella," supported by Land Forces. Union, 10 killed, 27 wounded; Confed., 15 killed. Union, Com. Buchanan killed; Confed. Gunboat "Cotton" destroyed.
Bayou Teché, or Irish Bens, and Bisland, La., April 12 to 14, 1863. U. S. Gunboats supporting Land Forces.
Bayport, Fla., April 4, 1863. Boat Exp. under Lieut.-Com. McCantey.
Bear Creek, Ala., April 12, 1862. Advance of Tooops, supported by U. S. Strs. "Tyler" and "Lexington."
Behring Strait, June 20 to 28, 1865. 20 U. S. Whalers destroyed by Confed. Str. "Shenandoah."
Behring Strait, Nov. 5 and 6, 1865.

Confed. Str. "Shenandoah" surrenders.
Bell's Mill, Cumberland River, Tenn., Dec. 3 and 4, 1864. U. S. Naval Flotilla, under Lieut.-Com. Fitch, defeats a portion of Hood's Army.
Bell's Mill, Cumberland River, Tenn., Dec. 6, 1864. Second action by Naval Flotilla.
Berwick Bay, La., April 14, 1863. U. S. Str. "Estrella" and other vessels destroy Confed. Strs. "Diana," "Queen of the West," and "Hart," previously captured from U. S. Forces.
Black River and Ouachita River, La., Feb. 29 to March 5, 1864. Exp. of U. S. Str. "Osage" and other vessels.
Black River, Tensas River, and Ouachita River, La., July 12 to 20, 1863. Naval Exp. under Lt.-Com. Selfridge, resulting in the capture and destruction of four Confed. Steamers and large quantities of Military Stores.
Blair's Landing, Red River, La., April 12, 1864. (See Pleasant Hill.)
Blakeley River, Ala., March 28, 1865. U. S. Monitor "Milwaukee" sunk by a torpedo.
Blakeley River, Ala., March 29, 1865. U. S. Monitor "Osage" sunk by a torpedo.
Bluffton, S. C., June 4, 1863. Destroyed by U. S. Str. "Com. McDonough," assisted by Land Forces.
Bolivar, Miss., Sept. 20, 1862. (See Prentiss.)
Broad River, S. C., April 8, 1863. U.S. Str. "Geo. Washington" destroyed by Confed. Troops.
Brown's Landing, St. John's River, Fla., May 22, 1864. U. S. Str. "Ottawa" engages Confed. Forces.
Brunswick, St. Simon's, and Jekyl Islands, Ga., March 9 and 10, 1862. U. S. Str. "Mohican" and other vessels attack and occupy.
Bubel's Bay, S. C., Feb. 11 to 19, 1865. Naval Force under Capt. Ridgely support Exp. of Troops under Gen. Potter.

Buffington Island, or St. George's Creek, Ohio, July 19, 1863. U. S. Str. "Moose" assists in the capture of Morgan's Raiders.
Bute La Rose, La., April 20, 1863. Captured by U. S. Strs. "Estrella," "Clifton," "Arizona," and "Calhoun," assisted by Troops.

Cape Fear River, N. C., Oct. 11, 1862. U. S. Str. "Maratauga" attacked by Confeds.
Cape Fear River, N. C., June 23 to 26, 1864. Boat Exp.
Cape Fear River, N. C., Jan. 20, 1865. U. S. Str. "Monticello" captures blockade Runners "Stag" and "Charlotte."
Cape Fear River, N. C., Feb. 17 to 19, 1865. (See Fort Anderson.)
Cape Hatteras Inlet, N. C., Aug. 28, 1861. (See Fort Hatteras.)
Calcasieu Bayou, La., May 6, 1864. U. S. Strs. "Granite City" and "Wave" captured by Confed. Troops and Battery.
Cane River, La., April 26, 1864. U. S. Strs. "Cricket" and "Fort Hindman" attack Confed. Battery.
Cedar Keys, Fla., Jan. 16, 1862. U. S. Naval Exp. make an attack.
Cedar Keys, Fla., Oct. 6, 1862. Salt Works destroyed by Exp. from U. S. Strs. "Somerset" and "Tahoma."
Chalmette, La., April 25, 1862. Farragut's Fleet silence Confed. Battery.
Charleston, S. C., April 3, 1861. Schooner "Rhoda H. Shannon" fired on by Morris Island Battery.
Charleston, S. C., June 20, 1862. 2d Stone Fleet sunk.
Charleston, S. C., Jan. 31, 1863. (Off Charleston at 4 A. M.) U.S. Blockading Squadron "Mercedita," "Keystone State," "Quaker City," "Housatonic," "Augusta," and "Memphis" attacked by Confed. Ironclads "Palmetto State" and "Chicora."
Charleston, S. C., April 7, 1863. Bombardment of Fort Sumter by U. S. Ironclads "Keokuk," "Weehawken," "Passaic," "Montauk," "Patapsco," "New Ironsides," "Nantucket," and "Nahant." Union, 2 killed, 20 wounded; Confed., 4 killed, 10 wounded.
Charleston, S. C., Aug. 31, 1863. Confed. Str. "Sumter" sunk by guns of Fort Moultrie.
Charleston, S. C., Sept. 7, 1863. (Near Charleston.) U. S. Str. "Weehawken" runs around and sustains the fire of Fort Moultrie.
Charleston, S. C., Dec. 6, 1863. U. S. Monitor "Weehawken" sunk off Morris Island.
Charleston, S. C., Feb. 18, 1865. Surrender of Fort Sumter and other Confed. Batteries and evacuation of the city.
Charleston Harbor, S. C., Jan. 9, 1861. U. S. Str. "Star of the West" fired on.
Charleston Harbor, S. C., Dec. 19, 1861. Stone Fleet sunk by Capt. Davis.
Charleston Harbor, S. C., Nov. 16 and 17, 1863. Bombardment of Cumming's Point Battery by Fort Moultrie.
Charleston Harbor, S. C., Jan. 15, 1865. U. S. Monitor "Patapsco" destroyed by a torpedo.
Charleston Harbor, S. C., Feb. 17, 1865. U. S. Batteries on Morris Island bombard Sullivan's Island and Fort Moultrie.
Cherbourg, France, June 19, 1864. (See Off Cherbourg.)
Chesapeake and Albemarle Canal, N. C., April 23 and 24, 1862. Closed by U. S. Navy.
Chesapeake Bay, May 8, 1861. U. S. Str. "Harriet Lane" captures Confed. Privateer.
Chicamicomico, N. C., Oct. 5, 1861. Naval Force supports the 29th Ind. Inf.
Chickahominy River, Va., July 30, 1862. Recon. of U. S. Steamers from Harrison's Landing.
Chincoteague Inlet, Va., Oct. 5, 1861. U. S. Str. "Louisiana" destroys Confed. Privateer.

LIST OF NAVAL ENGAGEMENTS.

Chowan River, N. C., March 1 and 2, 1864. U. S. Strs. "Southfield" and "Whitehead" rescue the Gunboat "Bombshell."

Chowan River, N. C., July 28 and 29, 1864. Exp. of Troops supported by U. S. Str. "Whitehead."

Chuckatuck, Va., April 22, 1863. Crew of U. S. Str. "Com. Barney" engaged.

Citronelle, Ala., May 4, 1865. Surrender of Confed. Naval Forces to Admiral Thatcher.

Clarendon, White River, Ark., June 24, 1864. U. S. Str. "Queen City" captured and destroyed by Confed. Forces, who were afterward attacked by U. S. Strs. "Tyler," "Naumkeag," and "Fawn."

Cobb's Point, N. C., Feb. 10, 1862. (See Elizabeth City.)

Coggin's Point (opposite Harrison's Landing), Va., July 31, 1862. U. S. Gunboat Fleet. Union, 10 killed, 15 wounded; Confed., 1 killed, 6 wounded.

Columbia, Ark., June 1, 1864. U. S. Str. "Exchange" engages Confed. Batteries.

Combahee River, S. C., Jan. 26, 1865. U. S. Str. "Dai Ching" destroyed after an engagement with a Confed. Battery.

Commerce, Miss., Jan. 14, 1863. U. S. Str. "Forest Queen" captured by Guerrillas.

Confed. Str. "Nashville" destroyed by U. S. Monitor "Montauk," Feb. 28, 1863.

Corpus Christi, Tex., Aug. 12 to 18, 1862. U. S. Strs. "Corypheus," "Sachem," and other vessels engage the Confed. Forces.

Craney Island, Va., May 11, 1862. (Off Craney Island.) Confed. Ironclad "Merrimac" destroyed by her Crew.

Crew of U. S. Str. "Seneca" captures "City of Beauford," Nov. 8, 1861.

Cumberland River, Tenn., Feb. 13, 1862. U. S. Str. "Carondolet" attacks Fort Donelson.

Cumberland River, Tenn., Dec. 3 and 4, 1864. (See Bell's Mill.)

Cumberland River, Tenn., Dec. 6, 1864. (See Bell's Mill.)

Cypress Bend, Miss., June 22, 1863. Engagement of U. S. Gunboats.

DAUPHIN Island, Ala., Aug. 6, 1864. (See Fort Gaines.)

Devaux Neck, S. C., Dec. 6 to 9, 1864. Naval Brigade supporting U. S. Troops.

Donaldsonville, La., June 28, 1863. U. S. Strs. "Winona" and "Princess Royal," assisted by 28th Me. Inf. and Convalescents.

Donaldsonville, La., July 7, 1863. U. S. Strs. "Monongahela" and "New London" engage Confed. Batteries. Com. Reed killed.

Dover, Tenn., Feb. 3, 1863. U. S. Str. "Lexington" and other vessels engage Confed. Forces.

Duck Creek, Tenn., Aug. 18, 1862. U. S. Strs. "Skylark" and "Sally" attacked and burned by Guerrillas.

Duck River Shoals, Tenn., April 24, 1863. (See Little Rock Landing.)

Dunn's Bayou, Red River, La., May 5, 1864. U. S. Gunboat "Signal," U. S. Str. "Covington," and U. S. Transport "Warner," with 56th Ohio Inf. on board. Union, 35 killed, 65 wounded, 150 missing.

Drewry's Bluff, James River, Va., May 15, 1862. U. S. Strs. "Galena," "Port Royal," "Naugatuck," "Monitor," and "Aroostook" attack Fort Darling.

Dutch Gap, James River, Va., Aug. 5, 1863. U. S. Gunboats "Com. Barney" and "Cohassett." Union, 3 killed, 1 wounded.

Dutch Gap, James River, Va., Aug. 16, 1864. U. S. Naval Fleet support Troops.

EASTPORT, Tenn. River, Miss., Oct. 10, 1864. U. S. Strs. "Key West" and "Undine" engage Confed. Forces.

Edisto Island, S. C., April 18, 1862. U. S. Str. "Crusader" supporting Land Forces.
Elizabeth City, or Cobb's Point, N. C., Feb. 10, 1862. U. S. Gunboats "Delaware," "Underwriter," "Louisiana," "Seymour," "Hetzel," "Shawseen," "Valley City," "Putnam," "Com. Perry," "Ceres," "Morse," "White Head," and "Brinker," engage Confed. Batteries and fleets. Union, 3 killed.
Eltham's Landing, or West Point, Va., May 7, 1862. U. S. Str. "Wachussett" and other vessels support Gen. Franklin.
Eunice, Ala., June 13, 1863, destroyed by U. S. Str. "Marmora."
Exp. up Steele's Bayou, Miss., March 14 to 24, 1863. U. S. Strs. "Louisville," "Cincinnati," "Mound City," "Caron lelet," "Pittsburg," and 4 Mortar Boats, Admiral Porter commanding, assisted by 2d Div., 15th Army Corps, under Gen. Sherman.
Exp. up the Yazoo River, Miss., Feb. 1 to March 8, 1864. Portion of Admiral Porter's Fleet, co-operating with Land Forces.

FLOUR Bluff, Tex., Sept. 14, 1862. Lieut. Kitridge and boat's crew captured.
Folly Inlet, S. C., Jan. 3, 1864. U. S. Str. "Fahkee" engages the Confed. Troops.
Folly Inlet, N. C., Jan. 11, 1864. (See Lockwood.)
Folly River, S. C., Feb. 10, 14, 17, and 18, 1865.
Foot of Miss. River, June 30, 1861. U. S. Str. "Brooklyn" chases Blockade Runner "Sumter."
Fort Anderson, Paducah, Ky., March 25, 1864. U. S. Strs. "Peosta" and "Paw Paw," assisted by Land Forces.
Fort Anderson, Cape Fear River, N.C., Feb. 17 to 19, 1865. Attacked and captured by Admiral Porter's Fleet, in co-operation with the 23d and 24th Army Corps.
Fort Caswell, N. C., Feb. 23, 1863. U. S. Strs. "Dakota" and "Monticello."
Fort Clifton, James River, Va., June 9, 1864. U. S. Str. "Com. Perry" engages the Fort.
Fort Clifton, James River, Va., June 16, 1864. 2d attack on the Fort by the U. S. Str. "Com. Perry."
Fort Darling, James River, Va., May 15, 1862. U. S. Gunboats "Galena," "Port Royal," "Naugatauck," "Monitor," and "Aristook." Union, 12 killed, 14 wounded ; Confed., 7 killed, 8 wounded.
Fort De France, Martinique, Nov. 19, 1862. Confed. Str. "Alabama" eludes the U. S. Str. "San Jacinto."
Fort De Russey, Gordon's Landing, Red River, La., May 4, 1863. Attacked by U. S. Str. "Albatross."
Fort De Russey, Red River, La., May 5, 1863. Occupied by Squadron under Ad. Porter.
Fort De Russey, Red River, La., March 14, 1864. U. S. Str. "Eastport" and other vessels destroyed the barrier below the Fort.
Fort De Russey, Red River, La., March 14 and 15, 1864. Miss. Squadron and detachments of 16th and 17th Army Corps capture and occupy.
Fort Donelson, or Dover, Tenn., Feb. 14 to 16, 1862. 7 U. S. Strs. supporting Troops under Brig.-Gen. U. S. Grant, resulting in the capture of the Fort. Union, 446 killed, 1,735 wounded, 150 missing; Confed., 231 killed, 1,007 wounded, 13,829 prisoners.
Fort Fisher, N. C., Aug. 23, 1863. Bombarded by U. S. Str. "Minnesota."
Fort Fisher, N. C., Dec. 23 and 24, 1864. Attempt to blow up the Fort by exploding the Powder-boat "Louisiana."
Fort Fisher, N. C., Dec. 24, 1864. Bombardment opened by North Atlantic Squadron into Ad. Porter.

Fort Fisher, N. C., Dec. 25, 1864. 2d day's bombardment. 10th Corps and North Atlantic Squadron. Union, 8 killed, 38 wounded; Confed., 3 killed, 55 wounded, 280 prisoners.

Fort Fisher, N. C., Jan. 13 to 15, 1865. Bombardment opened by a Fleet of 52 Men-of-War, carrying 600 heavy guns begun on the 13th inst., when troops were landed under Gen. Perry, captured Jan. 15, after three days' bombardment by assault. Union, 184 killed, 749 wounded; Confed., 4,000 killed and wounded, 2,083 captured.

Fort Gaines, Dauphin Island, Mobile Bay, Ala., Aug. 6, 1864. Shelled by U. S. Str. "Chickasaw."

Fort Gaines, Mobile Bay, Ala., Aug. 8, 1864. Surrenders to U. S. Fleet under Ad. Farragut.

Fort Gregg, or Battery Gregg and Fort Sumter, S. C., Sept. 2, 1863. Engaged by U. S. Str. "New Ironsides."

Fort Grimball, Stone River, S. C., July 16, 1863. U. S. Str. "Pawnee," and other vessels make an attack.

Fort Hatteras, N. C., Aug. 28, 1861. (Cape Hatteras Inlet.) Forts Hatteras and Clarke attacked by Com. Stringham's Fleet.

Fort Hatteras, N. C., Aug. 29, 1861. 2d Attack by fleet, assisted by 3 regiments of N. Y. Troops, resulting in surrender of the Forts.

Fort Heiman, Tenn., Oct. 28, 1864. Attacked by Union Gunboats.

Fort Henry, Tenn., Feb. 6, 1862. Captured by U. S. Gunboats "Essex," "Carondelet," "St. Louis," "Cincinnati," "Connestoga," "Tyler," and "Lexington." Union, 40 wounded; Confed., 5 killed, 11 wounded.

Fort Hinman, Arkansas Post, Ark., Jan. 10 and 11, 1863. U. S. Gunboats aiding the Land Forces under Gen. Sherman.

Fort Macon, N. C., April 25 and 26, 1862. U. S. Strs. "Daylight," "State of Georgia," "Chippewa,"

and "Gemsbok," bombard April 25, and the Fort surrenders April 26 to Gen. Parke, supported by Troops and U. S. Navy.

Fort McAllister, Great Ogeechee River, Ga., Jan. 27, 1863. U. S. Monitor "Montauk" and U. S. Strs. "Seneca" and "Dawn" bombard. Confed. Str. "Nashville" destroyed.

Fort McAllister, Genesis Point, Ga., Feb. 1, 1863. 2d Attack by U. S. Monitors "Montauk," "Patapsco," "Nahant," and "Passaic."

Fort McAllister, Genesis Point, Ga., March 3, 1863. Bombarded by U. S. Monitors "Montauk," "Passaic," "Patapsco," and "Nahant."

Fort McRee, Pensacola, Fla., Nov. 22, 1861. U. S. Strs. "Niagara" and "Richmond" make an attack.

Fort Pemberton, Miss., March 13 to April 5, 1863. U. S. Gunboats "Chillicothe" and "De Kalb," supporting 13th and 17th Army Corps.

Fort Pickens, Pensacola, Fla., Nov. 23, 1861. U. S. Strs. "Niagara" and "Richmond" bombard the Fort.

Fort Pillow, Tenn., April 14, 1862. Bombarded by U. S. Vessels.

Fort Pillow, Tenn., May 10, 1862. (See Plum Point Bend.)

Fort Pillow, or Fort Wright, Tenn., June 3 to 5, 1862. Captured by U. S. Strs. "Benton," "Louisville," "Carondelet," "Cairo," "St. Louis," "Pittsburg," and "Mound City."

Fort Powhattan, Va., July 13, 1863. Occupied by U. S. Fleet under Ad. Lee.

Fort Pulaski, Ga., April 10 and 11, 1862. Detachment from U. S. Str. "Wabash," assisting Land Forces.

Fort Strong, Cape Fear River, N. C., Feb 21, 1865. Naval Force assisting Gen. Terry's Troops.

Fort Sumter, S. C., Aug. 17 to 23, 1863. Naval Squadron under Ad. Dahlgren, and Battery on Morris Island bombard the Fort.

Fort Sumter, S. C., Aug. 23, 1863. Attack by 5 U. S. Monitors.

Fort Sumter, S. C., Sept. 1 and 2, 1863.

LIST OF NAVAL ENGAGEMENTS. 211

Attack at night by U. S. Str. "New Ironsides" and U. S. Monitors.
Fort Sumter, S. C., Sept. 8 and 9, 1863. Attack at night by 413 Marines and Sailors, under Comdr. Stevens. Union, 3 killed, 114 missing.
Fort Sumter, S. C., Sept. 27, 1863. Bombarded by Batteries on Morris Island and the U. S. Fleet.
Fort Sumter, S. C., Sept. 28, 1863. Bombarded by U. S. Monitors.
Fort Sumter, S. C., Oct. 26, 1863. Joint attack by the Forts on Morris Island and the U. S. Fleet.
Fort Sumter, S. C., Oct. 27, 1863. U. S. Monitors bombard the Fort.
Forts Gaines and Morgan, Ala., Aug. 5 to 23, 1864. 13th Corps and Ad. Farragut's Fleet. Union, 75 killed, 100 drowned by sinking of the "Tecumseh," 170 wounded; Confed., 2,344 captured.
Forts Jackson and St. Phillip, La., April 18 to 24, 1862. Bombarded by U. S. Vessels "Norfolk," "Picket," "O. H. Lee," "Para," "C. P. Williams," "Arletta," "Bacon," "Sophonia," "T. A. Ward," "M. J. Carleton," "Matthew Vassar," "Geo. Mangham," "Orvetta," "Sydney C. Jones," "Adolph Hugel," "John Griffiths," "Sarah Benen," "Racer," "Sea Foam," "Henry James," and "Dan Smith," and the U. S. Mortar Flotilla, under Comdr. David D. Porter.
Forts Jackson and St. Phillip, La., April 16, 1862.
Forts Jackson and St. Phillip, La., April 20, 1862. U. S. Strs. "Pinola" and "Itasca" break through the obstructions below the Fort,
Forts Jackson and St. Phillip, La., April 28, 1862. The Forts surrender to Com. David D. Porter.
Forts Roseden and Beaulieu, Vernon River, Ga., Dec. 14 to 21, 1864. Attacked by U. S. Strs. "Sonoma," "John Griffith," and "Winona."
Fort Wagner, Morris Island, S. C., July 10 to Sept. 6, 1863. Attacked and bombarded for almost 2 months by U. S. Navy, under Ad. Dahlgren, and U. S. Troops of the Dep't of the South under Maj.-Gen. Gillmore.
Fort Wagner, Charleston Harber, S. C., July 10, 1863. U. S. Monitors "Catskill," "Montauk," "Nahant," and "Weehawken" make an attack.
Fort Wagner, S. C., July 18, 1863. 2d bombardment and attack by 6 U. S. Monitors under Ad. Dahlgren, and 2d assault by U. S. Troops.
Fort Wagner, S. C., July 20, 1863. U. S. Str. "New Ironsides" engages the Fort.
Fort Wagner, S. C., July 22, 1863. U. S. Strs. "Nantucket" and "Ottawa" engage the Fort.
Fort Wagner, S. C., July 24, 1863. 2d attack by U. S. Ironclads.
Fort Wagner, S. C., July 25, 1863. Three U. S. Gunboats engage the Fort.
Fort Wagner, S. C., Aug. 6, 1863. U. S. Str. "Marblehead" engages the Fort.
Fort Wagner, S. C., Aug. 8, 1863. U. S. Strs. "Ottawa," "Mahaska," and "Marblehead" engage the Fort.
Fort Wagner, S. C., Aug. 11, 1863. U. S. Strs. "Patapsco" and "Catskill" bombard the Fort.
Fort Wagner, Fort Sumter, and Fort Gregg, S. C., Aug. 17, 1863. 7 Ironclads and 7 Wooden Vessels attack the Forts. Comdr. Geo. W. Rodgers killed.
Fort Wagner and Battery Gregg, Morris Island, S. C., Sept. 6 and 7, 1863. Evacuated by the Confeds. at night.
Fort Washington, near Fort Washington, May 19, 1861. Confed. Schooners carrying Troops captured by U. S. Str. "Freeborn."
Fort Wright, Tenn., June 3 to 5, 1862. (See Fort Pillow.)
Four Mile Creek, Va., June 30, 1864. U. S. Str. "Hunchback" and U. S. Monitor "Saugus."
Four Mile Creek, James River, Va., July 16, 1864. U. S. Str. "Mendota" engages a Confed. Battery.

Four Mile Creek, James River, Va., July 28, 1864 U. S. Strs. "Mendota" and "Agawam."

Four Mile Creek, James River, Va., Aug. 13, 1864. U. S. Strs. "Agawam" and "Hunchback" engage Confed. Batteries.

Franklin, Va., Oct. 3, 1862. U. S. Strs. "Com. Perry," "Hunchback," and "Whitehead," aided by Gen. Spear's Troops made an attack.

Freestone Point, Va., Sept. 25, 1861. U. S. Strs. "Jacob Bell" and "Seminole."

Freestone Point, Va., Dec. 9, 1861. The Potomac Flotilla engage the Confed. Forces.

G ALVESTON, Texas, Aug. 3, 1861. U. S. Str. "South Carolina" engages Confed. Batteries.

Galveston, Texas, Nov. 7 and 8, 1861. Crew of U. S. Str. "Santee" burn Confed. Privateer "Royal Yacht," at night.

Galveston, Texas, May 15, 1862. Attack by Naval Force.

Galveston, Texas, Oct. 9, 1862, surrenders to U. S. Str. "Westfield" and other vessels.

Galveston, Texas, Jan. 1, 1863. Three Companies 42d Mass. Inf. and U. S. Gunboats "Westfield," "Harriet Lane," "Owasca," "Sachem," "Clifton" and "Coryphaeus." Union, 600 killed, wounded, and missing. Confed., 50 killed and wounded. Comdrs. Renshaw and Wainwright killed. U. S. Str. "Harriet Lane" captured. U. S. Gunboat "Westfield" destroyed.

Galveston, Texas, Jan. 11, 1863. (Near Galveston.) U. S. Str. "Hatteras" sunk by Confed. Privateer "Alabama."

Genesis Point, Ga., Feb. 1, 1863. (See Fort McAllister.)

Genesis Point, Ga., March 3, 1863. (See Fort McAllister.)

Georgetown, S. C., Feb. 23, 1865. Detachment from U. S. Vessels seize and occupy the town.

Gloucester C. H., and Ware River, Va., April 8 and 9, 1863. Exp. by U. S. Str. "Com. Morris" and Troops.

Gloucester Point, Va., May 9, 1861. U. S. Str. "Yankee" attacks Confed. Battery.

Gordon's Landing, Red River, La., Feb. 14, 1863. U. S. Str. "Queen of the West" captures Confed. Str. "New Era." The "Queen of the West" runs aground within range of a Confed. Battery and is abandoned. Str. "De Sota" destroyed.

Gordon's Landing, Red River, La., May 4, 1863. (See Fort De Russey.)

Grand Ecore, Red River, La., April 3, 1864. Ad. Porter's Fleet occupies.

Grand Gulf, Miss., June 9, 1862. Confed. Batteries engaged by U. S. Strs. "Wissahickon" and "Itasca."

Grand Gulf, Miss., June 10, 1862. Bombarded by portion of Ad. Farragut's Fleet.

Grand Gulf, Miss., March 19, 1863. Ad. Farragut and U. S. Str. "Hartford" passes by Confed. Batteries.

Grand Gulf, Miss., March 30, 1863. U. S. Str. "Hartford" and other vessels, under Ad. Farragut, pass down the Miss. by the Confed. Batteries.

Grand Gulf, Miss., April 1, 1863. Engagement by U. S. Strs. "Hartford," "Switzerland," and "Albatross" supporting U. S. Troops.

Grand Gulf, Miss., April 29, 1863. Attacked by 7 U. S. Ironclads under Ad. Porter.

Grand Gulf, Miss., May 3, 1863. Ad. Porter's Fleet attack and the Confeds. evacuate.

Grant's Pass, Ala., Sept. 12, 1863. U. S. Strs. "Genessee," "Calhoun," and "Jackson."

Grant's Pass, Miss. Sound, Ala., Feb. 17 to 29, 1864. U. S. Mortar Boats, under Ad. Farragut, bombard Fort Powell.

Great Ogeechee River, Ga., Jan. 27, 1863. (See Fort McAllister.)

Grimball, S. C., April 29, 1862. U. S. Str. "E. D. Hale" captures Confed. Battery.

HAINES' Bluff, Miss., April 29 to May 1, 1863. U. S. Str. "Black Hawk" and other vessels make an attack.
Haines' Bluff, Miss., May 18, 1863. Evacuated after an attack by Army and U. S. Fleet.
Hamilton, N. C., July 9, 1862. U. S. Gunboats "Perry," "Ceres," and "Shawsoen," and 9th N. Y. Inf. Union, 1 killed, 20 wounded.
Hampton Roads, Va., June 5, 1861. U. S. Str. "Harriet Lane" attacks Confed. Batteries.
Hampton Roads, Va., March 8, 1862. U. S. Frigates "Cumberland" and "Congress" sunk by the Confed. Ram "Merrimac." Union, 250 killed and drowned.
Hampton Roads, Va., March 9, 1862. Confed. Ram "Merrimac" defeated by U. S. Ironclad "Monitor."
Hampton Roads, Va., March 9, 1862. U. S. Str. "Minnesota," assisted by Troops, attack Confed. Fleet and Batteries.
Hampton Roads, Va., April 11, 1862. Confed. Ironclad "Merrimac" captures three small vessels.
Harrisonburg, La., March 2, 1864. Miss. Squadron under Ad. Porter.
Harrison's Landing, James River, Va., Aug. 4, 1864. (Near Harrison's Landing.) U. S. Strs. "Osceola" and "Miami."
Head of the Passes, Miss. River, La., Oct. 12, 1861. U. S. Strs. "Richmond," "Vincennes," "Preble," and "Water Witch" engage Confed. Fleet.
Helena, Ark., July 4, 1863. U. S. Gunboat "Tyler" supporting Gen. Prentiss' Troops.
Hertford, N.C., Jan. 30, 1863. Recon. by Troops and U. S. Str. "Com. Perry."
Hill's Point, N. C., April 5, 1863. Bombarded by U. S. Fleet.
Horse Landing, St. John's River, Fla., May 23, 1864. U. S. Steam Tug "Columbine" captured.
Howlett's, near Dutch Gap, James River, Va., June 21, 1864. Four U. S. Monitors engage Confed. Battery.

INDIANOLA, Tex., Oct. 26, 1862. Captured by U. S. Strs. "Clifton" and "Westfield."
Island No. 10, Miss. River, March 16, 1862. Attacked by U. S. Gunboats and Mortar Boats.
Island No. 10, Miss. River, April 4 and 5, 1862. U. S. Str. "Carondelet" runs the Confed. Batteries at night.
Island No. 10, Tenn., April 6 and 7, 1862. U. S. Str. "Pittsburg" runs the Confed. Batteries at night.
Island No. 10, Tenn., April 8, 1862. Captured by U. S. Fleet under Flag Officer A. H. Foote, and Army under Maj.-Gen. Pope.
Island No. 82, Miss. River, May 18, 1863. U. S. Transport "Crescent City" attacked by Guerrillas.

JACKSONVILLE, Fla., Feb. 5 to April 14, 1864. Joint Exp. of Fleet under Ad. Dahlgren and Troops under Gen. Gillmore. U. S. Strs. "Pawnee," "Mahaska," "Unadilla," "Ottawa," and "Norwich" remain at Jacksonville.
James Island, S. C., June 8, 1862. Eight U. S. Gunboats and Troops make recon.
James Island, S. C., July 16, 1863. (See Secessionville.)
James River, S. C., May 8, 1862. U. S. Strs. "Galena," "Aroostook," and "Port Royal."
James River, Va., Aug. 4 to 7, 1863. Recon. by U. S. Fleet and Troops.
James and Nansemond Rivers, Va., April 14 and 15, 1864. Exp. by U. S. Gunboats and Launches supported by Troops.
James River, Va., May 5, 1864. U. S. Ironclads and Gunboats support the Troops at City Point and Bermuda Hundred.
James River, near Four Mile Creek, Va., May 6, 1864. U. S. Gunboat "Com. Jones" destroyed by a torpedo. Union, 23 killed, 48 wounded.
James River, Va., May 7, 1864. U. S.

Str. "Shawseen" destroyed by Confed. Batteries.
James River, near Dutch Gap, Va., June 21, 1864. U. S. Fleet engaged.
James River, Va., May 24, 1864. (See Wilson's Wharf Landing.)
James River, Va., July 14 to Aug. 4, 1864. Numerous engagements by U. S. Strs. "Pequod," "Mendota," "Agawam," and other vessels with Confed. Batteries.
James River, Va., Oct. 22, 1864. Union Batteries attacked by Confed. Gunboats.
Jamesville, Roanoke River, N. C., Dec. 9, 1864. U. S. Str. "Otsego" sunk by a torpedo.
Jekyl Island, Ga., March 9 and 10, 1862. (See Brunswick.)
John's Island, Stone River, S. C., Dec. 25, 1863. (See Legarsville.)

KINNAKEET, Cape Hatteras, N. C., Oct. 5, 1861. U. S. Str. "Monticello" attacks Ga. Troops.

LAKE Ocala, Fla., Dec. 2, 1863. U. S. Naval Exp. destroys Salt Works.
Lamaco, Tex., Nov. 1, 1862. U. S. Strs. "Clifton" and "Westfield" bombard the town.
Legarsville, John's Island, Stone River, S. C., Dec. 25, 1863. Confed. Batteries attack U. S. Str. "Marblehead."
Little River, S. C., Jan. 5, 1863. Confed. earthworks captured by Naval Force under Lieut. Cushing.
Little Rock Landing, or Duck River Shoals, Tenn., April 24, 1863. Ellet's Miss. Ram Fleet.
Lockwood's (off Lockwood's), Folly Inlet, S. C., Jan. 11, 1864. U. S. Str. "Iron Age" destroyed.
Lower Nansemond River, Va., April 12 to 26, 1863. U. S. Str. "Com. Barney" and Flotilla.

Lower Yazoo River, Miss., Nov. 22, 1862. U. S. Fleet under Capt. Walker.
Lucas' Bend, Miss. River, Sept. 10, 1861. U. S. Strs. "Lexington" and "Conestoga."
Lynnhaven Bay, Va., Oct. 10, 1861. U. S. Str. "Daylight" engages Confed. Battery.

MACHODOC Creek, Potomac River, Va., June 14, 1861. Schooner "Kean" burned.
Malvern Hill, James River, Va., July 14, 1864. U. S. Strs. "Pequod" and "Com. Morris" engage Confed. Battery.
Marlborough Point, Va., July 29, 1861. U. S. Strs. "Yankee" and "Reliance."
Mattapony River, Va., March 9 to 13, 1864. U. S. Str. "Morse" and other vessels co-operate with Troops.
Matthew's Co., Va., Oct. 5 to 7, 1863. U. S. Fleet co-operate with Troops.
Matthew's C. H., Va., Dec. 12, 1862. Recon. by portion of the Crew of the U. S. Str. "Mahaska" and N. Y. Troops.
Matthias' Point, Va., June 27, 1861. U. S. Gunboats "Freeborn," "Reliance," and "Pawnee" make an attack. Union, 1 killed, 4 wounded.
Matthias' Point, Va., July 29, 1861. U. S. Str. "Freeborn" supports Troops in an attack on Confed. Battery.
McIntosh Co. C. H., Ga., Aug. 2 to 4, 1864. Boat Exp. from U. S. Str. "Saratoga."
Memphis, Tenn., June 6, 1862, U. S. Gunboats "Benton," "Louisville," "Carondelet," "St. Louis," and "Cairo," and Rams "Queen of the West" and "Monarch" capture or destroy 7 Confed. Gunboats.
Metagorda Bay, Tex., Dec. 29 to 31, 1863. U. S. Gunboats "Monongahela," "Sciota," and other vessels, assisted by a detachment of 13th Me. Inf.

Milliken's Bend, or Ashland, La., June 6 to 8, 1863. U. S. Strs. "Choctaw" and "Lexington" supporting Troops.
Mississippi River, near Lucas' Bend, Mo., Jan. 11, 1862. U. S. Strs. "Essex" and "St. Louis" engage Confed. Gunboats.
Mississippi River (below Forts Jackson and St. Phillip), La., March 28, 1862. U. S. Gunboats "Kennebec" and "Wissahickon."
Mississippi River (above Island No. 10), April 1 and 2, 1862. Boat attack on a Confed. Fort, resulting in its capture.
Mississippi River (below Vicksburg), La., Feb. 24, 1863. U. S. Gunboat "Indianola" captured by Confeds. Union, 1 killed, 1 wounded; Confed., 35 killed.
Mississippi River (below New Orleans), April 24, 1865. Confed. Ram "Webb" was destroyed by U. S. Gunboats "Manhattan" and "Lafayette."
Mississippi Sound, Oct. 19, 1861. Engagement between U. S. Str. "Massachusetts" and Confed. Str. "Florida."
Mississippi Sound, La., Feb. 17 to 29, 1864. (See Grant's Pass.)
Mobile, Ala., May 26, 1861. Blockade established by U. S. Str. "Powhattan."
Mobile, Ala., Sept. 4, 1862. Confed. Str. "Florida" runs the blockade on the U. S. Vessels "Oneida," "Rachel Seaman," and "Winona."
Mobile, Ala., April 8 and 9, 1865. Troops under Gen. Canby and a Naval Force attack and capture Spanish Fort and Fort Alexis.
Mobile, Ala., April 12, 1865. Occupied by U. S. Land and Naval Forces.
Mobile Bay, Ala., Jan. 9, 1864. U. S. Fleet under Ad. Trenchard engages Fort Morgan.
Mobile Bay, Ala., Feb. 17 to 29, 1864. (See Grant's Pass.)
Mobile Bay, Ala., July 5 and 6, 1864. Confed. Blockade Runner "Ivanhoe" destroyed by an exp. in boat from Ad. Farragut's Squadron at night.
Mobile Bay, Ala., Aug. 5, 1864. U. S. Strs. "Hartford," "Brooklyn," "Octorora," "Ossippee," "Itasca," "Oneida," "Galena," "Metacoma," "Richmond," "Port Royal," "Lackawanna," "Seminole," "Monongahela," and "Tecumseh," under Ad. Farragut, pass Confed. Forts Morgan and Gaines. Union Str. "Tecumseh" sunk; Confed. Ram "Tennessee" captured.
Mobile Bay, Ala., Aug. 22, 1864. U. S. Troops and Navy Forces attack Fort Morgan, resulting in surrender of Fort Morgan Aug. 23.
Mobile Bay, Ala., April 11, 1865. Forts Huger and Tracey captured by U. S. Land and Navy Forces.
Mobile Bay, Ala., April 14, 1865. U. S. Vessels "Ada," "Laura," "Itasca," "Rose," and "Sciota" destroyed by a torpedo.
Mobile Harbor, Ala., Aug. 5 to 23, 1864. (See Forts Gaines and Morgan.)
Morris Island, Charleston Harbor, S. C., July 10, 1863. Boats from U. S. Fleet assist in landing Troops.
Morris Island, S. C., July 28 to Aug. 2, and Aug. 13 to 15, 1863. Bombardment by U. S. Fleet.
Mosquito Inlet, Fla., March 21 and 22, 1862. Recon. by U. S. Gunboats "Penguin" and "Henry Andrews." Union, 8 killed, 8 wounded.
Mouth of Red River, La., April 1 to 6, 1863. Blockaded by U. S. Str. "Hartford."
Murrell's Inlet, S. C., April 27, 1863. Exp. in boats from U. S. Str. "Monticello."
Mustang Island, Aranzas Pass, Texas, Nov. 17, 1863. Captured by U. S. Str. "Monongahela" and Troops under Gen. Ransom.

N ANSEMOND River, Va., April 14 and 15, 1864. (See James River.)
Narrows, Wilmington River, Ga., Jan.

27 to 29, 1862. U. S. Strs. "Ottawa," "Seneca," "Isaac H. Smith," "Potomski," "Ellen," and "Western World," with 2,400 troops under Gen. Wright make an attack.

Natchez, Miss., May 13, 1862. Captured by U. S. Gunboat "Iroquois."

Neuse River, N. C., Dec. 12 to 16, 1862. Recon. by U. S. Strs. "Delaware," "Shawseen," "Lockwood," and "Seymour," and Army Transports "Ocean Wave," "Allison," "Port Royal," and "North State," co-operating with Gen. Foster.

Neuse River, N. C., Dec. 13, 1862. U. S. Vessels "Allison" and "Manchester" engage Confed. Battery.

Neuse River, N. C., Feb. 2, 1864. U. S. Vessel "Underwriter" captured and destroyed by the Confeds.

Newbern, N. C., March 14, 1863. U. S. Gunboat "Hetzel" and other vessels assist Troops under Maj.-Gen. Foster in repelling a Confed. Attack.

New Inlet, N. C., May 6 and 7, 1864. (Off New Inlet.) Confed. Ram "Raleigh" attacks U. S. Blockading Squadron.

New Orleans, La., May 26, 1861. U. S. Gunboat "Brooklyn" establishes a blockade.

New Orleans, La., April 24, 1862. Union Fleet under Ad. Farragut, pass the Forts below New Orleans at 3.30 A. M.

New Madrid, Mo., March 18, 1862. Confed. Battery engaged by 5 U. S. Gunboats and 4 Mortar Boats.

New Madrid, Mo., April 7, 1862. (Below New Madrid.) U. S. Gunboats "Carondelet" and "Pittsburg" attack Confed. Batteries.

New River Inlet, N. C., Nov. 23 to 25, 1862. Recon. by U. S. Str. "Ellis."

New Topsail Inlet, N. C., Aug. 22, 1863. Exp. from U. S. Str. "Shokokon," in boats.

North and South Edisto River, S. C., Dec. 17 to 21, 1861. Recon. by U. S. Strs. "Pawnee," "Unadilla," and "Pembina," and "Vixen."

North Edisto River, S. C., Feb. 24, 1862. Naval Force under Lieut. Rhuid attack a Confed. Battery.

OFF Charleston, S. C., July 28, 1861. U. S. Str. "St. Lawrence" sinks Confed. Privateer "Petrel."

Off Charleston, S. C., Oct. 6, 1861. U. S. Str. "Flag" captured Confed. Schooner "Alert."

Off Charleston, S. C., Feb. 17, 1864. U. S. Str. "Houstonic" sunk by a Confed. Torpedo Boat.

Off Cherbourg, France, June 19, 1864. U. S. Str. "Kearsarge" under Capt. Winslow destroys and sinks the Confed. Privateer "Alabama," under Capt. Semmes. Union, 3 wounded; Confed., 175 killed, wounded, and missing.

Off Georgetown, S. C., March 1, 1865. U. S. Flagship "Harvest Moon" destroyed by a torpedo.

Off Ferrol, Spain, March 21 to 23, 1865. Engagement between U. S. Strs. "Niagara" and "Sacramento," and the Confed. Ram "Stonewall."

Off Fort Morgan, Ala., May 18, 1863. Exp. from U. S. Str. "R. R. Cuyler" destroys Confed. Schooner "Isabel."

Off Mobile, Ala., Jan. 16, 1863. Confed. Str. "Florida" passes the U. S. Blockading Squadron.

Off New Inlet, N. C., Aug. 1, 1863. U. S. Gunboat "Iroquois" and other vessels captures Confed. Str. "Kate."

Off Palatka, Fla., March 21 and 29, 1864. U. S. Str. "Ottawa" engages Confed. Forces.

Off Panama, Nov. 11, 1864. Forces from U. S. Str. "Lancaster" seizes a party of Confeds. on Steamer "Salvador."

Off Shore, May 25, 1864. Attempt to destroy Confed. Ram "Albemarle" by torpedoes.

Off St. Pierre, Martinique, Nov. 23, 1861. Confed. Privateer "Sumter" escapes from U. S. Str. "Iroquois."

Ogeechee River, Ga., July 27, 1862.

LIST OF NAVAL ENGAGEMENTS. 217

Exp. by U. S. Gunboats "Paul Jones," "Unadilla," "Huron," and "Madgie."
Ouachita River, La., July 12 to 20, 1863, and Feb. 29 to March 5, 1864. (See Black River.)
Ossabaw Sound, Ga., Dec. 11. 1861. Recon. by U. S. Strs. "Ottawa," "Seneca," "Pembina," and "Henry Andrews."
Ossabaw Sound, Ga., June 3, 1864. U. S. Str. "Water Witch" captured by the Confeds.

PAMLICO Sound, N. C., Oct. 1, 1861. U. S. Tender "Fanny" captured by the Confeds.
Palmyra, Tenn., April 4, 1863. Destroyed by U.S. Gunboat "Lexington."
Pamunkey River, Va., May 17, 1862. Recon. by U. S. Str. "Sebago" and other vessels.
Pamunkey River, Va., May 29 to June 23, 1864. (See White House.)
Pass Christian, Miss., May 25, 1862. U. S. Str. "New London" engages 2 Confed. Vessels.
Pass Christian, Miss., April 4, 1862. U. S. Strs. "New London," "J. P. Jackson," and "Henry Lewis" engage a Confed. Naval Force.
Patonic Creek, Va., Aug. 23, 1861. U. S. Strs. "Yankee" and "Release" attack Confed. Batteries.
Pattersonville, La., March 28, 1863. U. S. Gunboat "Diana" with detachment of 12th Conn. and 160th N. Y. Inf. on board captured by the Confeds. Union, 4 killed, 14 wounded, 99 missing.
Patrol of the Tenn. River, March 27 to April 27, 1863. U. S. Gunboat "Lexington" and other vessels under Lieut.-Comdr. Fitch, resulting in six engagements and a number of skirmishes.
Pensacola, Fla., Sept. 14, 1861. Confed. Privateer "Judah" destroyed by the U. S. Flagship "Colorado." Union, 13 killed, 15 wounded.

Piankatauk River, Va., Aug. 17, 1863. Exp. by U. S. Strs. "Gen. Putnam" and "Com. Jones."
Pittsburg Landing, Tenn., March 2, 1862. U. S. Gunboats "Lexington" and "Tyler," supporting the 32d Ill. Inf. Union, 5 killed, 5 wounded; Confed., 20 killed, 200 wounded.
Pittsburg Landing, Tenn., April 6 and 7, 1862. (See Shiloh.)
Pleasant Hill, or Blair's Landing, Red River, La., April 12, 1864. U. S. Gunboats "Osage" and "Lexington" and a portion of the 17th Army Corps. Union, 7 wounded; Confed., 200 killed and wounded.
Plum Point Bend, near Fort Pillow, Tenn., May 10, 1862. U. S. Gunboats "Cincinnati," "Mound City," and "Cairo" engage 8 Confed. Gunboats.
Plymouth, N. C., Dec. 10, 1862. U. S. Strs. "Southfield" and "Com. Perry" repel a Confed. attack.
Plymouth, N. C., April 17 to 20, 1864, U. S. Gunboats "Miami" and "Southfield" support Troops in repelling Confed. attack.
Plymouth, N. C., April 19 and 20, 1864. Confed. Ram "Albemarle" attacks U. S. Fleet. Gunboat "Southfield" sunk and U. S. Strs. "Miami," "Ceres," and "Whitehead" retreat.
Plymouth, N. C., Oct. 27 and 28, 1864. Naval Exp. of 13 men. under Lieut. Cushing destroy the Confed. Ram "Albemarle" at night.
Plymouth, N. C., Oct. 31, 1864. Captured by U. S. Gunboats "Shamrock," "Com. Hill," "Otsego," "Wyalusing" and "Tacony."
Point Lookout, Va., May 13, 1864. Seamen from the Potomac Flotilla support a Land Force.
Port Hudson, Miss. River, La., March 14, 1863. Bombarded by U. S. Fleet under Ad. Farragut and Troops under Gen. Banks.
Port Hudson, La., March 14 and 15, 1863. Ad. Farragut with U. S. Strs. "Hartford" and "Albatross" pass the Forts. U. S. Str. "Mississippi" destroyed.

218   LIST OF NAVAL ENGAGEMENTS.

Port Hudson, La., May 8 to June 26, 1863. Bombarded by U. S. Gunboat "Essex" and the Mortar Flotilla.
Port Hudson, La., June 9 to July 2, 1863. Bombarded by Naval Battery under Lieut.-Comdr. Terry.
Portland, Me., June 27, 1863. U. S. Revenue Cutter "Caleb Cushing" captured by an exp. from Confed. Tender "Archer."
Port Royal, S. C., Nov. 7, 1861. U. S. Vessels "Wabash," "Susquehanna," "Mohican," "Pawnee," "Seminole," "Isaac Smith," "Ottawa," "Unadilla," "Pembina," "Vandalia," "Dieuville," "Seneca," "Penguin," and "Augusta" bombard and capture Forts Beauregard and Walker. Union, 8 killed, 23 wounded; Confed., 11 killed, 39 wounded.
Port Royal Ferry, Coosaw River, S. C., Jan. 1 and 2, 1862. U. S. Gunboats "Ottawa," "Unadilla," "Isaac Smith," "Vixen," "Pembina," and "Pawnee," support Land Forces.
Potomac River, Va., June 24, 1861. Confeds. attack U. S. Strs. "Monticello" and "Quaker City."
Potomac River, Va., June 29, 1861. U. S. Str. "St. Nicholas" captured by the Confeds.
Prentiss and Bolivar, Miss., Sept. 20, 1862. U. S. Ram "Queen of the West" and Army Transport and the 23d Ill. Inf. attack Confeds.
Profit Island, Miss. River, La., June 14, 1862. U. S. Gunboat "Winona," engages Confed. Battery.

R APPAHANNOCK River, Va., Feb. 21, 1863. Recon. by U. S. Gunboats "Freeborn" and "Dragon."
Rappahannock River, Va., April 18 to 22, 1864. Exp. by the Potomac Flotilla.
Red River, Ark., Jan. 14, 1863. U. S. Str. "Queen of the West" captured by the Confeds.
Red River, La., Feb. 3, 1863. U. S.

Str. "Queen of the West" captured three Confed. vessels.
Red River, La., Feb. 17 to 21, 1863. Blockaded by U. S. Str. "Indianola."
Red River, La., April 16 to May 4, 1863. Blockaded by U. S. Str. "Hartford" under Ad. Farragut.
Red River, La., May 3, 1863. Exp. by U. S. Gunboats "Albatross," "Estrella," and "Arizona."
Red River, La., March 14, 1864. (See Fort De Russey.)
Red River, La., March 14 and 15, 1864. (See Fort De Russey.)
Red River, La., April 3, 1864. (See Grand Ecore.)
Red River, La., April 15, 1864. U. S. Gunboat "Eastport" sunk by a torpedo.
Red River, La., April 26, 1864. (See Cane River.)
Red River, La., May 9, 1864. U. S. Strs. "Lexington," "Neosho," "Fort Hindman," and "Osage" pass through Col. Bailey's Dam.
Red River, La., May 12, 1864. U. S. Gunboats "Mound City," "Carondelet," and "Pittsburg" pass through Col. Bailey's Dam.
Red River, La., May 13, 1864. U. S. Strs. "Louisville," "Chillicothe," and "Ozark" pass through Col. Bailey's Dam.
Red River, La., June 3, 1864. Confed. Naval Forces surrender to U. S. Fleet.
Red River Exp. March 7 to May 15, 1864. Ad. Porter's Fleet support the Troops under Gen. Banks.
Richmond, La., June 15, 1863. Ellet's Miss. Marine Brigade supports Gen. Mower's Troops.
Roanoke Island, N. C., Feb. 7 and 8, 1862. U. S. Gunboats "Southfield," "Delaware," "Stars and Stripes," "Louisiana," "Hetzel," "Com. Perry," "Underwriter," "Valley City," "Com. Barney," "Hunchback," "Ceres," "Putnam," "Morse," "Lockwood," "J. N. Seymour," "Granite," "Brinker," "Whitehead," "Shawseen," "Picket," "Pioneer," "Bazar," "Vidette," and

LIST OF NAVAL ENGAGEMENTS.

"Chasseur" under Com. Goldborough, supporting Troops under Gen. Burnside. Roanoke surrenders Feb. 8. Union, 35 killed, 200 wounded; Confed., 16 killed, 39 wounded, 2,527 captured.
Roanoke River, N. C., May 5, 1864. (See Albemarle Sound.)

SABINE Pass, Tex., Sept. 24 and 25, 1862. Confed. Forts captured by U. S. Strs. "Rachel Seaman," "Henry James," and "Kensington."
Sabine Pass, Tex., Jan. 21, 1863. (Off Sabine Pass.) U. S. Strs. "Morning Light" and "Velocity" captured by the Confeds.
Sabine Pass, Tex., April 18, 1863. Exp. from U. S. Gunboats "New London" and "Cayuga" in boats.
Sabine Pass, Tex., Sept. 8, 1863. U. S. Strs. "Clifton," "Sachem," "Arizona," and "Granite City" co-operate with the 19th Corps under Gen. Franklin. U. S. Strs. "Sachem" and "Clifton" captured.
Savannah, Ga., May 28, 1861. U. S. Str. "Union" establishes a blockade.
Savannah, Ga., Dec. 12, 1864. Communications established between Gen. Sherman and the U. S. Fleet.
Scuppernong River, N. C., Sept. 29, 1864. U. S. Str. "Valley City" engages the Confed. Forces.
Secessionville, James Island, S. C., July 16, 1863. U. S. Str. "Com. McDonough" engages Confed. Batteries.
Sewell's Point, Va., May 18 and 19, 1861. U. S. Strs. "Monticello" and "Federal" engage Confed. Batteries.
Sewell's Point, Va., May 8, 1862. U. S. Fleet engages Confed. Battery.
Shiloh, Tenn., April 6 and 7, 1862. U. S. Gunboats "Tyler" and "Lexington" support the Troops under Gen. Sherman.
Siege of Fort Wagner (Morris Island), S. C., July 10 to Sept. 6, 1863. Fleet

under Ad. Dahlgren supports Gen. Gillmore's forces.
Siege of Mobile, Ala., March 26 to April 9, 1865. (See Spanish Fort.)
Siege of Port Hudson, La., May 27 to July 9, 1863. Ad. Farragut's Fleet support the 19th Corps.
Siege of Vicksburg, Miss., May 18 to July 4, 1863. Ad. Porter's Fleet assists the Land Forces under Gen. Grant.
Simon's Bluff, S. C., June 21, 1862. Attack by U. S. Strs. "Crusader" and "Planter" and Land Forces.
Sinnisport, La., June 4, 1863. Destroyed by U. S. Ram "Switzerland."
Smithfield, Va., Feb. 1, 1864. Detachment from U. S. Str. "Minnesota" assists a Land Force. U. S. Army Transport "Smith Briggs" captured by the Confeds.
Smithville, N. C., Feb. 29 to March 1, 1864. Boat Exp. from U. S. Str. "Monticello."
Smyrna, Fla., July 28, 1863. Destroyed by U. S. Fleet.
Spanish Fort, Ala., March 26 to April 9, 1865. U. S. Fleet supporting the 13th and 16th Army Corps.
Stone River, S. C., May 20, 1862. Occupied by U. S. Str. "Unadilla" and other vessels.
Stone River, S. C., Jan. 30, 1863. U. S. Str. "Isaac Smith" captured by Confed. Batteries.
Stone River, S. C., July 1 to 10, 1864. U. S. Navy under Ad. Dahlgren co-operates with Gen. Schimmelfennig's Troops.
St. Andrew's, Fla., Dec. 11, 1863. Occupied by U. S. Str. "Wrestler."
St. Charles, White River, Ark., June 17, 1862. U. S. Gunboats "Lexington," "Mound City," "Conestoga," and "St. Louis," assisted by the 43d and 46th Ind. Inf. Boiler of Str. "Mound City" explodes, killing or wounding 150 out of her crew of 175.
St. George's Creek, Ohio, July 19, 1863. (See Buffington Island.)
St. Helena Sound, S. C., Nov. 25 to 28, 1861. Advance and attack by U. S.

14

Gunboats "Pawnee," "Unadilla," "Pembina," and "Vixen."
St. Helena Sound, S. C., Dec. 5 to 9, 1861. Recon. by U. S. Gunboats "Pawnee," "Unadilla," "Pembina," and "Vixen."
St. John's Bluff, Fla., Oct. 3, 1862. U. S. Fleet under Com. Steadman, assisted by Troops, captures a Confed. Battery.
St. John's River, Fla., June 8, 1862. Engagement by U. S. Strs. "Seneca" and "Patroon."
St. John's River and Ocklawaha, Fla., March 9 to 23, 1864. Exp. by U. S. Str. "Columbine" and the Steam Launch of the "Pawnee."
St. John's River, Fla., May 22 to 28, 1864. Exp. of U. S. Strs. "Ottawa" and "Columbine."
St. John's River, Fla., May 22, 1864. (See Brown's Landing.)
St. John's River, Fla., May 23, 1864. (See Horse Landing.)
St. Mary's, Fla., Nov. 9, 1862. Bombarded by U. S. Gunboat "Mohawk."
St. Simon's, Ga., March 9 and 10, 1862. (See Brunswick.)
Sun Flower River, Miss., May 24 to 31, 1863.
Swainsboro', N. C., Aug. 14 and 15, 1862. Recon. by U. S. Strs. "Wilson" and "Ellis," aided by Troops.

Nov. 4, 1864. U. S. Strs. "Key West," "Tawah," and "Elfin" burned.
Tensas River, La., July 12 to 20, 1863. (See Black River.)
Togodo Creek, North Edisto, S. C., Feb. 9, 1864. U. S. Gunboats "Pawnee" and "Sonoma" engage Confed. Batteries.
Trent's Reach, James River, Va., Jan. 23 and 24, 1865. Confed. Strs. "Virginia," "Richmond," "Fredericksburg," "Drewry," "Torpedo," "Scorpion," "Walsh," and "Hornet" attempt to pass obstructions in the river.
Trent's Reach, James River, Va., Jan. 24, 1865. U. S. Strs. "Onondaga" and "Massasoit" engage the Confed. Squadron.
Trent's Reach Bar, James River, Va., June 15 to 18, 1864. Obstructions placed in the River by the Naval Force, under orders from Gen. Grant.
Tulifing Cross Roads, S. C., Dec. 6, 7, and 9, 1864. Naval Brigade under Com. Preble assists Troops under Gen. J. B. Hatch.
Tunica Bend, La., June 16, 1864. U. S. Strs. "Gen. Bragg" and "Naiad" engage Confed. Battery.
Turkey Bend, James River, Va., May 7, 1864. U. S. Str. "Shawseen" destroyed by Confed. Batteries.

TAMPA, Fla., Nov. 3, 1862. Bombarded by U. S. Gunboat "Tahoma."
Tampa Bay, Fla., Oct. 17, 1863. Two Confed. Blockade Runners destroyed by U. S. Gunboats "Tahoma" and "Adele." Union, 3 killed, 10 wounded.
Tennessee River, Ala., Feb. 6 to 10, 1862. Recon. of U. S. Strs. "Conestoga," "Tyler," and "Lexington" up the Tennessee River to Florence, resulting in the capture of 3 Confed. Steamers and the burning of 6.
Tennessee River, near Johnsonville,

UPPER Nansemond River, Va., April 12 to 25, 1863. Recon. and Skirmishes by U. S. Gunboat "Stepping Stone" and Flotilla.
Up the Ocklawaha River, Fla., March 9 to 23, 1864. (See St. John's River.)
Urbana, Va., May 12 and 13, 1864. Recon. by a portion of the Potomac Flotilla.
U. S. Str. "Essex" destroys Confed. Ram "Arkansas," Aug. 6, 1862.
U. S. Str. "Empress," Miss., engaged Aug. 10, 1864.
U. S. Str. "Niagara" captured by Confed. Str. "Georgia," Aug. 15, 1864.

VERNON River, Ga., Dec. 14 to 21, 1864. (See Fort Roseden.)
Vernon River, Ga., Dec. 21, 1864. U. S. Fleet compels the evacuation of Forts Roseden and Beaulieu.
Vicksburg, Miss., June 26, 1862. Attack by Com. Porter's Mortar Fleet.
Vicksburg, Miss., June 28, 1862. U. S. Fleet under Ad. Farragut pass Confed. Batteries. U. S. Strs. "Brooklyn," "Kennebec," and "Katahdin" fail to pass.
Vicksburg, Miss., July 15, 1862. Second passage of the Confed. Batteries by Farragut's Fleet.
Vicksburg, Miss., July 22, 1862. U. S. Gunboat "Essex" and Ram "Queen of the West" pass the Confed. Batteries and attack the Confed. Ram "Arkansas."
Vicksburg, Miss., Feb. 2, 1863. U. S. Ram "Queen of the West" passes the Confed. Batteries.
Vicksburg, Miss., Feb. 13, 1863. U. S. Ram "Queen of the West" attacks the Confed. Batteries.
Vicksburg, Miss., Feb. 18, 1863. Bombarded by the U. S. Mortar Fleet.
Vicksburg, Miss., Feb. 25, 1863. U. S. Gunboat "Switzerland" passes the Confed. Batteries and U. S. Ironclad "Lancaster" destroyed.
Vicksburg, Miss., April 16 and 17, 1863. U. S. Fleet under Ad. Porter passes the Confed. Batteries at night.
Vicksburg, Miss., May 19 to 22, 1863. U. S. Fleet bombards Confed. Batteries.
Vicksburg, Miss., May 20 to July 3, 1863. Continuous bombardment by U. S. Mortar Fleet.
Vicksburg, Miss., May 22, 1863. Joint attack on the Confed. Fortifications and Water Batteries by U. S. Troops and Gunboats.
Vicksburg, Miss., May 27, 1863. U. S. Gunboat "Gen. Price" and other vessels bombard the Confed. hill batteries.
Vicksburg, Miss., May 27, 1863. Attack by U. S. Gunboat "Cincinnati" resulting in the sinking of the vessel.

Vicksburg, Miss., June 5 to July 4, 1863. Bombardment almost continuously by the U. S. Naval Shore Battery.
Vicksburg, Miss, June 20, 1863. Bombarded by U. S. Fleet.

WALKIN'S Bluff, James River, Va., June 20, 1862. U. S. Gunboat "Jacob Bell" engages Confed. Batteries.
Ware River, Va., April 8 and 9, 1863. (See Gloucester C. H.)
Warrenton, Miss., May 10 to 13, 1863. Attacked by U. S. Gunboat "Mound City."
Warsaw Sound, Ga., Dec. 5 and 6, 1861. Recon. by U. S. Gunboats "Ottawa," "Seneca," and "Pembina."
Warsaw Sound, Ga., Jan. 26, 1862. Recon. by U. S. Gunboats "Ottawa," "Seneca," "Western World," "Potomski," "Isaac H. Smith," and "Ellen."
Warsaw Sound, Ga., June 17, 1863. Confed. Gunboat "Atlanta" captured by U. S. Ironclad "Weehawken." Confed., 1 killed, 17 wounded, 145 prisoners.
Washington, N. C., March 30 to April 16, 1863. Engagement by U. S. Strs. "Louisiana" "Hunchback," and other vessels, supporting the Troops under Gen. Foster.
Washito River, April 30, 1864. Recon. by U. S. Squadron.
Waterproof, La., Nov. 21, 1863. Attack by U. S. Gunboat "Welcome."
Waterproof, La., Feb. 13 to 15, 1864. U. S. Gunboat "Forest Rose" supporting the 49th U. S. Colored Troops repel three Confed. attacks. Union, 8 killed, 14 wounded; Confed., 15 killed.
West Point, White River, Ark., Aug. 14, 1863. U. S. Gunboats "Lexington," "Cricket," and "Mariner" with the 32d Iowa Inf. make an attack. Union, 2 killed, 7 wounded.

West Point, Va., May 7, 1862. (See Eltham's Landing.)
Whitehall Point, La., July 10, 1863. U. S. Gunboat "New London" supported by the "Monongahela" and "Essex" engages the Confeds.
White House, Pamunkey River, Va., May 29 to June 23, 1864. U. S. Squadron co-operates with Troops.
White River, Ark., June 17, 1862. (See St. Charles.)
White River, Ark., Jan. 12 to 22, 1863. Exp. by U. S. Gunboat "De Kalb" and other vessels.
White River, Ark., Aug. 13 to 16, 1863. Recon. by U. S. Str. "Lexington" and other vessels.
White River, Ark., June 22,1864. U. S. Gunboat "Lexington" supports 3 Companies of the 12th Ohio Inf.
Wilcox's Wharf, James River, Va., Aug. 3, 1864. U. S. Gunboat "Miami" engages Confed. Battery.
Williamson, Roanoke River, Va., July 13, 1863. Bombarded by U. S. Fleet.
Wilmington River, Ga., Jan. 27 to 29, 1862. (See Narrows.)
Wilson's Wharf Landing, James River, Va., May 24. 1864. U. S. Strs. "Dawn" and "Mayflower" co-operate with Troops in repelling Confed. attack.

Y ASL A L' Outre, Miss., April 6, 1863. U. S. Str. "Fox" captured.
Yales' Point, Va., July 18, 1863. Attack by U. S. Strs. "Jacob Bell," "Resolute," and "Teaser;" Mortar Boat "Dan Smith" and U. S. Troops.
Yazoo City, Miss., May 13, 1863. Captured by U. S. Fleet.
Yazoo City, Miss., May 20 to 23, 1863. Exp. by U. S. Gunboat "De Kalb" and other vessels.
Yazoo City, Miss., July 13, 1863. Recaptured by U. S. Gunboat "De Kalb" and two other Ironclads, supported by U. S. Troops. The "De Kalb" sunk by a torpedo.
Yazoo City, Miss., March 5, 1864. U.

S. Strs. "Petrel" and "Momora" repel Confed. attack.
Yazoo City, Miss., April 21, 1864. U. S. Strs. "Petrel" and "Prairie Bird" engage Confed. Forces.
Yazoo Pass, Miss., Feb. 20 to April 10, 1863. Recon. by U. S. Str. "Chillicothe" and other vessels.
Yazoo River, Miss., July 15, 1862. Attempt to destroy the Confed. Ram "Arkansas" by U. S. Gunboats "Carondelet," "Tyler," "Queen of the West," and "Essex," aided by Troops. Union. 13 killed, 36 wounded. Confed., 5 killed, 9 wounded.
Yazoo River, Miss., Dec. 12, 1862. Exp. by U. S. Strs. "Cairo," "Pittsburg," "Marmora," "Signal," and "Queen of the West." The "Cairo" sunk by a torpedo.
Yazoo River, Miss., Dec. 24 to 27, 1862. Torpedoes removed by U. S. Naval Force.
Yazoo River, Miss., Dec., 27, 1862. U. S. Str. "Benton" and other vessels engage Confed. Batteries.
Yazoo River, Miss., Dec. 28, 1862. Attacked by U. S. Gunboats.
Yazoo River, Miss., March 11 and 16, 1863. (Near Greenwood.) Attack on Fort Pemberton by a Naval Force.
Yazoo River, and Sunflower River, Miss., May 21 to 24, 1863. Exp. by U. S. Gunboat "De Kalb" and other vessels.
Yazoo River, Miss., March 9 to April 22, 1864. Operations by U. S. Squadron under Lieut.-Com. Owen.
Yazoo River, Miss., April 22, 1864. U. S. Str. "Petrel" captured by the Confeds.
York River, Va., May 4, 1862. U. S. Str. "Wachusett" and other vessels make an attack.
York River, Va., May 25, 1863. Confeds. fire upon the U. S. Mail Boat "Swan."
York River, May 26, 1863. U. S. Str. "Morse" destroys property along the river in retaliation for the U. S. Mail Boat "Swan" being fired upon.

PART IV.

DOCUMENTARY EVIDENCE.

HONORABLE DISCHARGE.

THE majority of the certificates of Honorable Discharge issued by the Government to the Union soldiers have been so defaced by time and wear that to-day they are scarcely legible.

This documentary evidence of the services rendered by the "brave boys in blue" during the dark days of rebellion, suffering, and bloodshed which marked the years from '61 to '65 will increase in value to the soldier's descendants as the years go by. It is but natural, therefore, that sons and daughters of veterans should wish to preserve a copy of this written testimony of their father's loyalty to his country, and that the original should be filed away under lock and key, with other valuable papers, to prevent its being lost or destroyed.

The blank forms immediately following will enable each soldier's family to preserve in book form, for ready reference, an exact copy of the father's honorable discharge.

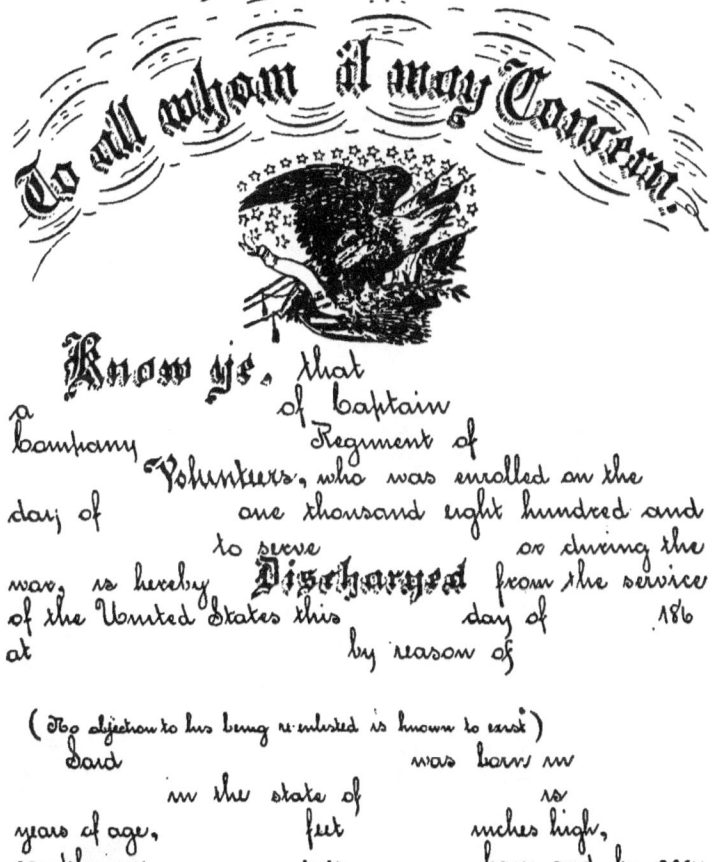

Honorable Discharge
from the
United States Navy

This is to Certify, That No.

enlisted   18
at   for three years,
years of age,   feet   inches high,
    eyes,   hair,   complexion.
has   born at

"As a Testimonial of Fidelity and Obedience", is this day "Honorably Discharged" from the United States and from the Naval Service of the United States. **Now**, according to the provisions of the second section of the Act approved March 2nd, 1855, if within three months from this date, the above described   shall present this his "Honorable Discharge" at any United States Naval Rendezvous, and if found physically qualified, and shall re-enlist for three years or longer, then he shall be entitled to pay during the said three months equal to that which he would have been entitled if he had been employed in actual Service.

Approved.   } Commanding
                                Officer.
————————————   Paymaster.

REMINISCENCES.

" 'Tis sweet to remember, I would not forego
The charm which the past o'er the present can throw,
For all the gay visions that Fancy may weave,
Which, in their illusions, shine but to deceive."

This little two-year old Son of Veteran wants facts, not fiction, and by the aid of the Colonel's spectacles thinks he is getting them.

The following blank and ruled pages intended for preserving to future generations personal memoirs of the war, newspaper clippings relative to his regiment, reunions, camp fires, G. A. R. encampments and other reminiscences which the soldier or any member of his family may desire to preserve, will increase in value as the years go by, and will be much more satisfactory to his children and his children's children than for them to be obliged to draw on their imagination for these particulars.

PART V.

PENSIONS.

Pensions issued to the survivors of the war for the preservation of the Union are not alms. They are but part of the debt the American Nation owes its soldiers and sailors. Pensions are life annuities, the premiums having been fully paid up with the close of the war in 1865.

All civilized nations have issued pensions in some form to those who risked their lives in the country's defense and honor. It is, comparatively, a modern idea, to issue them to survivors of wars who were not wounded in battle.

Civilization, however, has advanced with rapid strides in our day. The prevailing patriotism, deep sense of justice and overgrowing gratitude of the American people to those who fought the country's battles, have caused our law-givers to issue pensions to survivors of all our wars.

The statistics at the close of this volume will show, somewhat in detail, the amounts paid out for pensions from 1861 to 1898 inclusive.

Perhaps the accusation, that large sums of money are paid out yearly by this munificent Government to unworthy recipients in the form of pensions, is well founded. Doubtless there have been some fraud and deception. All patriotic citizens regret this fact, but the unanimity of sentiment in this great, rich country, great in a mighty, free, homogeneous, law-abiding people, great in progress, in material productions, in accumulated wealth, does not begrudge the veterans their just claim upon the bounty of the Nation.

The circumstances which justify the issuing of $150,000,000 in pensions in 1899 are peculiar to this country. We are just beginning to comprehend the value of the *priceless legacy preserved to us by the valor of the Boys in Blue.*

The outcome of the struggle in the great war for the preservation of the Union depended wholly upon the number of soldiers which could be promptly rallied under "Old Glory" for its defense. It was a war between giants. No soldiers ever faced a braver, more determined, unconquerable foe, for were they not our own brothers? Were they not Americans as ourselves? Who knew to do and dare better than they?

Oh, the cost, in blood and treasure to the Great Republic, of that war of the States! The deep silence of the national cemeteries speak, in part, for the dead. How many other thousands sleep where they perished and lie where they fell! What pen shall truthfully describe the horrors of the prison pen?

Let one who questions the validity of the ex-soldiers' claim on the Nation's bounty, weigh, in the balance, the exposures, fatigues, excitements, toils, privations, hardships of any great campaign, as the one against Atlanta in the summer of 1864. And this is but one specimen of the many campaigns during those four memorable years. With iron will and nerves of steel, under the creative stimulus of patriotic zeal, against a mighty array of armed heroes as courageous and determined as themselves, they ceaselessly kept up the fight with ever-increasing demands upon heart, brain and brawn, and when the reaction came, came multitudes of incurable ailments, which, for more than a quarter of a century, have baffled the skill of scientists and of the most learned physicians in the land.

The Nation awoke to this truth, at last, when a justice-loving people, from a deep sense of abiding gratitude ever growing upon them, instructed their representatives in Congress to pass the Pension Law of June 27, 1890.

The men who fought to save the Union are not looters of the Treasury; they are patriots. They are devoted to the interests of the whole country, as they were from '61 to '65. They earnestly wish to keep in close touch with the true spirit of America and American institutions. From their inmost heart they desire to be the *Grand Army of the Republic*, grand in every sense of the term. They desire to be to the Nation what the Old Guard was to Napoleon.

In 1961 societies will be organized as *Sons and Daughters of the Civil War*, as now "Sons and Daughters of the Revolution." It will be then a mark of distinction to trace with reverential pride the records of the service of their ancestors. Why shall it not be so now?

> "Seven Grecian cities contended for the birthplace of Homer dead,
> In which cities the living Homer was obliged to beg his bread."

We adorn with floral offerings the funeral caskets containing the precious bodies of our loved ones, flowers we frequently denied to them living. What tender, loving words we write as epitaphs for those whose services we greatly undervalued while living!

Shall the gratitude of the American people, to those who preserved the Union, be measured otherwise than by the financial ability of this great people to respond to the demands of just pension legislation?

We are only paying interest on part of the debt we owe the veterans. The principal we can never pay.

When the war closed between the States the public debt was one-tenth of the wealth of the country. It is now one-seventieth. A new Nation of 40,000,000 has been added to the population. Then the accumulated wealth of the country was $20,000,000,000; now it is nearly four times that aggregate. May we not consider the $60,000,000,000 as the gain in material resources since the war?

The Boys in Blue preserved the Nation in its political unity as one people, as God intended it should be. Have they not earned a small percentage for life on this added capital to the stock of the country? One hundred and fifty million dollars, the sum estimated to pay for pensions during the fiscal year ending June 30, 1899, is but one-fourth of one per cent interest on this vast sum saved and added to the resources of the Republic. This principal will ever increase to infinity, this percentage will ever decrease to zero.

Shall any true patriot begrudge to the veterans for a very few years more this small percentage of the vast, ever-growing financial resources of this Nation?

Nay, verily, the time approaches when with unanimous voice the American Congress shall take one step further, and from the rock of never-failing financial resources shall cause to issue forth a copious stream to be known in history as the "*Service Pension Law*," which shall flow in continuous volume to make glad the hearts and homes of the survivors of the War for the Union, until, one by one, they shall answer the last roll-call, and, in obedience to the summons of the Great Commander, they shall be "mustered out."

The verdict of history shall be: "They fought a good fight;" they kept inviolate the faith our Fathers pledged at Lexington and Bunker Hill. They made possible Washington's prophecy, that our glorious Star-Spangled Banner should wave over a nation of freemen a thousand years,

"That the Sons of Columbia shall never be slaves,
While the earth bears a plant or the sea rolls its waves."

High in the American soldier's Temple of Fame shall be written these words: "'They met and overcame the greatest rebellion the world ever saw. The stake for which they contended was the greatest ever submitted to the arbitrament of arms. They maintained the political unity of the States. They solved the mooted question of man's capacity for self-government. They broke the fetters of human slavery. They caused the dawn of Universal Liberty. They have helped carry out Lincoln's divine injunction at Gettysburg, 'With malice toward none, with charity for all.' They have received the New South with open arms. 'These men shall pass away as a tale that is told, but their work shall endure forever.'"

In accordance with the spirit of the foregoing article on the subject of pensions, the publishers of this Manual stand ready and willing to serve their patrons.

In response to inquiries, they will, to the best of their knowledge and ability, furnish their patrons information relative to pensions, —*free of charge.*

☞**Address** all inquiries to

U.S. ARMY AND NAVY HISTORICAL ASS'N.

No. 629 F Street, N. W.,

Washington, D. C.

PENSION STATISTICS.

NUMBER OF PENSIONERS ON THE ROLLS FOR THE FISCAL YEAR ENDING
JUNE 30, 1898.

Also the amount distributed in each State and Territory and the total amount paid to soldiers who served in the Civil War and now reside in foreign countries.

STATE.	No.	AMOUNT.	STATE.	No.	AMOUNT.
Alabama	3,780	$505,098.27	Nebraska	17,627	$2,764,084.78
Alaska	65	8,970.14	Nevada	264	37,292.73
Arizona	619	87,895.31	N. Hampshire	9,204	1,392,039.09
Arkansas	10,949	1,521,527.82	New Jersey	20,775	2,555,095.89
California	16,981	2,442,231.65	New Mexico	1,483	219,114 38
Colorado	7,307	1,001,617.20	New York	89,051	12,619,366.22
Connecticut	12,015	1,410,115.59	No. Carolina	4,064	561,292.50
Delaware	2,740	419,917.57	North Dakota	1,769	232,030 93
Dist. of Columbia	8,629	1,532,120.97	Ohio	105,864	16,166,264.16
Florida	3,121	426,058.07	Oklahoma	6,627	933,787.91
Georgia	3,770	495,737.07	Oregon	4,932	712,008.86
Idaho	1,248	177,297.17	Pennsylvania	104,376	13,164,211.79
Illinois	70,767	10,371,293.73	Rhode Island	4,402	519,129.51
Indiana	67,139	10,902,433.06	So. Carolina	1,743	227,332.94
Indian Territory	2,682	369,728.01	South Dakota	4,842	638,856.04
Iowa	37,977	5,549,978.61	Tennessee	18,434	2,732,349 25
Kansas	41,629	6,472,994.49	Texas	8,000	1,042,628.40
Kentucky	28,980	4,309,049.75	Utah	796	115,171.58
Louisiana	5,285	868,234.65	Vermont	9,635	1,504,170.78
Maine	20,935	3,127,655.53	Virginia	8,797	1,352,384.37
Maryland	12,905	1,789,363.91	Washington	5,336	780,977.54
Massachusetts	38,692	5,606,197.45	West Virginia	12,953	2,058,753 48
Michigan	45,436	7,209,436.93	Wisconsin	28,197	4,308,186.05
Minnesota	16,650	2,420,956.67	Wyoming	708	104,818.03
Mississippi	4,122	555,126.80	For. Countries	4,371	669,862.56
Missouri	53,649	7,455,681.72			
Montana	1,392	203,951.89	Grand total	993,714	144,651,879.80

PENSION CLAIMS, PENSIONS AND DISBURSEMENTS.
EACH YEAR
From June 30, 1862, to June 30, 1898, inclusive.

Year Ending June 30.	Total No. of applications filed.	Total No. of claims allowed.	Year Ending June 30.	Pensioners on the Roll and amounts paid yearly, including expense.	
				Total No. on roll.	Disbursements.
1862............	2,487	462	1862.........	* 8,159	$790,385.00
1863............	49,332	7,884	1863.........	14,791	1,025,140.00
1864............	53,599	39,487	1864.........	51,135	4,564,617.00
1865............	72,684	40,171	1865.........	85,986	8,525,153.00
1866............	65,256	50,177	1866.........	126,722	13,459,996.00
1867............	36,753	36,482	1867.........	153,183	18,619,956.00
1868............	20,768	28,921	1868.........	169,643	24,010,982.00
1869............	26,066	23,196	1869.........	187,963	28,422,884.00
1870............	24,851	18,221	1870.........	198,686	27,780,812.00
1871............	43,969	16,562	1871.........	207,495	33,077,384.00
1872............	26,391	34,333	1872.........	232,229	30,169,341.00
1873............	18,303	16,052	1873.........	238,411	29,185,290.00
1874............	16,734	10,462	1874.........	236,241	30,593,750.00
1875............	18,704	11,152	1875.........	234,821	29,683,117.00
1876............	23,523	9,977	1876.........	232,137	28,351,600.00
1877............	22,715	11,326	1877.........	222,104	28,580,157.00
1878............	44,587	11,962	1878.........	223,998	26,844,415.00
1879............	57,118	31,346	1879.........	242,755	33,780,526 00
1880............	141,466	19,545	1880.........	250,802	57,240,540.00
1881............	31,116	27,394	1881.........	268,830	50,626,539.00
1882............	40,939	27,664	1882.........	285,697	54,296,281.00
1883............	48,776	38,162	1883.........	303,658	60,431,973.00
1884............	41,785	34,192	1884.........	322,756	57,273,537.00
1885............	40,918	35,767	1885.........	345,125	65,693,707.00
1886............	49,895	40,857	1886.........	365,783	64,584,270.00
1887............	72,465	55,194	1887.........	406,007	74,815,486.85
1888............	75,726	60,252	1888.........	452,557	79,646,146.37
1889............	81,220	51,912	1889.........	489,725	88,275,113.28
1890............	105,044	66,637	1890.........	537,944	106,493,890.19
1891............	363,799	156,486	1891.........	676,160	118,548,959 71
1892............	198,345	224,047	1892.........	876,068	141,086,211.84
1893............	119,361	121,630	1893.........	966,012	158,155,342.51
1894............	40,148	39,085	1894.........	969,544	140,772,163.78
1895............	37,060	39,185	1895.........	970,524	140,959,076.37
1896............	33,749	40,374	1896.........	970,678	139,280,078.15
1897............	39,847	50,101	1897.........	976,014	139,949,717.35
1898............	37,524	52,648	1898.........	993,714	145,748,865.56
Total......	2,212,940	1,579,314	Total...	....	2,283,213,737.63

* NOTE.—In 1861, the total number of pensions in force on account of previous wars, was 8,636, and the amount paid out during the year was $1,072,462.00.

www.ingramcontent.com/pod-product-compliance
Lightning Source LLC
Chambersburg PA
CBHW020800230426
43666CB00007B/788